The Haynes
Duramax
Diesel Engine
Repair Manual

by Jeff Killingsworth
and John H Haynes

Member of the Guild of Motoring Writers

Models covered:

All 2001 through 2019 GM 6.6L Duramax V8 diesel engines

Haynes Publishing Group
Sparkford Nr Yeovil
Somerset BA22 7JJ England

Haynes North America, Inc
859 Lawrence Drive
Newbury Park, CA 91320 USA

www.haynes.com

(10331 - 11X5)

ABCDE
FGH

Acknowledgements

The Federal-Mogul Corporation supplied the illustrations of various engine bearing wear conditions. Wiring diagrams provided exclusively for Haynes North America, Inc. by HaynesPro B.V. and Bosch Automotive Service Solutions. Technical writers who contributed to this project include Mike Stubblefield, Trip Aiken, and Scott "Gonzo" Weaver. Mechanical work and photography was provided by Mark Henderson.

© **Haynes North America, Inc. 2013, 2019**
With permission from J.H. Haynes & Co. Ltd.

A book in the Haynes Automotive Repair Manual Series

Printed in Malaysia

ISBN-13: 978-1-62092-384-9
ISBN-10: 1-62092-384-X

Library of Congress Control Number: 2019953054

While every attempt is made to ensure that the information in this manual is correct, no liability can be accepted by the authors or publishers for loss, damage or injury caused by any errors in, or omissions from, the information given.

Contents

About this manual

Its purpose

The purpose of this manual is to help you get the best value from your vehicle. It can do so in several ways. It can help you decide what work must be done, even if you choose to have it done by a dealer service department or a repair shop; it provides information and procedures for routine maintenance and servicing; and it offers diagnostic and repair procedures to follow when trouble occurs.

We hope you use the manual to tackle the work yourself. For many simpler jobs, doing it yourself may be quicker than arranging an appointment to get the vehicle into a shop and making the trips to leave it and pick it up. More importantly, a lot of money can be saved by avoiding the expense the shop must pass on to you to cover its labor and overhead costs. An added benefit is the sense of satisfaction and accomplishment that you feel after doing the job yourself.

Using the manual

The manual is divided into Chapters. Each Chapter is divided into numbered Sections, which are headed in bold type between horizontal lines. Each Section consists of consecutively numbered paragraphs.

At the beginning of each numbered Section you will be referred to any illustrations which apply to the procedures in that Section. The reference numbers used in illustration captions pinpoint the pertinent Section and the Step within that Section. That is, illustration 3.2 means the illustration refers to Section 3 and Step (or paragraph) 2 within that Section.

Procedures, once described in the text, are not normally repeated. When it's necessary to refer to another Chapter, the reference will be given as Chapter and Section number. Cross references given without use of the word "Chapter" apply to Sections and/or paragraphs in the same Chapter. For example, "see Section 8" means in the same Chapter.

References to the left or right side of the vehicle assume you are sitting in the driver's seat, facing forward.

Even though we have prepared this manual with extreme care, neither the publisher nor the author can accept responsibility for any errors in, or omissions from, the information given.

NOTE

A **Note** provides information necessary to properly complete a procedure or information which will make the procedure easier to understand.

CAUTION

A **Caution** provides a special procedure or special steps which must be taken while completing the procedure where the Caution is found. Not heeding a Caution can result in damage to the assembly being worked on.

WARNING

A **Warning** provides a special procedure or special steps which must be taken while completing the procedure where the Warning is found. Not heeding a Warning can result in personal injury.

Model years, RPO codes, VIN numbers and design changes

The Duramax diesel engine is a common-rail direct injection engine configuration with a high-volume, high-pressure solenoid-type injector system. The fuel pressure can reach as high as 29,000 psi (2,000 bars), which promotes nearly perfect fuel atomization for a much cleaner burn in the combustion chamber and reduces particulate emissions out of the exhaust.

Even though all of the Duramax diesel engines covered by this manual are a 6.6 liter, 32 valve V8, they have gone through some dramatic changes since their introduction.

Engine changes can be identified by using the RPO code (Regular Production Option) or by the 8th digit of the VIN (Vehicle Identification Number). You can use the following guide to establish the evolution and changes and/or which version of the Duramax diesel you're working on by way of the 8th VIN or RPO. Not all the changes are listed, just some of the major differences.

It may be important to know the exact RPO or 8th VIN digit when ordering replacement components or for certain procedures, because of these design changes.

2001-2004.5: RPO LB7, VIN 1

The LB7 featured all aluminum heads and a fixed geometry turbo @ 300hp and 520 ft lbs. of torque. The LB7 utilized a fuel junction block. The LB7 cooled the Fuel Injector Control Module (FICM) with diesel fuel running through it. The LB7 fuel injectors are mounted under the valve covers.

2004.5-2006: RPO LLY, VIN 2

The LLY came from the factory with 310hp @ 605 ft lbs. of torque, and an improved valve design which made injector servicing more accessible. LLY does not use a fuel junction block. The LLY and later models have the injectors outside of the valve covers. The LLY also cooled the Fuel Injector Control Module (FICM) with diesel fuel running through it. The LLY and later models use a Garrett variable-vane turbocharger.

2006-2007.5: RPO LBZ, VIN D

The LBZ design cranked out 360hp @ 650 ft lbs. of torque with larger connecting rods, a new piston design, and improved heads. The LBZ and later models no longer used a Fuel Injector Control Module (FICM).

2007.5-2010.5: RPO LMM, VIN 6

LMM offered 365hp @ 660 ft lbs. of torque. The LMM is the first Duramax design utilizing a Diesel Particulate Filter (DPF), a Diesel Oxidation Catalyst (DOC), and a Selective Catalyst Reduction (SCR) system. Injector nozzles for the LMM can be determined by counting the holes in the injector nozzles. The LMM uses 6 holes in each of the injector nozzles while all previous models used 7 holes. The engine block and rods were strengthened for the increased horsepower and torque as well as having a redesigned head gasket.

2010.5-2012: RPO LGH, VIN L

The LGH changes include being B20 fuel compatible, larger oil pump, stronger engine block, new piston design, new quick-disconnect charge air cooler (intercooler), and additional engine Diagnostic Trouble Codes (DTC's) (Over 160 new codes added). The idle speed was dropped to 640 rpm for 2011 trucks (van idle speed changed to 600 rpm). The LGH had newly designed piezoelectric injectors with orange colored wire looms as well.

2011-2016: RPO LML, VIN 8

All the changes made on the LGH were carried over to the LML engines. The LML serpentine drivebelt can be tricky to install correctly. The LML and the LGH engines' PCV system uses an enhanced oil separator which incorporates a Crankcase Depression Regulator (CDR). The regulator limits the amount of vacuum drawn by the PCV. With the CDR in working order, the possibility of crankcase oil being sucked into the combustion chambers any time the air filter or intake air passages are clogged can be greatly reduced. The Glow Plug Control Module (GPCM) was also relocated to the right side of the engine on the alternator bracket.

2017-2019: RPO L5P, VIN Y

The L5P has an impressive 445hp @ 910 ft lbs. of torque. This latest redesigned turbo-diesel not only has the performance, but is quieter and smoother than previous models. A much stronger engine block, increased oil and coolant flow and capacity, and an all new EGR system with a single cooler and integrated bypass.

How diesel engines are different

There are many similarities between diesel and gasoline engines but it's the differences involved with the ignition of the fuel that makes the servicing and repairing of a diesel engine unique. The diesel engines covered by this manual operate on the same four-stroke principle (intake, compression, power and exhaust) as most gasoline powered engines. But, instead of igniting the fuel and air in the cylinder during the third (power) stroke by introducing a spark from the spark plug as on a gasoline engine, the diesel engine uses compression ignition. Compression ignition occurs when the extremely high compression ratio of the diesel engine (17.5: 1 in the case of the Duramax as opposed to a normally aspirated gasoline engine ratio which averages about 9.5:1) compresses the air in the cylinder until it's hot enough (around 1000-degrees F) to ignite when fuel is injected.

A gasoline engine has both an ignition system and air/fuel mixture induction system for controlling engine speed. In principle the diesel is much simpler because it needs only the fuel injection pump and injectors for delivering the fuel at the precise moment when ignition can occur. An unrestricted supply of air is supplied by the intake manifold. In practice, however, the Duramax diesel engine uses a highly refined common rail electronic fuel injection system controlled by a computerized engine management system. This adds to the complexity, but the result is an extremely efficient, powerful engine.

Another unique feature of diesel engines is that an electric glow plug system operates when starting the engine and until combustion chamber temperatures sufficient to sustain self-ignition are reached. Starting fluid must never be used, because the glow plugs remain hot when the intake valves are open and can ignite the fluid, causing a flame to travel back through the intake manifold. Personal injury and/or engine damage could occur.

Diesel fuel comes from a lower petroleum distillate than gasoline and it lubricates the fuel pump and injectors, reducing wear in the engine. The cetane number of diesel fuel indicates its ignition quality; the higher the number, the faster it burns, making for easier starting and smoother running. Diesel fuel contains more energy and burns more air per volume than gasoline, which partially accounts for a diesel's greater efficiency. For more information on diesel fuel, and the requirements/compatibility with the Duramax engines covered by this manual, see Chapter 3.

There are, however, several disadvantages to diesel fuel. It contains paraffins (waxes), its volatility is affected by temperature more than gasoline is, it absorbs moisture readily and it contains more sulfur than gasoline (although the current diesel fuels that are available are far lower in sulfur content than diesel fuel of years past). At lower temperatures (10-degrees F and below) number two diesel fuel will become cloudy (this is called the cloud point) because the paraffins crystallize, clogging the fuel filter. If cold enough, the fuel can't be poured or pumped (pour point), so different blends of fuel are required for summer and winter driving.

Water in diesel fuel can corrode the injectors and encourage bacteria (which feed off the sulfur) to grow in the fuel, leading to contamination problems. The sulfur can also accelerate wear because it forms corrosive deposits in the engine. Consequently, devices such as water sensors and separators are used in diesel fuel systems and care must be taken to change the fuel filter and engine oil and filter on a regular basis.

Gasoline engines use intake manifold vacuum to operate components such as the brake booster. Since diesel engines have unrestricted air intake, there is very little vacuum. In some cases, vacuum pumps are required to operate accessories, although in most of the vehicles covered by this manual, such devices are operated electrically or hydraulically.

Diesel engines offer several advantages over gasoline engines, particularly in the area of fuel efficiency, low-speed torque and reliability. One of the reasons diesel engines tend to get better mileage than gasoline engines is because they burn fuel more completely. Diesel fuel exhaust actually has fewer hydrocarbons and less carbon monoxide than gasoline exhaust.

Glossary of terms

A

Additive - A material added to fuels and lubricants, designed to improve their properties such as viscosity, cetane, pour point, film strength, etc.

Afterglow - The period during which the glow plugs continue to operate after the engine is started.

Ambient - Surrounding on all sides.

Atmospheric pressure - The weight of the air, usually expressed as pressure; the air pressure at sea level is 14.7 psi.

Atomization - Breaking up of the fuel into fine particles, so it can be mixed with air.

B

BDC - Bottom Dead Center.

Biocide - A bacteria-killing compound used in diesel fuel.

Black smoke - Incompletely burned fuel in the exhaust.

Blow-by - A leakage or loss of pressure past the piston into the crankcase.

Blue smoke - Caused by blow-by allowing crankcase oil in the combustion chamber due to bad rings, valve seals, or other faulty components.

BTU - British Thermal Unit.

By-pass oil filter - An oil filter that removes soot and carbon by continually filtering 20 percent of the engine oil.

C

Calibration - Adjusting the rate, speed and timing of fuel delivery in an injection system.

Cetane number - The number indicating the ignition quality of diesel fuel, similar to the octane rating of gasoline.

Ceton filter - A sock-type filter in the fuel tank capable of wicking diesel fuel, but not water; keeps water from the rest of the fuel system until the sock is 90 percent submerged in water.

Clearance volume - At Top Dead Center, the volume measurement of a combustion chamber.

Cloud point - The temperature at which paraffin crystals in diesel fuel separate out of solution and start to crystallize.

Coalescing action - The process of smaller water droplets merging together into larger droplets which takes place in a water separator.

Compression ignition - The burning an air/fuel mixture in the combustion chamber by compressing it sufficiently to raise its temperature above the flash point of the fuel and injecting into the combustion chamber so that it begins to burn spontaneously.

Compression ratio - The clearance volume of an engine cylinder divided by its total volume.

D

Delivery lines - High-pressure fuel lines used to carry fuel from the injection pump to the injector nozzles.

Diesel Exhaust Fluid (DEF) - A solution of urea and deionized water that is injected into the exhaust system of vehicles equipped with a Selective Catalyst Reduction system (SCR) to reduce NOx emissions.

Diesel fuel - A petroleum-based middle distillate suitable as a fuel for diesel engines.

Diesel Oxidation Catalyst (DOC) - A device installed in the exhaust system of some diesel-powered vehicles, similar to a catalytic converter, which reduces Hydrocarbon (HC) and carbon monoxide (CO) emissions.

Diesel Particulate Filter (DPF) - A device installed in the exhaust system of some diesel-powered vehicles that reduces the amount of particulate matter (soot) that is emitted from the tailpipe.

Diffusion - Mixing the molecules of two gases by thermal agitation.

Diode - An electronic device that permits current to flow through it in one direction only.

Dispersant - Dispersing or scattering in various directions; a state of matter in which finely divided particles of one substance (disperse phase) are suspended in another (dispersion medium) substance.

Dissipated - Scattered in various directions.

Dribble - Insufficiently atomized fuel issuing from the nozzle at or immediately following the end of the main injection phase.

Duration - The period of time during which anything lasts.

E

Eccentric - One circle within another circle not having the same center.
Exhaust Gas Recirculation (EGR) - Redirecting exhaust gases back into the combustion chamber to reduce peak combustion temperatures.

F

Flash point - The temperature at which fuel self-ignites.
Fuel return line - The fuel line that returns excess fuel from the injectors back to the fuel tank or inlet side of the injector pump.

G

Glow plug - An electrical heating device that helps diesel engines start and run smoothly when cold by creating heat in the combustion chamber.

I

Injection pump - A pump which delivers fuel to the fuel injectors at extremely high pressure so the injectors can overcome compression in the cylinders and begin the combustion process.
Injector opening pressure - The point at which injection pump fuel pressure overcomes nozzle valve-spring resistance, or combustion chamber pressure, so that fuel is injected into the pre-combustion chamber.
In-line fuel heater - A heating element which is integral to the fuel line. This heat warms the fuel prior to the filter to keep paraffin crystals from stopping fuel flow.

M

Manometer - Instrument used for measuring the pressure of liquids and gases.
Micron - One-millionth of a meter.
Moisture content - The amount of water contained in diesel fuel.

N

NOx - Oxides of nitrogen, a pollutant; a component of diesel exhaust.
Number one diesel fuel - Diesel fuel used in cold climates; sometimes blended with number two diesel fuel to increase number one's energy and two's cold-weather performance.
Number two diesel fuel - Diesel fuel used in moderate climates.

O

Orifice - A restriction to flow in a line or tube.

P

Paraffin - A semi-transparent, waxy mixture of hydrocarbons, derived principally from the distillation of petroleum; any hydrocarbon of the methane series.
PCV - Positive Crankcase Ventilation.
Peak pressure period - The phase of diesel combustion lasting from about five degrees before top dead center to about 10 degrees after top dead center; the majority of diesel fuel burns during this period.
Positive Crankcase Ventilation (PCV) system - A system for crankcase ventilation that returns crankcase blow-by gases to the intake manifold where they are sent to the combustion chambers for re-burning.
Pour point - The temperature at which diesel fuel can no longer be poured or pumped.
Pre-glow - The period of time when the glow plugs are heating to operating temperature.

S

Sock - The fuel pick-up strainer in the fuel tank. The sock is made of saran, so water won't enter until the sock is virtually engulfed in water.
Supply pump - A pump that transfers fuel from the tank and delivers it to the injection pump.
Swirl - Rotation of the mass of air as it enters the cylinder is known as swirl. This is one form of turbulence.

V

Vacuum pump - A device for creating vacuum to power various systems such as power brakes and other components.
Viscosity - A liquid's resistance to flow.

W

Water separator - A device for removing water from the fuel, located in the fuel line of diesel engines.
White smoke - Unburned fuel emitted by the exhaust that indicates low combustion chamber temperatures.

Buying parts

Replacement parts are available from many sources. Our advice concerning them is as follows::

Retail auto parts stores: Good auto parts stores will stock frequently needed components which wear out relatively fast, such as clutch components, exhaust systems, brake parts, tune-up parts, etc. These stores often supply new or reconditioned parts on an exchange basis, which can save a considerable amount of money. Discount auto parts stores are often very good places to buy materials and parts needed for general vehicle maintenance such as oil, grease, filters, spark plugs, belts, touch-up paint, bulbs, etc. They also usually sell tools and general accessories, have convenient hours, charge lower prices and can give you knowledgeable answers to your questions. To be sure of obtaining the correct parts, have engine and chassis numbers available and, if possible, take the old parts along for positive identification.

Authorized dealer parts department: This is the best source for parts which are unique to the vehicle and not generally available elsewhere.

Prices for most parts tend to be higher than at retail auto parts stores.

Auto recyclers or salvage yards: Auto recyclers and salvage yards are good sources for components that are specific to the vehicle and not subject to wear, such as fenders, bumpers, trim pieces, etc. You can expect substantial savings by going this route, and self-service salvage yards offer still more savings if you're willing to bring your own tools and pull the part(s) yourself.

Warranty information: If the vehicle is still covered under warranty, be sure that any replacement parts purchased - regardless of the source - do not invalidate the warranty! In most cases, replacement parts, even from aftermarket suppliers, are designed to meet manufacturer specifications. If in doubt, check with the parts supplier.

Because of a Federally mandated extended warranty that covers the emissions control system components, check with your dealer about warranty coverage before working on any emissions-related systems.

To be sure of obtaining the correct parts, have engine and chassis numbers available and, if possible, take the old parts along for positive identification.

Tools and equipment

For some home mechanics, the idea of using the correct tool is completely foreign. They'll cheerfully tackle the most complex overhaul procedures with only a set of cheap open-end wrenches of the wrong type, a single screwdriver with a worn tip, a large hammer and an adjustable wrench. Though they often get away with it, this cavalier approach is stupid and dangerous. It can result in relatively minor annoyances like stripped fasteners, or cause catastrophic consequences like blown engines. It can also result in serious injury.

A complete assortment of good tools is a given for anyone who plans to overhaul engines. If you don't already have most of the tools listed below, the initial investment may seem high, but compared to the spiraling costs of routine maintenance and repairs, it's a deal. Besides, you can use a lot of the tools around the house for other types of mechanical repairs. We've included a list of the tools you'll need and a detailed description of what to look for when shopping for tools and how to use them correctly. We've also included a list of the special factory tools you'll need for engine rebuilding.

Buying tools

There are two ways to buy tools. The easiest and quickest way is to simply buy an entire set. Tool sets are often priced substantially below the cost of the same individually priced tools - and sometimes they even come with a tool box. When purchasing such sets, you often wind up with some tools you don't need or want. But if low price and convenience are your concerns, this might be the way to go. Keep in mind that you're going to keep a quality set of tools a long time (maybe the rest of your life), so check the tools carefully; don't skimp too much on price, either. Buying tools individually is usually a more expensive and time-consuming way to go, but you're more likely to wind up with the tools you need and want. You can also select each tool on its relative merits for the way you use it.

You can get most of the hand tools on our list from the tool department of any large department store or hardware store chain that sells hand tools. Blackhawk, Cornwell, Craftsman, KD, Proto, Lisle and SK are relatively inexpensive, good-quality choices. Specialty tools are available from mechanics' tool companies such as Snap-on, Mac, Matco, Kent-Moore, OTC, etc. These companies also supply the other tools you need, but they'll probably be more expensive.

Also consider buying second-hand tools from garage sales or used tool outlets. You may have limited choice in sizes, but you can usually determine from the condition of the tools if they're worth buying. You can end up with a number of unwanted or duplicate tools, but it's a cheap way of putting a basic tool kit together, and you can always sell off any surplus tools later.

Until you're a good judge of the quality levels of tools, avoid mail order firms (excepting Sears and other name-brand suppliers), flea markets and swap meets. Some of them offer good value for the money, but many sell cheap, imported tools of dubious quality. Like other consumer products counterfeited in the Far East, these tools run the gamut from acceptable to unusable.

If you're unsure about how much use a tool will get, the following approach may help. For example, if you need a set of combination wrenches but aren't sure which sizes you'll end up using most, buy a cheap or medium-priced set (make sure the jaws fit the fastener sizes marked on them). After some use over a period of time, carefully examine each tool in the set to assess its condition. If all the tools fit well and are undamaged, don't bother buying a better set. If one or two are worn, replace them with high-quality items - this way you'll end up with top-quality tools where they're needed most and the cheaper ones are sufficient for occasional use. On rare occasions you may conclude the whole set is poor quality. If so, buy a better set, if necessary, and remember never to buy that brand again.

In summary, try to avoid cheap tools, especially when you're purchasing high-use items like screwdrivers, wrenches and sockets. Cheap tools don't last long. Their initial cost plus the additional expense of replacing them will exceed the initial cost of better-quality tools.

Hand tools

Note: *The information that follows is for early-model engines with only Standard fastener sizes. On some late-model engines, you'll need Metric wrenches, sockets and Allen wrenches. Generally, manufacturers began integrating metric fasteners into their vehicles around 1975.*

A list of general-purpose hand tools you need for general engine work

Adjustable wrench - 10-inch
Allen wrench set (1/8 to 3/8-inch or 4 mm to 10 mm)
Ball peen hammer - 12 oz (any steel hammer will do)
Box-end wrenches
Brass hammer
Brushes (various sizes, for cleaning small passages
Combination (slip-joint) pliers - 6-inch
Center punch

Cold chisels - 1/4 and 1/2-inch
Combination wrench set (1/4 to 1-inch)
Extensions - 1-, 6-, 10- and 12-inch
E-Z out (screw extractor) set
Feeler gauge set
Files (assorted)
Floor jack
Gasket scraper
Hacksaw and assortment of blades
Impact screwdriver and bits
Locking pliers
Micrometer(s) (one-inch)
Phillips screwdriver (no. 2 x 6-inch)
Phillips screwdriver (no. 3 x 8-inch)
Phillips screwdriver (stubby - no. 2)
Pin punches (1/16, 1/8, 3/16-inch)
Piston ring removal and installation tool
Pliers - lineman's
Pliers - needle-nose
Pliers - snap-ring (internal and external)
Pliers - vise-grip
Pliers - diagonal cutters
Ratchet (reversible)
Scraper (made from flattened copper tubing)
Scribe
Socket set (6-point)
Soft-face hammer (plastic/rubber, the biggest you can buy)
Standard screwdriver (1/4-inch x 6-inch)
Standard screwdriver (5/16-inch x 6-inch)
Standard screwdriver (3/8-inch x 10-inch)
Standard screwdriver (5/16-inch - stubby)
Steel ruler - 6-inch
Straightedge - 12-inch
Tap and die set
Thread gauge
Torque wrench (same size drive as sockets)
Torx socket(s)
Universal joint
Wire brush (large)
Wire cutter pliers

What to look for when buying hand tools and general purpose tools

Wrenches and sockets

Wrenches vary widely in quality. One indication of their cost is their quality: The more they cost, the better they are. Buy the best wrenches you can afford. You'll use them a lot.

Start with a set containing wrenches from 1/4 to 1-inch in size. The size, stamped on the wrench **(see illustration)**, indicates the distance across the nut or bolt head, or the distance between the wrench jaws - not the diameter of the threads on the fastener - in inches. For example, a 1/4-inch bolt usually has a 7/16-inch hex head - the size of the wrench required to loosen or tighten it. However, the relationship between thread diameter and hex size doesn't always hold true. In some instances, an unusually small hex may be used to discourage over-tightening or because space around the fastener head is limited. Conversely, some fasteners have a disproportionately large hex-head.

Wrenches are similar in appearance, so their quality level can be difficult to judge just by looking at them. There are bargains to be had, just as there are overpriced tools with well-known brand names. On the other hand, you may buy what looks like a reasonable value set of wrenches only to find they fit badly or are made from poor-quality steel.

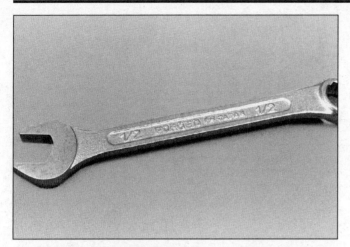

One quick way to determine whether you're looking at a quality wrench is to read the information printed on the handle - if it says "chrome vanadium" or "forged," it's made out of the right material

The size stamped on a wrench indicates the distance across the nut or bolt head (or the distance between the wrench jaws) in inches, not the diameter of the threads on the fastener

With a little experience, it's possible to judge the quality of a tool by looking at it. Often, you may have come across the brand name before and have a good idea of the quality. Close examination of the tool can often reveal some hints as to its quality. Prestige tools are usually polished and chrome-plated over their entire surface, with the working faces ground to size. The polished finish is largely cosmetic, but it does make them easy to keep clean. Ground jaws normally indicate the tool will fit well on fasteners.

A side-by-side comparison of a high-quality wrench with a cheap equivalent is an eye opener. The better tool will be made from a good quality material, often a forged/chrome-vanadium steel alloy **(see illustration)**. This, together with careful design, allows the tool to be kept as small and compact as possible. If, by comparison, the cheap tool is thicker and heavier, especially around the jaws, it's usually because the extra material is needed to compensate for its lower quality. If the tool fits properly, this isn't necessarily bad - it is, after all, cheaper - but in situations where it's necessary to work in a confined area, the cheaper tool may be too bulky to fit.

Open-end wrenches

Because of its versatility, the open-end wrench is the most common type of wrench. It has a jaw on either end, connected by a flat handle section. The jaws either vary by a size, or overlap sizes between consecutive

wrenches in a set. This allows one wrench to be used to hold a bolt head while a similar-size nut is removed. A typical fractional size wrench set might have the following jaw sizes: 1/4 x 5/16, 3/8 x 7/16, 1/2 x 9/16, 9/16 x 5/8 and so on.

Typically, the jaw end is set at an angle to the handle, a feature which makes them very useful in confined spaces; by turning the nut or bolt as far as the obstruction allows, then turning the wrench over so the jaw faces in the other direction, it's possible to move the fastener a fraction of a turn at a time **(see illustration)**. The handle length is generally determined by the size of the jaw and is calculated to allow a nut or bolt to be tightened sufficiently by hand with minimal risk of breakage or thread damage (though this doesn't apply to soft materials like brass or aluminum).

Common open-end wrenches are usually sold in sets and it's rarely worth buying them individually unless it's to replace a lost or broken tool from a set. Single tools invariably cost more, so check the sizes you're most likely to need regularly and buy the best set of wrenches you can afford in that range of sizes. If money is limited, remember that you'll use open-end wrenches more than any other type - it's a good idea to buy a good set and cut corners elsewhere.

Box-end wrenches

Box-end wrenches **(see illustration)** have ring-shaped ends with a 6-point (hex) or 12-point (double hex) opening **(see illustration)**. This allows

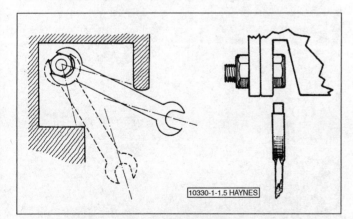

Open-end wrenches can do several things other wrenches can't - for example, they can be used on bolt heads with limited clearance (left) and they can be used in tight spots where there's little room to turn a wrench by flipping the offset jaw over every few degrees of rotation

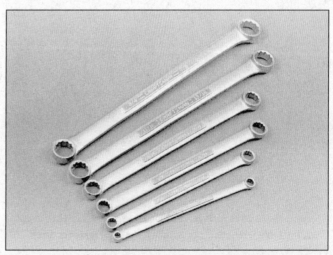

Box-end wrenches have a ring-shaped box at each end - when space permits, they offer the best combination of grip and strength

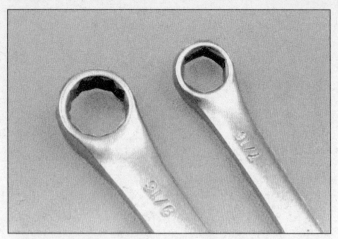

Box-end wrenches are available in 12 (left) and 6-point (right) openings; even though the 12-point design offers twice as many wrench positions, buy the 6-point first - it's less likely to strip off the corners of a nut or bolt head

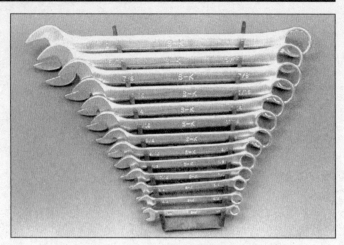

Buy a set of combination wrenches from 1/4 to 1 inch

the tool to fit on the fastener hex at 15 (12-point) or 30-degree (6-point) intervals. Normally, each tool has two ends of different sizes, allowing an overlapping range of sizes in a set, as described for open-end wrenches.

Although available as flat tools, the handle is usually offset at each end to allow it to clear obstructions near the fastener, which is normally an advantage. In addition to normal length wrenches, it's also possible to buy long handle types to allow more leverage (very useful when trying to loosen rusted or seized nuts). It is, however, easy to shear off fasteners if not careful, and sometimes the extra length impairs access.

As with open-end wrenches, box-ends are available in varying quality, again often indicated by finish and the amount of metal around the ring ends. While the same criteria should be applied when selecting a set of box-end wrenches, if your budget is limited, go for better-quality open-end wrenches and a slightly cheaper set of box-ends.

Combination wrenches

These wrenches **(see illustration)** combine a box-end and open-end of the same size in one tool and offer many of the advantages of both. Like the others, they're widely available in sets and as such are probably a better choice than box-ends only. They're generally compact, short-handled tools and are well suited for tight spaces where access is limited.

Adjustable wrenches

Adjustable wrenches **(see illustration)** come in several sizes. Each size can handle a range of fastener sizes. Adjustable wrenches aren't as effective as one-size tools and it's easy to damage fasteners with them. However, they can be an invaluable addition to any tool kit - if they're used with discretion. Note: If you attach the wrench to the fastener with the movable jaw pointing in the direction of wrench rotation **(see illustration)**, an adjustable wrench will be less likely to slip and damage the fastener head.

The most common adjustable wrench is the open-end type with a set of parallel jaws that can be set to fit the head of a fastener. Most are controlled by a threaded spindle, though there are various cam and spring-loaded versions available. Don't buy large tools of this type; you'll rarely be able to find enough clearance to use them.

Ratchet and socket sets

Ratcheting socket wrenches **(see illustration)** are highly versatile. Besides the sockets themselves, many other interchangeable accessories - extensions, U-drives, step-down adapters, screwdriver bits, Allen bits, crow's feet, etc. - are available. Buy six-point sockets - they're less likely to slip and strip the corners off bolts and nuts. Don't buy sockets with extra-thick walls - they might be stronger but they can be hard to use on recessed fasteners or fasteners in tight quarters. Buy a 3/8-inch drive for work on the outside of the engine. It's the one you'll use

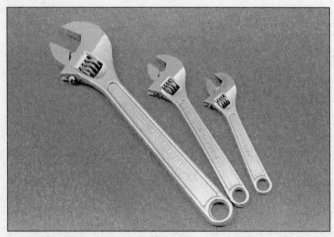

Adjustable wrenches can handle a range of fastener sizes - they're not as good as single-size wrenches but they're handy for loosening and tightening those odd-sized fasteners for which you haven't yet bought the correct wrench

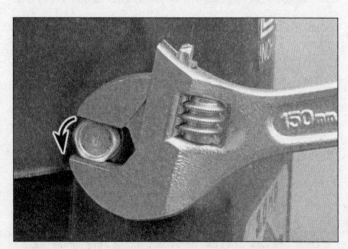

When you use an adjustable wrench, make sure the movable jaw points in the direction the wrench is being turned so the wrench doesn't distort and slip off the fastener head

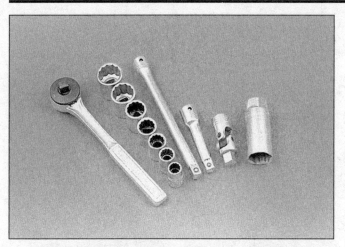

A typical ratchet and socket set includes a ratchet, a set of
sockets, a long and a short extension, a universal joint
and a spark plug socket

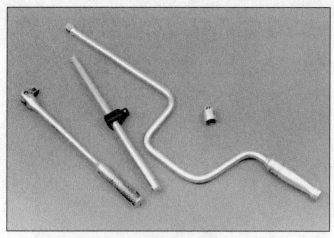

Lots of other accessories are available for ratchets:
From left to right, a breaker bar, a sliding T-handle,
a speed handle and a 3/8-to-1/4-inch adapter

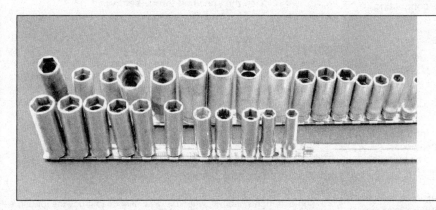

Deep sockets enable you to loosen
or tighten an elongated fastener,
or to get at a nut with a long bolt
protruding from it

most of the time. Get a 1/2-inch drive for overhaul work. Although the
larger drive is bulky and more expensive, it has the capacity of accept-
ing a very wide range of large sockets. Later, you may want to consider
a 1/4-inch drive for little stuff like ignition and carburetor work. Interchangeable sockets consist of a forged-steel alloy cylinder with a hex
or double-hex formed inside one end. The other end is formed into the
square drive recess that engages over the corresponding square end of
various socket drive tools.

Sockets are available in 1/4, 3/8, 1/2 and 3/4-inch drive sizes. A
3/8-inch drive set is most useful for engine repairs, although 1/4-inch
drive sockets and accessories may occasionally be needed.

The most economical way to buy sockets is in a set. As always,
quality will govern the cost of the tools. Once again, the "buy the
best" approach is usually advised when selecting sockets. While this
is a good idea, since the end result is a set of quality tools that should
last a lifetime, the cost is so high it's difficult to justify the expense for
home use. As far as accessories go, you'll need a ratchet, at least
one extension (buy a three or six-inch size), a spark plug socket
and maybe a T-handle or breaker bar. Other desirable, though less
essential items, are a speeder handle, a U-joint, extensions of various other lengths and adapters from one drive size to another (see
illustration). Some of the sets you find may combine drive sizes;
they're well worth having if you find the right set at a good price, but
avoid being dazzled by the number of pieces.

Above all, be sure to completely ignore any label that reads "86-
piece Socket Set," which refers to the number of pieces, not to the number of sockets (sometimes even the metal box and plastic insert are
counted in the total!).

Apart from well-known and respected brand names, you'll have to
take a chance on the quality of the set you buy. If you know someone
who has a set that has held up well, try to find the same brand, if pos-

sible. Take a pocketful of nuts and bolts with you and check the fit in
some of the sockets. Check the operation of the ratchet. Good ones
operate smoothly and crisply in small steps; cheap ones are coarse and
stiff - a good basis for guessing the quality of the rest of the pieces.

One of the best things about a socket set is the built-in facility for
expansion. Once you have a basic set, you can purchase extra sockets
when necessary and replace worn or damaged tools. There are special
deep sockets for reaching recessed fasteners or to allow the socket to
fit over a projecting bolt or stud (see illustration). You can also buy
screwdriver, Allen and Torx bits to fit various drive tools (they can be

Standard and Phillips bits, Allen-head and Torx drivers will
expand the versatility of your ratchet and extensions even further

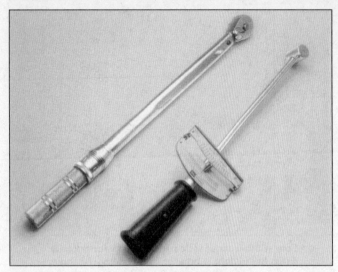

Torque wrenches (click-type on left, beam-type on right) are the only way to accurately tighten critical fasteners like connecting rod bolts, cylinder head bolts, etc.

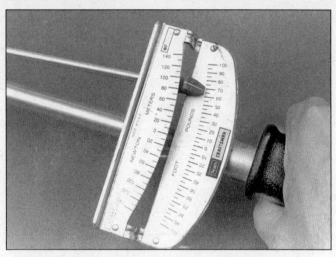

The deflecting beam-type torque wrench is inexpensive and simple to use - just tighten the fastener until the pointer points to the specified torque setting

very handy in some applications) **(see illustration)**. Most socket sets include a special deep socket for 14 millimeter spark plugs. They have rubber inserts to protect the spark plug porcelain insulator and hold the plug in the socket to avoid burned fingers.

Torque wrenches

Torque wrenches **(see illustration)** are essential for tightening critical fasteners like rod bolts, main bearing cap bolts, head bolts, etc. Attempting an engine overhaul without a torque wrench is an invitation to oil leaks, distortion of the cylinder head, damaged or stripped threads or worse.

There are two types of torque wrenches - the beam type, which indicates torque loads by deflecting a flexible shaft and the click type (see illustrations), which emits an audible click when the torque resistance reaches the specified resistance.

Torque wrenches are available in a variety of drive sizes and torque ranges for particular applications. For engine rebuilding, 0 to 150 ft-lbs should be adequate. Keep in mind that click types are usually more accurate (and more expensive).

Impact drivers

The impact driver **(see illustration)** belongs with the screwdrivers, but it's mentioned here since it can also be used with sockets (impact drivers normally are 3/8-inch square drive). As explained later, an impact driver works by converting a hammer blow on the end of its handle into a sharp twisting movement. While this is a great way to jar a seized fastener loose, the loads imposed on the socket are excessive. Use sockets only with discretion and expect to have to replace damaged ones on occasion.

Using wrenches and sockets

Although you may think the proper use of tools is self-evident, it's worth some thought. After all, when did you last see instructions for use supplied with a set of wrenches?

Which wrench?

Before you start tearing an engine apart, figure out the best tool for the job; in this instance the best wrench for a hex-head fastener. Sit down with a few nuts and bolts and look at how various tools fit the bolt heads.

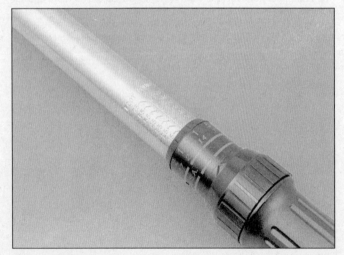

Click type torque wrenches can be set to give at a preset torque, which makes them very accurate and easy to use

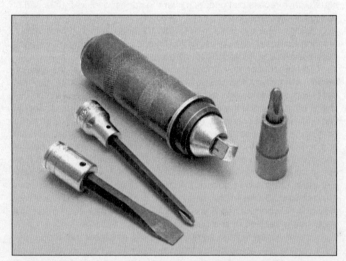

The impact driver converts a sharp blow into a twisting motion - this is a handy addition to your socket arsenal for those fasteners that won't let go - you can use it with any bit that fits a 3/8-inch drive ratchet

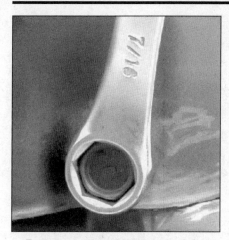

Try to use a six-point box wrench (or socket) whenever possible - its shape matches that of the fastener, which means maximum grip and minimum slip

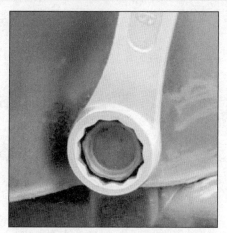

Sometimes a six-point tool just doesn't offer you any grip when you get the wrench at the angle it needs to be in to loosen or tighten a fastener - when this happens, pull out the 12-point sockets or wrenches - but remember: they're much more likely to strip the corners off a fastener

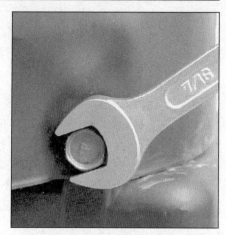

Open-end wrenches contact only two sides of the fastener and the jaws tend to open up when you put some muscle on the wrench handle - that's why they should only be used as a last resort

A golden rule is to choose a tool that contacts the largest area of the hex-head. This distributes the load as evenly as possible and lessens the risk of damage. The shape most closely resembling the bolt head or nut is another hex, so a 6-point socket or box-end wrench is usually the best choice **(see illustration)**. Many sockets and box-end wrenches have double hex (12-point) openings. If you slip a 12-point box-end wrench over a nut, look at how and where the two are in contact. The corners of the nut engage in every other point of the wrench. When the wrench is turned, pressure is applied evenly on each of the six corners **(see illustration)**. This is fine unless the fastener head was previously rounded off. If so, the corners will be damaged and the wrench will slip. If you encounter a damaged bolt head or nut, always use a 6-point wrench or socket if possible. If you don't have one of the right size, choose a wrench that fits securely and proceed with care.

If you slip an open-end wrench over a hex-head fastener, you'll see the tool is in contact on two faces only **(see illustration)**. This is acceptable provided the tool and fastener are both in good condition. The need for a snug fit between the wrench and nut or bolt explains the recommendation to buy good-quality open-end wrenches. If the wrench jaws, the bolt head or both are damaged, the wrench will probably slip, rounding off and distorting the head. In some applications, an open-end wrench is the only possible choice due to limited access, but always check the fit of the wrench on the fastener before attempting to loosen it; if it's hard to get at with a wrench, think how hard it will be to remove after the head is damaged.

The last choice is an adjustable wrench or self-locking plier/wrench (Vise-Grips). Use these tools only when all else has failed. In some cases, a self-locking wrench may be able to grip a damaged head that no wrench could deal with, but be careful not to make matters worse by damaging it further.

Bearing in mind the remarks about the correct choice of tool in the first place, there are several things worth noting about the actual use of the tool. Make sure the wrench head is clean and undamaged. If the fastener is rusted or coated with paint, the wrench won't fit correctly. Clean off the head and, if it's rusted, apply some penetrating oil. Leave it to soak in for a while before attempting removal.

It may seem obvious, but take a close look at the fastener to be removed before using a wrench. On many mass-produced machines, one end of a fastener may be fixed or captive, which speeds up initial assembly and usually makes removal easier. If a nut is installed on a stud or a bolt threads into a captive nut or tapped hole, you may have

only one fastener to deal with. If, on the other hand, you have a separate nut and bolt, you must hold the bolt head while the nut is removed. In some areas this can be difficult, particularly where engine mounts are involved. In this type of situation you may need an assistant to hold the bolt head with a wrench while you remove the nut from the other side. If this isn't possible, you'll have to try to position a box-end wrench so it wedges against some other component to prevent it from turning.

Be on the lookout for left-hand threads. They aren't common, but are sometimes used on the ends of rotating shafts to make sure the nut doesn't come loose during engine operation (most engines covered by this book don't have these types of fasteners). If you can see the shaft end, the thread type can be checked visually. If you're unsure, place your thumbnail in the threads and see which way you have to turn your hand so your nail unscrews from the shaft. If you have to turn your hand counterclockwise, it's a conventional right-hand thread.

Beware of the upside-down fastener syndrome. If you're loosening a fastener from the under side of a something, it's easy to get confused about which way to turn it. What seems like counterclockwise to you can easily be clockwise (from the fastener's point of view). Even after years of experience, this can still catch you once in a while.

In most cases, a fastener can be removed simply by placing the wrench on the nut or bolt head and turning it. Occasionally, though, the condition or location of the fastener may make things more difficult. Make sure the wrench is square on the head. You may need to reposition the tool or try another type to obtain a snug fit. Make sure the engine you're working on is secure and can't move when you turn the wrench. If necessary, get someone to help steady it for you. Position yourself so you can get maximum leverage on the wrench.

If possible, locate the wrench so you can pull the end towards you. If you have to push on the tool, remember that it may slip, or the fastener may move suddenly. For this reason, don't curl your fingers around the handle or you may crush or bruise them when the fastener moves; keep your hand flat, pushing on the wrench with the heel of your thumb. If the tool digs into your hand, place a rag between it and your hand or wear a heavy glove.

If the fastener doesn't move with normal hand pressure, stop and try to figure out why before the fastener or wrench is damaged or you hurt yourself. Stuck fasteners may require penetrating oil, heat or an impact driver or air tool.

Using sockets to remove hex-head fasteners is less likely to result in damage than if a wrench is used. Make sure the socket fits snugly

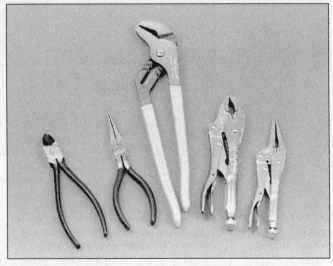

A typical assortment of the types of pliers you need to have in your box - from the left: diagonal cutters (dikes), needle-nose pliers, Channel-lock pliers, Vise-Grip pliers, needle-nose Vise Grip pliers

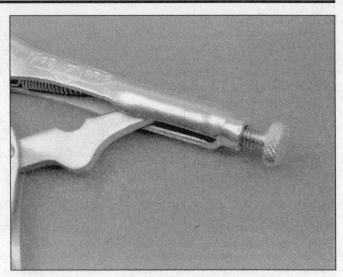

To adjust the jaws on a pair of Vise-Grips, grasp the part you want to hold with the jaws, tighten them down by turning the knurled knob on the end of one handle and snap the handles together - if you tightened the knob all the way down, you'll probably have to open it up (back it off) a little before you can close the handles

over the fastener head, then attach an extension, if needed, and the ratchet or breaker bar. Theoretically, a ratchet shouldn't be used for loosening a fastener or for final tightening because the ratchet mechanism may be overloaded and could slip. In some instances, the location of the fastener may mean you have no choice but to use a ratchet, in which case you'll have to be extra careful.

Never use extensions where they aren't needed. Whether or not an extension is used, always support the drive end of the breaker bar with one hand while turning it with the other. Once the fastener is loose, the ratchet can be used to speed up removal.

Pliers

Some tool manufacturers make 25 or 30 different types of pliers. You only need a fraction of this selection **(see illustration)**. Get a good pair of slip-joint pliers for general use. A pair of needle-nose models is handy for reaching into hard-to-get-at places. A set of diagonal wire cutters (dikes) is essential for electrical work and pulling out cotter pins. Vise-Grips are adjustable, locking pliers that grip a fastener firmly - and won't let go - when locked into place. Parallel-jaw, adjustable pliers have angled jaws that remain parallel at any degree of opening. They're also referred to as Channel-lock (the original manufacturer) pliers, arc-joint pliers and water pump pliers. Whatever you call them, they're terrific for gripping a big fastener with a lot of force.

Slip-joint pliers have two open positions; a figure eight-shaped, elongated slot in one handle slips back-and-forth on a pivot pin on the other handle to change them. Good-quality pliers have jaws made of tempered steel and there's usually a wire-cutter at the base of the jaws. The primary uses of slip-joint pliers are for holding objects, bending and cutting throttle wires and crimping and bending metal parts, not loosening nuts and bolts.

Arc-joint or Channel-lock pliers have parallel jaws you can open to various widths by engaging different tongues and grooves, or channels, near the pivot pin. Since the tool expands to fit many size objects, it has countless uses for engine and equipment maintenance. Channel lock pliers come in various sizes. The medium size is adequate for general work; small and large sizes are nice to have as your budget permits. You'll use all three sizes frequently.

Vise-Grips (a brand name) come in various sizes; the medium size with curved jaws is best for all-around work. However, buy a large and small one if possible, since they're often used in pairs. Although this tool

falls somewhere between an adjustable wrench, a pair of pliers and a portable vise, it can be invaluable for loosening and tightening fasteners - it's the only pliers that should be used for this purpose.

The jaw opening is set by turning a knurled knob at the end of one handle. The jaws are placed over the head of the fastener and the handles are squeezed together, locking the tool onto the fastener **(see illustration)**. The design of the tool allows extreme pressure to be applied at the jaws and a variety of jaw designs enable the tool to grip firmly even on damaged heads **(see illustration)**. Vise-Grips are great for removing fasteners that have been rounded off by badly-fitting wrenches.

As the name suggests, needle-nose pliers have long, thin jaws designed for reaching into holes and other restricted areas. Most needle-nose, or long-nose, pliers also have wire cutters at the base of the jaws.

Look for these qualities when buying pliers: Smooth operating handles and jaws, jaws that match up and grip evenly when the handles are closed, a nice finish and the word "forged" somewhere on the tool.

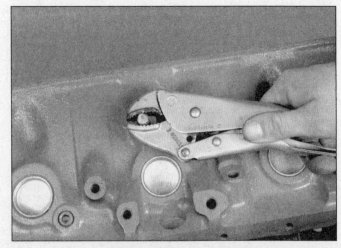

It you're persistent and careful, most fasteners can be removed with Vise-Grips

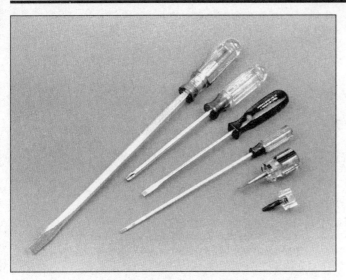

Screwdrivers come in myriad lengths, sizes and styles

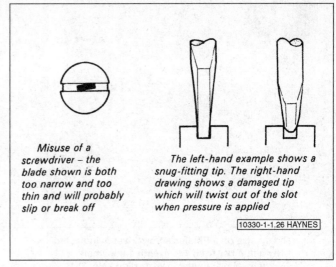

Standard screwdrivers - wrong size (left), correct fit in screw slot (center) and worn tip (right)

Screwdrivers

Screwdrivers **(see illustration)** come in a wide variety of sizes and price ranges. Anything from Craftsman on up is fine. But don't buy screwdriver sets for ten bucks at discount tool stores. Even if they look exactly like more expensive brands, the metal tips and shafts are made with inferior alloys and aren't properly heat treated. They usually bend the first time you apply some serious torque.

A screwdriver consists of a steel blade or shank with a drive tip formed at one end. The most common tips are standard (also called straight slot and flat-blade) and Phillips. The other end has a handle attached to it. Traditionally, handles were made from wood and secured to the shank, which had raised tangs to prevent it from turning in the handle. Most screwdrivers now come with plastic handles, which are generally more durable than wood.

The design and size of handles and blades vary considerably. Some handles are specially shaped to fit the human hand and provide a better grip. The shank may be either round or square and some have a hex-shaped bolster under the handle to accept a wrench to provide more leverage when trying to turn a stubborn screw. The shank diameter, tip size and overall length vary too. As a general rule, it's a good idea to use the longest screwdriver possible, which allows the greatest possible leverage.

If access is restricted, a number of special screwdrivers are designed to fit into confined spaces. The stubby screwdriver has a specially shortened handle and blade. There are also offset screwdrivers and special screwdriver bits that attach to a ratchet or extension.

The important thing to remember when buying screwdrivers is that they really do come in sizes designed to fit different size fasteners. The slot in any screw has definite dimensions - length, width and depth. Like a bolt head or a nut, the screw slot must be driven by a tool that uses all of the available bearing surface and doesn't slip. Don't use a big wide blade on a small screw and don't try to turn a large screw slot with a tiny, narrow blade. The same principles apply to Allen heads, Phillips heads, Torx heads, etc. Don't even think of using a slotted screwdriver on one of these heads! And don't use your screwdrivers as levers, chisels or punches! This kind of abuse turns them into very bad screwdrivers.

Standard screwdrivers

These are used to remove and install conventional slotted screws and are available in a wide range of sizes denoting the width of the tip and the length of the shank (for example: a 3/8 x 10-inch screwdriver is 3/8-inch wide at the tip and the shank is 10-inches long). You should have a variety of screwdrivers so screws of various sizes can be dealt

with without damaging them. The blade end must be the same width and thickness as the screw slot to work properly, without slipping. When selecting standard screwdrivers, choose good-quality tools, preferably with chrome moly, forged steel shanks. The tip of the shank should be ground to a parallel, flat profile (hollow ground) and not to a taper or wedge shape, which will tend to twist out of the slot when pressure is applied **(see illustration)**.

All screwdrivers wear in use, but standard types can be reground to shape a number of times. When reshaping a tip, start by grinding the very end flat at right angles to the shank. Make sure the tip fits snugly in the slot of a screw of the appropriate size and keep the sides of the tip parallel. Remove only a small amount of metal at a time to avoid overheating the tip and destroying the temper of the steel.

Phillips screwdrivers

Phillips screws are sometimes installed during initial assembly with air tools and are next to impossible to remove later without ruining the heads, particularly if the wrong size screwdriver is used. And don't use other types of cross-head screwdrivers (Torx, Posi-drive, etc.) on Phillips screws - they won't work.

The only way to ensure the screwdrivers you buy will fit properly, is to take a couple of screws with you to make sure the fit between the screwdriver and fastener is snug. If the fit is good, you should be able to angle the blade down almost vertically without the screw slipping off the tip. Use only screwdrivers that fit exactly - anything else is guaranteed to chew out the screw head instantly.

The idea behind all cross-head screw designs is to make the screw and screwdriver blade self-aligning. Provided you aim the blade at the center of the screw head, it'll engage correctly, unlike conventional slotted screws, which need careful alignment. This makes the screws suitable for machine installation on an assembly line (which explains why they're sometimes so tight and difficult to remove). The drawback with these screws is the driving tangs on the screwdriver tip are very small and must fit very precisely in the screw head. If this isn't the case, the huge loads imposed on small flats of the screw slot simply tear the metal away, at which point the screw ceases to be removable by normal methods. The problem is made worse by the normally soft material chosen for screws.

To deal with these screws on a regular basis, you'll need high-quality screwdrivers with various size tips so you'll be sure to have the right one when you need it. Phillips screwdrivers are sized by the tip number and length of the shank (for example: a number 2 x 6-inch Phillips screwdriver has a number 2 tip - to fit screws of only that size recess - and the shank is 6-inches long). Tip sizes 1, 2 and 3 should

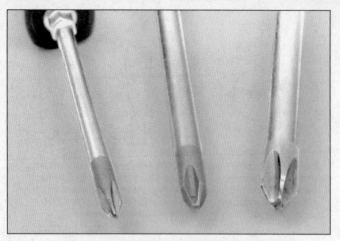

The tip size on a Phillips screwdriver is indicated
by a number from 1 to 4, with 1 the smallest
(left - No. 1; center - No. 2; right - No. 3)

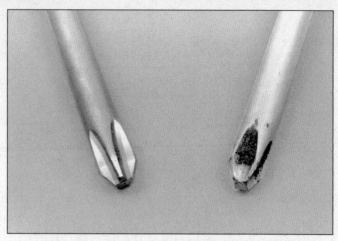

New (left) and worn (right) Phillips screwdriver tips

be adequate for engine repair work (see illustration). If the tips get worn or damaged, buy new screwdrivers so the tools don't destroy the screws they're used on (see illustration).

Here's a tip that may come in handy when using Phillips screwdrivers - if the screw is extremely tight and the tip tends to back out of the recess rather than turn the screw, apply a small amount of valve lapping compound to the screwdriver tip so it will grip the screw better.

Hammers

Resorting to a hammer should always be the last resort. When nothing else will do the job, a medium-size ball peen hammer, a heavy rubber mallet and a heavy soft-brass hammer (see illustration) are often the only way to loosen or install a part.

A ball-peen hammer has a head with a conventional cylindrical face at one end and a rounded ball end at the other and is a general purpose tool found in almost any type of shop. It has a shorter neck than a claw hammer and the face is tempered for striking punches and chisels. A fairly large hammer is preferable to a small one. Although it's possible to find small ones, you won't need them very often and it's much easier to control the blows from a heavier head. As a general rule, a single 12 or 16-ounce hammer will work for most jobs, though occasionally larger or smaller ones may be useful.

A soft-face hammer is used where a steel hammer could cause damage to the component or other tools being used. A steel hammer head might crack an aluminum part, but a rubber or plastic hammer can

be used with more confidence. Soft-face hammers are available with interchangeable heads (usually one made of rubber and another made of relatively hard plastic). When the heads are worn out, new ones can be installed. If finances are really limited, you can get by without a soft-face hammer by placing a small hardwood block between the component and a steel hammer head to prevent damage.

Hammers should be used with common sense; the head should strike the desired object squarely and with the right amount of force. For many jobs, little effort is needed - simply allow the weight of the head to do the work, using the length of the swing to control the amount of force applied. With practice, a hammer can be used with surprising finesse, but it'll take a while to achieve. Initial mistakes include striking the object at an angle, in which case the hammer head may glance off to one side, or hitting the edge of the object. Either one can result in damage to the part or to your thumb, if it gets in the way, so be careful. Hold the hammer handle near the end, not near the head, and grip it firmly but not too tightly.

Check the condition of your hammers on a regular basis. The danger of a loose head coming off is self-evident, but check the head for chips and cracks too. If damage is noted, buy a new hammer - the head may chip in use and the resulting fragments can be extremely dangerous. It goes without saying that eye protection is essential whenever a hammer is used.

Punches and chisels

Punches and chisels (see illustration) are used along with a hammer for various purposes in the shop. Drift punches are often simply a length of round steel bar used to drive a component out of a bore in the

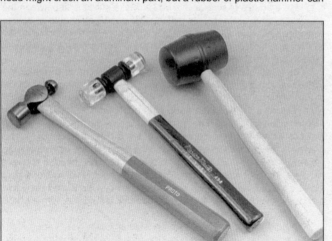

A ball-peen hammer, soft-face hammer and rubber mallet
(left-to-right) will be needed for various tasks (any steel
hammer can be used in place of the ball peen hammer)

Cold chisels, center-punches, pin punches and line-up
punches (left-to-right) will be needed sooner
or later for many jobs

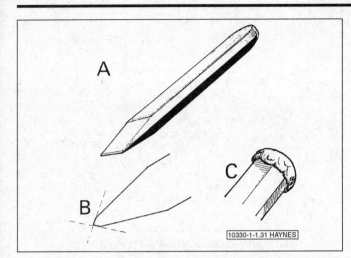

A typical general purpose cold chisel (A) - note the angle of the cutting edge (B), which should be checked and resharpened on a regular basis; the mushroomed head (B) is dangerous and should be filed to restore it to its original shape

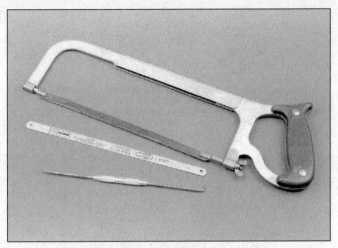

Hacksaws are handy for little cutting jobs like sheet metal and rusted fasteners

engine or equipment it's mounted on. A typical use would be for removing or installing a bearing or bushing. A drift of the same diameter as the bearing outer race is placed against the bearing and tapped with a hammer to knock it in or out of the bore. Most manufacturers offer special drifts for the various bearings in a particular engine. While they're useful to a busy dealer service department, they are prohibitively expensive for the do-it-yourselfer who may only need to use them once. In such cases, it's better to improvise. For bearing removal and installation, it's usually possible to use a socket of the appropriate diameter to tap the bearing in or out; an unorthodox use for a socket, but it works.

Smaller diameter drift punches can be purchased or fabricated from steel bar stock. In some cases, you'll need to drive out items like corroded engine mounting bolts. Here, it's essential to avoid damaging the threaded end of the bolt, so the drift must be a softer material than the bolt. Brass or copper is the usual choice for such jobs; the drift may be damaged in use, but the thread will be protected.

Punches are available in various shapes and sizes and a set of assorted types will be very useful. One of the most basic is the center punch, a small cylindrical punch with the end ground to a point. It'll be needed whenever a hole is drilled. The center of the hole is located first and the punch is used to make a small indentation at the intended point. The indentation acts as a guide for the drill bit so the hole ends up in the right place. Without a punch mark, the drill bit will wander and you'll find it impossible to drill with any real accuracy. You can also buy automatic center punches. They're spring loaded and are pressed against the surface to be marked, without the need to use a hammer.

Pin punches are intended for removing items like roll pins (semi-hard, hollow pins that fit tightly in their holes). Pin punches have other uses, however. You may occasionally have to remove rivets or bolts by cutting off the heads and driving out the shanks with a pin punch. They're also very handy for aligning holes in components while bolts or screws are inserted.

Of the various sizes and types of metal-cutting chisels available, a simple cold chisel is essential in any mechanic's workshop. One about 6-inches long with a 1/2-inch wide blade should be adequate. The cutting edge is ground to about 80-degrees (see illustration), while the rest of the tip is ground to a shallower angle away from the edge. The primary use of the cold chisel is rough metal cutting - this can be anything from sheet metal work (uncommon on engines) to cutting off the heads of seized or rusted bolts or splitting nuts. A cold chisel is also useful for turning out screws or bolts with messed-up heads.

All of the tools described in this section should be good quality items. They're not particularly expensive, so it's not really worth trying to save money on them. More significantly, there's a risk that with cheap tools, fragments may break off in use - a potentially dangerous situation.

Even with good-quality tools, the heads and working ends will inevitably get worn or damaged, so it's a good idea to maintain all such tools on a regular basis. Using a file or bench grinder, remove all burrs and mushroomed edges from around the head. This is an important task because the build-up of material around the head can fly off when it's struck with a hammer and is potentially dangerous. Make sure the tool retains its original profile at the working end, again, filing or grinding off all burrs. In the case of cold chisels, the cutting edge will usually have to be reground quite often because the material in the tool isn't usually much harder than materials typically being cut. Make sure the edge is reasonably sharp, but don't make the tip angle greater than it was originally; it'll just wear down faster if you do.

The techniques for using these tools vary according to the job to be done and are best learned by experience. The one common denominator is the fact they're all normally struck with a hammer. It follows that eye protection should be worn. Always make sure the working end of the tool is in contact with the part being punched or cut. If it isn't, the tool will bounce off the surface and damage may result.

Hacksaws

A hacksaw (see illustration) consists of a handle and frame supporting a flexible steel blade under tension. Blades are available in various lengths and most hacksaws can be adjusted to accommodate the different sizes. The most common blade length is 10-inches.

Most hacksaw frames are adequate. There's little difference between brands. Pick one that's rigid and allows easy blade changing and repositioning.

The type of blade to use, indicated by the number of teeth per inch (TPI) (see illustration), is determined by the material being cut.

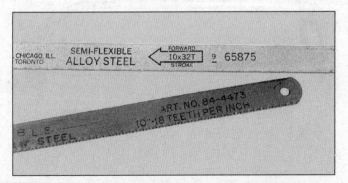

Hacksaw blades are marked with the number of teeth per inch (TPI) - use a relatively coarse blade for aluminum and thicker items such as bolts or bar stock; use a finer blade for materials like thin sheet steel

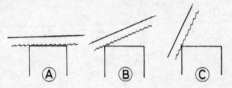

When cutting thin materials, check that at least three teeth are in contact with the workpiece at any time. Too coarse a blade will result in a poor cut and may break the blade. If you do not have the correct blade, cut at a shallow angle to the material

The correct cutting angle is important. If it is too shallow (A) the blade will wander. The angle shown at (B) is correct when starting the cut, and may be reduced slightly once under way. In (C) the angle is too steep and the blade will be inclined to jump out of the cut

10330-1-1.34 HAYNES

Correct procedure for use of a hacksaw

The rule of thumb is to make sure at least three teeth are in contact with the metal being cut at any one time **(see illustration)**. In practice, this means a fine blade for cutting thin sheet materials, while a coarser blade can be used for faster cutting through thicker items such as bolts or bar stock. When cutting thin materials, angle the saw so the blade cuts at a shallow angle. More teeth are in contact and there's less chance of the blade binding and breaking, or teeth breaking.

When you buy blades, choose a reputable brand. Cheap, unbranded blades may be perfectly acceptable, but you can't tell by looking at them. Poor quality blades will be insufficiently hardened on the teeth edge and will dull quickly. Most reputable brands will be marked "Flexible High Speed Steel" or a similar term, to indicate the type of material used **(see illustration)**. It is possible to buy unbreakable blades (only the teeth are hardened, leaving the rest of the blade less brittle).

Sometimes, a full-size hacksaw is too big to allow access to a frozen nut or bolt. On most saws, you can overcome this problem by turning the blade 90-degrees. Occasionally you may have to position the saw around an obstacle and then install the blade on the other side of

Good quality hacksaw blades are marked like this

it. Where space is really restricted, you may have to use a handle that clamps onto a saw blade at one end. This allows access when a hacksaw frame would not work at all and has another advantage in that you can make use of broken off hacksaw blades instead of throwing them away. Note that because only one end of the blade is supported, and it's not held under tension, it's difficult to control and less efficient when cutting.

Before using a hacksaw, make sure the blade is suitable for the material being cut and installed correctly in the frame **(see illustration)**. Whatever it is you're cutting must be securely supported so it can't move around. The saw cuts on the forward stroke, so the teeth must point away from the handle. This might seem obvious, but it's easy to install the blade backwards by mistake and ruin the teeth on the first few strokes. Make sure the blade is tensioned adequately or it'll distort and chatter in the cut and may break. Wear safety glasses and be careful not to cut yourself on the saw blade or the sharp edge of the cut.

Files

Files **(see illustration)** come in a wide variety of sizes and types for specific jobs, but all of them are used for the same basic function of removing small amounts of metal in a controlled fashion. Files are used by mechanics mainly for deburring, marking parts, removing rust, filing the heads off rivets, restoring threads and fabricating small parts.

File shapes commonly available include flat, half-round, round, square and triangular. Each shape comes in a range of sizes (lengths) and cuts ranging from rough to smooth. The file face is covered with rows

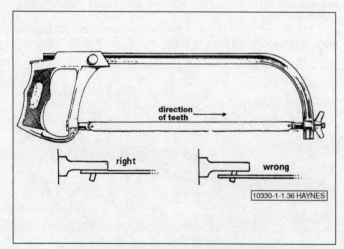

direction
of teeth

right

wrong

10330-1-1.36 HAYNES

**Correct installation of a hacksaw blade -
the tooth must point away from the handle
and butt against the locating lugs**

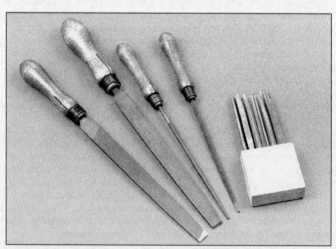

**Get a good assortment of files - they're handy for deburring,
marking parts, removing rust, filing the heads off rivets,
restoring threads and fabricating small parts**

Files are either single-cut (left) or double-cut (right) - generally speaking, use a single-cut file to produce a very smooth surface; use a double-cut file to remove large amounts of material quickly

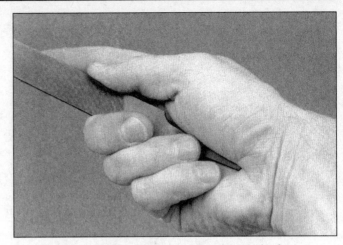

Never use a file without a handle - the tang is sharp and could puncture your hand

of diagonal ridges which form the cutting teeth. They may be aligned in one direction only (single cut) or in two directions to form a diamond-shaped pattern (double-cut) **(see illustration)**. The spacing of the teeth determines the file coarseness, again, ranging from rough to smooth in five basic grades: Rough, coarse, bastard, second-cut and smooth.

You'll want to build up a set of files by purchasing tools of the required shape and cut as they're needed. A good starting point would be flat, half-round, round and triangular files (at least one each - bastard or second-cut types). In addition, you'll have to buy one or more file handles (files are usually sold without handles, which are purchased separately and pushed over the tapered tang of the file when in use) **(see illustration)**. You may need to buy more than one size handle to fit the various files in your tool box, but don't attempt to get by without them. A file tang is fairly sharp and you almost certainly will end up stabbing yourself in the palm of the hand if you use a file without a handle and it catches in the work piece during use. Adjustable handles are also available for use with files of various sizes, eliminating the need for several handles **(see illustration)**.

Exceptions to the need for a handle are fine Swiss pattern files, which have a rounded handle instead of a tang. These small files are usually sold in sets with a number of different shapes. Originally intended for very fine work, they can be very useful for use in inaccessible areas. Swiss files are normally the best choice if piston ring ends require filing to obtain the correct end gap.

The correct procedure for using files is fairly easy to master. As with a hacksaw, the work should be clamped securely in a vise, if needed, to prevent it from moving around while being worked on. Hold the file by the handle, using your free hand at the file end to guide it and keep it flat in relation to the surface being filed. Use smooth cutting strokes and be careful not to rock the file as it passes over the surface. Also, don't slide it diagonally across the surface or the teeth will make grooves in the work piece. Don't drag a file back across the work piece at the end of the stroke - lift it slightly and pull it back to prevent damage to the teeth.

Files don't require maintenance in the usual sense, but they should be kept clean and free of metal filings. Steel is a reasonably easy material to work with, but softer metals like aluminum tend to clog the file teeth very quickly, which will result in scratches in the work piece. This can be avoided by rubbing the file face with chalk before using it. General cleaning is carried out with a file card or a fine wire brush. If kept clean, files will last a long time - when they do eventually dull, they must be replaced; there is no satisfactory way of sharpening a worn file.

Taps and dies

Taps

Tap and die sets **(see illustration)** are available in inch and metric sizes. Taps are used to cut internal threads and clean or restore damaged threads. A tap consists of a fluted shank with a drive square at one end. It's threaded along part of its length - the cutting edges are formed

Adjustable handles that will work with many different size files are also available

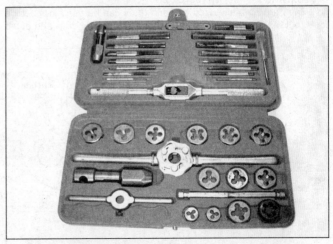

Tap and dies sets are available in inch and metric sizes - taps are used for cutting internal threads and cleaning and restoring damaged threads; dies are used for cutting, cleaning and restoring external threads

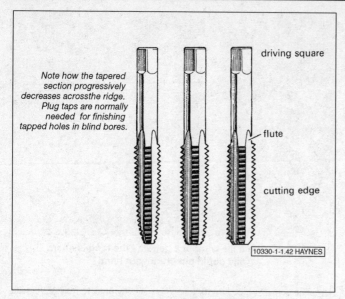

Note how the tapered section progressively decreases across the ridge. Plug taps are normally needed for finishing tapped holes in blind bores.

driving square

flute

cutting edge

10330-1-1.42 HAYNES

Taper, plug and bottoming taps (left-to-right)

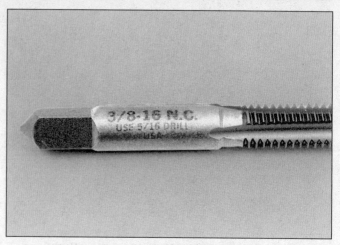

If you need to drill and tap a hole, the drill bit size to use for a given bolt (top) size is marked on the tap

where the flutes intersect the threads **(see illustration)**. Taps are made from hardened steel so they will cut threads in materials softer than what they're made of.

Taps come in three different types: Taper, plug and bottoming. The only real difference is the length of the chamfer on the cutting end of the tap. Taper taps are chamfered for the first 6 or 8 threads, which makes them easy to start but prevents them from cutting threads close to the bottom of a hole. Plug taps are chamfered up about 3 to 5 threads, which makes them a good all around tap because they're relatively easy to start and will cut nearly to the bottom of a hole. Bottoming taps, as the name implies, have a very short chamfer (1-1/2 to 3 threads) and will cut as close to the bottom of a blind hole as practical. However, to do this, the threads should be started with a plug or taper tap.

Although cheap tap and die sets are available, the quality is usually very low and they can actually do more harm than good when used on threaded holes in aluminum engines. The alternative is to buy high-quality taps if and when you need them, even though they aren't cheap, especially if you need to buy two or more thread pitches in a given size. Despite this, it's the best option - you'll probably only need taps on rare occasions, so a full set isn't absolutely necessary.

Taps are normally used by hand (they can be used in machine tools, but not when doing engine repairs). The square drive end of the tap is held in a tap wrench (an adjustable T-handle). For smaller sizes, a T-handled chuck can be used. The tapping process starts by drilling a hole of the correct diameter. For each tap size, there's a corresponding twist drill that will produce a hole of the correct size. This is important; too large a hole will leave the finished thread with the tops missing, producing a weak and unreliable grip. Conversely, too small a hole will place excessive loads on the hard and brittle shank of the tap, which can break it off in the hole. Removing a broken off tap from a hole is no fun! The correct tap drill size is normally marked on the tap itself or the container it comes in **(see illustration)**.

Dies

Dies are used to cut, clean or restore external threads. Most dies are made from a hex-shaped or cylindrical piece of hardened steel with a threaded hole in the center. The threaded hole is overlapped by three or four cutouts, which equate to the flutes on taps and allow metal waste to escape during the threading process. Dies are held in a T-handled holder (called a die stock) **(see illustration)**. Some dies are split at one point, allowing them to be adjusted slightly (opened and closed) for fine control of thread clearances.

Dies aren't needed as often as taps, for the simple reason it's normally easier to install a new bolt than to salvage one. However, it's often helpful to be able to extend the threads of a bolt or clean up damaged threads with a die. Hex-shaped dies are particularly useful for mechanic's work, since they can be turned with a wrench **(see illustration)** and are usually less expensive than adjustable ones.

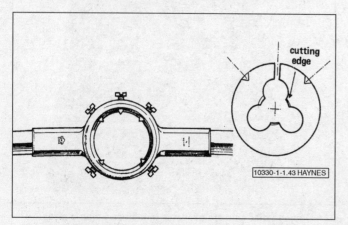

cutting edge

10330-1-1.43 HAYNES

A die (right) is used for cutting external threads (this one is a split-type/adjustable die) and is held in a tool called a die stock (left)

Hex-shaped dies are especially handy for mechanic's work because they can be turned with a wrench

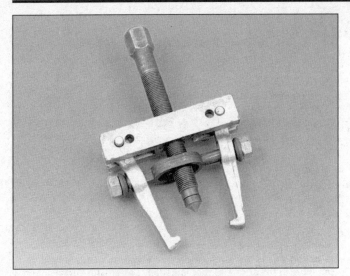

A two or three-jaw puller will come in handy for many tasks in the shop and can also be used for working on other types of equipment

The procedure for cutting threads with a die is broadly similar to that described above for taps. When using an adjustable die, the initial cut is made with the die fully opened, the adjustment screw being used to reduce the diameter of successive cuts until the finished size is reached. As with taps, a cutting lubricant should be used, and the die must be backed off every few turns to clear swarf from the cutouts.

Pullers

You'll need a general-purpose puller for engine rebuilding. Pullers can removed seized or corroded parts, bad bushes or bearings and dynamic balancers. Universal two- and three-legged pullers are widely available in numerous designs and sizes.

The typical puller consists of a central boss with two or three pivoting arms attached. The outer ends of the arms are hooked jaws which grab the part you want to pull off **(see illustration)**. You can reverse the arms on most pullers to use the puller on internal openings when necessary. The central boss is threaded to accept a puller bolt, which does the work. You can also get hydraulic versions of these tools which are capable of more pressure, but they're expensive.

You can adapt pullers by purchasing, or fabricating, special jaws for specific jobs. If you decide to make your own jaws, keep in mind that the pulling force should be concentrated as close to the center of the component as possible to avoid damaging it.

Before you use a puller, assemble it and check it to make sure it doesn't snag on anything and the loads on the part to be removed are distributed evenly. If you're dealing with a part held on the shaft by a nut, loosen the nut but don't remove it. Leaving the nut on helps prevent distortion of the shaft end under pressure from the puller bolt and stops the part from flying off the shaft when it comes loose.

Tighten a puller gradually until the assembly is under moderate pressure, then try to jar the component loose by striking the puller bolt a few times with a hammer. If this doesn't work, tighten the bolt a little further and repeat the process. If this approach doesn't work, stop and reconsider. At some point you must make a decision whether to continue applying pressure in this manner. Sometimes, you can apply penetrating oil around the joint and leave it overnight, with the puller in place and tightened securely. By the next day, the taper has separated and the problem has resolved itself.

If nothing else works, try heating the area surrounding the troublesome part with a propane or gas welding torch (We don't, however, recommend messing around with welding equipment if you're not already experienced in its use). Apply the heat to the hub area of the component you wish to remove. Keep the flame moving to avoid uneven heating and the risk of distortion. Keep pressure applied with the puller and make sure that you're able to deal with the resulting hot component and the puller jaws if it does come free. Be very careful to keep the flame away from aluminum parts.

If all reasonable attempts to remove a part fail, don't be afraid to give up. It's cheaper to quit now than to repair a badly damaged engine. Either buy or borrow the correct tool, or take the engine to a dealer and ask him to remove the part for you.

Drawbolt extractors

The simple drawbolt extractor is easy to make up and invaluable in every workshop. There are no commercially available tools of this type; you simply make a tool to suit a particular application. You can use a drawbolt extractor to pull out stubborn piston pins and to remove bearings and bushings.

To make a drawbolt extractor, you'll need an assortment of threaded rods in various sizes (available at hardware stores), and nuts to fit them. You'll also need assorted washers, spacers and tubing. For things like piston pins, you'll usually need a longer piece of tube.

Some typical drawbolt uses are shown in the accompanying line drawings **(see illustration)**. They also reveal the order of assembly of the various pieces. The same arrangement, minus the tubular spacer section, can usually be used to install a new bushing or piston pin. Using the tool is quite simple. Just make sure you get the bush or pin square to the bore when you install it. Lubricate the part being pressed into place, where appropriate.

Pullers for use in blind bores

Bushings or bearings installed in blind holes often require special pullers. Some bearings can be removed without a puller if you heat the engine or component evenly in an oven and tap it face down on a clean wooden surface to dislodge the bearing. Wear heavy gloves to protect yourself when handling the heated components. If you need a puller to do the job, get a slide-hammer with interchangeable tips. Slide hammers range from universal two or three-jaw puller arrangements to special bearing pullers. Bearing pullers are hardened steel tubes with a flange around the bottom edge. The tube is split at several places, which allows a wedge to expand the tool once it's in place. The tool fits inside the bearing inner race and is tightened so the flange or lip is locked under the edge of the race.

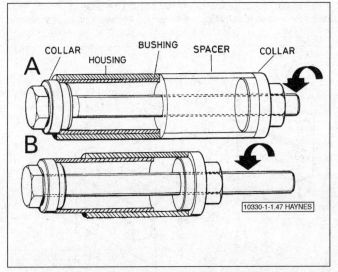

Typical drawbolt uses: in (A), the nut is tightened to pull the collar and bushing into the large spacer; in (B), the spacer is left out and the drawbolt is repositioned to install the new bushing

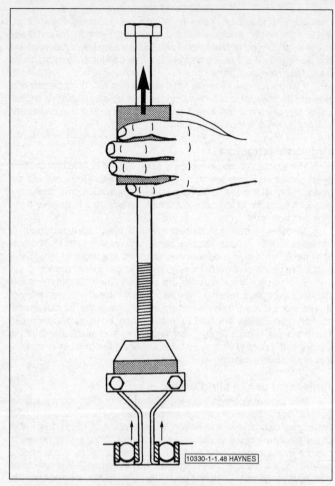

A slide hammer with special attachments can be used for removing bearings and bushings from blind holes

The slide-hammer consists of a steel shaft with a stop at its upper end. The shaft carries a sliding weight which slides along the shaft until it strikes the stop. This allows the tool holding the bearing to drive it out of the bore **(see illustration)**. A bearing puller set is an expensive and

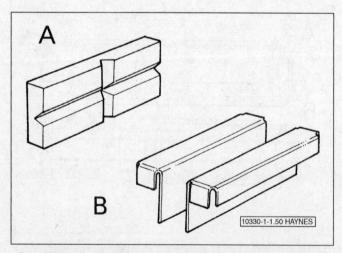

Sometimes, the parts you have to jig up in the vise are delicate, or made of soft materials - to avoid damaging them, get a pair of fiberglass or plastic "soft laws" (A) or fabricate your own with 1/8-inch thick aluminum sheet (B)

A bench vise is one of the most useful pieces of equipment you can have in the shop - bigger is usually better with vises, so get a vise with jaws that open at least four inches

infrequently-used piece of equipment, so take the engine to a dealer and have the bearings/bushings replaced.

Bench vise

The bench vise **(see illustration)** is an essential tool in a shop. Buy the best quality vise you can afford. A good vise is expensive, but the quality of its materials and workmanship are worth the extra money. Size is also important - bigger vises are usually more versatile. Make sure the jaws open at least four inches. Get a set of soft jaws to fit the vise as well - you'll need them to grip engine parts that could be damaged by the hardened vise jaws **(see illustration)**.

Power tools

Really, the only power tool you absolutely need is an electric drill. But if you have an air compressor and electricity, there's a wide range of pneumatic and electric hand tools to make all sorts of jobs easier and faster.

Air compressor

An air compressor **(see illustration)** makes most jobs easier and faster. Drying off parts after cleaning them with solvent, blowing out passages in a block or head, running power tools - the list is endless. Once

Although it's not absolutely necessary, an air compressor can make many jobs easier and produce better results, especially when air powered tools are available to use with it

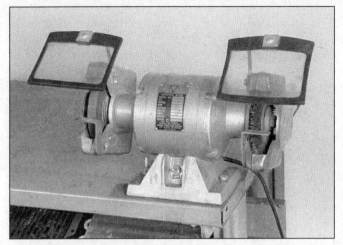

Another indispensable piece of equipment is the bench grinder (with a wire wheel mounted on one arbor) - make sure it's securely bolted down and never use it with the rests or eye shields removed

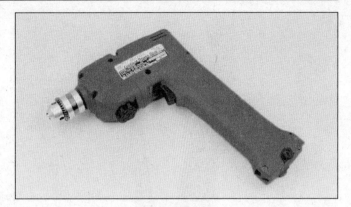

Electric drills can be cordless (above) or 115-volt, AC-powered (below)

you buy a compressor, you'll wonder how you ever got along without it. Air tools really speed up tedious procedures like removing and installing cylinder head bolts, crankshaft main bearing bolts or vibration damper (crankshaft pulley) bolts.

Bench-mounted grinder

A bench grinder **(see illustration)** is also handy. With a wire wheel on one end and a grinding wheel on the other, it's great for cleaning up fasteners, sharpening tools and removing rust. Make sure the grinder is fastened securely to the bench or stand, always wear eye protection when operating it and never grind aluminum parts on the grinding wheel.

Electric drills

Countersinking bolt holes, enlarging oil passages, honing cylinder bores, removing rusted or broken off fasteners, enlarging holes and fabricating small parts - electric drills **(see illustration)** are indispensable for engine work. A 3/8-inch chuck (drill bit holder) will handle most jobs. Collect several different wire brushes to use in the drill and make sure you have a complete set of sharp metal drill bits **(see illustration)**. Cordless drills are extremely versatile because they don't force you to work near an outlet. They're also handy to have around for a variety of non-mechanical jobs.

Twist drills and drilling equipment

Drilling operations are done with twist drills, either in a hand drill or a drill press. Twist drills (or drill bits, as they're often called) consist of a round shank with spiral flutes formed into the upper two-thirds to clear the waste produced while drilling, keep the drill centered in the hole and finish the sides of the hole.

The lower portion of the shank is left plain and used to hold the drill in the chuck. In this section, we will discuss only normal parallel shank drills **(see illustration)**. There is another type of bit with the plain

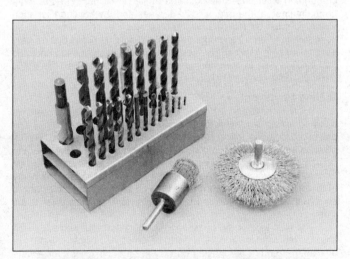

Get a set of good quality drill bits for drilling holes and wire brushes of various sizes for cleaning up metal parts - make sure the bits are designed for drilling in metal

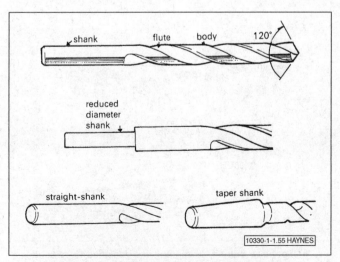

A typical drill bit (top), a reduced shank bit (center), and a tapered shank bit (bottom right)

Drill bits in the range most commonly used are available in fractional sizes (left) and number sizes (right) so almost any size hole can be drilled

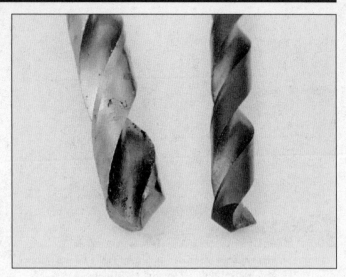

If a bit gets dull (left), discard it or resharpen it so it looks like the bit on the right

end formed into a special size taper designed to fit directly into a corresponding socket in a heavy-duty drill press. These drills are known as Morse Taper drills and are used primarily in machine shops.

At the cutting end of the drill, two edges are ground to form a conical point. They're generally angled at about 60-degrees from the drill axis, but they can be reground to other angles for specific applications. For general use the standard angle is correct - this is how the drills are supplied.

When buying drills, purchase a good-quality set (sizes 1/16 to 3/8-inch). Make sure the drills are marked "High Speed Steel" or "HSS". This indicates they're hard enough to withstand continual use in metal; many cheaper, unmarked drills are suitable only for use in wood or other soft materials. Buying a set ensures the right size bit will be available when it's needed.

Twist drill sizes

Twist drills are available in a vast array of sizes, most of which you'll never need. There are three basic drill sizing systems: Fractional, number and letter **(see illustration)** (we won't get involved with the fourth system, which is metric sizes).

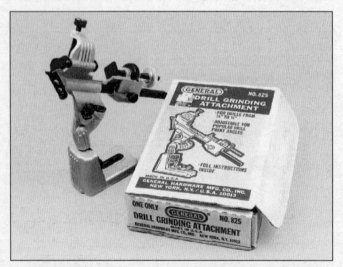

Inexpensive drill bit sharpening jigs designed to be used with a bench grinder are widely available - even if you only use it to resharpen drill bits, it'll pay for itself quickly

Fractional sizes start at 1/64-inch and increase in increments of 1/64-inch. Number drills range in descending order from 80 (0.0135-inch), the smallest, to 1 (0.2280-inch), the largest. Letter sizes start with A (0.234-inch), the smallest, and go through Z (0.413-inch), the largest.

This bewildering range of sizes means it's possible to drill an accurate hole of almost any size within reason. In practice, you'll be limited by the size of chuck on your drill (normally 3/8 or 1/2-inch). In addition, very few stores stock the entire range of possible sizes, so you'll have to shop around for the nearest available size to the one you require.

Sharpening twist drills

Like any tool with a cutting edge, twist drills will eventually get dull **(see illustration)**. How often they'll need sharpening depends to some extent on whether they're used correctly. A dull twist drill will soon make itself known. A good indication of the condition of the cutting edges is to watch the waste emerging from the hole being drilled. If the tip is in good condition, two even spirals of waste metal will be produced; if this fails to happen or the tip gets hot, it's safe to assume that sharpening is required.

With smaller size drills - under about 1/8-inch - it's easier and more economical to throw the worn drill away and buy another one. With larger (more expensive) sizes, sharpening is a better bet. When sharpening twist drills, the included angle of the cutting edge must be maintained at the original 120-degrees and the small chisel edge at the tip must be retained. With some practice, sharpening can be done freehand on a bench grinder, but it should be noted that it's very easy to make mistakes. For most home mechanics, a sharpening jig that mounts next to the grinding wheel should be used so the drill is clamped at the correct angle **(see illustration)**.

Drilling equipment

Tools to hold and turn drill bits range from simple, inexpensive hand-operated or electric drills to sophisticated and expensive drill presses. Ideally, all drilling should be done on a drill press with the work piece clamped solidly in a vise. These machines are expensive and take up a lot of bench or floor space, so they're out of the question for many do-it-yourselfers. An additional problem is the fact that many of the drilling jobs you end up doing will be on the engine itself or the equipment it's mounted on, in which case the tool has to be taken to the work.

The best tool for the home shop is an electric drill with a 3/8-inch chuck. Both cordless and AC drills (that run off household current) are available. If you're purchasing one for the first time, look for a well-known, reputable brand name and variable speed as minimum requirements. A 1/4-inch chuck, single-speed drill will work, but it's worth paying a little more for the larger, variable speed type.

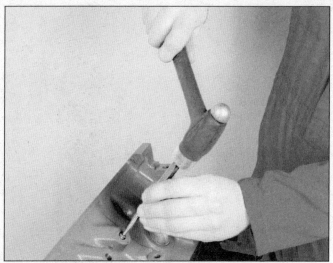

Before you drill a hole, use a centerpunch to make an
indentation for the drill bit so it won't wander

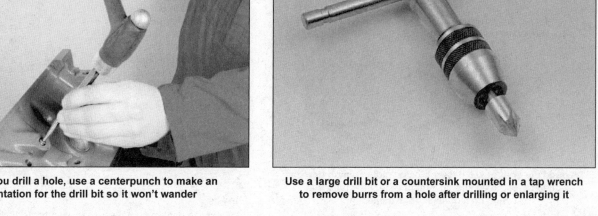

Use a large drill bit or a countersink mounted in a tap wrench
to remove burrs from a hole after drilling or enlarging it

All drills require a key to lock the bit in the chuck. When removing
or installing a bit, make sure the cord is unplugged to avoid accidents.
Initially, tighten the chuck by hand, checking to see if the bit is centered
correctly. This is especially important when using small drill bits which
can get caught between the jaws. Once the chuck is hand tight, use the
key to tighten it securely - remember to remove the key afterwards!

Drilling and finishing holes
Preparation for drilling
If possible, make sure the part you intend to drill in is securely
clamped in a vise. If it's impossible to get the work to a vise, make sure
it's stable and secure. Twist drills often dig in during drilling - this can
be dangerous, particularly if the work suddenly starts spinning on the
end of the drill. Obviously, there's little chance of a complete engine or
piece of equipment doing this, but you should make sure it's supported
securely.

Start by locating the center of the hole you're drilling. Use a center
punch to make an indentation for the drill bit so it won't wander. If you're
drilling out a broken-off bolt, be sure to position the punch in the exact
center of the bolt **(see illustration)**.

If you're drilling a large hole (above 1/4-inch), you may want to
make a pilot hole first. As the name suggests, it will guide the larger drill
bit and minimize drill bit wandering. Before actually drilling a hole, make
sure the area immediately behind the bit is clear of anything you don't
want drilled.

Drilling
When drilling steel, especially with smaller bits, no lubrication is
needed. If a large bit is involved, oil can be used to ensure a clean cut
and prevent overheating of the drill tip. When drilling aluminum, which
tends to smear around the cutting edges and clog the drill bit flutes, use
kerosene as a lubricant.

Wear safety goggles or a face shield and assume a comfortable,
stable stance so you can control the pressure on the drill easily. Position the drill tip in the punch mark and make sure, if you're drilling by
hand, the bit is perpendicular to the surface of the work piece. Start drilling without applying much pressure until you're sure the hole is positioned correctly. If the hole starts off center, it can be very difficult to
correct. You can try angling the bit slightly so the hole center moves in
the opposite direction, but this must be done before the flutes of the bit
have entered the hole. It's at the starting point that a variable-speed drill
is invaluable; the low speed allows fine adjustments to be made before
it's too late. Continue drilling until the desired hole depth is reached or
until the drill tip emerges at the other side of the work piece.

Cutting speed and pressure are important - as a general rule,
the larger the diameter of the drill bit, the slower the drilling speed
should be. With a single-speed drill, there's little that can be done to
control it, but two-speed or variable speed drills can be controlled.
If the drilling speed is too high, the cutting edges of the bit will tend
to overheat and dull. Pressure should be varied during drilling. Start
with light pressure until the drill tip has located properly in the work.
Gradually increase pressure so the bit cuts evenly. If the tip is sharp
and the pressure correct, two distinct spirals of metal will emerge
from the bit flutes. If the pressure is too light, the bit won't cut properly, while excessive pressure will overheat the tip.

Decrease pressure as the bit breaks through the work piece.
If this isn't done, the bit may jam in the hole; if you're using a hand-
held drill, it could be jerked out of your hands, especially when using
larger size bits.

Once a pilot hole has been made, install the larger bit in the chuck
and enlarge the hole. The second bit will follow the pilot hole - there's
no need to attempt to guide it (if you do, the bit may break off). It is
important, however, to hold the drill at the correct angle.

After the hole has been drilled to the correct size, remove the burrs
left around the edges of the hole. This can be done with a small round
file, or by chamfering the opening with a larger bit or a countersink **(see
illustration)**. Use a drill bit that's several sizes larger than the hole and
simply twist it around each opening by hand until any rough edges are
removed.

Enlarging and reshaping holes
The biggest practical size for bits used in a hand drill is about 1/2-
inch. This is partly determined by the capacity of the chuck (although it's
possible to buy larger drills with stepped shanks). The real limit is the
difficulty of controlling large bits by hand; drills over 1/2-inch tend to be
too much to handle in anything other than a drill press. If you have to
make a larger hole, or if a shape other than round is involved, different
techniques are required.

If a hole simply must be enlarged slightly, a round file is probably
the best tool to use. If the hole must be very large, a hole saw will be
needed, but they can only be used in sheet metal.

Large or irregular-shaped holes can also be made in sheet metal
and other thin materials by drilling a series of small holes very close
together. In this case the desired hole size and shape must be marked
with a scribe. The next step depends on the size bit to be used; the idea
is to drill a series of almost touching holes just inside the outline of the
large hole. Center punch each location, then drill the small holes. A cold
chisel can then be used to knock out the waste material at the center of

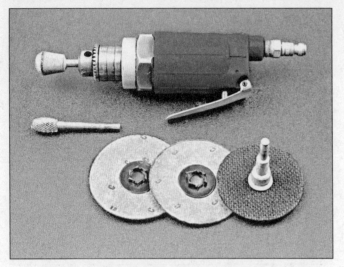

A good die grinder will deburr blocks, radius piston domes, chamfer oil holes and do a lot of other little jobs that would be tedious if done manually

the hole, which can then be filed to size. This is a time consuming process, but it's the only practical approach for the home shop. Success is dependent on accuracy when marking the hole shape and using the center punch.

High-speed grinders

A good die grinder **(see illustration)** will deburr blocks, radius piston domes and chamfer oil holes ten times as fast as you can do any of these jobs by hand.

Safety items that should be in every shop

Fire extinguishers

Buy at least one fire extinguisher **(see illustration)** before doing any maintenance or repair procedures. Make sure it's rated for flammable liquid fires. Familiarize yourself with its use as soon as you buy it - don't wait until you need it to figure out how to use it. Have it checked and recharged at regular intervals. Refer to the safety tips at the end of this Chapter for more information about the hazards of gasoline and other flammable liquids.

Buy at least one fire extinguisher before you open shop - make sure it's rated for flammable liquid fires and KNOW HOW TO USE IT!

Gloves

If you're handling hot parts or metal parts with sharp edges, wear a pair of industrial work gloves to protect yourself from burns, cuts and splinters **(see illustration)**. Wear a pair of heavy duty rubber gloves (to protect your hands when you wash parts in solvent).

Safety glasses or goggles

Never work on a bench or high-speed grinder without safety glasses **(see illustration)**. Don't take a chance on getting a metal sliver in your eye. It's also a good idea to wear safety glasses when you're washing parts in solvent.

Special diagnostic tools

These tools do special diagnostic tasks. They're indispensable for determining the condition of your engine. If you don't think you'll use them frequently enough to justify the investment, try to borrow or rent them, or split the cost with a friend who also wants to get into engine rebuilding. We've listed only those tools and instruments generally available to the public, not the special tools manufactured for dealer service departments. Occasional references to special tools may be included in the text of this manual. But we'll try to provide you with another way of doing the job without the special tool, if possible. However, when there's no alternative, you'll have to borrow or buy the tool or have the job done by a professional.

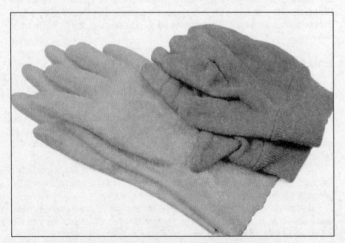

Get a pair of heavy work gloves for handling hot or sharp-edged objects and a pair of rubber gloves for washing parts with solvent

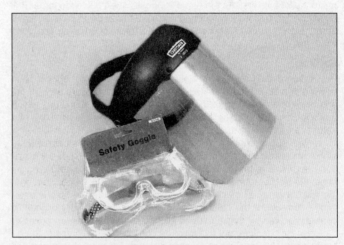

One of the most important items you'll need in the shop is a face shield or safety goggles, especially when you're hitting metal parts with a hammer, washing parts in solvent or grinding something on the bench grinder

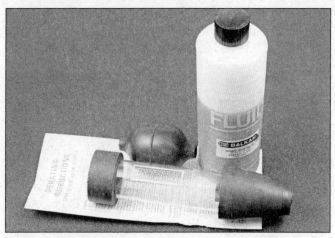

The combustion leak block tester tests for cracked blocks, leaky gaskets, cracked heads and warped heads by detecting combustion gases in the coolant

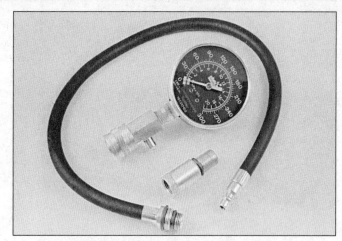

The compression gauge indicates cylinder pressure in the combustion chamber - you'll need to get one made for diesels (because of their higher compression)

Combustion leak block tester

The combustion leak block tester **(see illustration)** tests for cracked blocks, leaky gaskets, cracked heads and warped heads by detecting combustion gasses in the coolant. For information on using this tool, see Chapter 3.

Compression gauge

The compression gauge **(see illustration)** indicates cylinder pressure in the combustion chamber. The adapter (depending on engine) screws into the glow plug hole. **Warning:** *Because diesel engines have very high compression, a special diesel compression gauge is required.*

Cooling system pressure tester

The cooling system pressure tester **(see illustration)** checks for leaks in the cooling system.

Leakdown tester

The leakdown tester **(see illustration)** indicates the rate at which pressure leaks past the piston rings, the valves and/or the head gasket, in a combustion chamber.

Multimeter

The multimeter **(see illustration)** combines the functions of a volt-meter, ammeter and ohmmeter into one unit. It can measure voltage, amperage or resistance in an electrical circuit.

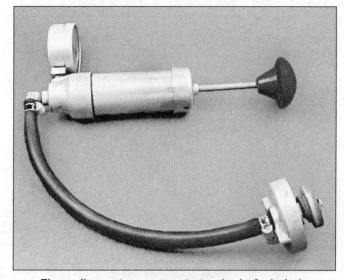

The cooling system pressure tester checks for leaks in the cooling system by pressurizing the system and measuring the rate at which it leaks down

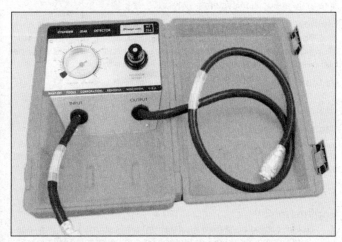

The leakdown tester indicates the rate at which pressure leaks past the piston rings, the valves and/or the head gasket

The multimeter combines the functions of a volt-meter, ammeter and ohmmeter into one unit - it can measure voltage, amperage or resistance in an electrical circuit

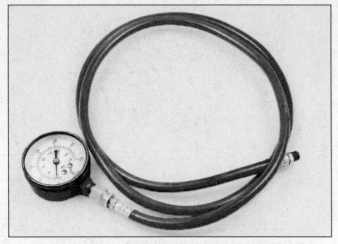

The oil pressure gauge, which screws into an oil pressure sending unit hole in the block or head, measures the oil pressure in the lubrication system

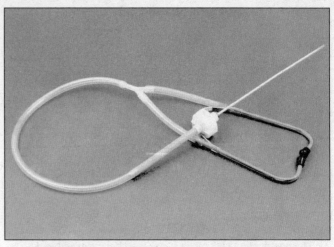

The stethoscope amplifies engine sounds, allowing you to pinpoint possible sources of trouble such as bad bearings, excessive play in the crank, rod knocks, etc.

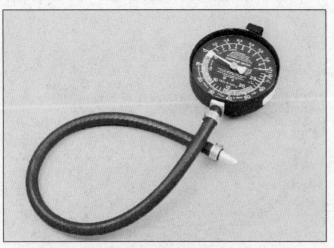

The vacuum gauge indicates intake manifold vacuum, in inches of mercury (in-Hg)

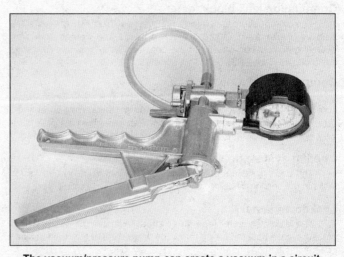

The vacuum/pressure pump can create a vacuum in a circuit, or pressurize it, to simulate the actual operating conditions

Get an engine hoist that's strong enough to easily lift your engine in and out of the engine compartment - an adapter, like the one shown here, can be used to change the angle of the engine as it's being removed or installed

Oil pressure gauge

The oil pressure gauge **(see illustration)** indicates the oil pressure in the lubrication system.

Stethoscope

The stethoscope **(see illustration)** amplifies engine sounds, allowing you to pinpoint possible sources of pending trouble such as bad bearings, excessive play in the crank, rod knock, etc.

Vacuum gauge

The vacuum gauge **(see illustration)** indicates intake manifold vacuum, in inches of mercury (in-Hg).

Vacuum/pressure pump

The hand-operated vacuum/pressure pump **(see illustration)** can create a vacuum, or build up pressure, in a circuit to check components that are vacuum or pressure operated.

Engine rebuilding tools

Engine hoist

Get an engine hoist **(see illustration)** that's strong enough to easily lift your engine in and out of the engine compartment. A V8 diesel is far too heavy to remove and install any other way. And you don't even want to think about the possibility of dropping an engine!

Get an engine stand sturdy enough to firmly support the engine
while you're working on it. Stay away from three-wheeled
models - they have a tendency to tip over more
easily - get a four-wheeled unit

A clutch alignment tool is necessary if you plan to install
a rebuilt engine mated to a manual transmission

Engine stand

A V8 diesel is too heavy and bulky to wrestle around on the floor
or the workbench while you're disassembling and reassembling it. Get
an engine stand (see illustration) sturdy enough to firmly support the
engine. Even if you plan to work on small blocks, it's a good idea to buy
a stand beefy enough to handle big blocks as well. Try to buy a stand
with four wheels, not three. The center of gravity of a stand is high, so
it's easier to topple the stand and engine when you're cinching down
head bolts with a two-foot long torque wrench. Get a stand with big
casters. The larger the wheels, the easier it is to roll the stand around
the shop. Wheel locks are also a good feature to have. If you want the
stand out of the way between jobs, look for one that can be knocked
down and slid under a workbench.

Engine stands are available at rental yards; however, the cost of
rental over the long period of time you'll need the stand (often, weeks)
is frequently as high as buying a stand.

Clutch alignment tool

The clutch alignment tool (see illustration) is used to center the
clutch disc on the flywheel.

Cylinder surfacing hone

After boring the cylinders, you need to put a cross-hatch pattern
on the cylinder walls to help the new rings seat properly. A flex hone
with silicone carbide balls laminated onto the end of wire bristles (see
illustration) will give you that pattern. Even if you don't bore the cylinders, you must hone the cylinders, since it breaks the glaze that coats
the cylinder walls.

Cylinder ridge reamer

If the engine has a lot of miles, the top compression ring will likely
wear the cylinder wall and create a ridge at the top of each cylinder (the
unworn portion of the bore forms the ridge). Carbon deposits make the
ridge even more pronounced. The ridge reamer (see illustration) cuts
away the ridge so you can remove the piston from the top of the cylinder without damaging the ring lands.

A cylinder hone like the one shown here is easier to use,
but not as versatile as the type that has three
spring-loaded stones

If there are ridges at the top of the cylinder wall created
by the thrust side of the piston at the top of its travel,
use a ridge reamer to remove them

The best universal ring compressor is the plier-type - to fit different bore sizes, simply insert different size compressor bands in the plier handles

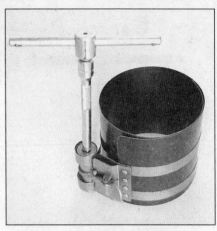

The band-type ring compressor is as easy to use as the plier type but is more likely to snag a ring

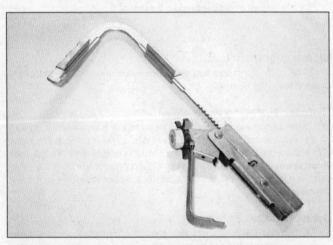

Sometimes you find that you can re-use the same pistons even when the rings need to be replaced - but the piston ring grooves in the old pistons are usually filthy. To clean them properly, you may need a piston ring groove cleaning tool

Piston ring compressor

Trying to install the pistons without a ring compressor is almost impossible.

The best universal ring compressor is the plier-type, like the one manufactured by K-D Tools **(see illustration)**. To accommodate different bore sizes, simply insert different size compressor bands in the plier handles. Plier-type spring compressors allow you to turn the piston with one hand while tapping it into the cylinder bore with a hammer handle.

The band type ring compressor **(see illustration)** is the cheapest of the two, and will work on a range of piston sizes, but it's more likely to snag a ring.

Piston ring groove cleaner

If you're reusing old pistons, you'll want to clean the carbon out of the ring grooves. This odd-looking tool **(see illustration)** has a cutting bit that digs the stuff out.

Piston ring expander

This plier-like tool **(see illustration)** pushes the ends of the ring apart so you can slip it over the piston crown and into its groove.

Valve spring compressor

The valve spring compressor **(see illustration)** compresses the

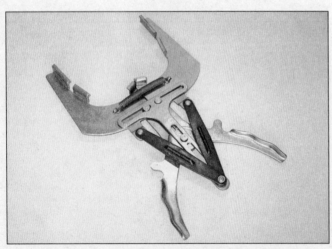

The piston ring expander pushes the ends of each ring apart so you can slip it over the piston crown and into its groove without scratching the piston or damaging the ring

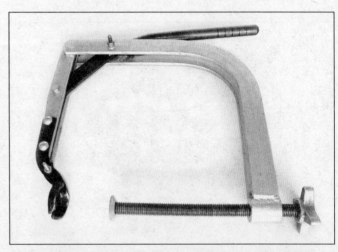

The valve spring compressor compresses the valve springs so you can remove the keepers and the retainer - the C-type (shown) reaches around to the underside of the head and pushes against the valve as it compresses the spring

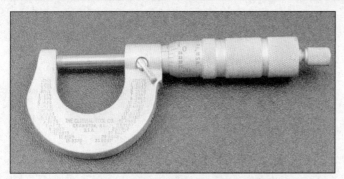

The one-inch micrometer is an essential precision measuring device for determining the dimensions of a piston pin, valve spring shim, thrust washer, etc.

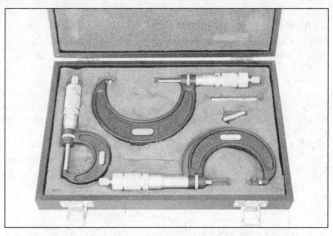

Get a good-quality micrometer set if you can afford it - this set has four micrometers ranging in size from one to four inches

valve springs so you can remove the keepers and the retainer. For engine overhaul, if you can afford it, get a C-clamp type that's designed to de-spring the head when it's off the engine. Cheaper types also work, but they're more time consuming to use.

Precision measuring tools

Think of the tools in the following list as the final stage of your tool collection. If you're planning to rebuild an engine, you've probably already accumulated all the screwdrivers, wrenches, sockets, pliers and other everyday hand tools that you need. You've also probably collected all the special-purpose tools necessary to tune and service your specific engine. Now it's time to round up the stuff you'll need to do your own measurements when you rebuild that engine.

The tool pool strategy

If you're reading this book, you may be a motorhead, but engine rebuilding isn't your life - it's a hobby. You may just want to save some money, have a little fun and learn something about engine building. If that description fits your level of involvement, think about forming a tool pool with a friend or neighbor who wants to get into engine rebuilding, but doesn't want to spend a lot of money. For example, you can buy a set of micrometers and the other guy can buy a dial indicator and a set of small hole gauges.

Start with the basics

It would be great to own every precision measuring tool listed here, but you don't really need a machinist's chest crammed with exotic calipers and micrometers. You can often get by just fine with nothing more than a feeler gauge, modeling clay and Plastigage. Even most professional engine builders use only three tools 95-percent of the time: a one-inch outside micrometer, a dial indicator and a six-inch dial caliper. So start your collection with these three items.

Micrometers

When you're rebuilding an engine, you need to know the exact thickness of a sizeable number of pieces. Whether you're measuring the diameter of a piston pin or the thickness of a valve spring shim or a thrust washer, your tool of choice should be the trusty one-inch outside micrometer **(see illustration)**.

Insist on accuracy to within one ten-thousandths of an inch (0.0001-inch) when you shop for a micrometer. You'll probably never need that kind of precision, but the extra decimal place will help you decide which way to round off a close measurement.

High-quality micrometers have a range of one inch. Eventually, you'll want a set **(see illustration)** that spans four, or even five, ranges: 0 to 1-inch, 1 to 2-inch, 2 to 3-inch and 3-to-4-inch. On engines bigger than about 350 cu. in., you'll also probably need a 4-to-5-inch. These five micrometers will measure the thickness of any part that needs to be measured for an engine rebuild. You don't have to run out and buy all five of these babies at once. Start with the one-inch model, then, when you have the money, get the next size you need (the 3 to 4-inch size or 4 to 5-inch is a good second choice - they measure piston diameters).

Digital micrometers **(see illustration)** are easier to read than conventional micrometers, are just as accurate and are finally starting to become affordable. If you're uncomfortable reading a conventional micrometer (see sidebar), then get a digital.

Unless you're not going to use them very often, stay away from micrometers with interchangeable anvils **(see illustration)**. In theory, one of these can do the work of five or six single-range micrometers. The trouble is, they're awkward to use when measuring little parts, and changing the anvils is a hassle.

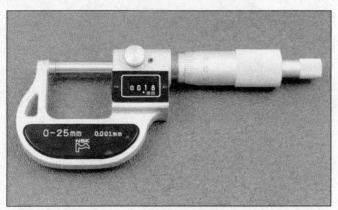

Digital micrometers are easier to read than conventional micrometers, are just as accurate and are finally starting to become affordable

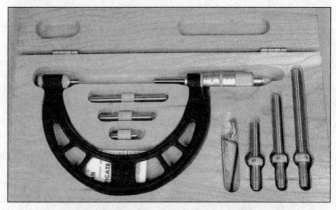

Avoid micrometer sets with interchangeable anvils - they're awkward to use when measuring small parts and changing the anvils is a hassle

How to read a micrometer

The outside micrometer is without a doubt the most widely used precision measuring tool. It can be used to make a variety of highly accurate measurements without much possibility of error through misreading, a problem associated with other measuring instruments, such as vernier calipers.

Like any slide caliper, the outside micrometer uses the double contact of its spindle and anvil **(see illustration)** touching the object to be measured to determine that object's dimensions. Unlike a caliper, however, the micrometer also features a unique precision screw adjustment which can be read with a great deal more accuracy than calipers.

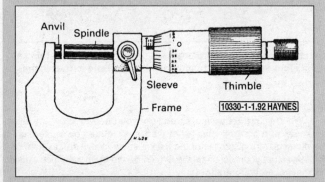

This diagram of a typical one-inch micrometer shows its major components

Why is this screw adjustment so accurate? Because years ago toolmakers discovered that a screw with 40 precision machined threads to the inch will advance one-fortieth (0.025) of an inch with each complete turn. The screw threads on the spindle revolve inside a fixed nut concealed by a sleeve.

On a one-inch micrometer, this sleeve is engraved longitudinally with exactly 40 lines to the inch, to correspond with the number of threads on the spindle. Every fourth line is made longer and is numbered one-tenth inch, two-tenths, etc. The other lines are often staggered to make them easier to read.

The thimble (the barrel which moves up and down the sleeve as it rotates) is divided into 25 divisions around the circumference of its beveled edge and is numbered from zero to 25. Close the micrometer spindle till it touches the anvil: You should see nothing but the zero line on the sleeve next to the beveled edge of the thimble. And the zero line of the thimble should be aligned with the horizontal (or axial) line on the sleeve. Remember: Each full revolution of the spindle from zero to zero advances or retracts the spindle one-fortieth or 0.025-inch. Therefore, if you rotate the thimble from zero on the beveled edge to the first graduation, you will move the spindle 1/25th of 1/40th, or 1/25th of 25/1000ths, which equals 1/1000th, or 0.001-inch.

Remember: Each numbered graduation on the sleeve represents 0.1-inch, each of the other sleeve graduations represents 0.025-inch and each graduation on the thimble represents 0.001-inch. Remember those three and you're halfway there.

For example: Suppose the 4 line is visible on the sleeve. This represents 0.400-inch. Then suppose there are an additional three lines (the short ones without numbers) showing. These marks are worth 0.025-inch each, or 0.075-inch. Finally, there are also two marks on the beveled edge of the thimble beyond the zero mark, each good for 0.001-inch, or a total of 0.002-inch. Add it all up and you get 0.400 plus 0.075 plus 0.002, which equals 0.477-inch.

Some beginners use a "dollars, quarters and cents" analogy to simplify reading a micrometer. Add up the bucks and change, then put a decimal point instead of a dollar sign in front of the sum!

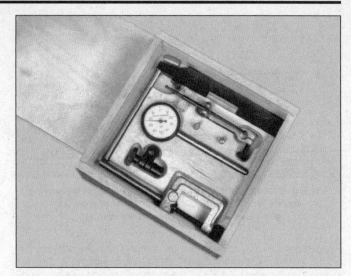

The dial indicator is indispensable for degreeing crankshafts, measuring valve lift, piston deck clearance, crankshaft endplay and a host of other critical measurements

Dial indicators

The dial indicator **(see illustration)** is another measuring mainstay. It's indispensable for degreeing camshafts, measuring valve lift, piston deck clearances, crankshaft endplay and all kinds of other little measurements. Make sure the dial indicator you buy has a probe with at least one inch of travel, graduated in 0.001-inch increments. And get a good assortment of probe extensions up to about six inches long. Sometimes, you need to screw a bunch of these extensions together to reach into tight areas like pushrod holes.

Buy a dial indicator set that includes a flexible fixture and a magnetic stand **(see illustration)**. If the model you buy doesn't have a magnetic base, buy one separately. Make sure the magnet is plenty strong. If a weak magnet comes loose and the dial indicator takes a tumble on a concrete floor, you can kiss it good-bye. Make sure the arm that attach the dial indicator to the flexible fixture is sturdy and the locking clamps are easy to operate.

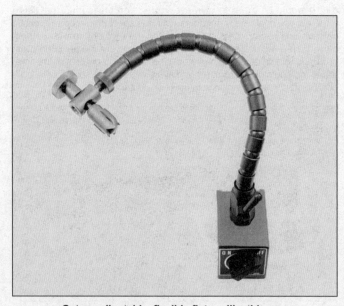

Get an adjustable, flexible fixture like this one, and a magnetic base, to ensure maximum versatility from your dial indicator

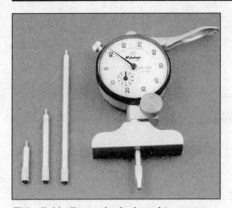

This dial indicator is designed to measure depth, such as deck height when the piston is below the block surface - with a U-shaped bridge (the base seen here is removable), you can measure the deck height of pistons that protrude above the deck (U-shaped bridges are also useful for checking the flatness of a block or cylinder head)

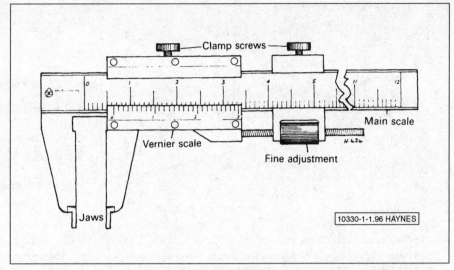

Vernier calipers aren't quite as accurate as micrometers, but they're handy for quick measurements and relatively inexpensive, and because they've got jaws that can measure internal and external dimensions, they're versatile

Some dial indicators are designed to measure depth **(see illustration)**. They have a removable base that straddles a hole. This setup is indispensable for measuring deck height when the piston is below the block surface. To measure the deck height of pistons that protrude above the deck, you'll also need a U-shaped bridge for your dial indicator. The bridge is also useful for checking the flatness of a block or a cylinder head.

Calipers

Vernier calipers **(see illustration)** aren't quite as accurate as a micrometer, but they're handy for quick measurements and they're relatively inexpensive. Most calipers have inside and outside jaws, so you can measure the inside diameter of a hole, or the outside diameter of a part.

Better-quality calipers have a dust shield over the geared rack that turns the dial to prevent small metal particles from jamming the mechanism. Make sure there's no play in the moveable jaw. To check, put a thin piece of metal between the jaws and measure its thickness with the metal close to the rack, then out near the tips of the jaws. Compare your two measurements. If they vary by more than 0.001-inch, look at another caliper - the jaw mechanism is deflecting.

If your eyes are going bad, or already are bad, vernier calipers can be difficult to read. Dial calipers **(see illustration)** are a better choice. Dial calipers combine the measuring capabilities of micrometers with the convenience of dial indicators. Because they're much easier to read quickly than vernier calipers, they're ideal for taking quick measurements when absolute accuracy isn't necessary. Like conventional vernier calipers, they have both inside and outside jaws which allow you to quickly determine the diameter of a hole or a part. Get a six-inch dial caliper, graduated in 0.001-inch increments.

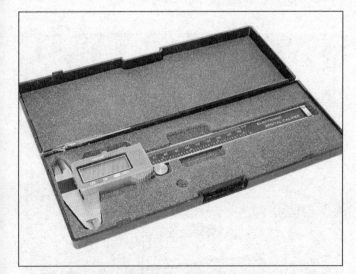

Dial calipers area lot easier to read than conventional vernier calipers, particularly if your eyesight isn't as good as it used to be!

How to read a vernier caliper

On the lower half of the main beam, each inch is divided into ten numbered increments, or tenths (0.100-inch, 0.200-inch, etc.). Each tenth is divided into four increments of 0.025-inch each. The vernier scale has 25 increments, each representing a thousandth (0.001) of an inch.

First read the number of inches, then read the number of tenths. Add to this 0.025-inch for each additional graduation. Using the English vernier scale, determine which graduation of the vernier lines up exactly with a graduation on the main beam. This vernier graduation is the number of thousandths which are to be added to the previous readings.

For example, let's say:

1) *The number of inches is zero, or 0.000-inch;*
2) *The number of tenths is 4, or 0.400-inch;*
3) *The number of 0.025's is 2, or 0.050-inch; and*
4) *The vernier graduation which lines up with a graduation on the main beam is 15, or 0.015-inch.*
5) *Add them up:*
   0.000
   0.400
   0.050
   0.015
6) *And you get: 0.46-inch.*

That's all there is to it!

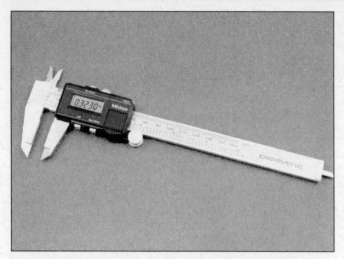

The latest calipers have a digital readout that is even easier to read than a dial caliper - another advantage of digital calipers is that they have a small microchip that allows them to convert instantaneously from inch to metric dimensions

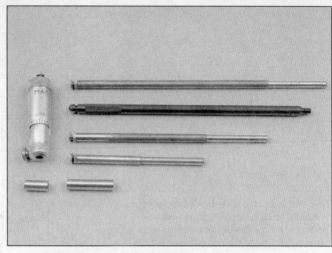

Inside micrometers are handy for measuring holes with thousandth-of-an-inch accuracy

The latest calipers **(see illustration)** have a digital LCD display that indicates both inch and metric dimensions. If you can afford one of these, it's the hot setup.

Inside micrometers

Cylinder bores, main bearing bores, connecting rod big ends - automotive engines have a lot of holes that must be measured accurately within a thousandth of an inch. Inside micrometers **(see illustration)** are used for these jobs. You read an inside micrometer the same way you read an outside micrometer. But it takes more skill to get an accurate reading.

To measure the diameter of a hole accurately, you must find the widest part of the hole. This involves expanding the micrometer while rocking it from side to side and moving it up and down. Once the micrometer is adjusted properly, you should be able to pull it through the hole with a slight drag. If the micrometer feels loose or

binds as you pull it through, you're not getting an accurate reading.

Fully collapsed, inside micrometers can measure holes as small as one inch in diameter. Extensions or spacers are added for measuring larger holes.

Telescoping snap gauges **(see illustration)** are used to measure smaller holes. Simply insert them into a hole and turn the knurled handle to release their spring-loaded probes, which expand out to the walls of the hole, turn the handle the other way and lock the probes into position, then pull the gauge out. After the gauge is removed from the hole, measure its width with an outside micrometer.

For measuring really small holes, such as valve guides, you'll need a set of small hole gauges **(see illustration)**. They work the same way as telescoping snap gauges, but instead of spring-loaded probes, they have expanding flanges on the end that can be screwed in and out by a threaded handle.

Telescoping snap gauges are used to measure smaller holes simply insert them into a hole, turn the knurled handle to release their spring-loaded probes out to the wall, turn the handle to lock the probes into position, pull out the gauge and measure the length from the tip of one probe to the tip of the other probe with a micrometer

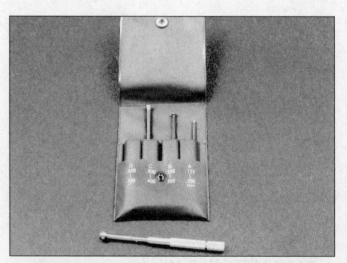

To measure really small holes, such as valve guides, you need a set of small hole gauges - to use them, simply stick them into the hole, turn the knurled handle until the expanding flanges are contacting the walls of the hole, pull out the gauge and measure the width of the gauge at the flanges with a micrometer

The dial bore gauge is more accurate and easier to use then an inside micrometer or telescoping snap gauges, but it's expensive - using various extensions, most dial gauges have a range of measurement from just over one inch to six inches or more

Metric thread sizes	Ft-lbs	Nm
M-6	6 to 9	9 to 12
M-8	14 to 21	19 to 28
M-10	28 to 40	38 to 54
M-12	50 to 71	68 to 96
M-14	80 to 140	109 to 154

Pipe thread sizes		
1/8	5 to 8	7 to 10
1/4	12 to 18	17 to 24
3/8	22 to 33	30 to 44
1/2	25 to 35	34 to 47

U.S. thread sizes		
1/4 – 20	6 to 9	9 to 12
5/16 – 18	12 to 18	17 to 24
5/16 – 24	14 to 20	19 to 27
3/8 – 16	22 to 32	30 to 43
3/8 – 24	27 to 38	37 to 51
7/16 – 14	40 to 55	55 to 74
7/16 – 20	40 to 60	55 to 81
1/2 – 13	55 to 80	75 to 108

Dial bore gauge

The dial bore gauge (see illustration) is more accurate and easier to use - but more expensive - than an inside micrometer for checking the roundness of the cylinders, and the bearing bores in main bearing saddles and connecting rods. Using various extensions, most dial bore gauges have a range of just over 1-inch in diameter to 6 inches or more. Unlike outside micrometers with interchangeable anvils, the accuracy of bore gauges with interchangeable extensions is unaffected. Bore gauges accurate to 0.0001-inch are available, but they're very expensive and hard to find. Most bore gauges are graduated in 0.0005-inch increments. If you use them properly, this accuracy level is more than adequate.

Storage and care of tools

Good tools are expensive, so treat them well. After you're through with your tools, wipe off any dirt, grease or metal chips and put them away. Don't leave tools lying around in the work area. General purpose hand tools - screwdrivers, pliers, wrenches and sockets - can be hung on a wall panel or stored in a tool box. Store precision measuring instruments, gauges, meters, etc. in a tool box to protect them from dust, dirt, metal chips and humidity.

Fasteners

Fasteners - nuts, bolts, studs and screws - hold parts together. Keep the following things in mind when working with fasteners: All threaded fasteners should be clean and straight, with good threads and unrounded corners on the hex head (where the wrench fits). Make it

a habit to replace all damaged nuts and bolts with new ones. Almost all fasteners have a locking device of some type, either a lockwasher, locknut, locking tab or thread adhesive. Don't reuse special locknuts with nylon or fiber inserts. Once they're removed, they lose their locking ability. Install new locknuts.

Flat washers and lockwashers, when removed from an assembly, should always be replaced exactly as removed. Replace any damaged washers with new ones. Never use a lockwasher on any soft metal surface (such as aluminum), thin sheet metal or plastic.

Apply penetrant to rusted nuts and bolts to loosen them up and prevent breakage. Some mechanics use turpentine in a spout-type oil can, which works quite well. After applying the rust penetrant, let it work for a few minutes before trying to loosen the nut or bolt. Badly rusted fasteners may have to be chiseled or sawed off or removed with a special nut breaker, available at tool stores.

If a bolt or stud breaks off in an assembly, it can be drilled and removed with a special tool commonly available for this purpose. Most automotive machine shops can perform this task, as well as other repair procedures, such as the repair of threaded holes that have been stripped out.

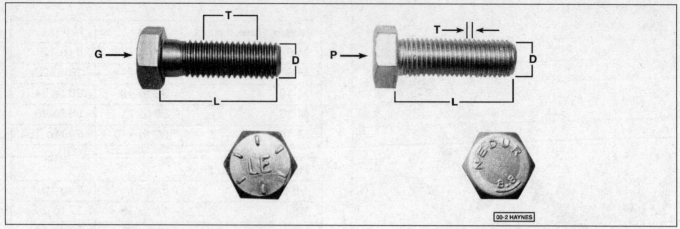

Standard (SAE and USS) bolt dimensions/grade marks

G   *Grade marks (bolt strength)*
L   *Length (in inches)*
T   *Thread pitch (number of threads per inch)*
D   *Nominal diameter (in inches)*

Metric bolt dimensions/grade marks

P   *Property class (bolt strength)*
L   *Length (in millimeters)*
T   *Thread pitch (distance between threads in millimeters)*
D   *Diameter*

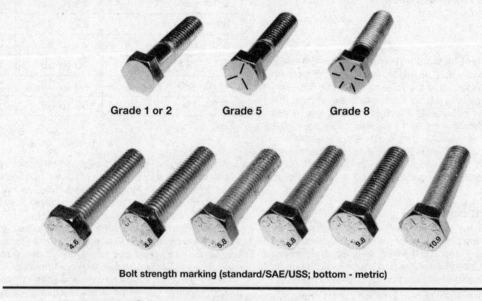

Grade 1 or 2   Grade 5   Grade 8

Bolt strength marking (standard/SAE/USS; bottom - metric)

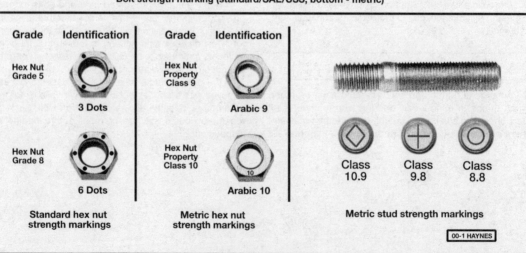

Grade	Identification
Hex Nut Grade 5	3 Dots
Hex Nut Grade 8	6 Dots

Standard hex nut strength markings

Grade	Identification
Hex Nut Property Class 9	Arabic 9
Hex Nut Property Class 10	Arabic 10

Metric hex nut strength markings

Class 10.9   Class 9.8   Class 8.8

Metric stud strength markings

Bolt strength markings

Fastener sizes

For a number of reasons, automobile manufacturers are making wider and wider use of metric fasteners. Therefore, it's important to be able to tell the difference between standard (sometimes called U.S. or SAE) and metric hardware, since they cannot be interchanged.

All bolts, whether standard or metric, are sized in accordance with their diameter, thread pitch and length (see illustration). For example, a standard 1/2 - 13 x 1 bolt is 1/2 inch in diameter, has 13 threads per inch and is 1 inch long. An M12 - 1.75 x 25 metric bolt is 12 mm in diameter, has a thread pitch of 1.75 mm (the distance between threads) and is 25 mm long. The two bolts are nearly identical, and easily confused, but they are not interchangeable.

In addition to the differences in diameter, thread pitch and length, metric and standard bolts can also be distinguished by examining the bolt heads. The distance across the flats on a standard bolt head is measured in inches; the same dimension on a metric bolt or nut is sized in millimeters. So don't use a standard wrench on a metric bolt, or vice versa.

Most standard bolts also have slashes radiating out from the center of the head (see illustration) to denote the grade or strength of the bolt, which is an indication of the amount of torque that can be applied to it. The greater the number of slashes, the greater the strength of the bolt. Grades 0 through 5 are commonly used on automobiles. Metric bolts have a property class (grade) number, rather than a slash, molded into their heads to indicate bolt strength. In this case, the higher the number, the stronger the bolt. Property class numbers 8.8, 9.8 and 10.9 are commonly used on automobiles.

Strength markings can also be used to distinguish standard hex nuts from metric hex nuts. Many standard nuts have dots stamped into one side, while metric nuts are marked with a number (see illustrations). The greater the number of dots, or the higher the number, the greater the strength of the nut.

Metric studs are also marked on their ends (see illustration) according to property class (grade). Larger studs are numbered (the same as metric bolts), while smaller studs carry a geometric code to denote grade. It should be noted that many fasteners, especially Grades 0 through 2, have no distinguishing marks on them. When such is the case, the only way to determine whether it's standard or metric is to measure the thread pitch or compare it to a known fastener of the same size.

Standard fasteners are often referred to as SAE, as opposed to metric. However, it should be noted that SAE technically refers to a non-metric fine thread fastener only. Coarse thread non-metric fasteners are referred to as USS sizes.

Since fasteners of the same size (both standard and metric) may have different strength ratings, be sure to reinstall any bolts, studs or nuts removed from your vehicle in their original locations. Also, when replacing a fastener with a new one, make sure that the new one has a strength rating equal to or greater than the original.

Tightening sequences and procedures

Most threaded fasteners should be tightened to a specific torque value (see accompanying charts). Torque is the twisting force applied to a threaded component such as a nut or bolt. Overtightening the fastener can weaken it and cause it to break, while under-tightening can cause it to eventually come loose. Bolts, screws and studs, depending on the material they are made of and their thread diameters, have specific torque values, many of which are noted in the Specifications at the beginning of each Chapter. Be sure to follow the torque recommendations closely. For fasteners not assigned a specific torque, a general torque value chart is presented here as a guide. These torque values are for dry (unlubricated) fasteners threaded into steel or cast iron (not aluminum). As was previously mentioned, the size and grade of a fastener determine the amount of torque that can safely be applied to it. The figures listed here are approximate for Grade 2 and Grade 3 fasteners. Higher grades can tolerate higher torque values.

If fasteners are laid out in a pattern - such as cylinder head bolts, oil pan bolts, differential cover bolts, etc. - loosen and tighten them in sequence to avoid warping the component. Where it matters, we'll show you this sequence. If a specific pattern isn't that important, the following rule-of-thumb guide will prevent warping.

First, install the bolts or nuts finger-tight. Then tighten them one full turn each, in a crisscross or diagonal pattern. Then return to the first one and, following the same pattern, tighten them all one-half turn. Finally, tighten each of them one-quarter turn at a time until each fastener has been tightened to the proper torque. To loosen and remove the fasteners, reverse this procedure.

How to remove broken fasteners

Sooner or later, you're going to break off a bolt inside its threaded hole. There are several ways to remove it. Before you buy an expensive extractor set, try some of the following cheaper methods first.

First, regardless of which of the following methods you use, be sure to use penetrating oil. Penetrating oil is a special light oil with excellent penetrating power for freeing dirty and rusty fasteners. But it also works well on tightly torqued broken fasteners.

If enough of the fastener protrudes from its hole - and if it isn't torqued down too tightly - you can often remove it with vise-grips or a small pipe wrench. If that doesn't work, or if the fastener doesn't provide sufficient purchase for pliers or a wrench, try filing it down to take a wrench, or cut a slot in it to accept a screwdriver **(see illustration)**. If you still can't get it off - and you know how to weld - try welding a flat piece of steel, or a nut, to the top of the broken fastener. If the fastener is broken off flush with - or below - the top of its hole, try tapping it out with a small, sharp punch. If that doesn't work, try drilling out the broken fastener with a bit only slightly smaller than the inside diameter of the hole. For example, if the hole is 1/2-inch in diameter, use a 15/32-inch drill bit. This leaves a shell which you can pick out with a sharp chisel.

If THAT doesn't work, you'll have to resort to some form of screw extractor, such as an E-Z-Out **(see illustration)**. Screw extractors are sold in sets which can remove anything from 1/4-inch to 1-inch bolts or studs. Most extractors are fluted and tapered high-grade steel. To use a screw extractor, drill a hole slightly smaller than the O.D. of the extractor you're going to use (extractor sets include the manufacturer's recommendations for what size drill bit to use with each extractor size). Then screw in the extractor **(see illustration)** and back it - and the broken fastener - out. Extractors are reverse-threaded, so they won't unscrew when you back them out.

A word to the wise: Even though an E-Z-Out will usually save your bacon, it can cause even more grief if you're careless or sloppy. Drilling the hole for the extractor off-center, or using too small, or too big, a bit for the size of the fastener you're removing will only make things worse. So be careful!

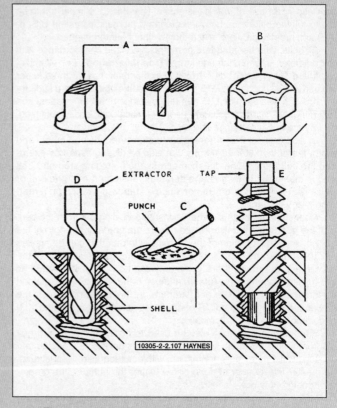

There are several ways to remove a broken fastener

A)   File it flat or slot it
B)   Weld on a nut
C)   Use a punch to unscrew it
D)   Use a screw extractor (like an E-Z-Out)
E)   Use a tap to remove the shell

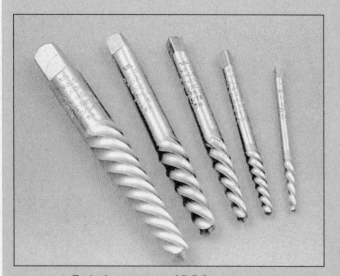

Typical assortment of E-Z-Out extractors

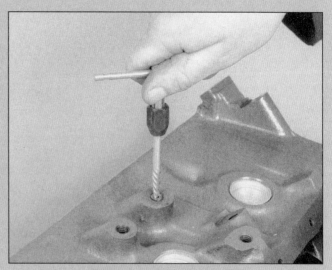

**When screwing in the E-Z-Out,
make sure it's centered properly**

How to repair broken threads

Sometimes, the internal threads of a nut or bolt hole can become stripped, usually from overtightening. Stripping threads is an all-too-common occurrence, especially when working with aluminum parts, because aluminum is so soft that it easily strips out. Over-tightened spark plugs are another common cause of stripped threads.

Usually, external or internal threads are only partially stripped. After they've been cleaned up with a tap or die, they'll still work. Sometimes, however, threads are badly damaged. When this happens, you've got three choices:

1) Drill and tap the hole to the next suitable oversize and install a larger diameter bolt, screw or stud.

2) Drill and tap the hole to accept a threaded plug, then drill and tap the plug to the original screw size. You can also buy a plug already threaded to the original size. Then you simply drill a hole to the specified size, then run the threaded plug into the hole with a bolt and jam nut. Once the plug is fully seated, remove the jam nut and bolt.

3) The third method uses a patented thread repair kit like Heli-Coil or Slimsert. These easy-to-use kits are designed to repair damaged threads in spark plug holes, straight-through holes and blind holes. Both are available as kits which can handle a variety of sizes and thread patterns. Drill the hole, then tap it with

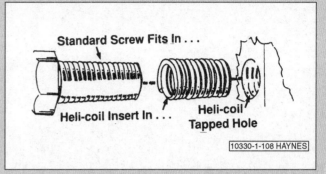

To install a Heli-Coil, drill out the hole, tap it with the special included tap and screw in the Heli-Coil

the special included tap. Install the Heli-Coil (see illustration) and the hole is back to its original diameter and thread pitch.

Regardless of which method you use, be sure to proceed calmly and carefully. A little impatience or carelessness during one of these relatively simple procedures can ruin your whole day's work and cost you a bundle if you wreck an expensive head or block.

Component disassembly

Disassemble components carefully to help ensure that the parts go back together properly. Note the sequence in which parts are removed. Make note of special characteristics or marks on parts that can be installed more than one way, such as a grooved thrust washer on a shaft. It's a good idea to lay the disassembled parts out on a clean surface in the order in which you removed them. It may also be helpful to make sketches or take instant photos of components before removal.

When you remove fasteners from a component, keep track of their locations. Thread a bolt back into a part, or put the washers and nut back on a stud, to prevent mix-ups later. If that isn't practical, put fasteners in a fishing tackle box or a series of small boxes. A cupcake or muffin tin, or an egg crate, is ideal for this purpose - each cavity can hold the bolts and nuts from a particular area (oil pan bolts, valve cover bolts, engine mount bolts, etc.). A pan of this type is helpful when working on assemblies with very small parts, such as the carburetor or valve train. Mark each cavity with paint or tape to identify the contents.

When you unplug the connector(s) between two wire harnesses, or even two wires, it's a good idea to identify the two halves with numbered pieces of masking tape - or a pair of matching pieces of colored electrical tape - so they can be easily reconnected.

Gasket sealing surfaces

Gaskets seal the mating surfaces between two parts to prevent lubricants, fluids, vacuum or pressure from leaking out between them. Gaskets are often coated with a liquid or paste-type gasket sealing compound before assembly. Age, heat and pressure can cause the two parts to stick together so tightly that they're difficult to separate. Often, you can loosen the assembly by striking it with a soft-face hammer near the mating surfaces. You can use a regular hammer if you place a block of wood between the hammer and the part, but don't hammer on cast or delicate parts that can be easily damaged. When a part refuses to come off, look for a fastener that you forgot to remove.

Don't use a screwdriver or pry bar to pry apart an assembly. It can easily damage the gasket sealing surfaces of the parts, which must be smooth to seal properly. If prying is absolutely necessary, use an old broom handle or a section of hard wood dowel.

Once the parts are separated, carefully scrape off the old gasket and clean the gasket surface. You can also remove some gaskets with a wire brush. If some gasket material refused to come off, soak it with rust penetrant or treat it with a special chemical to soften it, then scrape it off. You can fashion a scraper from a piece of copper tubing by flattening and sharpening one end. Copper is usually softer than the surface being scraped, which reduces the likelihood of gouging the part. The mating surfaces must be clean and smooth when you're done. If the gasket surface is gouged, use a gasket sealer thick enough to fill the scratches when you reassemble the components. For most applications, use a non-drying (or semi-drying) gasket sealer.

Hose removal tips

Warning: If the vehicle is equipped with air conditioning, do not disconnect any of the A/C hoses without first having the system depressurized by a dealer service department or a service station (see the Haynes "Automotive Heating and Air Conditioning Manual").

The same precautions that apply to gasket removal also apply to hoses. Avoid scratching or gouging the surface against which the hose mates, or the connection may leak. Take, for example, radiator hoses. Because of various chemical reactions, the rubber in radiator hoses can bond itself to the metal spigot over which the hose fits. To remove a hose, first loosen the hose clamps that secure it to the spigot. Then, with slip-joint pliers, grab the hose at the clamp and rotate it around the spigot. Work it back and forth until it is completely free, then pull it off. Silicone or other lubricants will ease removal if they can be applied between the hose and the outside of the spigot. Apply the same lubricant to the inside of the hose and the outside of the spigot to simplify installation. Snap-On and Mac Tools sell hose removal tools - they look like bent ice picks - which can be inserted between the spigot and the radiator hose to break the seal between rubber and metal.

As a last resort - or if you're planning to replace the hose anyway - slit the rubber with a knife and peel the hose from the spigot. Make sure you don't damage the metal connection.

If a hose clamp is broken or damaged, don't reuse it. Wire-type clamps usually weaken with age, so it's a good idea to replace them with screw-type clamps whenever a hose is removed.

Automotive chemicals and lubricants

A wide variety of automotive chemicals and lubricants - ranging from cleaning solvents and degreasers to lubricants and protective sprays for rubber, plastic and vinyl - is available.

Cleaners

Brake system cleaner

Brake system cleaner removes grease and brake fluid from brake parts like disc brake rotors, where a spotless surfaces is essential. It leaves no residue and often eliminates brake squeal caused by contaminants. Because it leaves no residue, brake cleaner is often used for cleaning engine parts as well.

Carburetor and choke cleaner

Carburetor and choke cleaner is a strong solvent for gum, varnish and carbon. Most carburetor cleaners leave a dry-type lubricant film which will not harden or gum up. So don't use carb cleaner on electrical components.

Degreasers

Degreasers are heavy-duty solvents used to remove grease from the outside of the engine and from chassis components. They're usually sprayed or brushed on. Depending on the type, they're rinsed off either with water or solvent.

Demoisturants

Demoisturants remove water and moisture from electrical components such as alternators, voltage regulators, electrical connectors and fuse blocks. They are non-conductive, non-corrosive and nonflammable.

Electrical cleaner

Electrical cleaner removes oxidation, corrosion and carbon deposits from electrical contacts, restoring full current flow. It can also be used to clean spark plugs, carburetor jets, voltage regulators and other parts where an oil-free surface is necessary.

Lubricants

Assembly lube

Assembly lube is a special extreme pressure lubricant, usually containing moly, used to lubricate high-load parts (such as main and rod bearings and cam lobes) for initial start-up of a new engine. The assembly lube lubricates the parts without being squeezed out or washed away until the engine oiling system begins to function.

Graphite lubricants

Graphite lubricants are used where oils cannot be used due to contamination problems, such as in locks. The dry graphite will lubricate metal parts while remaining uncontaminated by dirt, water, oil or acids. It is electrically conductive and will not foul electrical contacts in locks such as the ignition switch.

Heat-sink grease

Heat-sink grease is a special electrically non-conductive grease that is used for mounting electronic ignition modules where it is essential that heat is transferred away from the module.

Moly penetrants

Moly penetrants loosen and lubricate frozen, rusted and corroded fasteners and prevent future rusting or freezing.

Motor oil

Motor oil is the lubricant formulated for use in engines. It normally contains a wide variety of additives to prevent corrosion and reduce foaming and wear. Motor oil comes in various weights (viscosity ratings) from 5 to 80. The recommended weight of the oil depends on the season, temperature and the demands on the engine. Light oil is used in cold climates and under light load conditions. Heavy oil is used in hot climates and where high loads are encountered. Multi-viscosity oils are designed to have characteristics of both light and heavy oils and are available in a number of weights from 0W-20 to 20W-50. Some home mechanics use motor oil as an assembly lube, but we don't recommend it, because motor oil has a relatively thin viscosity, which means it will slide off the parts long before the engine is fired up.

Silicone lubricants

Silicone lubricants are used to protect rubber, plastic, vinyl and nylon parts.

Wheel bearing grease

Wheel bearing grease is a heavy grease that can withstand high loads and friction, such as wheel bearings, balljoints, tie-rod ends and universal joints. It's also sticky enough to hold parts like the keepers for the valve spring retainers in place on the valve stem when you're installing the springs.

White grease

White grease is a heavy grease for metal-to-metal applications where water is present. It stays soft under both low and high temperatures (usually from -100 to +190-degrees F), and won't wash off or dilute when exposed to water. Another good "glue" for holding parts in place during assembly.

Sealants

Anaerobic sealant

Anaerobic sealant is much like RTV in that it can be used either to seal gaskets or to form gaskets by itself. It remains flexible, is solvent resistant and fills surface imperfections. The difference between an anaerobic sealant and an RTV-type sealant is in the curing. RTV cures when exposed to air, while an anaerobic sealant cures only in the absence of air. This means that an anaerobic sealant cures only after the assembly of parts, sealing them together.

RTV sealant

RTV sealant is one of the most widely used gasket compounds. Made from silicone, RTV is air curing, it seals, bonds, waterproofs, fills surface irregularities, remains flexible, doesn't shrink, is relatively easy to remove, and is used as a supplementary sealer with almost all low and medium temperature gaskets.

Thread and pipe sealant

Thread and pipe sealant is used for sealing hydraulic and pneumatic fittings and vacuum lines. It is usually made from a Teflon compound, and comes in a spray, a paint-on liquid and as a wrap-around tape.

Chemicals

Anaerobic locking compounds

Anaerobic locking compounds are used to keep fasteners from vibrating or working loose and cure only after installation, in the absence of air. Medium strength locking compound is used for small nuts, bolts and screws that may be removed later. High-strength locking compound is for large nuts, bolts and studs which aren't removed on a regular basis.

Anti-seize compound

Anti-seize compound prevents seizing, galling, cold welding, rust and corrosion in fasteners. High-temperature anti-seize, usually made with copper and graphite lubricants, is used for exhaust system and exhaust manifold bolts.

Gas additives

Gas additives perform several functions, depending on their chemical makeup. They usually contain solvents that help dissolve gum and varnish that build up on carburetor, fuel injection and intake parts. They also serve to break down carbon deposits that form on the inside surfaces of the combustion chambers. Some additives contain upper cylinder lubricants for valves and piston rings, and others contain chemicals to remove condensation from the gas tank.

Oil additives

Oil additives range from viscosity index improvers to chemical treatments that claim to reduce internal engine friction. It should be noted that most oil manufacturers caution against using additives with their oils.

Safety first!

Regardless of how enthusiastic you may be about getting on with the job at hand, take the time to ensure that your safety is not jeopardized. A moment's lack of attention can result in an accident, as can failure to observe certain simple safety precautions. The possibility of an accident will always exist, and the following points should not be considered a comprehensive list of all dangers. Rather, they are intended to make you aware of the risks and to encourage a safety conscious approach to all work you carry out on your vehicle.

Essential DOs and DON'Ts

DON'T rely on a jack when working under the vehicle. Always use approved jackstands to support the weight of the vehicle and place them under the recommended lift or support points.

DON'T attempt to loosen extremely tight fasteners (i.e. wheel lug nuts) while the vehicle is on a jack - it may fall.

DON'T start the engine without first making sure that the transmission is in Neutral (or Park where applicable) and the parking brake is set.

DON'T remove the radiator cap from a hot cooling system - let it cool or cover it with a cloth and release the pressure gradually.

DON'T attempt to drain the engine oil until you are sure it has cooled to the point that it will not burn you.

DON'T touch any part of the engine or exhaust system until it has cooled sufficiently to avoid burns.

DON'T siphon toxic liquids such as gasoline, antifreeze and brake fluid by mouth, or allow them to remain on your skin.

DON'T inhale brake lining dust - it is potentially hazardous (see Asbestos below).

DON'T allow spilled oil or grease to remain on the floor - wipe it up before someone slips on it.

DON'T use loose fitting wrenches or other tools which may slip and cause injury.

DON'T push on wrenches when loosening or tightening nuts or bolts. Always try to pull the wrench toward you. If the situation calls for pushing the wrench away, push with an open hand to avoid scraped knuckles if the wrench should slip.

DON'T attempt to lift a heavy component alone - get someone to help you.

DON'T rush or take unsafe shortcuts to finish a job.

DON'T allow children or animals in or around the vehicle while you are working on it.

DO wear eye protection when using power tools such as a drill, sander, bench grinder, etc. and when working under a vehicle.

DO keep loose clothing and long hair well out of the way of moving parts.

DO make sure that any hoist used has a safe working load rating adequate for the job.

DO get someone to check on you periodically when working alone on a vehicle.

DO carry out work in a logical sequence and make sure that everything is correctly assembled and tightened.

DO keep chemicals and fluids tightly capped and out of the reach of children and pets.

DO remember that your vehicle's safety affects that of yourself and others. If in doubt on any point, get professional advice.

Steering, suspension and brakes

These systems are essential to driving safety, so make sure you have a qualified shop or individual check your work. Also, compressed suspension springs can cause injury if released suddenly - be sure to use a spring compressor.

Airbags

Airbags are explosive devices that can CAUSE injury if they deploy while you're working on the vehicle. Follow the manufacturer's instructions to disable the airbag whenever you're working in the vicinity of airbag components.

Asbestos

Certain friction, insulating, sealing, and other products - such as brake linings, brake bands, clutch linings, torque converters, gaskets, etc. - may contain asbestos or other hazardous friction material. Extreme care must be taken to avoid inhalation of dust from such products, since it is hazardous to health. If in doubt, assume that they do contain asbestos.

Fire

Remember at all times that gasoline is highly flammable. Never smoke or have any kind of open flame around when working on a vehicle. But the risk does not end there. A spark caused by an electrical short circuit, by two metal surfaces contacting each other, or even by static electricity built up in your body under certain conditions, can ignite gasoline vapors, which in a confined space are highly explosive. Do not, under any circumstances, use gasoline for cleaning parts. Use an approved safety solvent.

Always disconnect the battery ground (-) cable at the battery before working on any part of the fuel system or electrical system. Never risk spilling fuel on a hot engine or exhaust component. It is strongly recommended that a fire extinguisher suitable for use on fuel and electrical fires be kept handy in the garage or workshop at all times. Never try to extinguish a fuel or electrical fire with water.

Fumes

Certain fumes are highly toxic and can quickly cause unconsciousness and even death if inhaled to any extent. Gasoline vapor falls into this category, as do the vapors from some cleaning solvents. Any draining or pouring of such volatile fluids should be done in a well ventilated area.

When using cleaning fluids and solvents, read the instructions on the container carefully. Never use materials from unmarked containers.

Never run the engine in an enclosed space, such as a garage. Exhaust fumes contain carbon monoxide, which is extremely poisonous. If you need to run the engine, always do so in the open air, or at least have the rear of the vehicle outside the work area.

The battery

Never create a spark or allow a bare light bulb near a battery. They normally give off a certain amount of hydrogen gas, which is highly explosive.

Always disconnect the battery ground (-) cable at the battery before working on the fuel or electrical systems.

If possible, loosen the filler caps or cover when charging the battery from an external source (this does not apply to sealed or maintenance-free batteries). Do not charge at an excessive rate or the battery may burst.

Take care when adding water to a non maintenance-free battery and when carrying a battery. The electrolyte, even when diluted, is very corrosive and should not be allowed to contact clothing or skin.

Always wear eye protection when cleaning the battery to prevent the caustic deposits from entering your eyes.

Household current

When using an electric power tool, inspection light, etc., which operates on household current, always make sure that the tool is correctly connected to its plug and that, where necessary, it is properly grounded. Do not use such items in damp conditions and, again, do not create a spark or apply excessive heat in the vicinity of fuel or fuel vapor.

Secondary ignition system voltage

A severe electric shock can result from touching certain parts of the ignition system (such as the spark plug wires) when the engine is running or being cranked, particularly if components are damp or the insulation is defective. In the case of an electronic ignition system, the secondary system voltage is much higher and could prove fatal.

Hydrofluoric acid

This extremely corrosive acid is formed when certain types of synthetic rubber, found in some O-rings, oil seals, fuel hoses, etc. are exposed to temperatures above 750-degrees F (400-degrees C). The rubber changes into a charred or sticky substance containing the acid. Once formed, the acid remains dangerous for years. If it gets onto the skin, it may be necessary to amputate the limb concerned.

When dealing with a vehicle which has suffered a fire, or with components salvaged from such a vehicle, wear protective gloves and discard them after use.

Accidents and emergencies

Shop accidents range from minor cuts and skinned knuckles to serious injuries requiring immediate medical attention. The former are inevitable, while the latter are, hopefully, avoidable or at least uncommon. Think about what you would do in the event of an accident. Get some first aid training and have an adequate first aid kit somewhere within easy reach.

Think about what you would do if you were badly hurt and incapacitated. Is there someone nearby who could be summoned quickly? If possible, never work alone just in case something goes wrong.

If you had to cope with someone else's accident, would you know what to do? Dealing with accidents is a large and complex subject, and it's easy to make matters worse if you have no idea how to respond. Rather than attempt to deal with this subject in a superficial manner, buy a good First Aid book and read it carefully. Better yet, take a course in First Aid at a local junior college.

Conversion factors

Length (distance)

Inches (in)	X	25.4	= Millimeters (mm)	X 0.0394	= Inches (in)
Feet (ft)	X	0.305	= Meters (m)	X 3.281	= Feet (ft)
Miles	X	1.609	= Kilometers (km)	X 0.621	= Miles

Volume (capacity)

Cubic inches (cu in; in³)	X	16.387	= Cubic centimeters (cc; cm³)	X 0.061	= Cubic inches (cu in; in³)
Imperial pints (Imp pt)	X	0.568	= Liters (l)	X 1.76	= Imperial pints (Imp pt)
Imperial quarts (Imp qt)	X	1.137	= Liters (l)	X 0.88	= Imperial quarts (Imp qt)
Imperial quarts (Imp qt)	X	1.201	= US quarts (US qt)	X 0.833	= Imperial quarts (Imp qt)
US quarts (US qt)	X	0.946	= Liters (l)	X 1.057	= US quarts (US qt)
Imperial gallons (Imp gal)	X	4.546	= Liters (l)	X 0.22	= Imperial gallons (Imp gal)
Imperial gallons (Imp gal)	X	1.201	= US gallons (US gal)	X 0.833	= Imperial gallons (Imp gal)
US gallons (US gal)	X	3.785	= Liters (l)	X 0.264	= US gallons (US gal)

Mass (weight)

Ounces (oz)	X	28.35	= Grams (g)	X 0.035	= Ounces (oz)
Pounds (lb)	X	0.454	= Kilograms (kg)	X 2.205	= Pounds (lb)

Force

Ounces-force (ozf; oz)	X	0.278	= Newtons (N)	X 3.6	= Ounces-force (ozf; oz)
Pounds-force (lbf; lb)	X	4.448	= Newtons (N)	X 0.225	= Pounds-force (lbf; lb)
Newtons (N)	X	0.1	= Kilograms-force (kgf; kg)	X 9.81	= Newtons (N)

Pressure

Pounds-force per square inch (psi; lbf/in²; lb/in²)	X	0.070	= Kilograms-force per square centimeter (kgf/cm²; kg/cm²)	X 14.223	= Pounds-force per square inch (psi; lbf/in²; lb/in²)
Pounds-force per square inch (psi; lbf/in²; lb/in²)	X	0.068	= Atmospheres (atm)	X 14.696	= Pounds-force per square inch (psi; lbf/in²; lb/in²)
Pounds-force per square inch (psi; lbf/in²; lb/in²)	X	0.069	= Bars	X 14.5	= Pounds-force per square inch (psi; lbf/in²; lb/in²)
Pounds-force per square inch (psi; lbf/in²; lb/in²)	X	6.895	= Kilopascals (kPa)	X 0.145	= Pounds-force per square inch (psi; lbf/in²; lb/in²)
Kilopascals (kPa)	X	0.01	= Kilograms-force per square centimeter (kgf/cm²; kg/cm²)	X 98.1	= Kilopascals (kPa)

Torque (moment of force)

Pounds-force inches (lbf in; lb in)	X	1.152	= Kilograms-force centimeter (kgf cm; kg cm)	X 0.868	= Pounds-force inches (lbf in; lb in)
Pounds-force inches (lbf in; lb in)	X	0.113	= Newton meters (Nm)	X 8.85	= Pounds-force inches (lbf in; lb in)
Pounds-force inches (lbf in; lb in)	X	0.083	= Pounds-force feet (lbf ft; lb ft)	X 12	= Pounds-force inches (lbf in; lb in)
Pounds-force feet (lbf ft; lb ft)	X	0.138	= Kilograms-force meters (kgf m; kg m)	X 7.233	= Pounds-force feet (lbf ft; lb ft)
Pounds-force feet (lbf ft; lb ft)	X	1.356	= Newton meters (Nm)	X 0.738	= Pounds-force feet (lbf ft; lb ft)
Newton meters (Nm)	X	0.102	= Kilograms-force meters (kgf m; kg m)	X 9.804	= Newton meters (Nm)

Vacuum

Inches mercury (in. Hg)	X	3.377	= Kilopascals (kPa)	X 0.2961	= Inches mercury
Inches mercury (in. Hg)	X	25.4	= Millimeters mercury (mm Hg)	X 0.0394	= Inches mercury

Power

Horsepower (hp)	X	745.7	= Watts (W)	X 0.0013	= Horsepower (hp)

Velocity (speed)

Miles per hour (miles/hr; mph)	X	1.609	= Kilometers per hour (km/hr; kph)	X 0.621	= Miles per hour (miles/hr; mph)

Fuel consumption*

Miles per gallon, Imperial (mpg)	X	0.354	= Kilometers per liter (km/l)	X 2.825	= Miles per gallon, Imperial (mpg)
Miles per gallon, US (mpg)	X	0.425	= Kilometers per liter (km/l)	X 2.352	= Miles per gallon, US (mpg)

Temperature

Degrees Fahrenheit = ($°C \times 1.8$) + 32   Degrees Celsius (Degrees Centigrade; °C) = ($°F - 32$) x 0.56

*It is common practice to convert from miles per gallon (mpg) to liters/100 kilometers (l/100km), where mpg (Imperial) x l/100 km = 282 and mpg (US) x l/100 km = 235

DECIMALS to MILLIMETERS

Decimal	mm	Decimal	mm
0.001	0.0254	0.500	12.7000
0.002	0.0508	0.510	12.9540
0.003	0.0762	0.520	13.2080
0.004	0.1016	0.530	13.4620
0.005	0.1270	0.540	13.7160
0.006	0.1524	0.550	13.9700
0.007	0.1778	0.560	14.2240
0.008	0.2032	0.570	14.4780
0.009	0.2286	0.580	14.7320
0.010	0.2540	0.590	14.9860
0.020	0.5080	0.600	15.2400
0.030	0.7620	0.610	15.4940
0.040	1.0160	0.620	15.7480
0.050	1.2700	0.630	16.0020
0.060	1.5240	0.640	16.2560
0.070	1.7780	0.650	16.5100
0.080	2.0320	0.660	16.7640
0.090	2.2860	0.670	17.0180
0.100	2.5400	0.680	17.2720
0.110	2.7940	0.690	17.5260
0.120	3.0480	0.700	17.7800
0.130	3.3020	0.710	18.0340
0.140	3.5560	0.720	18.2880
0.150	3.8100	0.730	18.5420
0.160	4.0640	0.740	18.7960
0.170	4.3180	0.750	19.0500
0.180	4.5720	0.760	19.3040
0.190	4.8260	0.770	19.5580
0.200	5.0800	0.780	19.8120
0.210	5.3340	0.790	20.0660
0.220	5.5880	0.800	20.3200
0.230	5.8420	0.810	20.5740
0.240	6.0960	0.820	21.8280
0.250	6.3500	0.830	21.0820
0.260	6.6040	0.840	21.3360
0.270	6.8580	0.850	21.5900
0.280	7.1120	0.860	21.8440
0.290	7.3660	0.870	22.0980
0.300	7.6200	0.880	22.3520
0.310	7.8740	0.890	22.6060
0.320	8.1280	0.900	22.8600
0.330	8.3820	0.910	23.1140
0.340	8.6360	0.920	23.3680
0.350	8.8900	0.930	23.6220
0.360	9.1440	0.940	23.8760
0.370	9.3980	0.950	24.1300
0.380	9.6520	0.960	24.3840
0.390	9.9060	0.970	24.6380
0.400	10.1600	0.980	24.8920
0.410	10.4140	0.990	25.1460
0.420	10.6680	1.000	25.4000
0.430	10.9220		
0.440	11.1760		
0.450	11.4300		
0.460	11.6840		
0.470	11.9380		
0.480	12.1920		
0.490	12.4460		

FRACTIONS to DECIMALS to MILLIMETERS

Fraction	Decimal	mm	Fraction	Decimal	mm
1/64	0.0156	0.3969	33/64	0.5156	13.0969
1/32	0.0312	0.7938	17/32	0.5312	13.4938
3/64	0.0469	1.1906	35/64	0.5469	13.8906
1/16	0.0625	1.5875	9/16	0.5625	14.2875
5/64	0.0781	1.9844	37/64	0.5781	14.6844
3/32	0.0938	2.3812	19/32	0.5938	15.0812
7/64	0.1094	2.7781	39/64	0.6094	15.4781
1/8	0.1250	3.1750	5/8	0.6250	15.8750
9/64	0.1406	3.5719	41/64	0.6406	16.2719
5/32	0.1562	3.9688	21/32	0.6562	16.6688
11/64	0.1719	4.3656	43/64	0.6719	17.0656
3/16	0.1875	4.7625	11/16	0.6875	17.4625
13/64	0.2031	5.1594	45/64	0.7031	17.8594
7/32	0.2188	5.5562	23/32	0.7188	18.2562
15/64	0.2344	5.9531	47/64	0.7344	18.6531
1/4	0.2500	6.3500	3/4	0.7500	19.0500
17/64	0.2656	6.7469	49/64	0.7656	19.4469
9/32	0.2812	7.1438	25/32	0.7812	19.8438
19/64	0.2969	7.5406	51/64	0.7969	20.2406
5/16	0.3125	7.9375	13/16	0.8125	20.6375
21/64	0.3281	8.3344	53/64	0.8281	21.0344
11/32	0.3438	8.7312	27/32	0.8438	21.4312
23/64	0.3594	9.1281	55/64	0.8594	21.8281
3/8	0.3750	9.5250	7/8	0.8750	22.2250
25/64	0.3906	9.9219	57/64	0.8906	22.6219
13/32	0.4062	10.3188	29/32	0.9062	23.0188
27/64	0.4219	10.7156	59/64	0.9219	23.4156
7/16	0.4375	11.1125	15/16	0.9375	23.8125
29/64	0.4531	11.5094	61/64	0.9531	24.2094
15/32	0.4688	11.9062	31/32	0.9688	24.6062
31/64	0.4844	12.3031	63/64	0.9844	25.0031
1/2	0.5000	12.7000	1	1.0000	25.4000

Notes

Chapter 1 Maintenance

Contents

Specifications

Recommended lubricants and fluids

Note: *Listed here are manufacturer recommendations at the time this manual was written. Manufacturers occasionally upgrade their fluid and lubricant specifications, so check with your local auto parts store for current recommendations.*

Engine oil

    Type CK-4

    Viscosity

        Above 0-degrees F (-18-degrees C) 15W-40

        Below 0-degrees F (-18-degrees C) 5W-40

Coolant .... 50/50 mixture of DEX-COOL coolant and demineralized water

Capacities*
Engine oil (including filter) .... 10 quarts (9.5 liters)
Cooling system** .... Between 20.5 to 25.5 quarts (19.3 to 24 liters), depending on model

*All capacities approximate. Add as necessary to bring to appropriate level.
**Cooling system capacities vary depending on engine/transmission package, radiator and A/C system type. Add coolant as necessary to bring to appropriate level.

Torque specifications

	Ft-lbs	Nm
Engine oil drain plug		
13 mm head	18	25
16 mm head	62	84
Drivebelt tensioner mounting bolt		
LB7	30	41
LLY and later models	37	50

Engine compartment components (2500HD with LLY engine shown)

1	Brake fluid reservoir	6	Power steering fluid reservoir	11	Engine oil dipstick (not visible)
2	Underhood fuse/relay box	7	Drivebelt	12	Fuel filter/water separator (not visible)
3	Windshield washer fluid reservoir	8	Engine oil filler cap	13	Automatic transmission fluid dipstick
4	Battery	9	Air filter housing		(not visible)
5	Upper radiator hose	10	Coolant expansion tank		

1   Introduction

1   This Chapter is designed to help the home mechanic maintain the GM Duramax diesel engine with the goals of maximum performance, economy, safety and reliability in mind.

2   Included is a master maintenance schedule. It tells you what to do and when to do it. Each recommended service or maintenance procedure is explained later in this Chapter.

3   Servicing your engine in accordance with this sensible maintenance schedule will significantly prolong its service life. Keep in mind

that this is a comprehensive plan: servicing selected items - but skipping others - will not produce the same results.

4   When you service your engine, you'll find that many of the maintenance procedures can be grouped together because they're logically related, or because they're located next to each other.

5   Before you get started, read through the procedures you're planning to perform, familiarize yourself with the steps and gather up all the parts and tools you'll need. If it looks like you might run into problems during a particular job, seek advice from a mechanic or an experienced do-it-yourselfer.

2 Maintenance schedule

Every 250 miles (400 km) or weekly, whichever comes first

Check the engine oil level (Section 3)
Check the engine coolant level (Section 3)

Every 5000 miles (8000 km) or 6 months, whichever comes first

All items listed above, plus:
Change the engine oil and filter* (Section 4)
Check and engine drivebelt (Section 7)
Check the underhood hoses (Section 8)
Check the cooling system (Section 9)
Check the fuel system (Section 10)
Drain the water from the fuel filter/water separator (Section 11)
Check the exhaust system (Section 12)

Every 15,000 miles (24,000 km) or 12 months, whichever comes first

Check and service the batteries (Section 6)
Check and, if necessary, replace the air filter (Section 13)
Replace the fuel filter (Section 11)
Inspect and replace, if necessary, all underhood hoses (Section 8)

Every 100,000 miles (160,000 km) or 60 months, whichever comes first

Replace the engine coolant (Section 14)

* This item is affected by "severe" operating conditions as described below. If the vehicle is operated under severe conditions, perform all maintenance indicated with an asterisk (*) at 3000 mile/3 month intervals. Severe conditions exist if you mainly operate the vehicle.
In dusty areas
Towing a trailer
Idling for extended periods and/or driving at low speeds
When outside temperatures remain below freezing and most trips are less than four miles long

3   Fluid level checks

Note: *The following are fluid level checks to be done on a 250 mile or weekly basis. Regardless of intervals, be alert to fluid leaks under the vehicle which would indicate a fault to be corrected immediately.*
1   Fluids are an essential part of the lubrication and cooling systems. Because the fluids gradually become depleted and/or contaminated during normal operation of the vehicle, they must be periodically replenished. See this Chapter's Specifications before adding fluid to any of the following components.
Note: *The vehicle must be on level ground when fluid levels are checked.*

Engine oil

Refer to illustrations 3.4a, 3.4b and 3.6
2   The engine oil level is checked with a dipstick that extends through a tube and into the oil pan at the bottom of the engine.
3   The oil level should be checked before the vehicle has been driven, or about 5 minutes after the engine has been shut off. If the oil is checked immediately after driving the vehicle, some of the oil will remain in the upper engine components, resulting in an inaccurate reading on the dipstick.
4   Pull the dipstick out of the tube and wipe all the oil from the end with a clean rag or paper towel **(see illustration)**. Insert the clean dipstick all the way back into the tube, then pull it out again. Note the oil at

3.4a The engine oil dipstick is located on the right side of the engine

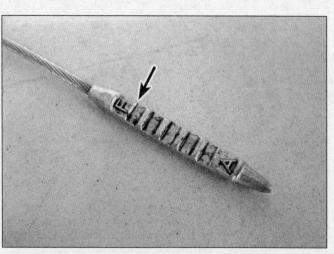

3.4b The oil level must be maintained near the "F" area on the dipstick, but not above it

3.6 Location of the oil filler cap - always make sure the area around the opening is clean before removing the cap to prevent dirt from contaminating the engine

3.9 The coolant expansion tank is located on the right side, near the air filter - make sure the level is up to the FULL COLD (early models) or MIN (later models) mark when the engine is cold

the end of the dipstick. The level should be near the "F" or FULL mark **(see illustration)**. If it's near the "A" or ADD mark, add oil as necessary to keep the level near the upper mark.

5   Do not overfill the engine by adding too much oil since this may result in oil foaming (which can cause engine damage), oil leaks or oil seal failures.

6   Unscrew and remove the oil filler cap to add oil **(see illustration)**.

7   Checking the oil level is an important preventive maintenance step. A consistently low oil level indicates oil leakage through damaged seals, defective gaskets or past worn rings or valve guides. If the oil looks milky or has water droplets in it, the cylinder head gasket(s) may be blown or the head(s) or block may be cracked. The engine should be checked immediately. The condition of the oil should also be checked. Whenever you check the oil level, slide your thumb and index finger up the dipstick before wiping off the oil. If you see small dirt or metal particles clinging to the dipstick, the oil should be changed.

Engine coolant

Refer to illustration 3.9

Warning: *Do not allow antifreeze to come in contact with your skin or painted surfaces of the vehicle. Flush contaminated areas immediately with plenty of water. Don't store new coolant or leave old coolant lying around where it's accessible to children or pets - they're attracted by its sweet smell. Ingestion of even a small amount of coolant can be fatal! Wipe up garage floor and drip pan coolant spills immediately. Keep antifreeze containers covered and repair leaks in the cooling system as soon as they are noted.*

8   All vehicles covered by this manual are equipped with a pressurized coolant expansion tank located at the right side of the engine compartment, and connected by hoses to the radiator and cooling system.

9   The coolant level in the expansion tank should be checked regularly. **Warning:** *Do not remove the expansion tank cap when the engine is warm.* The level in the tank varies with the temperature of the engine. When the engine is cold, the coolant level should be at or slightly above the FULL COLD mark (early models) or MIN mark (later models) on the tank **(see illustration)**. If it isn't, slowly unscrew the cap from the expansion tank and add the recommended coolant (see this Chapter's Specifications).

Warning: *If you hear pressure escaping from the tank as you unscrew the cap, wait until the hissing stops, then resume unscrewing the cap.*

10   Drive the vehicle and recheck the coolant level. If only a small amount of coolant is required to bring the system up to the proper level, water can be used. However, repeated additions of water will dilute the antifreeze and water solution. In order to maintain the proper ratio of antifreeze and water, always top up the coolant level with the correct mixture. An empty plastic milk jug or bleach bottle makes an excellent container for mixing coolant. Do not use rust inhibitors or additives.

11   If the coolant level drops consistently, there may be a leak in the system. Inspect the radiator, hoses, expansion tank cap, drain plugs and water pump (see Section 9). If no leaks are noted, have the expansion tank cap pressure tested by a service station.

12   Check the condition of the coolant as well. It should be relatively clear. If it's brown or rust colored, the system should be drained, flushed and refilled. Even if the coolant appears to be normal, the corrosion inhibitors wear out, so it must be replaced at the specified intervals.

Battery electrolyte

13   Most vehicles covered by this manual are equipped with batteries which are permanently sealed (except for vent holes) and have no filler caps. Water doesn't have to be added to these batteries at any time. If maintenance-type batteries are installed, the caps on the top of the batteries should be removed periodically to check for a low water level. This check is most critical during the warm summer months. Only add distilled water to the battery.

4   Engine oil and filter change

Refer to illustrations 4.3, 4.9, 4.14 and 4.18

1   Frequent oil changes are the most important preventive maintenance procedures that can be done by the home mechanic. As engine oil ages, it becomes diluted and contaminated, which leads to premature engine wear.

2   Although some sources recommend oil filter changes every other oil change, we feel that the minimal cost of an oil filter and the relative ease with which it is installed dictate that a new filter be installed every time the oil is changed.

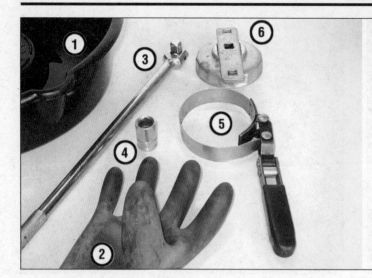

4.3 These tools are required when changing the engine oil and filter

1   *Drain pan* - It should be fairly shallow in depth, but wide to prevent spills
2   *Rubber gloves* - When removing the drain plug and filter, you will get oil on your hands (the gloves will prevent burns)
3   *Breaker bar* - Sometimes the oil drain plug is tight, and a long breaker bar is needed to loosen it
4   *Socket* - To be used with the breaker bar or a ratchet (must be the correct size to fit the drain plug - six-point preferred)
5   *Filter wrench* - This is a metal band-type wrench, which requires clearance around the filter to be effective
6   *Filter wrench* - This type fits on the bottom of the filter and can be turned with a ratchet or breaker bar (different-size wrenches are available for different types of filters)

3   Gather together all necessary tools and materials before beginning this procedure **(see illustration)**.

4   You should have plenty of clean rags and newspapers handy to mop up any spills. Access to the underside of the vehicle may be improved if the vehicle can be lifted on a hoist, driven onto ramps or supported by jackstands.

Warning: *Do not work under a vehicle that is supported only by a bumper, hydraulic or scissors type jack.*

5   If this is your first oil change, get under the vehicle and familiarize yourself with the locations of the oil drain plug and the oil filter. The engine and exhaust components will be warm during the actual work, so note how they are situated to avoid touching them when working under the vehicle.

6   Warm the engine to normal operating temperature. If the new oil or any tools are needed, use this warm up time to gather everything necessary for the job. The correct type of oil for your application can be found in this Chapter's Specifications.

7   With the engine oil warm (warm engine oil will drain better and more built up sludge will be removed with it), raise and support the vehicle. Make sure it's safely supported!

8   Move all necessary tools, rags and newspapers under the vehicle. Set the drain pan under the drain plug. Keep in mind that the oil will initially flow from the pan with some force; position the pan accordingly.

9   Being careful not to touch any of the hot exhaust components, use a wrench to remove the drain plug near the bottom of the oil pan **(see illustration)**. Depending on how hot the oil is, you may want to wear gloves while unscrewing the plug the final few turns.

10   Allow the old oil to drain into the pan.

11   After all the oil has drained, wipe off the drain plug with a clean rag. Small metal particles may cling to the plug and would immediately contaminate the new oil.

12   Clean the area around the drain plug opening and reinstall the plug. Tighten the plug securely with the wrench. If a torque wrench is available, use it to tighten the plug.

13   Move the drain pan into position under the oil filter.

14   Use the filter wrench to loosen the oil filter **(see illustration)**. Chain or metal band filter wrenches may distort the filter canister, but it doesn't matter since the filter will be discarded anyway.

15   Completely unscrew the old filter. Be careful - it's full of oil. Empty the oil inside the filter into the drain pan.

16   Compare the old filter with the new one to make sure they're the same type.

17   Use a clean rag to remove all oil, dirt and sludge from the area where the oil filter mounts to the engine. Check the old filter to make sure the rubber gasket isn't stuck to the engine. If the gasket is stuck to the engine (use a flashlight if necessary), remove it.

4.9 Use a proper size box-end wrench or socket to remove the oil drain plug to avoid rounding it off

4.14 Since the oil filter is on very tight, you'll need a special wrench for removal - DO NOT use the wrench to tighten the new filter

4.18 Lubricate the oil filter gasket with clean engine oil before installing the filter on the engine

4.30a The DIC should read 99 or 100 percent (depending on model) oil life remaining when properly reset

18   Apply a light coat of clean oil to the rubber gasket on the new oil filter **(see illustration)**.

19   Attach the new filter to the engine, following the tightening directions printed on the filter canister or packing box. Most filter manufacturers recommend against using a filter wrench due to the possibility of overtightening and damage to the seal.

20   Remove all tools, rags, etc. from under the vehicle, being careful not to spill the oil in the drain pan, then lower the vehicle.

21   Move to the engine compartment and locate the oil filler cap.

22   Pour seven quarts of fresh oil into the engine.

23   Wait a few minutes to allow the oil to drain into the pan, then check the level on the oil dipstick (see Section 3). If the oil level is above the ADD mark, start the engine and allow the new oil to circulate.

24   Turn off the engine. Wait about five minutes, then recheck the level on the dipstick. Add more oil as necessary.

25   During the first few trips after an oil change, make it a point to check frequently for leaks and proper oil level.

26   The old oil drained from the engine cannot be reused in its present state and should be disposed of. Check with your local auto parts store, disposal facility or environmental agency to see if they will accept the oil for recycling. After the oil has cooled it can be drained into a container (capped plastic jugs, topped bottles, milk cartons, etc.) for transport to one of these disposal sites. Don't dispose of the oil by pouring it on the ground or down a drain!

Oil Life Monitor

27   The Oil Life Monitor is a function of the PCM that tracks engine operating temperature and rpm. If the PCM determines that your engine's oil has been used long enough, an indicator that shows "CHANGE ENGINE OIL SOON" will light on the instrument panel.

28   When you change your engine oil and filter, whether you change it at the interval recommended in this Chapter or only when the light comes on, you will have to reset the system to make the indicator go out and allow the system to accurately calculate when the next oil change is due.

Vehicles without a Driver Information Center (DIC)

29   To reset, turn the ignition key to the Run position (not Start) with the engine off, then fully depress and let up the accelerator pedal three times within a five-second period. Turn the key to Off, then start the engine. If the "CHANGE ENGINE OIL SOON" message still appears, repeat the resetting procedure.

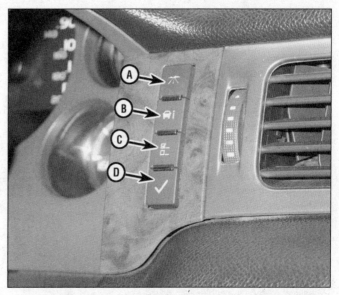

4.30b DIC buttons (on models so equipped) are trip/fuel (A), vehicle information (B), customization (C) and set/reset (D)

Vehicles equipped with a Driver Information Center (DIC)

Refer to illustrations 4.30a and 4.30b

30   To reset, turn the ignition key to the Run position (not Start) with the engine off, then press the DIC (Driver Information Center) vehicle information button **(see illustration)** to display the "OIL LIFE LEFT/ HOLD SET TO RESET" or "OIL LIFE REMAINING" message on the DIC, depending on model. Press the SET/RESET button (or the odometer trip reset button if your DIC doesn't have buttons) until 99 or 100 percent (depending on model) is displayed on the DIC **(see illustration)**. The system will chime three times, then the "CHANGE ENGINE OIL SOON" message will go out. Turn the key off; after a minute start the engine - if the CHANGE ENGINE OIL SOON message comes back on, repeat the procedure.

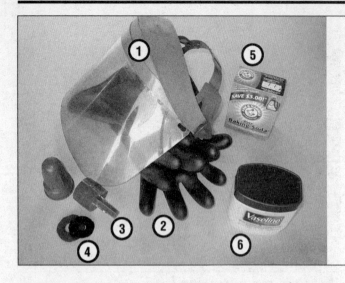

6.1 Tools and materials required for battery maintenance

1   **Face shield/safety goggles** - *When removing corrosion with a brush, the acidic particles can easily fly up into your eyes*
2   **Rubber gloves** - *Another safety item to consider when servicing the battery - remember that's acid inside the battery!*
3   **Battery terminal/cable cleaner** - *This wire brush cleaning tool will remove all traces of corrosion from the battery posts and cable clamps*
4   **Treated felt washers** - *Placing one of these on each post, directly under the cable clamps, will help prevent corrosion*
5   **Baking soda** - *A solution of baking soda and water can be used to neutralize corrosion*
6   **Petroleum jelly** - *A layer of this on the battery terminals will help prevent corrosion*

5   Battery cable check and replacement

Check

1   Periodically inspect the entire length of each battery cable for damage, cracked or burned insulation and corrosion. Poor battery cable connections can cause starting problems and decreased engine performance.
2   Check the cable to terminal connections at the ends of the cables for cracks, loose wire strands and corrosion. The presence of white, fluffy deposits under the insulation at the cable terminal connection is a sign the cable is corroded and should be replaced. Check the terminals for distortion, missing mounting bolts and corrosion.
3   Too much resistance in the battery cables will result in poor starter performance. Disconnect the battery feed at the shutoff solenoid so the engine won't start.
4   With the transmission in Neutral and the parking brake on, connect one voltmeter probe on the negative battery terminal and the other on a good ground, such as the frame. Operate the starter and check the voltage.
5   With the starter operating, check the voltage drop between the positive battery cable and the starter terminal stud.
6   Operate the starter again and check the voltage drop between the starter housing and the frame.
7   If there is a drop of over one volt during this check, disconnect the battery cables and clean the connectors. If the voltage drop is still excessive, replace the cables with new ones.

Replacement

8   When removing the cables, always disconnect the negative cable first and hook it up last or the battery may be shorted by the tool used to loosen the cable clamps. Even if only the positive cable is being replaced, be sure to disconnect the negative cable from the battery first.
9   Disconnect the old cables from the battery, then trace each of them to their opposite ends and detach them from the starter solenoid and ground terminals. Note the routing of each cable to ensure correct installation.
10   If you're replacing one or all of the old cables, take them with you when buying new cables. It's vitally important that you replace the cables with identical parts. Cables have characteristics that make them easy to identify: Positive cables are usually red, larger in cross section and have a larger diameter battery post clamp; ground cables are usually black, smaller in cross section and have a slightly smaller diameter clamp for the negative post.
11   Clean the threads of the solenoid or ground connection with a wire brush to remove rust and corrosion. Apply a light coat of battery terminal corrosion inhibitor, or petroleum jelly, to the threads to prevent future corrosion.

12   Attach the cable to the solenoid or ground connection and tighten the mounting nut/bolt securely.
13   Before connecting a new cable to the battery, make sure it reaches the battery post without having to be stretched.
14   Connect the positive cable first, followed by the negative cable.

6   Battery check, maintenance and charging

Warning: *Certain precautions must be followed when checking and servicing the batteries. Hydrogen gas, which is highly flammable, is always present in the battery cells, so don't smoke and keep open flames and sparks away from the batteries. The electrolyte inside the battery is actually dilute sulfuric acid, which will cause injury if splashed on your skin or in your eyes. It will also ruin clothes and painted surfaces. When removing the battery cables, always detach the negative cable first and hook it up last!*
Note: *These models use two batteries, connected in parallel. The batteries can be serviced and charged separately, but must be replaced in pairs.*

Check and maintenance

Refer to illustrations 6.1 and 6.6

1   Battery maintenance is an important procedure which will help ensure that you are not stranded because of dead batteries. Several tools are required for this procedure **(see illustration)**.
2   When checking/servicing the batteries, always turn the engine and all accessories off.
3   Sealed (sometimes called maintenance free), side terminal batteries are standard equipment on these vehicles. The cell caps cannot be removed, no electrolyte checks are required and water cannot be added to the cells. However, if a maintenance type aftermarket battery has been installed, the following maintenance procedure can be used.
4   Remove the caps and check the electrolyte level in each of the battery cells. It must be above the plates. There's usually a split ring indicator in each cell to indicate the correct level. If the level is low, add distilled water only, then reinstall the cell caps.
Caution: *Overfilling the cells may cause electrolyte to spill over during periods of heavy charging, causing corrosion and damage to nearby components.*
5   The external condition of each battery should be checked periodically. Look for damage such as a cracked case.
6   Check the tightness of the battery cable bolts **(see illustration)** to ensure good electrical connections. Inspect the entire length of each cable, looking for cracked or abraded insulation and frayed conductors.
7   If corrosion (visible as white, fluffy deposits) is evident, remove the cables from the terminals, clean them with a battery brush and reinstall them. Corrosion can be kept to a minimum by applying a layer of petroleum jelly or grease to the bolt threads.

6.6 Make sure the battery terminals on both batteries are tight

12   If you're using a charger with a rate higher than two amps, check the battery regularly during charging to make sure it doesn't overheat. If you're using a trickle charger, you can safely let the battery charge overnight after you've checked it regularly for the first couple of hours.

13   If the battery has removable cell caps, measure the specific gravity with a hydrometer every hour during the last few hours of the charging cycle. Hydrometers are available inexpensively from auto parts stores - follow the instructions that come with the hydrometer. Consider the battery charged when there's no change in the specific gravity reading for two hours and the electrolyte in the cells is gassing (bubbling) freely. The specific gravity reading from each cell should be very close to the others. If not, the battery probably has a bad cell(s).

14   Some batteries with sealed tops have built in hydrometers on the top that indicate the state of charge by the color displayed in the hydrometer window. Normally, a bright colored hydrometer indicates a full charge and a dark hydrometer indicates the battery still needs charging. Check the battery manufacturer's instructions to be sure you know what the colors mean.

15   If the battery has a sealed top and no built in hydrometer, you can hook up a digital voltmeter across the battery terminals to check the charge. A fully charged battery should read 12.6 volts or higher.

8   Make sure the battery carrier is in good condition and the hold down clamp is tight. If a battery is removed, make sure that no parts remain in the bottom of the carrier when it's reinstalled. When reinstalling the hold down clamp, don't overtighten the bolt.

9   Corrosion on the carrier, battery case and surrounding areas can be removed with a solution of water and baking soda. Apply the mixture with a small brush, let it work, then rinse it off with plenty of clean water.

10   Any metal parts of the vehicle damaged by corrosion should be coated with a zinc based primer, then painted.

Charging

Note: *These models have two batteries connected in parallel - each battery should be charged separately, after disconnecting the cables.*

11   Remove all of the cell caps (if equipped) and cover the holes with a clean cloth to prevent spattering electrolyte. Disconnect the negative battery cable and hook the battery charger leads to the battery posts (positive to positive, negative to negative), then plug in the charger. Make sure it is set at 12 volts if it has a selector switch.

7   Drivebelt check and replacement/tensioner replacement

Refer to illustrations 7.2 and 7.4

1   A serpentine belt is located at the front of the engine and plays an important role in the overall operation of the engine and its components. Due to its function and material make up, the belt is prone to wear and should be periodically inspected. The serpentine belt drives the alternator(s), power steering pump, vacuum pump and air conditioning compressor.

2   With the engine off, open the hood and use your fingers (and a flashlight, if necessary), to move along the belt checking for cracks and separation of the belt plies **(see illustration)**. Also check for fraying and glazing, which gives the belt a shiny appearance. Both sides of the belt should be inspected, which means you will have to twist the belt to check the underside.

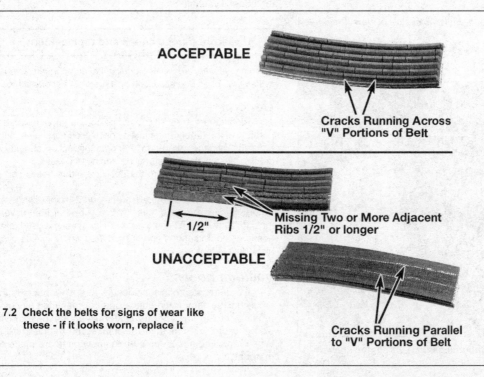

7.2 Check the belts for signs of wear like these - if it looks worn, replace it

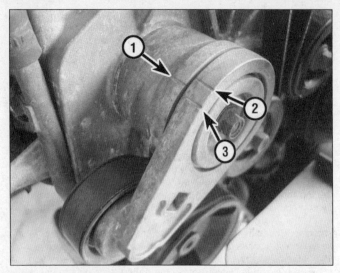

7.4 The drivebelt tensioner is equipped with belt wear marks. When the belt wears, the tensioner will move outward; when the maximum wear mark on the tensioner arm nears the stationary mark on the alternator bracket, the belt should be changed

1   Stationary mark
2   New belt
3   Change belt

3   Check the underside of the belt. They should be all the same depth, with none of the surfaces uneven.
4   The tension of the belt is maintained by a spring-loaded tensioner assembly and isn't adjustable. The belt should be replaced when the acceptable range marks on the moveable part of the tensioner move beyond the mark on the alternator bracket **(see illustration)**.

Drivebelt replacement

Refer to illustration 7.5

5   Remove the upper fan shroud (see Chapter 2, Section 4). Insert a 3/8-inch or 1/2-inch drive (as applicable) ratchet or breaker bar into the tensioner square and rotate the tensioner counterclockwise to release belt tension **(see illustrations)**.
Note: *Before removing the belt, make a sketch of how it is routed around the pulleys.*
Note: *On some models it is helpful to remove the upper fan shroud for access (see Chapter 2).*

7.8 Drivebelt tensioner mounting bolt (LB7 engine shown)

7.5 Use a 3/8-inch or 1/2-inch drive tool (as applicable) in the tensioner's square hole to rotate the tensioner arm for belt removal

6   Remove the belt from the tensioner and auxiliary components and slowly release the tensioner.
7   Route the new belt over the various pulleys, again rotating the tensioner to allow the belt to be installed, then release the belt tensioner. Make sure the belt seats properly in all of the pulleys.

Tensioner replacement

Refer to illustration 7.8

8   To replace a tensioner that has lost its spring tension, exhibits binding or has a worn-out pulley/bearing, remove the drivebelt (see Steps 5 and 6), remove the mounting bolt in the center of the tensioner arm **(see illustration)** and remove the tensioner.
9   When installing the tensioner, make sure the pin on the back of the tensioner engages with the hole in the alternator mounting bracket. Tighten the mounting bolt to the torque listed in this Chapter's Specifications.

8   Underhood hose check and replacement

Warning: *Never remove air conditioning components or hoses until the system has been depressurized by a licensed air conditioning technician.*

General

1   High temperatures in the engine compartment can cause the deterioration of the rubber and plastic hoses used for engine, accessory and emission systems operation. Periodic inspection should be made for cracks, loose clamps, material hardening and leaks.
2   Information specific to the cooling system hoses can be found in Section 9.
3   Some, but not all, hoses are secured to the fittings with clamps. Where clamps are used, check to be sure that they haven't lost their tension, allowing the hose to leak. If clamps aren't used, make sure the hose has not expanded and/or hardened where it slips over the fitting, allowing it to leak.

Vacuum hoses

4   It's quite common for vacuum hoses, especially those in the emissions system, to be color-coded or identified by colored stripes molded into them. Various systems require hoses with different wall thicknesses, collapse resistance and temperature resistance. When replacing hoses, be sure the new ones are made of the same material.

5   Often the only effective way to check a hose is to remove it completely from the vehicle. If more than one hose is removed, be sure to label the hoses and fittings to ensure correct installation.

6   When checking vacuum hoses, be sure to include any plastic T-fittings in the check. Inspect the fittings for cracks and the hose where it fits over the fitting for distortion, which could cause leakage.

7   A small piece of vacuum hose (1/4 inch inside diameter) can be used as a stethoscope to detect vacuum leaks. Hold one end of the hose to your ear and probe around vacuum hoses and fittings, listening for the hissing sound characteristic of a vacuum leak.

Warning: *When probing with the vacuum hose stethoscope, be very careful not to come into contact with moving engine components such as the drivebelts, cooling fan, etc.*

Fuel hose

Warning: *There are certain precautions that must be taken when inspecting or servicing fuel system components. Work in a well-ventilated area and do not allow open flames (cigarettes, appliance pilot lights, etc.) or bare light bulbs near the work area. Mop up any spills immediately and do not store fuel soaked rags where they could ignite.*

8   Check all rubber fuel lines for deterioration and chafing. Check especially for cracks in areas where the hose bends and just before fittings.

9   High quality fuel line specifically designed for carrying diesel fuel must be used for fuel line replacement. Never, under any circumstances, use unreinforced vacuum line, clear plastic tubing or water hose for fuel lines. Lines with quick-connect fittings must be replaced with genuine factory parts or equivalent.

10   Spring type clamps are commonly used on fuel lines. These clamps often lose their tension over a period of time, and can be sprung during removal. Replace all spring type clamps with screw clamps whenever a hose is replaced.

Metal lines

Warning: *Use extreme care when inspecting the fuel lines. The fuel is under very high pressure and spray from a leak can actually penetrate the skin, causing serious personal injury.*

11   Sections of metal line are used for fuel line between the fuel pump and the fuel injection unit and injectors. Check carefully to be sure that the lines have not been bent or crimped, and that cracks have not started in the lines.

12   If a section of metal fuel line between the fuel injection pump and the injectors must be replaced, use only direct replacement steel tubing from a dealer, since each line is a specific length.

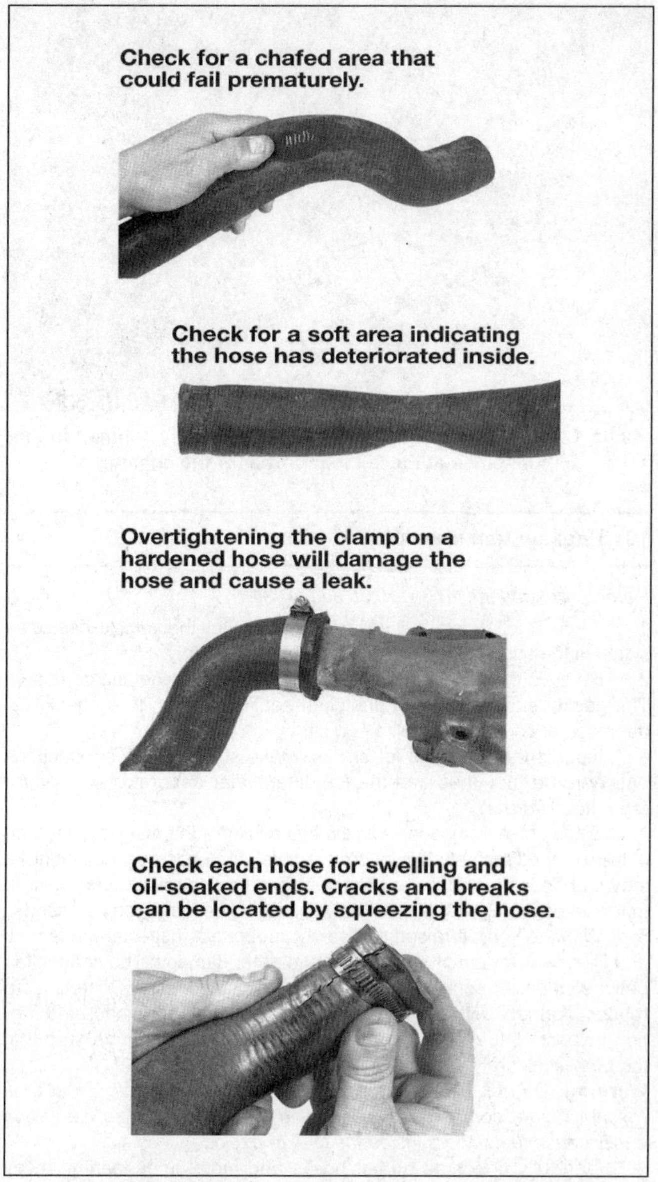

---

9   Cooling system check

Refer to illustration 9.4

Warning: *Wait until the engine is completely cool before beginning this procedure.*

Caution: *Never mix green-colored ethylene glycol antifreeze and orange-colored DEX-COOL silicate-free coolant because doing so will destroy the efficiency of the DEX-COOL coolant, which is designed to last for 100,000 miles or five years.*

1   Many major engine failures can be attributed to a faulty cooling system. The cooling system also cools the transmission fluid and thus plays an important role in prolonging transmission life.

2   The cooling system should be checked with the engine cold. Do this before the vehicle is driven for the day or after it has been shut off for at least three hours.

3   Remove the coolant pressure cap on the expansion tank by slowly unscrewing it. If you hear any hissing sounds (indicating there is still pressure in the system), wait until it stops. Thoroughly clean the cap, inside and out, with clean water. Also clean the filler neck on the expansion tank. All traces of corrosion should be removed. The coolant inside the expansion tank should be relatively transparent. If it is rust colored,

Check for a chafed area that could fail prematurely.

Check for a soft area indicating the hose has deteriorated inside.

Overtightening the clamp on a hardened hose will damage the hose and cause a leak.

Check each hose for swelling and oil-soaked ends. Cracks and breaks can be located by squeezing the hose.

9.4 Hoses, like drivebelts, have a habit of failing at the worst possible time - to prevent the inconvenience of a blown radiator or heater hose, inspect them carefully as shown here

the system should be drained and refilled (see Section 14). If the coolant level is not up to the Cold mark, add additional antifreeze/coolant mixture (see Section 3).

4   Carefully check the large upper and lower radiator hoses along with any smaller diameter heater hoses that run from the engine to the firewall. Inspect each hose along its entire length, replacing any hose that is cracked, swollen or shows signs of deterioration. Cracks may become more apparent if the hose is squeezed **(see illustration)**.

5   Make sure all hose connections are tight. A leak in the cooling system will usually show up as white or rust-colored deposits on the areas adjoining the leak.

6   Use compressed air or a soft brush to remove bugs, leaves, etc. from the front of the radiator or air conditioning condenser. Be careful not to damage the delicate cooling fins or cut yourself on them.

7   Every other inspection, or at the first indication of cooling system problems, have the cap and system pressure tested. If you don't have a pressure tester, most gas stations and repair shops will do this for a minimal charge.

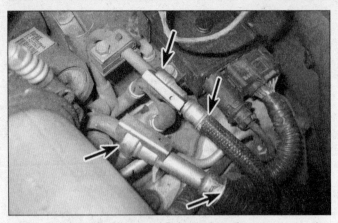

10.3a Check the fuel lines and fittings where they connect to the fuel pipes at the left rear corner of the engine

10.3b Check the fuel lines at the fuel filter/water separator

10   Fuel system check

Refer to illustrations 10.3a, 10.3b and 10.3c

1   If you smell diesel fuel while driving or after the vehicle has been sitting in the sun, inspect the fuel system immediately.
2   Remove the fuel filler cap and inspect if for damage and corrosion. The gasket should have an unbroken sealing imprint. If the gasket is damaged or corroded, install a new cap.
3   Inspect the fuel lines for cracks. Make sure that the connections between the fuel lines and the fuel filter/water separator are secure **(see illustrations)**.
4   Since some components of the fuel system - the fuel tank and part of the fuel feed and return lines, for example - are underneath the vehicle, they can be inspected more easily with the vehicle raised on a hoist. If that's not possible, raise the vehicle and support it securely on jackstands.
5   With the vehicle raised and safely supported, inspect the gas tank and filler neck for punctures, cracks and other damage. The connection between the filler neck and the tank is particularly critical. Sometimes a rubber filler neck will leak because of loose clamps or deteriorated rubber. Inspect all fuel tank mounting brackets and straps to be sure that the tank is securely attached to the vehicle.
Warning: *Do not, under any circumstances, try to repair a fuel tank (except rubber components). A welding torch or any open flame can easily cause fuel vapors inside the tank to explode.*
6   Carefully check all rubber hoses and metal lines leading away from the fuel tank.
Note: *Some rubber hoses are covered with braided wire for strength and protection.*

Check for loose connections, deteriorated hoses, crimped lines and other damage. Repair or replace damaged sections as necessary (see Chapter 3).

11   Fuel filter/water separator - water draining and filter replacement

Warning: *Diesel fuel is flammable, so take extra precautions when you work on any part of the fuel system. Don't smoke or allow open flames or bare light bulbs near the work area, and don't work in a garage where a gas-type appliance (such as a water heater or a clothes dryer) is present. Since diesel fuel is carcinogenic, wear fuel-resistant gloves when there's a possibility of being exposed to fuel, and, if you spill any fuel on your skin, rinse it off immediately with soap and water. Mop up any spills immediately and do not store diesel fuel-soaked rags where they could ignite. When you perform any kind of work on the fuel system, wear safety glasses and have a Class B type fire extinguisher on hand.*

Water in fuel draining

Refer to illustrations 11.1 and 11.3

1   If you're working on a van model or a 2017 or later truck model, raise the vehicle and support it securely on jackstands.
Note: *The fuel filter/water separator on these models is located under the vehicle on the frame rail, forward of the fuel tank.*
2   Working at the bottom of the filter assembly, connect a small clear hose to the petcock in the sensor **(see illustration)** then place the other end of the hose in a container.

10.3c Check the high-pressure fuel lines from the fuel rail to the injectors for seepage

11.1 Connect a hose to the petcock on the water-in-fuel sensor, then loosen the petcock

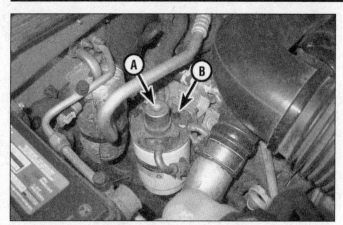

11.3 Location of the priming pump (A) and bleeder screw (B) (2016 and earlier truck models)

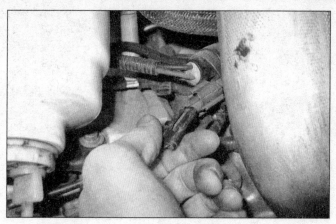

11.9 Disconnect the "water-in-fuel" sensor harness electrical connector

Note: *On 2016 and earlier truck models, removing the right inner fender splash shield improves access to the bottom of the filter.*

3   Open the petcock several turns until the water/fuel mixture starts to flow out of the hose.

4   On 2016 and earlier truck models, depress the priming pump **(see illustration)** at the top of the assembly to help push all the fluid out of the line. Repeat this step several times, each time allowing the priming pump to come back up before depressing it again.

5   Tighten the petcock and remove the hose.

6   To prime the system on van models and 2017 and later truck models:

a) *Turn the ignition to RUN for 30 seconds (don't attempt to start the engine).*

b) *Turn the ignition off, then crank the engine over for 15 seconds.*

c) *If the engine doesn't start, repeat a) and b).*

d) *If the engine doesn't start after performing a) and b) three times, switch off the ignition for one minute, then repeat a) and b).*

e) *When the engine starts, allow it to idle for a few minutes. If it is not running smoothly, it will likely smooth-out after this short period of time.*

Filter replacement

Refer to illustrations 11.9, 11.11 and 11.13

7   On 2016 and earlier truck models, loosen the wheel lug nuts for the right front wheel, raise the front of the vehicle and place it securely on jackstands. Remove the right front wheel and the inner fender splash shield fasteners. Remove the splash shield, or maneuver it until the filter can be accessed.

8   Drain the fuel from the fuel filter (see Steps 1 through 4).

9   Disconnect the "water-in-fuel" sensor electrical connector **(see illustration)**.

10   Move a drain pan into position under the fuel filter.

11   Use a filter wrench to loosen the fuel filter **(see illustration)**. Chain or metal band filter wrenches may distort the filter canister, but it doesn't

12   Completely unscrew the old filter. Be careful - it still has a lot of fuel in it. Empty the fuel inside the filter into the drain pan.

13   Unscrew the water-in-fuel sensor from the bottom of the filter **(see illustration)**.

14   Compare the old filter with the new one to make sure they're the same type.

15   Use a clean rag to remove all dirt from the area where the filter mounts to the fuel filter/heater housing.

Note: *Inspect the fuel filter/heater housing for debris. Any type of debris or contamination can cause leakage at the fuel filter.*

16   Apply a light coat of clean engine oil to the rubber gasket at each end of the new fuel filter.

17   Install the fuel-in-water sensor to the filter and tighten the sensor until the seal contacts the filter, then tighten it an additional 1/2-turn.

18   Attach the new filter to the fuel filter/fuel heater housing, following the tightening directions printed on the filter canister or packing box.

Caution: *Most filter manufacturers recommend against using a filter wrench due to the possibility of overtightening and damage to the seal.*

19   Connect the fuel-in-water senor harness connector.

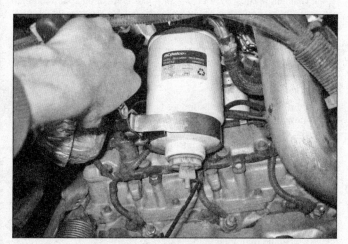

11.11 Use a filter wrench to loosen the fuel filter

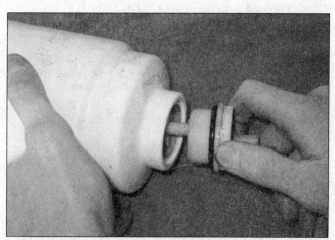

11.13 Unscrew the water-in-fuel sensor from the bottom of the filter

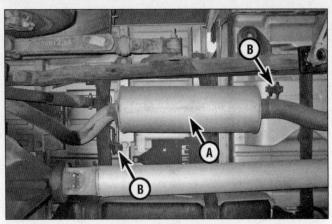

12.2a Inspect the muffler (A) and exhaust system hangers (B) for signs of deterioration

12.2b Inspect all flanged joints for loose fasteners and signs of exhaust gas leakage

2016 and earlier truck models

20 Prime the fuel system as follows:

a) *Unscrew the bleeder screw a few turns* **(see illustration 11.3)**.

b) *Depress the priming pump until fuel begins to leak from around the bleeder screw, then tighten the bleeder screw.*

c) *Depress the primer pump approximately 25 times or until the pump becomes hard to depress.*

d) *Try to start the engine. The engine may start and die again quickly. If it does, depress the primer pump again approximately 25 times, or until the pump becomes hard to depress.*

e) *Start the engine and allow to idle for several minutes.*

f) *Check for leaks and clear any trouble codes (see Chapter 6).*

Van models and 2017 and later truck models

21 To prime the system on these models, see Step 6.

Fuel Filter Life Monitor

22 The Fuel Filter Life Monitor is a function of the PCM that tracks engine operating hours and conditions. If the PCM determines that your fuel filter has been used long enough, an indicator that shows "FUEL FILTER LIFE" will light on the instrument panel.

23 When you change your filter, whether you change it at the interval recommended in this Chapter or only when the light comes on, you will have to reset the system to make the indicator go out and allow the system to accurately calculate when the next filter change is due.

2016 and earlier truck models

Vehicles without steering wheel controls and a Driver Information Center (DIC)

24 To reset, turn the ignition key to the Run position (not Start) with the engine off and wait 5 seconds.

25 Fully depress the accelerator pedal and brake pedal at the same time and hold for 10 seconds. Turn the key to Off; the system is reset.

26 Start the engine, if the "FUEL FILTER LIFE" message still appears, repeat the resetting procedure.

Vehicles equipped steering wheel controls and Driver Information Center (DIC)

27 To reset, press and hold the select button on the steering wheel control for five seconds; an indicator that shows "FUEL FILTER LIFE" will light on the instrument panel for 10 seconds and the system is reset.

28 Start the engine, if the "FUEL FILTER LIFE" message still appears, repeat the resetting procedure.

2017 and later models

Note: *The Fuel Filter Life will only display on the Driver Information Center (DIC) if the Ignition is On. The vehicle must be in Service Mode and the gear selector must be in Park.*

29 Display the Fuel Filter Life Remaining on the DIC. If the vehicle does not have DIC buttons, use the trip odometer reset stem.

30 Press and hold the SET/RESET button on the DIC, or the trip odometer reset stem if the vehicle does not have DIC buttons, for more than two seconds. The Fuel Filter Life Remaining will change to 100 percent.

31 Turn the key off and back on to verify the procedure

12 Exhaust system check

Refer to illustrations 12.2a and 12.2b

1 With the engine cold (at least three hours after the vehicle has been driven), check the complete exhaust system from the manifold to the end of the tailpipe. Be careful around the catalytic converter, which may be hot even after three hours. The inspection should be done with the vehicle on a hoist to permit unrestricted access. If a hoist isn't available, raise the vehicle and support it securely on jackstands.

2 Check the exhaust pipes and connections for signs of leakage and/or corrosion indicating a potential failure. Make sure that all brackets and hangers are in good condition and tight **(see illustrations)**.

3 Inspect the underside of the body for holes, corrosion, open seams, etc. which may allow exhaust gasses to enter the passenger compartment. Seal all body openings with silicone sealant or body putty.

4 Rattles and other noises can often be traced to the exhaust system, especially the hangers, mounts and heat shields. Try to move the pipes, mufflers and catalytic converter. If the components can come in contact with the body or suspension parts, secure the exhaust system with new brackets and hangers.

13 Air filter replacement

Refer to illustration 13.1

1 At the specified intervals, the air filter element should be replaced with a new one. The filter housing is equipped with an indicator that measures airflow; if the disc inside moves into the red zone, the filter is in need of replacement **(see illustration)**

Note: *If you drive in conditions that are particularly dusty, a filter change may be necessary before the normally recommended mileage interval.*

2005 and earlier models

Refer to illustrations 13.4a and 13.4b

2 The air filter is housed in a black plastic box mounted on the inner fenderwell in the right front of the engine compartment.

3 Disconnect the electrical connector from the Mass Air Flow/Intake Air Temperature (MAF/IAT) sensor (see Chapter 6).

13.1 If the disc inside of the air filter indicator moves near or into the red zone, replace the air filter element

4   Loosen the captive screws and pull the housing cover up, then lift the air filter element out of the housing (**see illustrations**). Wipe out the inside of the air filter housing with a clean rag.
5   Place the new filter element in the air filter housing. Make sure it seats properly in the groove of the housing.
6   Installation is the reverse of removal.

2006 through 2010 models
7   The air filter is housed in the round inlet housing at the right front of the engine compartment.
8   Remove the housing door screw and pull the door up, then pull back and lift the air filter element out of the housing. Wipe out the inside of the air filter housing with a clean rag.
9   With the filter at a slight angle, slide the front of the filter in while pushing down, until the rear of the element clicks into place.
Note: *Make sure it seats properly in the housing.*
10   Installation is the reverse of removal.

2011 and later models
11   The air filter is housed in a black plastic box mounted at the front of the engine compartment.
12   Loosen the two captive screws at the top of the housing and lift the housing cover up to disengage the tabs at the bottom of the cover. Lift the air filter element out of the housing. Wipe out the inside of the air filter housing with a clean rag.
13   Place the new filter element in the air filter housing. Make sure it seats properly in the groove of the housing.
14   Installation is the reverse of removal.

14   Cooling system servicing (draining, flushing and refilling)

Warning: *Do not allow antifreeze to come in contact with your skin or painted surfaces of the vehicle. Rinse off spills immediately with plenty of water. Antifreeze is highly toxic if ingested. Never leave antifreeze lying around in an open container or in puddles on the floor; children and pets are attracted by its sweet smell and may drink it. Check with local authorities on disposing of used antifreeze. Many communities have collection centers that will see that antifreeze is disposed of safely. Antifreeze is flammable under certain conditions - be sure to read the precautions on the container.*
Caution: *Never mix green-colored ethylene glycol antifreeze and orange-colored DEX-COOL silicate-free coolant because doing so will destroy the efficiency of the DEX-COOL coolant, which is designed to last for 100,000 miles or five years.*
Note: *Non-toxic coolant is available at local auto parts stores. Although the coolant is non-toxic when fresh, proper disposal is still required.*

Draining
Refer to illustration 14.3
Warning: *If the vehicle has just been driven, wait several hours to allow the engine to cool down completely before beginning this procedure.*
1   Periodically, the cooling system should be drained, flushed and refilled to replenish the antifreeze mixture and prevent formation of rust and corrosion, which can impair the performance of the cooling system and cause engine damage. When the cooling system is serviced, all hoses and the expansion tank cap should be checked and replaced if necessary.
2   Apply the parking brake and block the wheels.
3   Move a large container under the right corner of the radiator hose to catch the coolant. Unscrew the radiator drain plug (**see illustration**). Remove the expansion tank cap.
Caution: *The coolant will come out with force when the cap is removed.*
Note: *If the radiator is not equipped with a drain plug, slide the clamp back on the lower radiator hose and disconnect the hose from the radiator.*
4   While the coolant is draining, check the condition of the radiator hoses, heater hoses and clamps.
5   Replace any damaged clamps or hoses. Tighten the radiator drain plug.

Flushing
6   Fill the cooling system with clean water, following the *Refilling* procedure (see Steps 12 through 17).
7   Start the engine and allow it to reach normal operating temperature.
8   Turn the engine off and allow it to cool completely, then drain the system as described earlier.

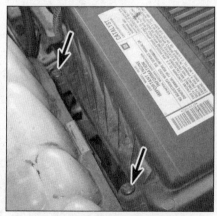

13.4a Loosen the screws (two of four shown) and lift up the air filter housing cover . . .

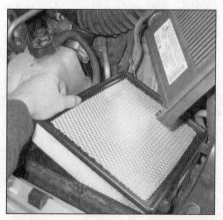

13.4b . . . then remove the filter element

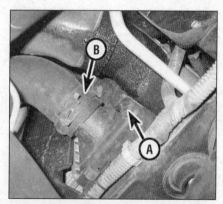

14.3 Location of the radiator drain plug (A). If your radiator isn't equipped with a drain plug, detach the lower radiator hose (B) from the radiator

14.13 Cooling system bleed bolt on the thermostat housing

9   Repeat Steps 6 through 8 until the water being drained is free of contaminants.

10   In severe cases of contamination or clogging of the radiator, remove the radiator (see Chapter 2) and have a radiator repair facility clean and repair it if necessary.

11   Many deposits can be removed by the chemical action of a cleaner available at auto parts stores. Follow the procedure outlined in the manufacturer's instructions.

Note: *When the coolant is regularly drained and the system refilled with the correct antifreeze/water mixture, there should be no need to use chemical cleaners or descalers.*

Refilling

Refer to illustration 14.13

12   Place the heater temperature control in the maximum heat position.

13   Be sure to use the proper coolant listed in this Chapter's Specifications. Unscrew the bleed bolt on the thermostat housing **(see illustration)**. Slowly fill the expansion tank with the recommended mixture of antifreeze and water until coolant flows from the bleed bolt hole, then install the bolt and tighten it securely. Continue to add coolant to the expansion tank until the level is up to the COLD mark.

14   Install the cap on the expansion tank. Start the engine and run it at approximately 2000 to 2500 rpm until the engine reaches normal operating temperature and the thermostats open.

15   Let the engine idle for three minutes.

16   Turn the engine off and let it cool. Add coolant to the expansion tank until the level is up to the COLD mark, repeat Steps 14 and 15, then turn the engine off.

17   Check the cooling system for leaks.

Service record

Date	Mileage	Work performed

Notes

Chapter 2
Cooling system

Contents

Specifications

General
Coolant type .... See Chapter 1
Coolant system capacity .... See Chapter 1

Torque specifications

Ft-lbs (unless otherwise indicated)   **Nm**

Note: *One foot-pound (ft-lb) of torque is equivalent to 12 inch-pounds (in-lbs) of torque. Torque values below approximately 15 ft-lbs are expressed in inch-pounds, because most foot-pound torque wrenches are not accurate at these smaller values.*

	Ft-lbs	Nm
Air conditioning compressor mounting bolts	37	50
Air conditioning compressor/power steering pump bracket bolts		
2005 through 2007	34	46
All others	37	50
Alternator bracket bolts/nuts	37	50
Alternator mounting bolts	See Chapter 5	
Block coolant drain plug	156 in-lbs	18
Charge air cooler bolts	15	21
Coolant expansion tank bolt/nut	80 in-lbs	9
Coolant heater bolt	18 in-lbs	2

Torque specifications (continued)

Ft-lbs (unless otherwise indicated)   **Nm**

Note: *One foot-pound (ft-lb) of torque is equivalent to 12 inch-pounds (in-lbs) of torque. Torque values below approximately 15 ft-lbs are expressed in inch-pounds, because most foot-pound torque wrenches are not accurate at these smaller values.*

	Ft-lbs	Nm
Crankshaft balancer bolt		
2002 and earlier	278	363
2003 and later		
Step 1	74	100
Step 2	Tighten an additional 105 degrees	
Fan clutch nut	41	56
Fan-to-fan clutch bolts	17	23
Fan pulley mounting bolts	34	46
Fuel line bracket bolt/nut	15	21
Idler pulley bolt		
LB7	27	34
All others	37	50
Oil fill tube bolts	18	25
Radiator bolts	18	25
Starter mounting bolts	See Chapter 5	
Thermostat bypass pipe-to-water pump bolts	15	21
Thermostat housing cover bolts		
LB7, LMM	15	21
All other variants	18	25
Thermostat housing crossover bolts/nuts	15	21
Turbocharger coolant bypass valve	44	60
Water outlet tube bolts	15	21
Water pump bolts		
2010 and earlier models	15	21
2011 and later models	18	25
Water pump outlet pipe nuts	15	21

1   General information

1   The Duramax 6.6L engine makes use of a pressurized cooling system with thermostatically controlled coolant circulation. Coolant is drawn from the radiator by a gear driven, impeller-type water pump mounted at the front of the block. Coolant flows to the heater core where it can be used to provide heat for the passenger compartment and window defrosting. The coolant is routed through a pipe containing the engine oil cooler, then to the rear engine cover, where flow is directed to both banks of the engine block. As the coolant passes through water jackets inside the engine block, heat is absorbed and carried away. Coolant is then circulated up to the cylinder heads, where additional heat is absorbed as the fluid flows through water jackets surrounding the combustion chambers and valve seats.

2   Coolant flows through the center housing of the turbocharger to cool it, too. As the engine warms up, a bypass valve in the turbocharger inlet hose inhibits coolant flow and allows the turbocharger to warm to operating temperature.

3   From the cylinder heads, the coolant flows to the thermostat housing, then on to the radiator. If the engine coolant temperature is under 185°F (85°C), the thermostats remain closed and coolant is directed to the water pump through the bypass pipe.

4   Two thermostats control and direct coolant flow in order to maintain the operating temperature of the engine. The thermostats make use of a wax-pellet to actuate a valve. As the wax pellet heats up, it expands and pushes against a rubber piston which opens the valve. As the wax is cooled, it contracts and a spring closes the valve. When the coolant temperature is below 180°F (82°C), both thermostats are closed and coolant flow is directed through the bypass port by the front thermostat. When the coolant exceeds 180°F (82°C), the front thermostat primary valve will begin to open and allow coolant to flow to the radiator where engine heat can be dissipated. As the coolant temperature increases to 185°F (85°C), a secondary valve in the front thermostat starts to close the bypass port and the rear thermostat starts to open, allowing more coolant to flow to the radiator where it is cooled before returning to the engine. The front thermostat opens completely when the coolant temperature reaches 203°F (95°C); the rear thermostat opens completely when the coolant temperature reaches 212°F (100°C).

5   The cooling system is sealed by the pressure cap, which contains a blow-off pressure valve and a vacuum atmospheric valve. By maintaining higher pressure within the system, it increases the boiling point of the coolant. If the coolant temperature goes above this increased boiling point, the extra pressure in the system forces the blow-off valve off its seat and allows excess pressure to escape the system.

6   The expansion tank serves as both the point at which fresh coolant is added to the cooling system to maintain the proper fluid level and as the point where coolant is circulated to allow air bubbles out of the system.

7   The Duramax engine is equipped with various sensors which will illuminate warning lights on the instrument panel to alert the operator of an overheating condition as well as a low coolant level.

2   Antifreeze - general information

Warning: *Do not allow antifreeze to come in contact with your skin or painted surfaces of the vehicle. Rinse off spills immediately with plenty of water. Antifreeze is highly toxic if ingested. Never leave antifreeze lying around in an open container or in puddles on the floor; children and pets are attracted by it's sweet smell and may drink it. Check with local authorities about disposing of used antifreeze. Many communities have collection centers which will see that antifreeze is disposed of safely. Never dump used antifreeze on the ground or pour it into drains.*
Caution: *The manufacturer recommends using only DEX-COOL coolant in this system. DEX-COOL is a long-lasting coolant designed for 100,000 miles or 5 years. Never mix green-colored ethylene glycol antifreeze and orange-colored DEX-COOL silicate-free coolant because doing so will destroy the efficiency of the DEX-COOL.*

1   The cooling system should be filled with a 50/50 mixture of DEX-COOL and water which will prevent freezing down to at

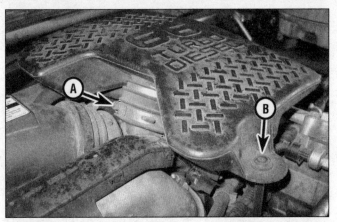

3.6 Loosen the hose clamp (A), then unscrew the bolt (B) and remove the resonator

least -20-degrees F. It also provides protection against corrosion and increases the coolant boiling point. The manufacturer states that DEX-COOL is good for up to five years, after which the cooling system should be drained, flushed and refilled with a fresh solution of DEX-COOL and water. The use of antifreeze solutions for periods of longer than five years is likely to cause damage and encourage the formation of rust and scale in the system.

2   Before adding antifreeze, check all hose connections, because antifreeze tends to leak through very minute openings. Engines don't normally consume coolant, so if the level goes down, find the cause and correct it.

3   Thermostats - check and replacement

Check

1   Before assuming a thermostat is to blame for a cooling system problem, check the coolant level (see Chapter 1) and temperature gauge (or light) operation.

2   If the engine seems to be taking a long time to warm up (based on heater output or temperature gauge operation), one or both thermostats may be stuck open. Replace the thermostats.

3   If the engine runs hot, use your hand to check the temperature of the upper radiator hose. If the hose isn't hot, but the engine is, one or both thermostats may be stuck closed, preventing the coolant inside the engine from escaping to the radiator. Replace the thermostats.
Caution: *Don't drive the vehicle without a thermostat. The computer may stay in open loop and emissions and fuel economy will suffer.*

4   If the hose is hot, it means the coolant is flowing to the radiator. Consult the *Troubleshooting* Section at the rear of this manual for cooling system diagnosis.

Replacement

Refer to illustrations 3.6, 3.10, 3.11, 3.12, 3.13, 3.17 and 3.18
Warning: *Wait until the engine is completely cool before beginning this procedure.*
Note: *Always replace the thermostats as a pair.*
Note: *The following procedure is the GM factory recommended procedure for removing the thermostat housing cover and replacing the thermostats. Some of these steps will be necessary for removal of other components as well. It is possible, however, to replace the thermostats without performing all of the steps listed here:*

   a) *Steps 8, 10 and 12 can be omitted, as well as the steps on reassembly that don't apply.*

   b) *Once the other Steps have been performed, the thermostat housing cover can be lifted up high enough to access the thermostats.*

5   Disconnect the cables from the negative terminals of both batteries (see Chapter 5, Section 1).

6   On models where it would interfere, remove the air intake resonator **(see illustration)**.

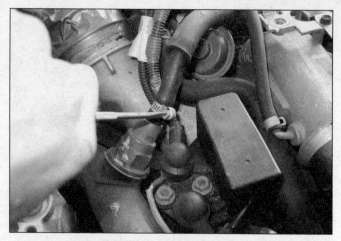

3.10 Loosen the clamp and disconnect the turbocharger cooling hose from the bypass valve

3.11 Water outlet tube-to-valve cover bolts

3.12 Coolant outlet tube-to-thermostat housing cover bolt

7   Partially drain the cooling system (see Chapter 1) to a point that is lower than the level of the thermostat housing cover. If the coolant is relatively new or in good condition, save it and reuse it. If it is to be replaced, see the **Warning** in Section 2.

8   Remove the upper radiator hose from the water outlet tube on the engine.

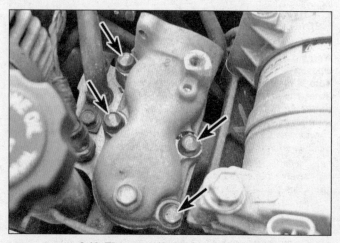

3.13 Thermostat housing cover bolts

Note: *On Kodiak, Topkick and some other models, you may have to remove the charge air inlet and outlet ducts from the air filter housing.*

9   Remove the bolt and bracket holding the wiring harness to the thermostat housing.

10   Disconnect the turbocharger cooling hose from the turbocharger bypass valve on the water outlet tube **(see illustration)**.

11   Remove the two bolts holding the water outlet tube to the valve cover **(see illustration)**.

Note: *On LLY and later engines, the bracket that holds the electrical connectors for the main engine wiring harness will have to be unbolted and repositioned for access to the rear bolt that holds the water outlet tube to the valve cover.*

12   Remove the bolt holding the coolant outlet tube to the thermostat housing **(see illustration)**. Detach the outlet tube from the engine and remove and discard the O-ring.

13   Remove the bolts holding the thermostat housing cover to the thermostat housing **(see illustration)**.

14   Remove the thermostat cover. If the cover is stuck, tap it gently with a soft-face hammer to jar it loose.

15   Note how the thermostats are installed (which end is facing up), then remove them along with the seals. Make sure the seals don't stick to the underside of the cover or in the housing.

16   Clean the mating surfaces of the thermostat housing and thermostat housing cover. Place a rag in the openings to prevent debris from falling into the housing.

17   If the new thermostats didn't come with their seals installed, install the seals around the flanges of the thermostats **(see illustration)**.

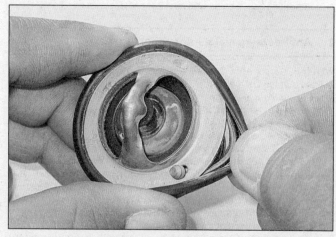

3.17 Install the rubber seal onto the flange of each thermostat

3.18 The thermostat with two vent holes is the rear thermostat, and the vent holes must be positioned at the rear of the housing

18 Install the new thermostats and seals to the thermostat housing. The rear thermostat is the one with two vent valves; these vent valves face toward the rear of the engine **(see illustration)**.
19 Reinstall the thermostat housing cover. Tighten the bolts to the torque listed in this Chapter's Specifications.
20 Install a new O-ring seal on the water outlet tube and reattach the tube.
21 The remainder of installation is the reverse of the removal procedure.
22 Refill the engine with coolant (see Chapter 1). Run the engine and check for leaks.

4   Engine cooling fan and fan clutch - check and replacement

Check

Warning: *While checking the fan, make sure that the engine is NOT started. If it is, you could be severely injured.*
Warning: *Before the fan clutch operation can be checked in Step 5, the engine must be warmed up to its normal operating temperature and then turned off. Even though the engine won't be running during this check, it's HOT! Make sure that you don't touch the engine itself during this check, or you could be burned.*
Warning: *Keep hands, tools and clothing away from the fan when the engine is running. To avoid injury or damage DO NOT operate the engine with a damaged fan. Do not attempt to repair fan blades - replace a damaged fan with a new one.*
1   Symptoms of fan clutch failure are continuous noisy operation, looseness, vibration and/or silicone fluid leaking from the clutch.

Cold engine checks
2   Rock the fan back and forth by hand to check for excessive bearing play.
3   With the engine cold, turn the blades by hand. The fan should turn freely.
4   Visually inspect for substantial fluid leakage from the fan clutch assembly, a deformed bi-metal spring (on the front of the clutch) or grease leakage from the cooling fan bearing. If any of these conditions exist, replace the fan clutch.

Hot engine check
5   Start the engine and allow it to warm up to its normal operating temperature. When the engine is fully warmed up, turn off the ignition switch. Turn the fan by hand. Some resistance should be felt. If the fan turns easily, replace the fan clutch.

4.7a Remove these two bolts and detach the Transmission Control Module (TCM) from the left side of the fan shroud

Fan and clutch removal and installation
Refer to illustrations 4.7a, 4.7b, 4.7c, 4.9a, 4.9b and 4.11
6   Disconnect the cables from the negative battery terminals.
7   Remove the upper fan shroud **(see illustrations)**.
Note: *2006 and later models have an additional, circular fan shroud surrounding the fan. Remove the shroud brackets bolts and reposition it. When reinstalling the circular shroud, be sure to center it in the fan opening, leaving a minimum of 1/4-inch all the way around the fan or damage will occur.*

4.7b Detach the refrigerant line from the right side of the shroud

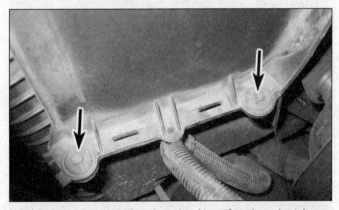

4.7c Remove the upper fan shroud-to-lower fan shroud retainers, then lift the shroud out. To remove the retainers, pull up on the center portion, then pry out the bottom portion

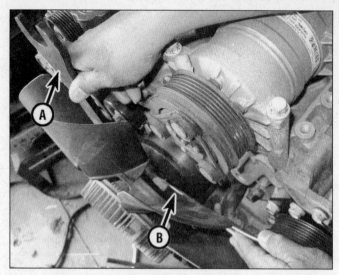

4.9a Unscrew the large fan nut with a wrench (A) while holding the pulley from turning. Here, a pin spanner (B) is being used, with the pins engaged with the holes in the face of the pulley . . .

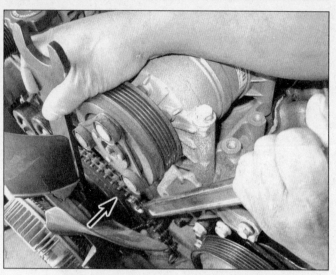

4.9b . . . and here, a chain wrench is being used to prevent the pulley from turning. Note the piece of old drivebelt being used to protect the surface of the pulley

8   On 2011 and later models with an electro-viscous fan clutch, disconnect the electrical connector from the clutch.
9   The fan clutch is held to the drive hub with a large nut. A large open-end wrench or adjustable wrench, and a means to hold the pulley from turning, are needed to remove the cooling fan. One way to prevent the pulley from turning is with a pin spanner that engages with the holes in the face of the pulley. The other method is to use a chain wrench wrapped around the pulley **(see illustrations)**. Hold the pulley stationary while loosening the nut with the large wrench.
Note: *The fan clutch hub nut is a normal right-hand thread (turn counterclockwise to loosen). In some cases the nut may be extremely tight. Hitting the wrench with a hammer, or using an air hammer on the large nut, can help to jar it loose.*
10   Once the nut is loose, spin the fan clutch off of the pulley and remove it from the engine compartment.
Caution: *Do not allow the fan to contact the radiator.*
11   If you're going to replace the fan or the clutch, remove the fan-to-fan clutch bolts **(see illustration)**.
Caution: *To prevent silicone fluid from draining from the clutch assem-*

bly into the fan drive bearing and ruining the lubricant, place the drive unit so that the shaft points UP.
12   Installation is the reverse of removal.

Fan pulley removal and installation

Refer to illustration 4.14
13   Remove the fan and clutch assembly (see Steps 6 through 11).
14   Disconnect the electrical connector from the camshaft position sensor **(see illustration)**.
15   Unscrew the fasteners and detach the pulley from the engine front cover.
16   Installation is the reverse of the removal procedure. Tighten the fasteners to the torque listed in this Chapter's Specifications.

5   Radiator and coolant expansion tank - removal and installation

Warning: *Wait until the engine is completely cool before beginning this procedure.*

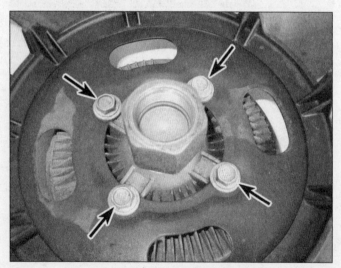

4.11 Fan-to-fan clutch bolts

4.14 Unplug the electrical connector from the camshaft position sensor, then remove the fan pulley mounting bolts

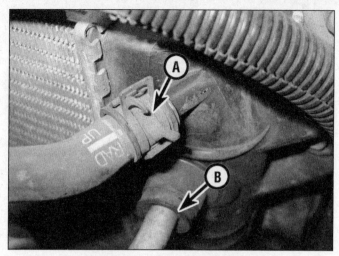

5.8a Expansion tank hose (A) and upper transmission cooler line (B)

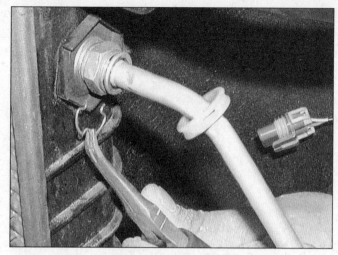

5.8b Unsnap the plastic collar, then pry off the retaining clip from the quick-connect fitting to disconnect the transmission cooler lines

Radiator

Removal

Refer to illustrations 5.8a, 5.8b and 5.10

1   Disconnect the cables from the negative terminals of both batteries (see Chapter 5, Section 1).
2   Drain the cooling system (see Chapter 1). If the coolant is relatively new or in good condition, save it and reuse it. If it is going to be replaced, see the **Warning** in Section 2.
3   Remove the upper fan shroud (see Section 4).

2007.5 (LMM) and later models

4   Remove the engine cooling fan and clutch assembly (see Section 4).
5   Remove the inlet and outlet ducts from the charge air cooler.
All models
6   Disconnect the radiator upper hose from the radiator.
7   Disconnect the radiator lower hose from the radiator.
8   Disconnect the expansion tank hose and the transmission cooler lines from the right side of the radiator **(see illustrations)**. To disconnect the transmission cooler lines from the radiator, simply unsnap the plastic collar from the quick-connect fitting, then pry off the quick-connect fitting retaining clip and remove the lines.
Note: *Do not remove the clips by pulling straight out. Hold one side in with your fingers while using a pick (with a bent tip) to pull the other side out, then rotate the clip off.*
Plug the ends of the lines to prevent fluid from leaking out after you disconnect them. Have a drip pan ready to catch any spills. Always be sure to inspect the O-rings on the cooler lines before reinstallation. Install clips the same way, not straight on.
Note: *Some vehicles may be equipped with an engine oil cooler mounted within the radiator, similar to the transmission cooler, but on the left side radiator tank. Disconnect the lines to the engine oil cooler in the same manner as the transmission cooler lines.*
9   Detach the lower fan shroud from the radiator.
10   Remove the radiator mounting bolts **(see illustration)**. On 2007.5 (LMM) and later models, the radiator is bolted to the charge air cooler; remove the four bolts and detach the radiator from the charge air cooler.
11   Carefully lift the radiator out.

Kodiak/TopKick trucks

12   These vehicles use a system of upper and lower support brackets to secure the radiator. Remove the bolts to the upper bracket, then remove the bracket and lift the radiator out. The rubber insulators should be replaced when re-installing the radiator.

5.10 Left side radiator mounting bolt - right side similar (2007 LBZ and earlier models)

Installation

13   Radiator installation is the reverse of removal. On 2007 and earlier models, make sure the lower rubber insulators are in good condition, in place and the radiator seats properly in them.
Note: *Prior to installation of the radiator, replace any damaged radiator hoses and hose clamps.*
14   Install new retaining clips onto the quick connect fittings before installing the transmission cooler lines. Rotate these clips into the recesses in the fitting, ensuring that the clip is engaged in all three slots, then snap the cooler lines into place by pushing the line straight into the quick connect fittings. Pull back sharply on the line to ensure it is held in place by the fitting. Don't forget to reinstall the plastic collars on the quick connect fittings as they lock the retaining clip in place. If the plastic collar is properly seated, the yellow band on the tube will not be visible.
15   Refill the cooling system (see Chapter 1) and check for leaks. Also check the engine oil and automatic transmission fluid levels.

Coolant expansion tank

Refer to illustrations 5.18a and 5.18b

16   Drain the cooling system as described in Chapter 1 until the expansion tank is empty. Refer to the coolant **Warning** in Section 2.

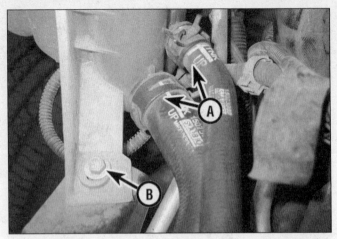

**5.18a Expansion tank hoses (A) and forward mounting bolt (B)
(2005 LLY model shown)**

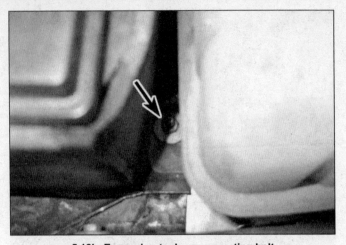

**5.18b Expansion tank rear mounting bolt
(2005 LLY model shown)**

17　Disconnect the electrical connection to the low coolant level sensor.
18　Detach the coolant hoses from the expansion tank. Unscrew the mounting fasteners, then remove the expansion tank **(see illustrations)**.
19　Prior to installation, make sure the tank is clean and free of debris which could be drawn into the radiator (wash it with soapy water and a brush if necessary, then rinse thoroughly).
20　Installation is the reverse of removal. Refill the cooling system (see Chapter 1) and check for leaks

6　Water pump - check and replacement

Warning: *Wait until the engine is completely cool before beginning this procedure.*
Note: *While replacing the water pump, there is a high probability that coolant could be accidentally introduced into the engine oil. It is a good idea to drain and replace the engine oil after completing the water pump replacement procedure.*

Check

Refer to illustration 6.2
1　A failure in the water pump can cause serious engine damage due to overheating.
2　The water pump is equipped with a small weep or vent hole **(see illustration)**. If the pump seal fails, coolant will flow from this hole.
3　If the water pump shaft bearings fail, there may be a howling sound near the water pump while the engine is running.

Removal

Refer to illustrations 6.12, 6.13, 6.15, 6.16, 6.17a, 6.17b, 6.19a and 6.19b
Note: *It's a good idea to place a sheet of cardboard or thin plywood against the engine side of the radiator to prevent accidentally damaging the radiator during this procedure.*
4　Disconnect the cables from the negative terminals of the batteries. (see Chapter 5, Section 1).
5　Loosen the front wheel lug nuts. Raise the front of the vehicle and support it securely on jackstands, then remove the wheels.
Note: *If you have a flywheel holding tool that does not require the starter motor to be removed, the right-front wheel does not have to be removed.*
6　Remove the inner fender splash shield(s).
7　Completely drain the coolant from the cooling system (see Chapter 1).
8　Remove the upper fan shroud (see Section 4).
9　Remove the fan and clutch assembly (see Section 4).
10　Remove the drivebelt (see Chapter 1).
11　Remove the starter (see Chapter 5).
Note: *Special tools are available from specialty tool manufacturers that attach to the bellhousing so the starter does not have to be removed.*
12　Using a 12-point 36 mm socket and long breaker bar on the crankshaft pulley bolt, turn the crankshaft until one of the **unthreaded** holes in the flywheel is exposed in the starter opening. Insert a long punch or rod into this hole to prevent the crankshaft from turning when performing the next Step **(see illustration)**.

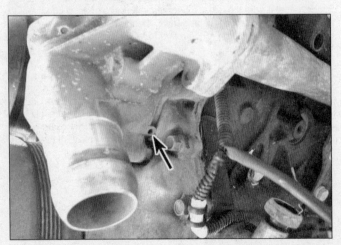

6.2 Location of the water pump weep hole

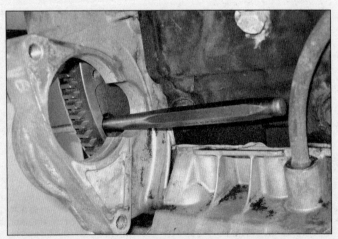

**6.12 Insert a long punch into one of the unthreaded holes
in the flywheel to prevent it from turning**

6.13 Use a long breaker bar and 12-point 36 mm socket toremove the crankshaft pulley bolt

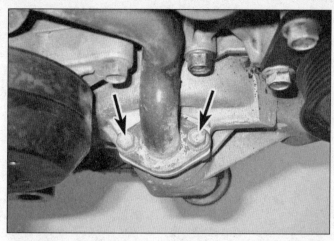

6.15 Thermostat bypass pipe bolts at the top of the water pump

13   Remove the crankshaft pulley bolt **(see illustration)**.
Note: *This bolt is extremely tight. At the very least, a long breaker bar will be required. Soak the area around the bolt head and around the large washer with penetrating oil and let it soak in for awhile. If you can't loosen the bolt with the breaker bar, try pounding on the breaker bar with a hammer as force is applied to it. If it just won't break loose, you'll have to use an impact wrench, which, in most cases, will require removal of the radiator for clearance.* Slide the pulley off the end of the crankshaft.
14   Loosen the clamp and remove the lower radiator hose from the bottom of the water pump.
15   Remove the two bolts that hold the thermostat bypass pipe to the top of the water pump **(see illustration)**. This pipe does not have to be removed completely to get the water pump out. However, if you do remove it, you will need a new O-ring for the top where it connects to the thermostat housing crossover.
Note: *Even if the bypass pipe isn't removed, just dislodging it from its normal resting place is enough to cause the O-ring to leak, so it's a good idea to replace the O-ring at this stage to prevent a leak after everything is put back together.*
16   Remove the two nuts that hold the water pump outlet pipe to the back of the water pump **(see illustration)**. If there is a wiring harness retainer on the inner stud, remove this too.
17   Remove the two water pump bolts and one nut **(see illustrations)**. Pay close attention to which bolt goes where, as they are different lengths.

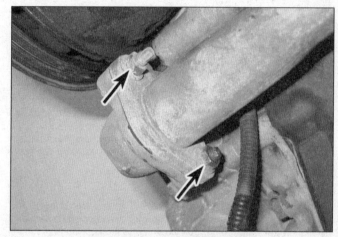

6.16 Water pump outlet pipe nuts

18   Remove the water pump by pulling it straight out of the front of the engine. Too much rotating or tipping the pump at this point could spill coolant into the engine oil. If the water pump outlet pipe gasket did not come off with the pump, remove the gasket from the pipe.

6.17a Remove the bolt at the top of the water pump (behind the thermostat pipe) . . .

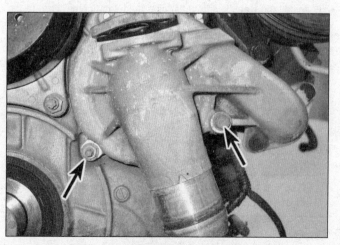

6.17b . . . and the remaining nut and bolt

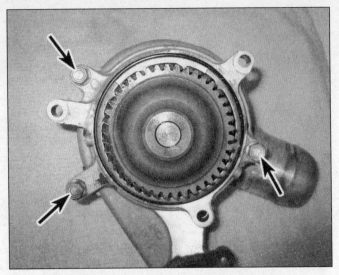

6.19a Remove the water pump-to-housing bolts . . .

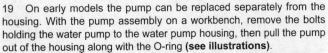

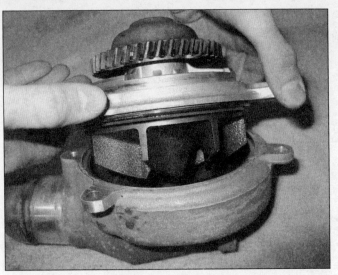

**6.19b . . . and separate the pump from the housing
(early models only)**

19   On early models the pump can be replaced separately from the housing. With the pump assembly on a workbench, remove the bolts holding the water pump to the water pump housing, then pull the pump out of the housing along with the O-ring **(see illustrations)**.
20   Clean and inspect the water pump housing. Pay close attention to the mating surfaces for damage or signs of leaks. Also, check the drive gear for chips or other damage and the pump shaft to see if its loose. Replace the pump and pump housing as necessary.
21   It's a good idea to remove the water outlet pipe from the oil cooler/ filter adapter and replace the O-ring to prevent the possibility of a coolant leak at that point.

Installation
22   If you're working on an early model and are installing a new pump into the housing, lubricate a new O-ring with clean engine coolant and install it on the water pump. Bolt the pump to the housing and tighten the fasteners to the torque listed in this Chapter's Specifications.
23   Install a new O-ring onto the pump housing, using clean coolant to lubricate it. Place a new gasket on the studs that connect the water pump outlet pipe to the oil cooler. Install a new O-ring on the top of the pump for the thermostat bypass pipe.
24   Install the water pump on the engine, making sure the pump is seated all the way. Use the correct length bolt in each location and tighten the bolts and nut to the torque listed in this Chapter's Specifications.
25   Install the water pump outlet pipe nuts and tighten them to the torque listed in this Chapter's Specifications. Don't forget to place the wiring harness retainer on the inside stud (if equipped).
26   Connect the thermostat bypass pipe to the top of the water pump and tighten the bolts to the torque listed in this Chapter's Specifications.
27   Reconnect the lower radiator hose to the water pump.
28   The remainder of installation is the reverse of removal. Don't forget to remove the cardboard from the radiator before you install the upper shroud. Tighten the crankshaft pulley bolt to the torque listed in the Chapter 7 Speciifcations.
29   Refill the cooling system (see Chapter 1). Run the engine and check for leaks.

7   Coolant temperature gauge sending unit - check and replacement

Check
1   The coolant temperature indicator system consists of a temperature gauge mounted in the dash and a coolant temperature sensor

mounted on the engine. This coolant temperature sensor doubles as an information sensor for the fuel and emissions systems.
2   If an overheating indication occurs, first check the coolant level in the system (see Chapter 1).
3   If the sensor is defective, a Diagnostic Trouble Code (DTC) will be set (see Chapter 6); replace it with a new one.
4   If the coolant temperature sensor is good, have the temperature gauge checked by a dealer service department. This test will require a scan tool to access the information as it is processed by the on-board computer.

Replacement
5   See Chapter 6 for the ECT sensor replacement procedure.

8   Coolant heater - check and replacement

Check
1   The coolant heater (an optional accessory), also referred to as an engine block heater, is a 110-volt electric heating element designed to aid engine starting in very cold conditions. It does this by heating the coolant inside the engine block. A power cord is routed from the heater to the front of the vehicle. There are two types of cords: one with an internal thermal switch that will shut the heater off above 0-degrees F (-18-degrees C), and another that will operate at all temperatures.
2   Before replacing the coolant heater, first inspect the cord for cuts, abrasions, burns or other obvious signs of damage. Use an ohmmeter to check for continuity in the cord. It is important to note that cords with the internal thermal switch will always show an open condition in temperatures above 0 degrees F (-18 degrees C). Alternatively, use an ohmmeter to test the heater for a short or ground. If the heater checks good, replace the cord.

Replacement
Warning: *Wait until the engine is completely cool before beginning this procedure.*
3   Disconnect the cables from the negative battery terminals (see Chapter 5, Section 1).
4   Drain the cooling system (see Chapter 1). If the coolant is relatively new or in good condition, save it and reuse it. If it is going to be replaced, see the **Warning** in Section 2.

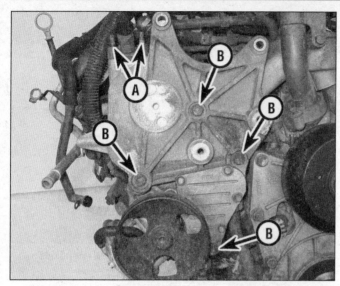

9.9 Detach the fuel pressure test port from the top of the alternator bracket (A), then remove the alternator mounting bracket bolts (B) (LB7 model shown)

9.10 Power steering/air conditioning compressor bracket bolts (it isn't necessary to remove the power steering pump from the bracket)

5   Loosen the right-front wheel lug nuts. Raise the front of the vehicle and support it securely on jackstands, then remove the right-front wheel.
6   Remove the right inner fender splash shield.
7   Remove the right-side engine mount (see Chapter 7).
8   Disconnect the cord from the coolant heater, then loosen the heater mounting bolt.
9   Be prepared for some coolant to drain out as you remove the heater from the engine block. Use pliers to pull the heater out of the block and be careful not to score or damage the surface of the opening, as any irregularities can lead to coolant leaks.

Installation

10   To install a new block heater, first inspect the core plug opening on the engine block to ensure it is smooth and free of any burrs, scratches, old sealant, paint, or any other debris.
11   Using a water resistant, high-temperature grease, coat the O-ring and the surface of the opening on the block.
12   Avoid contacting the inside walls of the engine block with the heater element.
13   With the heating element pointing to the top of the engine, insert and firmly push the heater into the engine block
14   Tighten the bolt on the heater until you can feel the two locking wings draw up tightly against the inner wall of the block. Be sure the heater does not rotate within the hole as you tighten the bolt.
15   Attach the cord and route it to the front of the vehicle. Don't allow the cord to come into contact with any moving parts or source of excessive heat such as the engine, exhaust, manifold, etc. Secure as needed using cable ties to keep the cord in place and prevent damage.
16   Re-install the right side engine mount.
17   The remainder of the installation is the reverse of the removal procedure.
18   Refill the engine with coolant (see Chapter 1). Run the engine and check for leaks.

---

9   Thermostat housing crossover - removal and installation

Warning: *Wait until the engine is completely cool before beginning this procedure.*

Removal

Refer to illustrations 9.9, 9.10, 9.11, 9.12, 9.13a and 9.13b
1   Disconnect the cables from the negative terminals of the batteries (see Chapter 5).
2   Drain the engine coolant (see Chapter 1).
3   Unbolt the air conditioning compressor and position it aside, without disconnecting the hoses.
4   Remove the fan and fan clutch assembly (see Section 4).
5   Remove the alternator (see Chapter 5).
6   Unbolt the water outlet pipe from the valve cover and thermostat housing, then detach it from the thermostat housing.
7   Disconnect the electrical connector from the Engine Coolant Temperature (ECT) sensor next to the thermostat housing cover. Also unbolt the wiring harness bracket from the thermostat housing cover.
8   Remove the idler pulley from the alternator bracket.
9   Unscrew the bolts and detach the fuel pressure test port from the alternator bracket, then unbolt the alternator bracket and move it out of the way **(see illustration)**.
10   Unbolt the power steering pump/air conditioning compressor bracket and move it out of the way **(see illustration)**.
11   Unbolt the fuel line bracket and the coolant pipe from the top of the thermostat housing crossover **(see illustration)**.

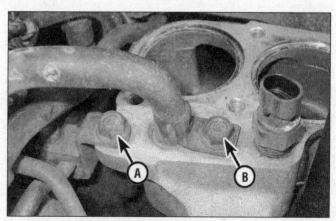

9.11 Fuel line bracket bolt (A) and coolant pipe bolt (B)

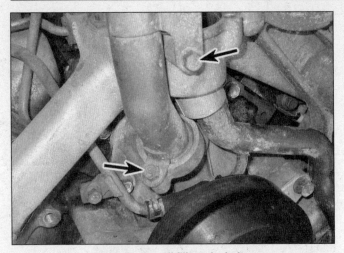

9.12   Engine oil filler tube bolts

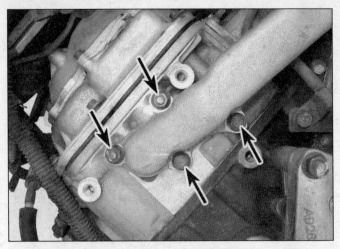

9.13a   Thermostat housing crossover bolts - right side

12   Remove the oil filler tube **(see illustration)**.

13   Remove the bolts from both sides of the thermostat housing crossover **(see illustrations)**, then detach the crossover from the cylinder heads.

Installation

14   Installation is the reverse of removal, noting the following points:

a)   *Use new O-rings wherever present. Lubricate coolant pipe O-rings with clean coolant, and lubricate the oil filler tube O-rings with clean engine oil.*

b)   *Tighten the thermostat housing crossover bolts to the torque listed in this Chapter's Specifications.*

c)   *Tighten the alternator mounting bracket and the power steering pump/air conditioning compressor mounting bolts to the torque listed in this Chapter's Specifications.*

d)   *Refill the cooling system (see Chapter 1).*

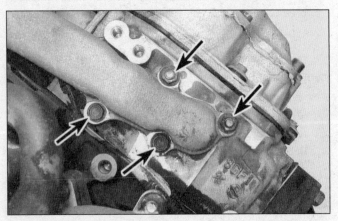

9.13b   Thermostat housing crossover bolts - left side

Chapter 3   Fuel system

Contents

Specifications

Torque specifications

Note: One foot-pound (ft-lb) of torque is equivalent to 12 inch-pounds (in-lbs) of torque. Torque values below approximately 15 ft-lbs are expressed in inch-pounds, because most foot-pound torque wrenches are not accurate at these smaller values.

	Ft-lbs (unless otherwise indicated)	Nm
Fuel filter/fuel heater element housing mounting bolts	15	20
Fuel Injection Control Module (FICM) (LB7 and LLY only)		
FICM mounting bolts		
2001 through 2003	18	24
2004 through 2006	168 in-lbs	19
FICM fuel line banjo bolts		
LB7	25	34
LLY	26	35
Fuel injection pump		
Pump driven gear nut		
All except L5P	52	71
L5P	55	75
Pump spacer bolts	15	20
Pump mounting bolts		
LB7, LLY and LBZ	15	20
LMM, LGH, LML and L5P	18	24

Torque specifications (continued)

Note: *One foot-pound (ft-lb) of torque is equivalent to 12 inch-pounds (in-lbs) of torque. Torque values below approximately 15 ft-lbs are expressed in inch-pounds, because most foot-pound torque wrenches are not accurate at these smaller values.*

	Ft-lbs (unless otherwise indicated)	Nm
Fuel injectors		
Injector bracket bolts		
LB7	37	50
LLY and later	22	30
Injector pipe fitting retainer bolts (LB7 only)	35 in-lbs	4
Fuel junction block mounting nuts (LB7 only)	18	24
Fuel pipes		
LB7		
Return line (low-pressure) banjo bolt fittings		
At fuel injectors	144 in-lbs	16
At cylinder head	144 in-lbs	16
At junction block	132 in-lbs	15
Fuel delivery (high-pressure) line threaded pipe fittings		
Return line at back end of fuel rail	32	43
Line between fuel injection pump and junction block	32	43
Fuel feed lines at fuel injectors	30	40
LLY, LBZ, LMM and LGH		
Fuel delivery (high-pressure) line threaded pipe fittings		
Line between fuel injection pump and left fuel rail	30	40
Balance pipe between fuel rails	30	40
Balance pipe retainer bolts	89 in-lbs	10
Fuel feed lines at fuel rails	30	40
Fuel feed lines at fuel injectors	30	40
LML and L5P		
Fuel delivery (high-pressure) line threaded pipe fittings	22	30
Fuel rail mounting bolts		
LB7	19	26
All others	18	24
Fuel rail pressure regulator		
LB7, LLY, LBZ, LMM, LGH and L5P		
First pass	35 in-lbs	4
Second pass	62 in-lbs	7
LML	89 in-lbs	10
Fuel rail pressure sensor		
2016 and earlier models	52	70
2017 and later models		
Step 1	15	
Step 2	Tighten an additional 15 degrees	
Fuel temperature sensor	16	22
Fuel rail balance pipe	18	25

1 General information

Warning: *Diesel fuel is flammable, so take extra precautions when you work on any part of the fuel system. Don't smoke or allow open flames or bare light bulbs near the work area, and don't work in a garage where a gas-type appliance (such as a water heater or a clothes dryer) is present. Since diesel fuel is carcinogenic, wear fuel-resistant gloves when there's a possibility of being exposed to fuel, and, if you spill any fuel on your skin, rinse it off immediately with soap and water. Mop up any spills immediately and do not store diesel fuel-soaked rags where they could ignite. When you perform any kind of work on the fuel system, wear safety glasses and have a Class B type fire extinguisher on hand.*

Fuel requirements

1 Prior to 1993, diesel fuel contained 0.2 to 0.4 percent sulfur by weight. In 1993, the EPA mandated that diesel fuel contain no more than 0.05 percent sulfur by weight. The new fuel, known as Low Sulfur Diesel (LSD) fuel, contained 500 ppm (parts-per-million) sulfur. In 2001 the EPA mandated even lower emissions that would reduce particulate pollution by 90 percent and reduce the sulfur content of diesel fuel by 97 percent. The EPA gave the oil industry six years to develop this new Ultra Low Sulfur Diesel (ULSD), which contains only 15 ppm sulfur. The new fuel became available on June 1, 2006, and by January 1, 2007 it was the only diesel fuel available. Not coincidentally, GM's first LMM engines started rolling off the assembly line the same day. Duramax diesels built prior to January 1, 2007 - LB7, LLY and 2006 LBZ engines - can use LSD or ULSD fuel. 2007 LBZ, LMM, LML and LGH engines, however, can use only ULSD.

2 Using LSD fuel in a 2007 LBZ or any LMM or later engine can damage the emission system, and the manufacturer might not cover damage caused by using the wrong fuel. Today, ULSD fuel should be the only fuel available, so this should no longer be a problem for current owners.

Fuel number

3 Diesel fuel is also classified in terms of its grade as Type A (or Number 1) and Type B (or Number 2). The grade structure, which refers to the fuel's viscosity, ensures a uniform standard for diesel fuel regardless of where it's sold. Type A/Number 1 diesel is a lighter, thinner, cold-weather blend that can be used safely ONLY when the temperature is below 0 degrees F (-18 degrees C). Type A/Number 1 should not be used unless it's really necessary, because it will hurt power and fuel economy. Using Type A/Number 1 in warmer weather can cause stalling and/or poor starting.

4 Type B/Number 2 was once the commonly used diesel fuel in Canada. But Canada, like the USA, also now classifies diesel fuel as either ULSD (which it recommends for both on-road and off-road use), or "Regular Sulfur Diesel" (RSD), which it recommends <u>only</u> for rail or marine applications. So make sure that you put ULSD - not RSD - fuel in your 2007 LBZ or any LMM or later Duramax engine.

Cetane number

5 The cetane number of diesel fuel - from 30 to 65 - indicates its "ignition value." The higher the cetane number, the easier the fuel ignites. If the cetane number is too low it might cause hard starting, engine knocking and/or puffs of white smoke during warm-ups and under a slight load.

Fuel recommendations

LB7, LLY and LBZ

6 Use No. 2 diesel fuel all the time, whether the temperature is above or below freezing. In the US, oil companies blend No. 2 diesel fuel to address climate differences. Don't use No. 1 unless the temperature is below zero and stays below zero. Even then, No. 1 fuel might cause a loss of power and/or poor mileage. Using No. 1 fuel in warmer temperatures can cause stalling, hard starting when the engine is already hot, and can damage the fuel injection system.

LMM and LML

7 Use only Ultra Low Sulfur Diesel (ULSD) fuel in these engines. (You can also safely use ULSD in older LB7, LLY and LBZ engines.) At a minimum, the diesel fuel you use should meet the latest ASTM specification D975 (Grade Low Sulfur) in the US. The Engine Manufacturers Association (EMA) also publishes guidelines identifying the properties of diesel fuel that improve engine performance and durability. EMA claims that fuels corresponding to its Recommended Guideline on Premium Diesel Fuel (FQP-1A) can improve starting, lower noise and improve performance.

Bio-Diesel fuel

8 Finally, so-called "Bio-Diesel," which is a blend of diesel and up to 20-percent non-diesel (usually a blend of vegetable oil and/or animal fats that have been chemically modified to reduce the likelihood of damage to the fuel system and/or emission controls). B5, or 5 percent non-diesel, can be safely used in the LB7, LLY, LBZ, LMM and LGH Duramax engines. B20, or 20 percent non-diesel, formulations can be used only in LML engines. GM does NOT recommend using a Bio-Diesel formulation using more than the specified percentage of vegetable oils/animal fats, or "*the use of unmodified bio-oils blended into diesel fuel at any concentration,*" because it could damage the fuel system and/or the engine. Any damage caused by the use of such fuel will not be covered by your warranty.

Fuel tank cap

9 All fuel systems covered in this manual use a pressure and vacuum regulating fuel tank cap. On vehicles with dual fuel tanks, there is a fuel cap for each tank. A check valve opens to vent when the tank pressure exceeds 2 psi, and opens to allow outside air into the tank when the vacuum inside the tank exceeds 1 inch Hg. The fuel tank cap on vehicles with gasoline engines has no vent, and it has a different vacuum valve opening point. So, to prevent system damage and driveability problems, be sure to replace a defective cap with the correct replacement cap for the diesel engine in your vehicle.

Balance (transfer) pump (dual fuel tank applications only)

10 On vehicles with dual fuel tanks, fuel is pumped to the engine only from the primary (front) fuel tank. A balance, or transfer, pump, which is located on the left frame rail, moves fuel from the secondary (rear) fuel tank to the primary tank when directed to do so by the ECM to maintain a balance between the two tanks, either to replenish the primary tank as fuel is consumed, or to balance fuel levels when the secondary fuel tank is filled. The ECM monitors the fuel level sending units in the two tanks and maintains five percent more fuel in the primary tank than in the secondary tank. If the secondary tank is filled, fuel is transferred to the primary tank until it has five percent more fuel than the secondary tank. If the primary tank is filled, the ECM allows the fuel to stay out of balance until the fuel level in the primary tank reaches the five-percent-more-than-the-secondary-tank level. Once the fuel in the primary tank reaches that level, the ECM begins to transfer fuel again from the secondary tank to the primary tank.

Note: *The following information describes the important components of the fuel system. If you don't see a certain component described in the section for your engine, it's because that component was unchanged from the previous model. Only changes to the fuel system are noted.*

LB7 engine (2001 through 2004)

Fuel level sending unit

11 The fuel level sending unit is located inside the fuel tank (on vehicles with dual fuel tanks, there is a fuel level sending unit inside each tank). It has two fittings on top: one goes to the fuel supply pipe and the other goes to the return pipe. A pick-up tube at the lower end of the unit draws fuel from the tank. A filter sock on the pick-up tube functions as a fuel "pre-filter." If the sock filter becomes clogged, a bypass on the sending unit maintains fuel flow. The ECM monitors the fuel level sending unit's signal circuit, which changes resistance in accordance with

the fuel level: On LB7 models, the resistance is 40 ohms when the fuel tank is empty and 250 ohms when it's full. On LLY and later models, it's just the opposite; the resistance is 250 ohms when the tank is empty and 40 ohms when it's full. If the sending unit's float arm sticks, there will be no signal variation; the ECM will interpret a fixed signal from the fuel level sending unit as a stuck float arm and will set a Diagnostic Trouble Code (DTC).

Fuel injection pump

12   The mechanical fuel injection pump, which is located in the front part of the intake valley, is driven by the camshaft gear. The injection pump assembly consists of two pumps - a low-pressure supply pump and a high-pressure delivery pump - and the Fuel Rail Pressure Regulator (FRPR).

13   The low-pressure pump, which is located in the rear part of the injection pump, draws fuel from the fuel tank, through the fuel filter/water separator and the Fuel Injection Control Module (FICM), then into the pump assembly. The low-pressure supply pump ensures an adequate supply of fuel volume to the high-pressure part of the pump through the FRPR. Fuel that isn't delivered to the high-pressure pump is routed to the low-pressure return system. The two main components of the low-pressure pump are two counter-rotating spur gears that draw fuel from the inlet port and pump it to the outlet port on the pressure side. The quantity of fuel delivered to the outlet port is governed by the engine speed.

14   The high-pressure pump, which is located in the front part of the injection pump, connects the low-pressure system to the high-pressure system. It consists of three pistons, arranged in a radial configuration, 120 degrees apart, driven by a cam eccentric to produce three delivery strokes of fuel per revolution. Fuel from the FRPR is compressed by the pistons and routed to a junction block that meters the high-pressure fuel to the injectors.

15   The Fuel Rail Pressure Regulator (FRPR) is an electronically operated valve located between the low-pressure supply pump and the high-pressure delivery pump. The FRPR is a "duty cycle" ECM-controlled solenoid (a duty cycle is the percent of time that the solenoid is turned on). The FRPR doesn't regulate fuel pressure; it controls the volume of fuel available to the high-pressure pump.

Fuel junction block

16   The fuel junction block, which is located on the left side of the intake manifold, distributes fuel to the fuel injectors in each cylinder bank. The junction block receives high-pressure fuel from the pump and sends it to both common fuel rails. Two important components - the fuel pressure relief valve and the fuel pressure sensor - are located on the junction block.

Fuel pressure relief valve

17   The fuel pressure relief valve, or pressure-limiting valve, is located on the fuel junction block on the left side of the intake manifold. The pressure relief valve protects the fuel system from excessively high pressure. If system pressure exceeds 27,557 psi, the pressure relief valve opens and routes fuel to a return pipe, lowering fuel pressure to a safe operating level.

Fuel pressure regulator

18   The fuel pressure regulator monitors and controls the fuel pressure inside the junction block and fuel rails. A diaphragm inside the pressure regulator alters sensor resistance in response to changes in fuel pressure. The ECM, which monitors this resistance, responds by sending a signal to the pressure regulator to alter fuel pressure.

Fuel rails and high-pressure fuel pipes

18   High-pressure fuel goes from the junction block to two fuel rails (also referred to as "common rails"). There's one fuel rail for each cylinder head. The fuel rails function as fuel reservoirs for the fuel injectors and reduce pressure oscillations produced by the fuel injection pump. The fuel rails might look big, but most of that bulk is because they have to be stout enough to contain the highly pressurized fuel; each rail actually holds only 16 cc of fuel!

19   There are 11 high-pressure fuel pipes: One pipe connects the fuel injection pump to the junction block; two pipes go from the junction block to the two fuel rails; and four pipes connect each fuel rail to its four injectors.

Warning: *Do NOT alter the configuration of any fuel pipe, because it could cause a high-pressure leak or restriction. And never under-torque or over-torque fuel pipe fittings, which could cause leaks and damage pipes.*

Fuel Injector Control Module (FICM)

20   The ECM-controlled Fuel Injector Control Module (FICM), which is mounted on the front of the right (passenger side) valve cover, turns the fuel injectors on and off. High-current injector drivers inside the FICM generate considerable heat, so the FICM is cooled by fuel from the fuel tank on its way to the fuel filter/water separator.

Fuel injectors

21   There are eight fuel injectors, one for each cylinder. The injectors are direct injection units: fuel is injected directly into the combustion chambers, not into the intake ports, so each injector is mounted in a sleeve in the cylinder head, above the piston. The injectors are electronically controlled by the Fuel Injector Control Module (FICM), which supplies the 93 volts/18 amps of current needed to fire each injector.

Fuel return pipes

22   There are 10 low-pressure fuel return pipes: one from the fuel injection pump, one from the pressure limiting valve on the junction block, and one from each fuel injector. The return pipes from the fuel injection pump and from the pressure limiting valve are external, so they're easy to find once you locate the component. The return pipes for the injectors are under the valve covers, so you have to remove a valve cover to service either injector return pipe. When servicing a fuel injector return pipe, be sure to use new banjo bolt gaskets and install the sealing washers right-side-up. If they're installed upside down they will leak. Also be sure to tighten the banjo bolts to the torque listed in this Chapter's Specifications. If one of these fittings leaks, it could fill up the crankcase with fuel. Finally, do NOT alter the fuel return pipe configurations, which could affect engine performance and/or cause injector damage.

Fuel cooler

23   Fuel from the fuel return pipes is routed back go the fuel tank through a fuel cooler located in-line with the main fuel return pipe, just ahead of the fuel tank. A diesel engine is already a warm environment for fuel, but on the Duramax, fuel gets even warmer because of high fuel pressure and because fuel is also used to cool the Fuel Injection Control Module (FICM).

Intake Air Heater (IAH)

24   The Intake Air Heater (IAH) is a heated coil located inside the air intake system. The IAH warms intake air during cold weather to reduce white smoke during warm-ups and after long decelerations. The IAH is powered through the same 175 amp fuse that powers the glow plugs, but has its own relay, which is powered when the ignition key is turned to START or RUN. On California models, the relays for the IAH and glow plugs, respectively, are separate; on Federal models the relays are in the same module, and must be replaced as a single assembly. If the engine emits white smoke during a cold start, the intake air heater or some component in the IAH circuit is probably malfunctioning.

LLY engine (2004.5 through 2006)

25   The fuel system on the LLY engine incorporates some improvements that enable it to meet stricter mandated emissions reductions for 2004. Major changes include the elimination of the junction block, a different valve cover design, new fuel injectors, relocation of the fuel return pipes and a new Fuel Injector Control Module (FICM). All of these changes together help to reduce hydrocarbons, NOx and particulates; and the LLY is more powerful, too.

Fuel rails and high pressure fuel pipes

26 The fuel rails themselves are similar to those used on the earlier engine, but there is no junction block, so the junction block components - the fuel pressure limiting valve and the Fuel Rail Pressure (FRP) sensor - are relocated to the fuel rails. The FRP sensor is now located on the middle of the right fuel rail, and the fuel pressure limiting valve is located on the rear of the left fuel rail. High pressure fuel is now routed to the left fuel rail, then goes through a crossover tube to the right fuel rail.

Valve covers

27 On the LLY engine, the two-piece valve covers are redesigned to leave the fuel injectors and the fuel rails exposed for easier service. On LB7 engines, you must remove the valve covers and the fuel return pipes in order to serve the injectors.

Fuel injectors

28 The completely redesigned fuel injectors used on the LLY engine are larger than the injectors used on the LB7 engine. The fuel return line has been moved from the side of the injector, inside the valve cover, to the top of the injector, where it can be accessed without removing the valve cover. The LLY injectors have seven nozzles, one more than the LB7 injectors. The injector nozzle pattern has been rotated 35-degrees to spray fuel directly at the tip of the glow plug, and the injector sleeves used on LB7 injectors have been eliminated.

Fuel return pipes

29 On LB7 engines, the fuel return pipes, like the injectors, can only be accessed by removing the valve covers. Because the fuel injectors are now located outside the valve cover on LLY engines, the two rigid steel return pipe assemblies used on LB7 engines have been replaced by braided rubber hoses that connect to the upper end of each injector with a cotter pin.

Fuel Injection Control Module (FICM)

30 The FICM on LLY engines is slightly different from the FICM used on LB7 engines. Cooling fuel now travels through the FICM from the upper part of the module and exits out the lower part of the unit (on the FICM used with LB7 engines, the cooling fuel entered and exited from the top of the unit). The new FICM also uses oscillators instead of capacitors to control the "hold" period - the interval of time during which each injector is open. The duration of the hold period determines how much fuel the injector delivers.

LBZ engine (2006.5 and 2007)

31 The fuel system on LBZ engines received a number of changes.

New ECM eliminates Fuel Injector Control Module (FICM)

32 One of the most significant changes on LBZ engines is the elimination of the Fuel Injector Control Module (FICM) used on previous engines. Unlike earlier ECM units used on the Duramax, the new Bosch ECM includes the high-current injector drivers needed to fire the fuel injectors, so the FICM is no longer used.

Intake Air Heater (IAH) and Intake Air Temperature (IAT 2) sensor

33 Unlike earlier intake air heaters, which were heated coil units, the new ECM-controlled Intake Air Heater (IAH) is a heated grid with much more surface area. The IAH reduces smoke and emissions during short trips and cold-weather operation. An Intake Air Temperature (IAT) sensor, which is located on the right side of the intake manifold, was added to enable the new ECM to fine-tune fuel adjustment and reduce emissions by improving control of the IAH. The new IAT sensor is referred to as "IAT 2." Don't confuse it with the primary IAT sensor, which is one of an array of information sensors used by the ECM (see Chapter 6 for more information on this and other information sensors).

Fuel rail assembly

34 The fuel rails on the LBZ engine are smaller than the fuel rails on

LB7 and LLY engines, and the Fuel Rail Pressure (FRP) sensor is relocated from the center of the right fuel rail (as on the LLY engine) to the rear of the right fuel rail.

Fuel injectors

35 The LBZ engine uses new fuel injectors. To achieve more precise fuel control the new ECM needs very specific information about each injector. Each injector is manufactured to the same specifications, but small manufacturing variations affect the flow rate. These variations are measured and encoded on the body of each injector. These codes must be stored in the ECM and Glow Plug Control Module (GPCM) so that the engine management system can establish a baseline for injection timing. If an injector must be replaced, or if the ECM or GPCM is replaced, the new injector flow rate measurements must be programmed into both modules with a factory scan tool. Do not remove injectors and install them in a different cylinder, because doing so will likely set Diagnostic Trouble Codes (DTCs).

36 On LB7 and LLY engines there are two groups of four cylinders because there is a single electrical power circuit for each group of four injectors. On the LBZ engine, each power circuit powers two injectors, which are paired as follows: 1 & 4; 2 & 5; 7 & 6; 8 & 3.

LMM engine (2007-1/2 to 2010)

37 The introduction of the LMM engine in 2007 was partly a response to new diesel fuel standards mandated by the Federal government. The fuel system on LMM engines is essentially the same as LBZ engines.

Fuel gauge labels and green fuel tank caps

38 Starting in 2007, the fuel gauges on all Duramax-powered vehicles were equipped with labels specifying "ULTRA LOW SULFUR DIESEL FUEL ONLY." These vehicles were also equipped with green gas tank caps to help prevent owners from accidentally putting gasoline in the tank. These caps are functionally identical to earlier caps.

LML and LGH engines (2010-1/2 to 2016)

39 These engines are improved versions of their LMM predecessor. Most of the improvements were made to optimize performance and emissions in response to the newly mandated Federal emission reductions for diesels, and can also be safely operated using up to a 20-percent bio-diesel fuel.

New piezo fuel injectors

40 One important change is new 29,000 psi *piezo* fuel injectors. Certain crystals are *piezoelectric* (when compressed or struck, they generate an electric charge); when an electric current runs through a piezoelectric crystal, the crystal changes shape slightly. When current is applied to the crystal element in a piezo injector, the crystal expands quickly, opening the injector nozzle and spraying high-pressure fuel into the combustion chamber. When current is cut, the piezo crystal contracts just as quickly, closing the nozzle. A piezo injector can operate five times faster than a conventional solenoid-type injector, allowing the ECM to control fuel injection cycles in milliseconds. The new injectors are very high-voltage, high-current components: it takes 160 volts to trigger the injector, and holding voltage is between 140 and 250 volts. The applied current is about 20 amps.

New fuel injection pump

41 The LML engine also uses a new version of the Bosch CP3 high-flow fuel injection pump designed to take advantage of the more precise fuel injectors.

Fuel system "hardening"

42 The inside surfaces of all fuel system components exposed to fuel have been "hardened" to enable the fuel system to tolerate up to 20 percent bio-diesel mixtures.

L5P engine (2017-2019)

43 The L5P has uses an electric fuel feed pump located in the fuel tank to supply the high-pressure fuel pump with fuel. Improved injectors are used, with the ability to fire up to seven times per ignition cycle.

2   Fuel system diagnosis

Refer to illustrations 2.1a, 2.1b and 2.1c

Warning: *The fuel system operates at anywhere from around 23,000 psi on LB7 engines to about 30,000 psi on LML/LGH engines. ALWAYS wear safety glasses when working around a fuel system in operation. And do NOT use your fingers to find fuel leaks! A fuel leak at pressure this high can penetrate your skin and enter your bloodstream, resulting in poisoning/infection and amputation or death.*

Warning: *Diesel fuel is flammable, so take extra precautions when you work on any part of the fuel system. See the Warning in Section 1.*

1   Correct diagnosis is the first and most essential component of every repair. Without it you can only successfully make the right repair by accident. There are several types of problems that can occur on diesel engines. Some of these problems (air leaks, for example) are typical of all internal combustion engines; other problems are unique to diesels.

2   Older, high-mileage engines that lose some compression and develop excessive blow-by gradually become more difficult to start. Low ambient temperatures aggravate the problem. If your Duramax starts to consume an excessive amount of oil, burns the valves, develops a knocking sound in the bottom end or some other abnormality, it might need some simple repair or it might need to be overhauled (see Chapters 7 and 8).

3   If your engine has been running normally, but then suddenly loses power or stalls, it might be caused by fuel starvation. If the engine has been running normally and still cranks well, but suddenly refuses to start or takes excessive cranking to start when the ambient temperature is cold, it's usually a glow plug problem (see Chapter 5).

4   See a pattern here? Problems that occur gradually over time are, more often than not, caused by mechanical wear. Problems that occur suddenly are more likely caused by a fuel or electrical component failure.

Preliminary checks: Always check the simple stuff first

• Make sure that there is clean, good quality diesel fuel in the fuel tank (and that it's the *right* diesel fuel for your engine).

• Always check the oil level. Make sure it's at the correct level and is the correct viscosity for the climate.
   Note: *On LB7 engines, the fuel injectors are located under the valve covers; an injector or return line leak can result in oil dilution (which would be indicated by a high oil level and thinned-out oil).*

• Make sure that the fuel filter(s) is clean.

• Make sure that there is no water in the separator(s).

• Make sure that the batteries are fully charged.

• If you have a scan tool, check and record any Diagnostic Trouble Codes (DTCs).
   Note: *Do not erase DTCs until after you have made repairs.*

No Start or Hard Start

• Verify that there is fuel in the tank, and that it is the specified fuel for your engine.

• Check for an air leak in a suction line hose or pipe.

• Check for a restriction in the fuel system. Inspect and, if necessary, replace the fuel filter.

• Check the fuel filter for signs of a paraffin deposit clogging it.

• Remove the outlet hose from the fuel filter adapter and splice in a section of clear tubing. Prime the fuel system with the pump on top of the filter adapter, then run the engine and see if there are air bubbles in the hose. If there are, there is an air leak somewhere between the fuel tank and the filter adapter.

• Using a vacuum/pressure gauge connected to the fuel test port **(see illustrations 2.1a, 2.1b and 2.1c)**, check the low-side suction. There should be no more than 5 inches Hg at wide-open throttle, and about 7 to 8 inches Hg under a load. If there is too much suction, the restriction might be a clogged fuel "sock" at the inlet end of the sending unit pick-up tube in the fuel tank. If there is too little suction, the engine could be sucking air somewhere. Look

for a leak in the air intake system. The low-pressure side of the fuel injection pump could be faulty, too.
   Note: *The plunger pump on the fuel filter adapter is a common source of air leaks.*

• Check the fuel system pressure (if the engine won't start, check the fuel pressure while cranking the engine). If the fuel pressure is okay, then either the problem is a fuel injector (or more than one injector), the fuel injection pump, the fuel pressure regulator (check it to make sure it's not stuck) or the fuel pressure relief valve (check to make sure that it's not leaking into the return system when the fuel rail pressure is 160 mPa).

• Before zeroing in on the high-pressure fuel injection pump, make sure that there are no high-pressure fuel leaks.

Black smoke

• Listen for an exhaust leak or a "boost leak" (a boost leak will sound like a high-pitched squeal under load).

• Inspect the air filter. If it's dirty, replace it.

• There might be a problem with the Exhaust Gas Recirculation (EGR) system or with the Mass Air Flow (MAF) sensor, or there might be an intake leak downstream from the MAF sensor (see Chapter 6).

• If you have a scan tool capable of doing so, with the engine idling, cut out one cylinder at a time and see if the black smoke disappears. If it does, that cylinder has a faulty injector.

Engine running rough, uneven idle, skipping or missing under load

• If you have a scan tool capable of doing a power balance test, cut out one cylinder at a time and see how it affects engine operation. If cutting out an injector doesn't affect engine operation, then that injector isn't working.

• A damaged head gasket or low compression could cause misfiring condition.

Engine knocking

• Clogged or defective injection nozzle(s)
• Incorrect fuel
• Defective injection pump
• Broken or worn piston rings
• Incorrect bearing clearance because of excessive bearing wear
• Damaged bearings

Engine surging or loping at idle

• Bad fuel pressure regulator
• Air in the fuel system

White or blue smoke at idle when cold

Note: *Depending on the altitude and the temperature, smoke should clear in less than one minute. Blue-white smoke that burns your eyes is unburnt fuel; white smoke usually indicates cold combustion, which can be caused by high altitude (less oxygen) and cold temperature.*

• Possible bad injector.

• Glow plug(s) not operating when cold.

• Excessive idle time (more than 20-percent) can cause white smoke when cold because of carbon build-up on the injector tips.

Dilution

• On LB7 engines, the injector return pipes are under the valve cover. Remove the valve covers, pressurize the return pipe and look for bubbles, or vacuum-test the return circuit for each head. Each return pipe should hold 15 inches Hg of vacuum.

• Also on LB7 engines, if you've recently replaced one or more injectors, remove the valve cover(s) and look for leaks in the return pipe(s) where the return pipe(s) connect to the injector(s).
   Note: *The green-coated injector return pipes are more susceptible to leaks than the polished steel pipes. You can also use a dye in the fuel and a black light kit to try to pinpoint leaks at the injectors.*

• Inspect the injectors for cracks.

• Look for a leak at the high-pressure pump driveshaft seal.

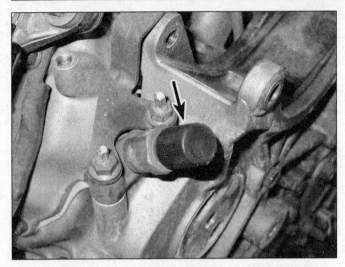

2.1a Fuel test port - LB7 engine (at the front of the right-side valve cover on the alternator bracket)

2.1b Fuel test port - LLY engine (behind the alternator)

Fuel supply and fuel filter housing

Note: *The fuel filter housing is on the suction side and it's prone to sucking air.*

- Install a vacuum/pressure gauge on the fuel test port **(see illustrations 2.1a, 2.1b and 2.1c).**
- Prime the fuel system with the primer pump on top of the fuel filter housing until the gauge indicates 10 psi, then check for external leaks. Repair any leaks. If the pressure drops from 10 psi to 2 psi in less than one minute, remove the fuel outlet line from the filter and cap it. Remove the "Ignition 1" relay and crank the engine for 2 to 15 second intervals; the fuel injection pump should pull at least 12 inches Hg of vacuum.
- Install clear hoses at the inlet and outlet side of the fuel filter housing. Re-prime the system, then start the engine. There should be little air going in or coming out of the fuel filter housing.
- Common places to look for air ingestion are: the filter housing, a plugged filter, the drain valve, and rubber hoses and connections. You must use clear lines to pinpoint where the air is coming from, then work your way back toward the fuel tank until you see no more air coming through the line.

High-pressure injection pump (CP3 pump)

Note: *Fuel pressure on the high-pressure side of the system can only be checked with a scan tool that has graphing capability.*

- Air leaks or restrictions - kinked hoses, for example - on the suction side of the pump will seriously affect pump output. So, with the engine running, inspect the inlet hoses for flattening or kinks that might be restricting fuel flow to the pump.
- Check for leaks at all fuel connections from the fuel tank to the fuel injection pump and tighten any loose connections, incorrectly installed or loose hose clamps or a hole in a braided fuel line.
- Before you condemn the pump for a starting issue, make sure that the high-pressure side of the fuel system is not leaking.
- If the system has been seriously contaminated with dirt or water, the injectors are probably damaged or ruined. And if they are, then the contamination came through the pump first, so it will very likely have to be replaced as well.
- One common sign that the pump has been damaged is its inability to supply sufficient fuel pressure when the engine is under a load, like pulling a trailer up a hill. If this happens, the ECM will set a P0087 (low fuel rail pressure) Diagnostic Trouble Code (DTC).

Fuel injectors

Note: *The injectors need about 2500 psi of fuel rail pressure to supply enough fuel to start the engine.*

2.1c Fuel test port - LML engine

Note: *Fuel pressure on the high-pressure side of the system can only be checked with a scan tool that has graphing capability.*

- With respect to injector return flow, an injector must not leak more than 5 ml in 15 seconds, and a cylinder bank must not leak more than 20 ml. With the Fuel Injector Control Module (FICM) disabled, operating pressure should be 114 to 135 MPa during cranking.
- GM doesn't provide a specification for injector return flow at idle, but reputable aftermarket shops claim that, on a good-running LB7, injector return flow at idle from one cylinder bank is 95-110 ml per minute at 21,000 psi.
- Excessive leakage from the injectors usually causes a starting problem, which can occur when the engine is hot or cold, but usually occurs when it's hot because the fuel is thinner.
- Excessive leakage from the injectors can also cause the ECM to set DTCs P0087, P0093 or P1093 (see Chapter 6 for explanations of these codes).
- If you're unable to increase fuel rail pressure at idle to 21,000 psi, the injectors are probably bad.
- Finally, replace any injectors that produce poor cylinder power, are noisy, produce smoke when momentarily deactivated by a scan tool, or that produce low fuel rail pressure during cranking.

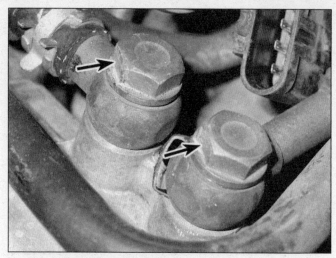

3.6a Typical fuel supply pipe banjo fittings, shown here at the Fuel Injection Control Module (FICM). Whenever reconnecting banjo fittings, new sealing washers should be used

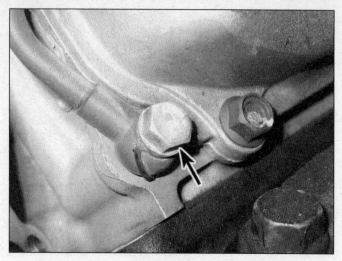

3.6b Typical low-pressure fuel return pipe banjo fitting

3 Fuel lines and fittings - general information

Warning: *Diesel fuel is flammable, so take extra precautions when you work on any part of the fuel system. See the Warning in Section 1.*
1   Always disconnect the cables from the negative battery terminals (see Chapter 5) before servicing fuel lines or fittings.
2   If you find signs of dirt or water in fuel lines during disassembly, disconnect the lines and blow them out with compressed air. And if the dirt or water is in the suction side of the fuel injection pump, then the pump and the injectors are very likely also contaminated.

Low-pressure fuel supply lines and fittings
3   The low-pressure fuel supply lines are made of rubber, steel and/or steel-braided materials.
4   Many of the low-pressure lines use hose clamps to secure them to fuel supply side components. Others use typical GM nylon or plastic quick-connect fittings. The procedure for releasing each type of quick-connect fitting will differ slightly (see the accompanying "Disconnecting Fuel Line Fittings" chart). But a few rules of thumb apply to all fittings:

   a) *Inspect the fitting for dirt. If the fitting is dirty, clean it off before disassembling it.*

3.7 Typical high-pressure fuel pipe threaded fitting

   b) *The seals in the fitting will stick to the fuel line as they age. Twist the fitting on the line, then push and pull the fitting until it moves freely.*
   c) *Always disconnect all fuel line fittings from a fuel system component before removing the component.*
   d) *When disconnecting a quick-connect fitting, inspect the condition of the retainer before reconnecting the fitting. The best strategy with respect to retainers is to simply replace the retainer every time that you disconnect the fitting.*
   e) *When you disconnect a fitting with an O-ring inside, inspect the O-ring before reconnecting the fitting. If it has been leaking or looks deteriorated, replace the line and fitting (in some cases, the fitting itself might be an integral, non-removable part of the fuel line, so you might have to replace an entire fuel line if a fitting is damaged or defective).*

5   The low-pressure lines are connected to the Fuel Injection Control Module (FICM) by banjo fittings. Always replace the sealing washers every time you disconnect these fittings. And be sure to use factory parts with the correct part numbers.

Banjo fittings and threaded high-pressure fuel supply pipes and fittings
Refer to illustrations 3.6a, 3.6b and 3.7
Warning: *Because the high-pressure steel fuel supply pipes used on Duramax engines are operated under very high pressure, it is critical that they be replaced with OEM pipes or approved aftermarket pipes of equivalent specification. These pipes cannot be replaced with aluminum or copper pipes, because they cannot be safely used when subjected to typical operating pressures.*
6   Most of the high-pressure fuel supply pipes, and even some of the low-pressure fuel return pipes, use banjo fittings **(see illustrations)**. Always replace the sealing washers every time you disconnect these fittings. And be sure to use factory parts with the correct part numbers.
7   Some steel fuel pipes have threaded fittings **(see illustration)**. When loosening these fittings to service or replace components:
   a) *Hold the stationary fitting with one wrench while loosening or tightening the nut with another.*
   b) *If you're going to replace one of these fittings, use original equipment parts or parts that meet original equipment standards.*

Disconnecting Fuel Line Fittings

Two-tab type fitting; depress both tabs with your fingers, then pull the fuel line and the fitting apart

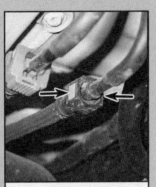

On this type of fitting, depress the two buttons on opposite sides of the fitting, then pull it off the fuel line

Threaded fuel line fitting; hold the stationary portion of the line or component (A) while loosening the tube nut (B) with a flare-nut wrench

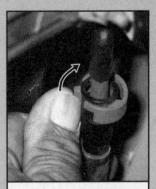

Plastic collar-type fitting; rotate the outer part of the fitting

Metal collar quick-connect fitting; pull the end of the retainer off the fuel line and disengage the other end from the female side of the fitting . . .

. . . insert a fuel line separator tool into the female side of the fitting, push it into the fitting and pull the fuel line off the pipe

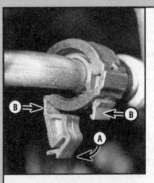

Some fittings are secured by lock tabs. Release the lock tab (A) and rotate it to the fully-opened position, squeeze the two smaller lock tabs (B) . . .

. . . then push the retainer out and pull the fuel line off the pipe

Spring-lock coupling; remove the safety cover, install a coupling release tool and close the tool around the coupling . . .

. . . push the tool into the fitting, then pull the two lines apart

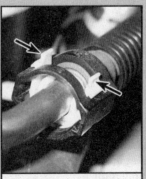

Hairpin clip type fitting: push the legs of the retainer clip together, then push the clip down all the way until it stops and pull the fuel line off the pipe

5.4 Use a large pair of water pump pliers to unscrew the fuel pump lock ring; if the lock ring is too tight to loosen this way, carefully tap it loose with a hammer and a brass punch

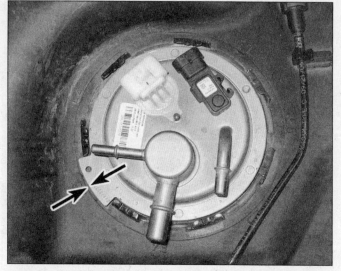

5.5 To ensure that the electrical connector, the fuel supply and return lines and the sending unit itself are oriented correctly when you install the fuel level sending unit, make alignment marks on the tank and the pump flange

4   Balance pump - check and replacement

Warning: *Diesel fuel is flammable, so take extra precautions when you work on any part of the fuel system. See the Warning in Section 1.*
Note: *The balance pump, which is only used on dual-tank vehicles, is located on the left frame rail.*

Check

1   If the combined fuel level increase in the primary (front) fuel tank and fuel level decrease in the secondary (rear) fuel tank is less than 0.7 gallons in 120 seconds, the ECM will set a Diagnostic Trouble Code (DTC) - P1172 (LB7, LLY and LBZ) or P2636 (LMM and later variants) - and turn on the Check Engine light.
Note: *Once the DTC has been set, the ECM will default the fuel gauge reading to EMPTY.*

Replacement

2   Unscrew the fuel filler cap to release any residual fuel tank pressure.
3   Raise the rear of the vehicle and place it securely on jackstands.
4   Disconnect the balance pump electrical connector.
5   Thoroughly clean the area surrounding the pump, then clean the inlet and outlet fittings on the pump, to protect the fuel pipes from contamination.
6   Disconnect the fuel pipe fittings. Cap the fuel pipes while they're disconnected from the balance pump.
7   Loosen the pump mounting bracket and slide the pump out of the bracket.
8   Installation is the reverse of removal.

5   Fuel level sending unit / transfer pump - removal and installation

Refer to illustrations 5.4, 5.5 and 5.7
Warning: *Diesel fuel is flammable, so take extra precautions when you work on any part of the fuel system. See the Warning in Section 1.*
Note: *Only 2017 and later truck models are equipped with an electric in-tank transfer (feed) pump, which is an integral part of the fuel tank module. All models are equipped with an in-tank fuel level sending unit.*

1   Disconnect the cables from the negative battery terminals (see Chapter 5).
2   Remove the fuel tank (see the Haynes manual for your specific vehicle).
3   Disconnect the fuel supply line quick-connect fittings from the fuel level sending unit mounting flange.
4   Using a pair of large water pump pliers, unscrew the fuel level sending unit lock ring by turning it counterclockwise **(see illustration)**. If the lock ring is tight, use a hammer and a brass punch to loosen it.
5   Note the orientation of the fuel level sending unit mounting flange and mark the orientation of the sending unit in relation to the fuel tank **(see illustration)** to ensure that the sending unit, the electrical connector and the fuel supply and return lines are correctly realigned when you install it again. If you're going to install a new sending unit, note the location of your alignment mark on the old sending unit flange and make a mark at the same spot on the new unit.
6   Carefully remove the sending unit from the fuel tank.
Caution: *Be careful not to damage the fuel level sensor float arm and float as you lift the fuel level sending unit assembly out of the tank.*
7   Remove and discard the old fuel level sending unit gasket **(see illustration)**.

5.7 Remove and discard the old gasket from the sending unit mounting flange and install a new one

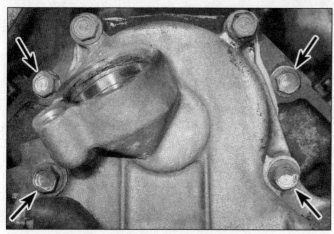

6.29 Fuel injection pump mounting bolts

6.30 To remove the fuel injection pump driven gear nut, immobilize the pump driven gear with a pin-type spanner wrench, then loosen the nut with a wrench

8   Before installing the fuel level sending unit assembly, be sure to install a new gasket.

9   Carefully insert the fuel level sending unit assembly into the fuel tank, align the mark that you made on the mounting flange with the mark you made on the tank and carefully seat the flange on the tank. Make sure that you don't damage the float arm or the float during installation. If the float arm is bent, the fuel level indicated on the fuel level gauge on the instrument cluster will be incorrect.

10   Installation is otherwise the reverse of removal.

6   Fuel injection pump - removal and installation

Warning: *Diesel fuel is flammable, so take extra precautions when you work on any part of the fuel system. See the Warning in Section 1.*

Warning: *The engine must be completely cool before beginning this procedure.*

Caution: *Before removing the fuel injection pump, remove the fuel pressure regulator and inspect the tip of the regulator for any metal debris. If there is ANY metal debris found, do NOT just replace just the injector pump. Replace the following components: fuel injection pump, fuel rails, all fuel injectors, fuel return lines, all high-pressure fuel pipes, indirect fuel injector, fuel feed pipes, and filters. Lower the fuel tank, pressure regulator, sensors, and flush the fuel tank out completely.*

Note: *In many cases the actual metal shavings may be too small to see with the naked eye. Take a paper towel and wipe the tip of the fuel regulator with it, then use the same paper towel to collect a small sample of the fuel from the return line. Allow the towel to dry, then place the paper towel in a microwave for a few seconds. If there are any metal particles present, you'll see the reaction in the microwave, or even small burn holes in the paper towel indicating a minute piece of metal was present.*

LB7

Removal

Refer to illustration 6.29

Caution: *Plug both ends of all disconnected fuel pipes and hoses to prevent contamination from entering.*

1   Disconnect the cables from the negative battery terminals (see Chapter 5).

2   Remove the air duct between the air filter housing and the turbocharger inlet housing. Stuff clean rags into the air intake duct to prevent dust from entering.

3   Drain the cooling system (see Chapter 1).

4   Remove the engine cooling fan (see Chapter 2).

5   Remove the drivebelt (see Chapter 1).

6   Remove the bolt that secures the positive battery cable junction box and set the junction box aside, then reposition the battery cables out of the way.

7   Disconnect all electrical connectors from the air conditioning compressor and from the power steering pump.

8   Unbolt the air conditioning compressor and the power steering pump and set them aside. Don't disconnect any air conditioning or power steering hoses.

9   Unbolt and remove the alternator mounting bracket.

10   Remove the oil filler tube (see Chapter 7).

11   Remove the air conditioning/power steering pump mounting bracket.

12   Remove the alternator (see Chapter 5).

13   Remove the thermostat housing, wiring harness, fuel test port and two mounting nuts.

14   Detach the Positive Crankcase Ventilation (PCV) catch tank from the PCV catch tank bracket (see Chapter 1, Section 15), and the bolt below it that secures the lower line; set the assembly aside.

15   Remove the turbocharger cooling hose return line clamp and hose.

16   Disconnect the upper radiator hose from the outlet pipe. Remove the bracket, set it aside and secure it to the valve cover, out of the way.

17   Remove the bolt that secures the wiring harness support bracket to the thermostat housing.

18   Disconnect the fuel pressure regulator electrical connector from the fuel injection pump, disconnect the Fuel Injection Control Module (FICM) electrical connectors and set the main wiring harness aside. Remove the FICM (see Section 11).

19   Move the wiring harness and harness tray to the rear and set them aside.

20   Disconnect the temperature sensor wire from the thermostat housing.

21   Remove the bolts that secure the heater inlet pipe to the fuel filter and the thermostat housing and remove the heater inlet pipe.

22   Remove the center intake manifold (see Chapter 7).

23   Remove the thermostat housing crossover (see Chapter 2).

24   Disconnect the hose to the turbocharger coolant feed line (see Chapter 4).

25   Disconnect the high-pressure fuel pipe from the fuel rail and injection pump (see Section 10).

26   Disconnect and remove the supply pipe and hose from the fuel injection pump and from the junction block.

27   Disconnect and remove the fuel return hose from the fuel injection pump.

28   Disconnect and remove the high-pressure pipe from the fuel injection pump and the junction block.

29   Unbolt the fuel injection pump **(see illustration)**. Use a couple of screwdrivers to gently pry the pump loose from the block. Make sure that you don't damage the mating surfaces of the pump or the block.

6.31 Use a small puller to remove the pump driven gear from its tapered shaft

Pump replacement

Refer to illustrations 6.30, 6.31, 6.32a, 6.32b and 6.33

30   If you're replacing the pump, you'll have to swap the driven gear to the new pump. Carefully secure the pump in a bench vise with soft copper or plastic jaw liners, or place the pump on a clean work surface and immobilize the pump driven gear with a pin-type spanner wrench **(see illustration)**. Loosen the driven gear nut and remove the nut and washer from the gear shaft.

31   Use a small puller to remove the driven gear from the tapered shaft **(see illustration)**.

32   The mounting adapter is secured to the fuel injection pump by three bolts on the backside of the pump **(see illustration)**. To remove the adapter, remove the three bolts, then remove the adapter and spacers with a small puller **(see illustration)**.

33   Remove the old O-ring from the nose of the fuel injection pump **(see illustration)** and install a new O-ring. Be sure to lubricate the new O-ring with clean engine oil.

34   Clean all mating surfaces, then install the three spacers and adapter. Install the three bolts and tighten them to the torque listed in this Chapter's Specifications.

35   Install the driven gear, the driven gear washer and nut, then tighten the nut to the torque listed in this Chapter's Specifications.

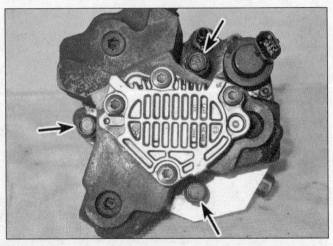

6.32a To detach the adapter from the fuel injection pump, remove these three bolts from the backside of the pump assembly

6.32b Remove the adapter from the fuel injection pump with a small puller (remove the old adapter O-ring so that you can insert the puller jaws into the O-ring recess)

6.33 Even if you're simply removing and installing the old fuel injection pump, be sure to replace this O-ring unless it's in good condition

6.36 Inspect the adapter O-ring and, if it's even slightly worn, replace it

Installation

Refer to illustration 6.36

36   Inspect the O-ring on the adapter **(see illustration)**. Unless it's in very good condition, replace it. Be sure to lubricate the new O-ring with clean engine oil.

37   Installation is the reverse of removal. Be sure to tighten all fasteners to the torque listed in this Chapter's Specifications. Refill the cooling system as described in Chapter 1.

LLY

Removal

38   Disconnect the cables from the negative battery terminals (see Chapter 5).

39   Remove the intake manifold cover.

40   Remove the air duct between the air filter housing and the turbocharger inlet housing. Stuff clean rags into the air intake duct to prevent dust from entering the duct.

41   Drain the cooling system (see Chapter 1).

42   Remove the engine cooling fan (see Chapter 2).

43   Remove the bolt that secures the positive battery cable junction box and set the junction box aside, then reposition the battery cables out of the way.

44   Disconnect all electrical connectors from the air conditioning compressor and the power steering pump, then unbolt the A/C compressor and the power steering pump and set them aside. Don't disconnect any air conditioning or power steering hoses.

45   Remove the alternator (see Chapter 5).

46   Remove the air conditioning compressor/power steering mounting bracket.

47   Remove the oil filler tube (see Chapter 7).

48   Remove the engine oil dipstick tube bracket bolt.

49   Remove the heater outlet hose bolt from the alternator mounting bracket.

50   Remove the drivebelt tensioner mounting bolt, then remove the tensioner (see Chapter 1).

51   Remove the alternator mounting bracket.

52   Remove the thermostat housing crossover (see Chapter 2).

53   Remove the turbocharger inlet elbow (see Chapter 4).

54   Disconnect the fuel balance pipe threaded fitting from the right fuel rail, remove the fuel balance pipe retaining bolt and remove the fuel balance pipe (see Section 10).

55   Disconnect the fuel rail inlet pipe from the fuel injection pump and the fuel rail, then remove the fuel rail inlet pipe (see Section 10).

56   Loosen the hose clamps and remove the hoses from the fuel pipes (see Section 10).

57   Remove the fuel injection pump mounting bolts **(see illustration 6.29)**. Use a couple of screwdrivers to gently pry the pump loose from the block. Make sure that you don't damage the mating surfaces of the pump or the block.

Pump replacement

58   Refer to Steps 30 through 35.

Installation

59   Installation is the reverse of removal. Be sure to tighten all fasteners to the torque listed in this Chapter's Specifications. Refill the cooling system as described in Chapter 1.

LBZ

Removal

60   Disconnect the cables from the negative battery terminals (see Chapter 5).

61   Remove the intake manifold cover.

62   Remove the air duct between the air filter housing and the turbocharger inlet housing. Stuff clean rags into the air intake duct to prevent dust from entering the duct.

63   Detach the wiring harness retainer from its bracket.

64   Remove the engine oil dipstick tube retaining bolt and bracket bolts and remove the bracket.

65   Drain the cooling system (see Chapter 1).

66   Remove the engine cooling fan (see Chapter 2).

67   Disconnect the battery cable junction block retaining bolt from the power steering pump mounting bracket, then set the battery cables aside.

68   Disconnect the air conditioning compressor clutch and the air conditioning cut-out switch electrical connectors.

69   Remove the air conditioning compressor mounting bolts, then set the compressor aside. Don't disconnect the air conditioning hoses.

70   Remove the power steering pump mounting bolts, then set the power steering pump aside. Don't disconnect the power steering pump hoses.

71   Remove the air conditioning compressor/power steering pump mounting bracket bolts and remove the mounting bracket.

72   Remove the bolt that secures the heater outlet hose to the alternator mounting bracket.

73   Remove the drivebelt tensioner (see Chapter 1).

74   Remove the alternator (see Chapter 6), then remove the alternator mounting bracket.

75   Remove the thermostat housing crossover (see Chapter 2).

76   Unscrew the threaded fittings that connect the fuel balance pipe to the two fuel rails. Remove the two fuel balance pipe retainer bolts and remove the fuel balance pipe.

77   Unscrew the threaded fittings that connect the fuel rail inlet pipe to the fuel injection pump and the left fuel rail, then remove the fuel inlet pipe (see Section 10).

78   Remove the center intake manifold (see Chapter 7).

79   Loosen the hose clamps that secure the fuel hoses to the fuel pipe and remove the hoses from the fuel pipe (see Section 10).

80   Remove the fuel injection pump mounting bolts **(see illustration).** Use a couple of screwdrivers to gently pry the pump loose from the block. Make sure that you don't damage the mating surfaces of the pump or the block.

Pump replacement

81   Refer to Steps 30 through 35.

Installation

82   Installation is the reverse of removal. Be sure to tighten all fasteners to the torque listed in this Chapter's Specifications. Refill the cooling system as described in Chapter 1

LMM

83   Disconnect the cables from the negative battery terminals (see Chapter 5).

84   Remove the thermostat crossover housing (see Chapter 2) and the center intake manifold (see Chapter 7).

85   Loosen the fuel hose clamps that connect the two hoses between the fuel injection pump and the fuel return pipe and the fuel injection fuel feed manifold, respectively, and remove both hoses.

86   Loosen the threaded fitting that connects the fuel feed pipe to the fuel injection pump and the left fuel rail, then remove the fuel feed pipe.

87   Remove the camshaft gear access plug from the engine front cover. Using a long breaker bar on the crankshaft balancer bolt, rotate the engine clockwise until the camshaft gear tension relief hole is visible through the access plug opening. Insert a long punch into the hole and pull it toward the right side of the engine as you remove the pump in the next step.

88   Remove the fuel injection pump bolts **(see illustration 6.29)**. Use a couple of screwdrivers to gently pry the pump loose from the block. Make sure that you don't damage the mating surfaces of the pump or the block.

Note: *You might have to rotate the pump slightly in order to remove it.*

Pump replacement

89   Refer to Steps 30 through 35.

Installation

90   Installation is the reverse of removal. Be sure to tighten all fasteners to the torque listed in this Chapter's Specifications. Refill the cooling system as described in Chapter 1.

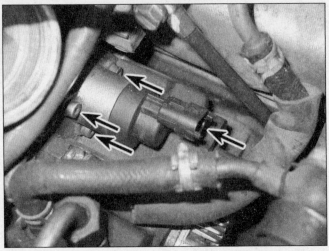

7.12 To remove the fuel pressure regulator, disconnect the electrical connector (already disconnected here) and remove the three mounting bolts (LB7 regulator shown, later units similar)

LML/LGH

Removal

91   Disconnect the cables from the negative battery terminals (see Chapter 5).

92   Remove the center intake manifold (see Chapter 2).

93   Remove the bolt that secures the high-pressure rail-to-fuel rail pipe.

94   Disconnect the threaded fittings at both ends of the high-pressure pipes that connect the fuel injection pump to the right fuel rail. Remove the bolt that secures the pipe and remove the pipe.

95   Unscrew the threaded fittings that connect the two high-pressure fuel pipes to the fuel injection pump and to right fuel rail, then remove the pipe.

96   Remove the front or rear Exhaust Gas Recirculation (EGR) valve cooler (see Chapter 6).

97   Unbolt and set aside the indirect fuel injector feed pipe from the injection pump.

98   Disconnect the electrical connectors from the top of the fuel injection pump.

99   Loosen the hose clamp and disconnect the fuel return and fuel feed hoses from the top of the fuel injection pump.

100   Remove the thermostat crossover housing (see Chapter 2).

101   Remove the camshaft gear access plug from the engine front cover.

102   Rotate the crankshaft until the fuel injection pump timing marks are aligned with the camshaft gear timing marks. There is one mark on the pump gear and there are two marks on the camshaft drive gear. The single mark on the pump gear must be between the two marks on the camshaft gear.

103   Note how the mounting bracket for the turbocharger cooler return pipe is installed with the lower right pump mounting bolt. Remove the four fuel injection pump mounting bolts and the turbocharger cooler return pipe bracket, then remove the pump.

Inspection

104   Remove the fuel pressure regulator from the pump and inspect the end of the regulator tip for metal debris.

Caution: *If you find any metal debris on the regulator tip, replace the fuel injection pump, the fuel rails, the fuel injectors, the fuel return line assembly, all high-pressure fuel pipes, the indirect fuel injector and the fuel feed pipes (including the pump to indirect injector).*

105   Inspect the condition of the fuel injection pump O-ring. If it's cracked, torn or damaged, replace it.

Installation

106   When installing the fuel injection pump, make sure that the timing marks on the camshaft gear are aligned with the timing mark on the pump gear as follows: Rotate the crankshaft until the two timings marks on the camshaft drive gear are in the center of the inspection hole, then lubricate the O-ring on the pump adapter. Install the pump so that the timing mark on the pump driven gear is between the two timing marks on the camshaft drive gear.

107   Install the turbocharger cooler return pipe bracket, install the four pump mounting bolts, then tighten the bolts to the torque listed in this Chapter's Specifications.

108   The remainder of installation is the reverse of removal. Refill the cooling system as described in Chapter 1.

L5P

109   Remove the center intake manifold (see Chapter 7).

110   Remove the coolant thermostat housing (see Chapter 2).

111   Remove the EGR return pipe.

112   Disconnect the electrical connections from the injection pump.

113   Remove the fuel return and feed pipes.

114   Remove the crossover fuel pipe. Discard the pipe and obtain a new one for installation. (The high-pressure pipes are only to be installed one time.)

115   Remove and discard the high-pressure fuel pipe connected to the fuel rails. Obtain a new pipe for installation.

116   Remove the bolts securing the injection pump to the engine.

117   Lift the pump from the engine.

118   Installation is the reverse of removal.

---

7   Fuel pressure regulator - removal and installation

Warning: *Diesel fuel is flammable, so take extra precautions when you work on any part of the fuel system. See the Warning in Section 1.*
Warning: *The engine must be completely cool before beginning this procedure.*

1   Disconnect the cables from the negative battery terminals (see Chapter 5).

LB7

Refer to illustration 7.12
Note: *The fuel pressure regulator is located on the upper back side of the fuel injection pump.*

2   Remove the air intake duct.

3   Remove the drivebelt (see Chapter 1).

4   Disconnect the electrical connectors from the air conditioning (A/C) compressor clutch and from the A/C cut-out switch. Remove the A/C compressor mounting bolts and move the compressor, with the hoses attached, to the right side of the engine compartment.

5   Remove the coolant outlet tube (see Chapter 2).

6   Remove both main engine wiring harness electrical connector bracket bolts and disconnect both connectors.

7   Disconnect the electrical connector from the Engine Coolant Temperature (ECT) sensor (see Chapter 6).

8   Disconnect the electrical connector from the Barometric Pressure (BARO) sensor (see Chapter 6).

9   Disconnect the electrical connectors from the glow plug relay (see Chapter 5).

10   Disconnect the electrical connector from the fuel rail temperature sensor (see Chapter 6).

11   Disconnect the electrical connectors from the left front and right front fuel injectors (see Section 12).

12   Disconnect the electrical connector from the fuel pressure regulator **(see illustration)**.

13   Disconnect the electrical connector from the oil level sensor (see Chapter 6).

14   Disconnect the Positive Crankcase Ventilation (PCV) hoses from both valve covers (see Chapter 6).

15   Reposition the clamp that secures the fuel inlet hose to the fuel injection pump, disconnect the inlet hose from the fuel feed distribution (block-off) block and set the hose aside.
16   Thoroughly clean the fuel pressure regulator and fuel injection pump with brake system cleaner.
17   Remove the three fuel pressure regulator mounting screws **(see illustration 7.12)** with a T25 TORX bit and remove the fuel pressure regulator.
18   Carefully inspect the bore and the mating surfaces of the regulator and the fuel injection pump.
19   Carefully inspect the condition of the O-rings. If they're even slightly damaged, replace them. Lubricate the new O-rings with clean engine oil before installing them.
20   When installing the regulator, make sure that you don't install it at an angle, which will damage the O-rings. Be sure to tighten the three T25 TORX mounting screws to the torque listed in this Chapter's Specifications.
21   Installation is otherwise the reverse of removal.

LLY and LBZ

Note: *The fuel pressure regulator is located on the upper back side of the fuel injection pump.*
22   Remove the air intake duct.
23   Disconnect the electrical connectors from the air conditioning (A/C) compressor clutch and from the A/C cut-out switch. Disconnect the electrical connectors from the alternator.
24   Remove the drivebelt (see Chapter 1).
25   Remove the A/C compressor mounting bolts and move the compressor, with the hoses attached, to the right side of the engine compartment. Remove the alternator mounting bolts and remove the alternator (see Chapter 5).
26   Remove both main engine wiring harness electrical connector bracket bolts and disconnect both connectors.
27   Disconnect the electrical connector from the Barometric Pressure (BARO) sensor (see Chapter 6).
28   Remove the main engine harness electrical connector retaining bolts and detach the main harness connectors from their retaining bracket.
29   Disconnect the electrical connector from the Engine Coolant Temperature (ECT) sensor (see Chapter 6, Section 6).
30   Remove the coolant outlet tube (see Chapter 2).
31   Disconnect the electrical connector from the fuel rail temperature sensor (see Chapter 6).
32   Disconnect the electrical connector from the fuel pressure regulator.
33   Disconnect the electrical connector from the oil level sensor (see Chapter 6).
34   Loosen the hose clamps and disconnect the hoses from the distribution block.
35   Refer to Steps 16 through 21.

LMM

Note: *The fuel pressure regulator is located on the upper back side of the fuel injection pump.*
36   Remove the alternator (see Chapter 5).
37   Remove the intake manifold tube (see Chapter 7).
38   Remove the coolant outlet tube (see Chapter 2).
39   Unbolt the air conditioning compressor and place the compressor and hoses on the right side of the engine compartment.
Warning: *Don't disconnect the refrigerant lines.*
40   Disconnect the electrical connectors from the Engine Coolant Temperature (ECT) sensors and set the ECT sensor connectors and wiring aside.
41   Disconnect the electrical connector from the fuel pressure regulator.
42   Loosen the hose clamps at both ends of the fuel hose between the fuel injection fuel feed manifold and the fuel injection pump, and remove the hose.
43   Refer to Steps 16 through 21.

LML/LGH

Note: *The fuel pressure regulator is located on top of the fuel injection pump.*
44   Remove the turbocharger (see Chapter 4).
45   Disconnect the electrical connector from the fuel pressure regulator.
46   Refer to Steps 16 through 21.

---

8   Fuel junction block and pressure relief valve - removal and installation

---

Refer to illustrations 8.13, 8.14a, 8.14b, 8.16a and 8.16b
Warning: *Diesel fuel is flammable, so take extra precautions when you work on any part of the fuel system. See the Warning in Section 1.*
Warning: *The engine must be completely cool before beginning this procedure.*
Caution: *The junction block has three rigid high-pressure fuel pipes connected to it by threaded fittings; none of these pipes are flexible, so you must either disconnect them at **both** ends or at least at their opposite end from the junction block, because if you bend, deform or kink any of these pipes in while removing or installing the junction block, one or more of them might break after the engine is reassembled and started. If you opt to simply disconnect them at their other ends and leave them connected to the junction block until after the junction block is removed, be sure to **loosen** the junction block end of each pipe before detaching the junction block from the intake manifold. For more information about the high-pressure fuel pipes and the locations and types of fittings they use, refer to Section 10.*
Note: *The fuel junction block, which is used only on LB7 models, is located at the left front corner of the valley between the cylinder heads and is mounted on the left intake manifold. Two fuel system devices are mounted on the junction block: the fuel pressure relief valve and the fuel rail pressure sensor. The pressure relief valve is not available separately at the time of publication; you can only replace it by replacing the junction block. The fuel rail pressure sensor is available separately; to replace it, see Section 9.*
1   Disconnect the cables from the negative battery terminals (see Chapter 5).
2   To give yourself more room to work, move the hood to its "service position" by moving the hood hinge bolts from their standard position to their service position holes.
3   Drain the cooling system (see Chapter 1).
4   Remove the upper intake manifold cover.
5   Remove the drivebelt (see Chapter 1).
6   Disconnect the electrical connectors from the air conditioning (A/C) compressor clutch and the A/C cut-out switch.
7   Remove the A/C compressor mounting bolts and, with the hoses still connected, reposition the A/C compressor in the right side of the engine compartment.

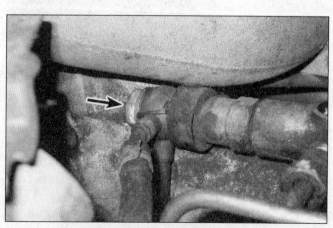

8.13 Fuel pressure relief valve banjo bolt

8.14a Threaded fittings for the high-pressure fuel line between the fuel injection pump and the junction block (LB7)

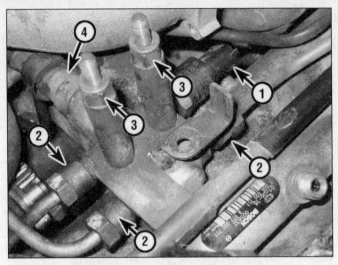

8.14b Fuel junction block details (LB7):

1   *Fuel rail pressure sensor (electrical connector already disconnected)*
2   *High-pressure fuel pipe threaded fittings*
3   *Fuel junction block mounting studs*
4   *Fuel pressure relief valve*

8   Disconnect the electrical connector from the left front fuel injector (see Section 12).

9   Loosen the hose clamp and disconnect the turbocharger coolant hose from the turbocharger bypass valve (see Chapter 4).

10   Remove the bolts that secure the coolant outlet tube to the left valve cover and to the thermostat housing and remove the coolant outlet tube. Remove and discard the old O-ring.

11   Reposition the Positive Crankcase Ventilation (PCV) hose clamp and disconnect the PCV hose from the upper valve cover (see Chapter 6).

12   Loosen the hose clamp that secures the charge air cooler inlet hose to the turbocharger, then twist the hose to loosen it and remove the hose.

Caution: *Do NOT use a screwdriver or some other tool to pry the hose loose. Doing so might tear or damage the hose.*

13   Remove the banjo bolt that secures the fuel pipe to the fuel pressure relief valve on the fuel junction block **(see illustration)**.

14   Unscrew the threaded fittings that secure the three high-pressure fuel pipes to the junction block, then unscrew the other end of the short pipe between the fuel injection pump and the junction block and remove that pipe now **(see illustrations)**.

15   Disconnect the threaded fittings from the other end of all high-pressure fuel lines (see Section 10).

Note: *Refer to the **Caution** at the beginning of this Section regarding disconnection of the high-pressure fuel lines at their opposite ends from the junction block.*

16   Remove the fuel junction block mounting studs **(see illustration)** and remove the fuel junction block **(see illustration)**.

17   Installation is the reverse of removal. Be sure to tighten all fasteners to the torque listed in this Chapter's Specifications.

8.16a Remove the two junction block mounting studs

8.16b Remove the fuel junction block only after you have already loosened and, if necessary, disconnected all of the high-pressure fuel line fittings

9 Fuel rail pressure sensor - removal and installation

Warning: *Diesel fuel is flammable, so take extra precautions when you work on any part of the fuel system. See the Warning in Section 1.*
Warning: *The engine must be completely cool before beginning this procedure.*

LB7

Note: *The fuel rail pressure sensor is located on the junction block.*
1   Remove the air conditioning (A/C) compressor.
Warning: *Don't disconnect the refrigerant lines.*
2   Disconnect the electrical connector from the fuel rail pressure sensor **(see illustration 8.14b)**.
3   Before removing the fuel rail pressure sensor, thoroughly clean the sensor and the surrounding area with brake system cleaner.
4   Unscrew the fuel rail pressure sensor from the junction block. Discard the old metal gasket.
5   Using a new metal gasket, carefully screw in the fuel rail pressure sensor and tighten it to the torque listed in this Chapter's Specifications.
Note: *Because of its location, the fuel rail pressure sensor might be difficult to tighten with a torque wrench alone. If you use a crow's foot to torque the sensor, make sure that the crow's foot is perpendicular to the torque wrench to ensure that the torque is correct.*
6   Reconnect the electrical connector to the fuel rail pressure sensor.
7   Install the A/C compressor.

LLY

Note: *The fuel rail pressure sensor is located on the right fuel rail.*
8   Remove the air filter housing outlet duct.
9   Remove the Exhaust Gas Recirculation (EGR) cooler tube (see Chapter 6).
10   Disconnect the fuel rail pressure sensor electrical connector.
11   Before removing the fuel rail pressure sensor, thoroughly clean the sensor and the surrounding area with brake system cleaner.
12   Unscrew the fuel rail pressure sensor from the right fuel rail.
13   Install the new fuel rail pressure sensor and tighten it to the torque listed in this Chapter's Specifications
14   Installation is otherwise the reverse of removal.

LBZ

Note: *The fuel rail pressure sensor is located on the back end of the right fuel rail.*
15   Remove the air filter housing outlet duct (see Chapter 1).
16   Remove the Exhaust Gas Recirculation (EGR) cooler tube (see Chapter 6).
17   Remove the EGR cooler tube heat protector bolt and remove the heat protector.
18   Disconnect the electrical connector from the fuel rail pressure sensor.
19   Before removing the fuel rail pressure sensor, thoroughly clean the sensor and the surrounding area with brake system cleaner, then blow dry the sensor and surrounding area with compressed air.
20   Unscrew and remove the old fuel rail pressure sensor from the right fuel rail.
21   Install the new fuel rail pressure sensor and tighten it to the torque listed in this Chapter's Specifications
22   Installation is otherwise the reverse of removal.

LMM

Note: *The fuel rail pressure sensor is located on the back end of the right fuel rail.*
23   Remove the Exhaust Gas Recirculation (EGR) valve cooler (see Chapter 6).
24   Remove the right exhaust manifold-to-turbocharger pipe (see Chapter 4).
25   Disconnect the engine wiring harness electrical connector from the fuel rail pressure sensor wiring harness extension electrical connector.
26   Remove the fuel rail pressure sensor wiring harness extension clip from the wiring harness bracket.
27   Remove the EGR valve cooler rear bracket retaining bolts and remove the bracket.
28   Disconnect the fuel rail pressure sensor wiring harness extension from the sensor.
29   Before removing the fuel rail pressure sensor, thoroughly clean the sensor and the surrounding area with brake system cleaner.
30   Unscrew the fuel rail pressure sensor from the right fuel rail.
31   Install the new fuel rail pressure sensor and tighten it to the torque listed in this Chapter's Specifications
32   Installation is otherwise the reverse of removal.

LML

Note: *The fuel rail pressure sensor is located at the back end of the left fuel rail.*
33   Remove the intake manifold heat shield bolts and remove the heat shield.
34   Disconnect the electrical connector from the fuel rail pressure sensor.
35   Before removing the fuel rail pressure sensor, thoroughly clean the sensor and the surrounding area with brake system cleaner.
36   Unscrew the fuel rail pressure sensor.
37   Install the new fuel rail pressure sensor and tighten it to the torque listed in this Chapter's Specifications.
38   Installation is otherwise the reverse of removal.

L5P

Warning: *If the noise cancelling foam was exposed to any fluids, such as diesel fuel or coolant, the foam must be replaced. Failure to replace the foam may result in an engine fire. To help avoid this issue, wrap a shop towel around the fuel rail pressure sensor and any open fuel lines to absorb any fuel that may leak out.*
Note: *The fuel rail pressure sensor is located at the front of the right fuel rail.*
39   Disconnect the negative battery cables and insulate the ends from the battery terminals.
40   Remove the throttle body (see Chapter 6).
41   Disconnect the electrical connector from the sensor.
42   Remove the fuel rail pressure sensor and obtain a new one for installation. Do NOT reuse the sensor.

10 Fuel rails and high-pressure fuel pipes - removal and installation

Warning: *Diesel fuel is flammable, so take extra precautions when you work on any part of the fuel system. See the Warning in Section 1.*
Warning: *The engine must be completely cool before beginning this procedure.*
Caution: *GM recommends using compressed air to blow off all fuel pipe and fuel injector fittings to remove all dirt, dust and debris before disconnecting them. If the fittings are still dirty, wipe them off with a clean shop rag. GM also recommends spraying lithium grease between the fuel injector pipes and fittings to help contain any dust or dirt that might still be present. Finally, every time you open up a fuel rail or any fuel pipe, immediately plug the opening to keep out dirt, dust and moisture. Failure to do so could cause serious engine damage and expensive repairs.*
Caution: *The high-pressure fuel pipes are designed for a one time use only. Never reuse the lines, as the crimping area will have already been crushed when it was tightened. ALWAYS install NEW high-pressure pipes if the pipes have been loosened or removed.*

LB7

1   Disconnect the cables from the negative battery terminals (see Chapter 5).
2   Drain the cooling system (see Chapter 1).

10.15 Fuel injector feed pipes (LB7 left cylinder head shown, right cylinder head same)

1   *Injector pipe fitting retainer bolts*
2   *Injector pipe fitting retainers*
3   *Fuel feed pipe fittings at injectors*
4   *Fuel feed pipe fittings at fuel rail*

10.17 Threaded fitting for the fuel feed pipe at the back end of the left fuel rail (1) and fuel rail mounting bolts (2) (LB7 shown)

Left fuel rail and fuel feed pipes

Refer to illustrations 10.15 and 10.17

3   Slide back the upper radiator hose clamps, then disconnect the upper hose from the radiator and the engine.

4   Remove the bolt that secures the positive battery cable junction box and move it aside.

5   Loosen the hose clamp that secures the charge air duct to the turbocharger and remove the duct.

6   Disconnect all three electrical connectors from the glow plug relay and remove the glow plug relay bracket.

7   Disconnect all electrical connectors in the engine wiring harness, remove the engine harness bracket and set the harness and bracket aside.

8   Disconnect the fuel inlet and return pipes. Remove the fuel pipe L-bracket.

9   Loosen the Positive Crankcase Ventilation (PCV) hose clamp, disconnect the PCV hose and move it aside (see Chapter 6).

10   Remove the coolant pipe from the thermostat housing (see Chapter 2).

11   Remove the drivebelt (see Chapter 1).

12   Remove the air conditioning (A/C) compressor mounting bolts and set the A/C compressor aside.

Warning: *Don't disconnect the refrigerant lines.*

13   Loosen and disconnect the threaded fittings at both ends of the high-pressure fuel pipe that connects the fuel injection pump to the junction block **(see illustration 8.14a)**.

14   Remove the fittings that connect the fuel junction block fuel pipes to the fuel rails **(see illustration 8.14b)**. Detach the junction block **(see illustration 8.16a and 8.16b)** and remove the junction block and fuel pipes.

15   Remove the fuel injector feed pipe retainer bolts and retainers **(see illustration)**.

16   Unscrew the fuel injector feed pipe threaded fittings and remove the injector feed pipes.

Note: *Mark the pipes with pieces of numbered tape so they can be returned to their original locations.*

17   Loosen and disconnect the threaded fitting for the fuel feed rear pipe from the back end of the fuel rail **(see illustration)**.

18   Remove the fuel rail mounting bolts **(see illustration 10.17)** and remove the fuel rails.

Caution: *Once the fuel rail, injector pipes and fuel rails are open, do NOT use compressed air to remove dirt, dust or debris.*

10.27 Threaded fitting for the fuel feed pipe at the front end of the right fuel rail (LB7 shown)

19   Inspect the sealing surfaces of all threaded fittings for excessive corrosion and damage to the sealing surfaces. If the sealing surface of any threaded fitting is corroded or damaged, replace the high-pressure pipe. If any fasteners are damaged in any way, replace them as well.

20   Installation is the reverse of removal. Be sure to tighten all fasteners and threaded fittings to the torque listed in this Chapter's Specifications.

Right fuel rail and fuel feed pipes

Refer to illustration 10.27

21   Remove the air filter housing outlet duct.

22   Loosen the Positive Crankcase Ventilation (PCV) hose clamp, disconnect the PCV hose and move it aside (see Chapter 6).

23   Remove the Fuel Injection Control Module (FICM) (see Section 11).

24   Remove the fuel filter (see Chapter 1).

25   Remove the Exhaust Gas Recirculation (EGR) valve (see Chapter 6).

26   Remove the fuel injector feed pipe threaded fittings **(see illustration 10.15)** and remove the injector feed pipes.

27   Loosen and disconnect the threaded fitting for the fuel feed pipe from the front end of the fuel rail **(see illustration)**.

28   Remove the fuel rail mounting bolts **(see illustration 10.17)** and remove the fuel rails.
Caution: *Once the injector pipes and fuel rails are open, do NOT use compressed air to remove dirt, dust or debris.*
29   Inspect the sealing surfaces of all threaded fittings for excessive corrosion and damage to the sealing surfaces. If the sealing surface of any threaded fitting is corroded or damaged, replace the high-pressure pipe. If any fasteners are damaged in any way, replace them as well.
30   Installation is the reverse of removal. Be sure to tighten all fasteners and threaded fittings to the torque listed in this Chapter's Specifications.

LLY and LBZ

Left fuel rail and fuel feed pipes

31   Remove the coolant outlet tube (see Chapter 2).
32   Remove the battery cable junction block bracket bolt and set the junction block and bracket aside.
33   Remove the charge air cooler inlet duct from the turbocharger (see Chapter 4, Section 3).
Caution: *After removing the charge air cooler inlet duct, immediately cover the opening in the turbocharger with tape to prevent dirt, dust or moisture from entering the turbo.*
34   Disconnect the fuel supply and return line quick-connect fittings (see Section 3).
35   Remove the fuel pipe bracket retaining nut and remove the fuel pipe bracket from its mounting stud.
36   Remove the Positive Crankcase Ventilation (PCV) hose and pipe (see Chapter 6).
37   Remove the air conditioning (A/C) compressor mounting bolts and set the A/C compressor aside. Don't disconnect the A/C hoses.
38   Remove the nut and two bolts that secure the fuel supply pipe. Remove the fuel supply pipe banjo bolt and washer from the Fuel Injection Control Module (FICM), then remove the fuel supply pipe.
39   Remove the two bolts that secure the fuel rail balance pipe, remove the threaded fitting on each end of the balance pipe, and remove the balance pipe from the fuel rails.
40   Disconnect the fuel injector return hose from the return/junction block pipe, then loosen the hose clamps and remove the fuel hoses from the return/junction block.
41   Loosen the hose clamp at the back end of the left fuel rail and disconnect the fuel hose.
42   Remove the return/junction block fuel pipe retainer bolt and retainers, then remove the return/junction block and fuel pipes.
43   Remove the fuel pipe retaining bracket bolts and remove the fuel pipe/bracket assembly.
44   Using compressed air, blow off the fuel injector pipes and fittings to remove all dirt, dust and debris. If the fittings are dirty, wipe them off with a clean shop rag.
45   Unscrew the threaded fittings at both ends of the fuel inlet pipe, then disconnect and remove the fuel inlet pipe from the fuel injection pump and left fuel rail.
46   Unscrew the threaded fittings that secure the fuel injector pipes to the fuel injectors, then remove the left fuel injector pipes.
Caution: *Once the injector pipes and fuel rails are open, do NOT use compressed air to remove dirt, dust or debris.*
47   Remove the fuel rail bolts and remove the left fuel rail and mounting bracket assembly.
48   Inspect the sealing surfaces of all threaded fittings for excessive corrosion and damage to the sealing surfaces. If the sealing surface of any threaded fitting is corroded or damaged, replace the high-pressure pipe. If any of the fasteners are damaged in any way, replace them.
49   Installation is the reverse of removal. Be sure to tighten the fuel rail mounting bolts and all fuel pipe threaded fittings and banjo bolts to the torque listed in this Chapter's Specifications.

Right fuel rail and fuel feed pipes

50   Remove the air filter housing outlet duct.
51   On LLY engines, remove the Fuel Injection Control Module (FICM) (see Section 11).
52   On LBZ engines, remove the dipstick tube retaining bolt, bracket bolts and bracket.

53   Remove the fuel filter (see Chapter 1).
54   Remove the Exhaust Gas Recirculation (EGR) valve cooler tube (see Chapter 6).
55   Remove the Positive Crankcase Ventilation (PCV) hose/pipe (see Chapter 6).
56   Using compressed air, blow off the fuel injector pipes and fittings to remove all dirt, dust and debris. If the fittings are dirty, wipe them off with a clean shop rag. GM recommends spraying lithium grease between the fuel injector pipes and fittings to help contain any dust or dirt in the air.
57   Remove the two bolts that secure the fuel rail balance pipe, remove the threaded fitting on each end of the balance pipe, and remove the balance pipe from the fuel rails.
58   Unscrew the threaded fittings that secure the fuel injector pipes to the fuel injectors, then remove the left fuel injector pipes.
Caution: *Once the injector pipes and fuel rails are open, do NOT use compressed air to remove dirt, dust or debris. Doing so could damage an injector.*
59   Remove the fuel rail bolts and remove the right fuel rail and mounting bracket assembly.
60   Inspect the sealing surfaces of all threaded fittings for excessive corrosion and damage to the sealing surfaces. If the sealing surface of any threaded fitting is corroded or damaged, replace the high-pressure pipe. If any of the fasteners are damaged in any way, replace them.
61   Installation is the reverse of removal. Be sure to tighten the fuel rail mounting bolts, all fuel pipe threaded fittings and banjo bolts to the torque listed in this Chapter's Specifications.

LMM

Left fuel rail and feed pipes

62   Remove the fuel line bracket retaining nut and remove the fuel line bracket from its mounting stud.
63   Remove the charge air cooler inlet pipe.
64   Remove the Positive Crankcase Ventilation (PCV) hose/pipe (see Chapter 6).
65   Disconnect and remove the right fuel rail feed pipe (this is the pipe that delivers high-pressure fuel from the left fuel rail to the right fuel rail).
66   Remove the fuel return pipe (see Section 13).
67   Remove the fuel pipe bracket bolt and bracket.
68   Using compressed air, blow off the fuel injector pipes and fittings to remove all dirt, dust and debris. If the fittings are dirty, wipe them off with a clean shop rag. GM recommends spraying lithium grease between the fuel injector pipes and fittings to help contain any dust or dirt in the air.
69   Loosen the threaded fittings for the left fuel rail feed pipe and remove the left fuel rail feed pipe (this is the pipe that delivers high-pressure fuel from the fuel injection pump to the left fuel rail).
70   Unscrew the threaded fittings that connect the fuel injector feed pipes to the fuel injectors, then remove the left fuel injector feed pipes.
Caution: *Once the injector pipes and fuel rails are open, do NOT use compressed air to remove dirt, dust or debris. Doing so could damage an injector.*
71   Remove the fuel rail mounting bolts and remove the fuel rail from its mounting bracket. Loosen the fuel hose clamp at the fuel rail, if necessary, and remove the fuel hose.
72   Installation is the reverse of removal. Be sure to tighten the fuel rail mounting bolts to the torque listed in this Chapter's Specifications.

Right fuel rail and fuel feed pipes

73   Remove the heater outlet pipe (this is the coolant pipe between the water pump and the expansion tank).
74   Remove the fuel filter/heater element assembly (see Section 15).
75   Remove the turbocharger coolant outlet pipe (see Chapter 4).
76   Disconnect the engine wiring harness electrical connector from the fuel rail fuel pressure sensor harness. Remove the clip that secures the fuel rail fuel pressure sensor wiring harness to the wiring harness bracket. Remove the bolts that secure the wiring harness bracket and remove the bracket.

77   Using compressed air, blow off the fuel injector pipes and fittings to remove all dirt, dust and debris. If the fittings are dirty, wipe them off with a clean shop rag. GM recommends spraying lithium grease between the fuel injector pipes and fittings to help contain any dust or dirt in the air.

78   Unscrew the threaded fittings that connect the fuel injector feed pipes to the fuel injectors, then remove the right fuel injector feed pipes. **Caution:** *Once the injector pipes and fuel rails are open, do NOT use compressed air to remove dirt, dust or debris. Doing so could damage an injector.*

79   Unscrew the threaded fitting that connects the right fuel rail from feed pipe to the right fuel rail.

80   Remove the fuel rail mounting bolts and remove the fuel rail its mounting bracket. Loosen the fuel hose clamp at the fuel rail, if necessary, and remove the fuel hose.

81   Installation is the reverse of removal. Be sure to tighten the fuel rail mounting bolts to the torque listed in this Chapter's Specifications.

LML/LGH

Left fuel rail and fuel injector feed pipes

82   Remove the front Exhaust Gas Recirculation (EGR) cooler (see Chapter 6).

83   Unscrew the fuel injector feed pipe threaded fittings from the left fuel rail and from the left bank injectors and remove the fuel injector feed pipes.

84   Disconnect the electrical connector from the fuel pressure relief valve at the front end of the left fuel rail.

85   Unscrew the threaded fitting that connects the high-pressure fuel pipe to the fuel rail.

86   Loosen the hose clamp that secures the fuel return hose to the left fuel rail and disconnect the fuel return hose.

87   Disconnect the electrical connector from the fuel pressure sensor at the back end of the left fuel rail.

88   Remove the left fuel rail heat shield fasteners, remove the two fuel rail mounting bolts, and remove the fuel rail and heat shield.

89   Installation is the reverse of removal.

Right fuel rail and fuel injector feed pipes

90   Remove the rear Exhaust Gas Recirculation (EGR) cooler (see Chapter 6).

91   Unscrew the fuel injector feed pipe threaded fittings from the right fuel rail and from the right bank injectors and remove the fuel injector feed pipes.

92   Remove the fuel rail mounting bolts and remove the fuel rail.

93   Installation is the reverse of removal.

L5P

Caution: *Debris can gather under the noise reducing covers. Prior to removing any fuel injection fuel feed pipes, use compressed air to blow any debris from the area. Wipe all fittings clean of any remaining debris. Avoid using compressed air to clean any debris once the lines or injectors have been removed.*

Right side

94   Remove the sound reducing covers.

95   Remove the right-side fuel injector fuel feed pipes.

96   Remove the rail-to-rail high-pressure pipe.

97   Remove the electrical connections.

98   Remove the fuel rail bolts.

99   Remove the fuel rail.

100 Installation is the reverse of removal. Tighten the fuel rail mounting bolts to the torque listed in this Chapter's Specifications. **Note:** *Prime the fuel system before attempting to restart.*

Left side

101 Remove the bank 2 fuel injector noise reducing cover.

102 Remove the fuel feed pipes and the rail-to-rail high-pressure fuel pipe.

103 Remove the fuel return pipe clip bolt.

11.5 Fuel Injection Control Module (FICM) banjo bolts (LB7 shown, LLY similar, except that one banjo bolt is on top and the other banjo bolt is at the bottom)

104 Disconnect the fuel return pipe from the fuel rail.

105 Remove the fuel return pipe washer.

106 Disconnect the electrical connections.

107 Remove the bolts securing the rail to the engine.

108 Remove the fuel rail.

109 Installation is the reverse of removal. Tighten the fuel rail mounting bolts to the torque listed in this Chapter's Specifications. **Note:** *Prime the fuel system before attempting to restart.*

11   Fuel Injection Control Module (FICM) - removal and installation

Warning: *Diesel fuel is flammable, so take extra precautions when you work on any part of the fuel system. See the Warning in Section 1.* **Note:** *The FICM is used only on LB7 and LLY engines.*

Removal

Refer to illustrations 11.5 and 11.6

1   Remove the fuel filler neck cap to relieve fuel tank pressure.

2   Disconnect the cables from the negative and positive battery terminals (see Chapter 5).

3   Remove the air filter housing outlet duct.

4   Cut and discard the large tie straps (if equipped) and remove them from the FICM.

5   Remove the fuel pipe banjo bolts from the FICM **(see illustration)** and disconnect the fuel pipes. Discard the old washers.

6   Remove the FICM mounting bolts and insulators from the FICM **(see illustration)**.

7   Once the FICM is detached from its mounting bracket, disconnect the FICM electrical connectors. **Caution:** *Do not break off the tab on the electrical connector.*

8   Remove the FICM.

Installation

Refer to illustration 11.10

9   Inspect the mounting bolt insulators. If they're cracked or torn, replace them.

10 Position the FICM on its mounting bracket and secure it with the insulators and mounting bolts **(see illustration)** but don't tighten them fully yet.

11 Using new washers, reconnect the fuel pipes to the FICM. Hand-tighten the banjo bolts but don't tighten them yet either.

12 Reconnect the electrical connectors to the FICM.

13 Tighten the FICM mounting bolts to the torque listed in this Chapter's Specifications.

11.6 FICM mounting bolt locations (LB7 shown, LLY similar)

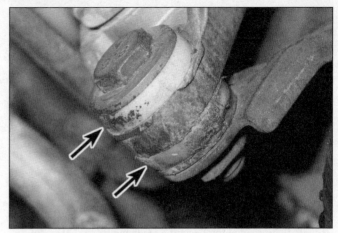

11.10 When installing the insulator/washers on the FICM mounting bolts, make sure they're installed just like this

14   Tighten the fuel pipe banjo bolts to the torque listed in this Chapter's Specifications.

15   The remainder of installation is the reverse of removal.

16   When everything is reassembled, close the fuel filler neck cap, then depress the fuel primer button 30 times. Attempt to start the engine. If the engine starts, but stalls, repeat this step again. Once the engine is running, check for any fuel leaks at the banjo bolts that connect the fuel hoses to the FICM.

12   Fuel injectors - removal and installation

Warning: *Diesel fuel is flammable, so take extra precautions when you work on any part of the fuel system. See the Warning in Section 1.*
Warning: *Wait until the engine is completely cool before beginning this procedure.*
Caution: *GM recommends using compressed air to blow off all fuel pipe and fuel injector fittings to remove all dirt, dust and debris before disconnecting them. If the fittings are still dirty, wipe them off with a clean shop rag. GM recommends spraying lithium grease between the fuel injector pipes and fittings to help contain any dust or dirt that might still be present. Finally, every time you open up a fuel rail or any fuel pipe, immediately plug the opening to keep out dirt, dust and moisture. Failure to do so could cause serious engine damage and expensive repairs.*

LB7
Removal
Refer to illustrations 12.4, 12.6, 12.8a and 12.8b
Note: *To remove a fuel injector, GM specifies a special fuel injector puller (GM #J44639) or a suitable equivalent from an aftermarket tool manufacturer like Snap-On. You might not be able to remove an injector without the special tool, and you might damage the injector if you attempt to remove it without such a tool. However, we used a medium-size prybar to perform this job and it worked well.*

1   Disconnect the cables from the negative battery terminals (see Chapter 5). Drain the cooling system (see Chapter 1).

2   Disconnect the fuel injector feed pipes from the fuel rail and the fuel injectors (see Section 10).

3   Remove the upper and lower valve covers from the cylinder head you are working on (see Chapter 7).

4   Clearly label the injector electrical connectors, then disconnect the electrical connectors from all the fuel injectors on the side you are working on **(see illustration),** and set the injector electrical harness aside.
Caution: *Failure to properly reconnect the injector connectors will result in severe engine damage.*

5   Unbolt the fuel injector return pipe **(see illustration 13.4)** from the fuel injectors and remove it.

6   Remove the bolt from the injector bracket **(see illustration).**

7   If you have the special factory injector puller tool, install it on the injector retainer, then install a wrench on the injector puller and remove the injector by prying *away from the injector.*

12.4 To disconnect the injector harness from each pair of injectors, remove these nuts from the injector terminals; be sure to note the positive and negative terminals of each injector to ensure correct reconnection - mark them if necessary (LB7)

12.6 Injector bracket bolts (LB7)

12.8a If you don't have the special factory injector puller tool (or a similar aftermarket tool), insert a medium-size prybar under the injector protrusion (arrow) on the opposite side from the retaining bracket and carefully lever the injector out of its bore

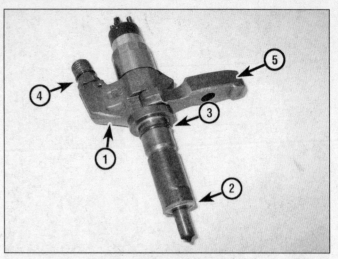

12.8b Fuel injector details:

1   *Position the pry bar under this protrusion to lever the injector out of the cylinder head*
2   *Copper compression washer - must be removed, discarded and replaced with a new compression washer (even if you're installing the old injector)*
3   *Injector O-ring (always replace)*
4   *Injector O-ring (always replace)*
5   *Injector retainer*

8   If you don't have the special factory injector puller tool, carefully insert the tip of a medium size prybar under the injector body protrusion on the opposite side from the retainer **(see illustrations)** and lever the injector up and out of its bore in the cylinder head.
9   Remove and discard the old injector copper compression washer and O-rings.
10   If the copper compression washer **(see illustration 12.8b)** doesn't come out with the injector, remove it now and discard it.
Caution: *Never re-use an old compression washer. Always install a new one.*

Injector sleeve
11   If the injector sleeve was pulled out of the cylinder head when you removed an injector, install the sleeve as follows.
12   Inspect the injector sleeve for scoring or other damage. If the sleeve is damaged, replace it.
13   Install two new injector sleeve O-rings on the injector sleeve. Apply GM part no. 12345493 adhesive to the tapered lower sealing portion of the sleeve.
14   Install the injector sleeve into the injector bore in the cylinder head with a brass drift. Carefully tap the sleeve into the head until it's fully seated.

Installation
15   If you're planning to install an old injector, before installing it, clean and inspect it as follows: Use a soft bristle non-metallic brush and engine cleaner to remove any deposits from the nozzle tip and the area that seats on the copper sealing washer. When the injector is clean, inspect the injector nozzle tip for any signs of discoloration - dark yellow, tan or blue - caused by excessive heat. If there are any signs of discoloration, replace the injector.
16   Install a new compression washer and new injector O-rings **(see illustration 12.8b)**, then insert the injector into its mounting sleeve. Install the injector bracket and tighten the bolt to the torque listed in this Chapter's Specifications.
17   Inspect the high-pressure injector feed pipe(s) for excessive corrosion or damaged sealing surfaces. If there is evidence of either condition, replace the feed pipe(s) (see Section 10).
18   Installation is otherwise the reverse of removal. Be sure to tighten all fuel pipe fittings to the torque listed in this Chapter's Specifications.
19   Refill the cooling system (see Chapter 1).

LLY and LBZ
Removal
Refer to illustrations 12.36a and 12.36b

Note: *To remove a fuel injector, you will need to obtain a special fuel injector puller (GM #J46594) or a suitable equivalent from an aftermarket tool manufacturer. You might not be able to remove an injector without this special tool*

Left cylinder head
20   Disconnect the cables from the negative battery terminals (see Chapter 5).
21   Remove the intake manifold cover.
22   Drain the cooling system (see Chapter 1).
23   Loosen the hose clamp and remove the charge air cooler inlet duct from the turbocharger.
24   Disconnect the main engine harness electrical connectors (lift up the connector latches before trying to disconnect the connectors). Open the harness clip, then remove the main engine harness connector retaining bolts and remove the connectors from the connector bracket.
25   Disconnect the barometric (BARO) sensor electrical connector (see Chapter 6).
26   Disengage the engine wiring harness from the clip on the main electrical harness bracket, remove the bracket bolts and remove the bracket.
27   Disconnect the glow plug controller electrical connector (see Chapter 5).
28   Disconnect the battery feed electrical connector from the glow plug controller (see Chapter 5).
29   Remove the Positive Crankcase Ventilation (PCV) hose and pipe.

Right cylinder head
30   Disconnect the cables from the negative battery terminals (see Chapter 5).
31   Remove the air filter housing outlet duct.
32   Loosen the hose clamp and remove the charge air cooler outlet duct from the intake.
33   Remove the fuel filter and filter mounting bracket (see Chapter 1 and Section 15 of this Chapter).
34   On LLY engines, remove the Fuel Injection Control Module (FICM) (see Section 11).

Either cylinder head
35   Read the **Caution** at the beginning of this Section regarding cleaning fittings and injectors before removal.
36   Unscrew the threaded fittings and disconnect the fuel feed pipes between the fuel rail(s) and the fuel injector(s) **(see illustrations)**.

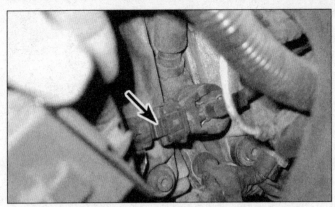

12.36a Fuel injector electrical connector - depress the tab to release (LLY shown)

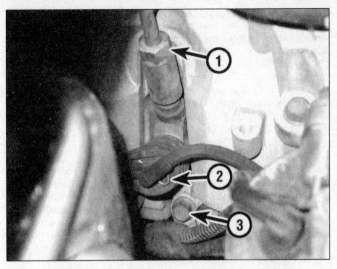

12.36b Fuel injector details - LLY and later models

1	Fuel feed pipe fitting	3 Injector retainer bolt
2	Return hose clip	

37   Remove the fuel return hose clips and disconnect the fuel return hose(s) from the injectors.

38   Clearly label all fuel injector electrical connectors to prevent reconnection to the wrong injector, then disconnect the electrical connectors from the injectors.

Caution: *Failure to properly reconnect the injector connectors will result in severe engine damage.*

39   Remove the fuel injector bracket bolt.

40   Install the special injector puller tool on the injector mounting bracket (see **Note** above).

41   Install a wrench on the injector puller and remove the injector by prying *away from the injector.* Alternatively, carefully pry the injector from its bore, being very careful not to damage the valve cover.

Caution: *When removing more than one fuel injector from an LBZ engine, make sure that you clearly mark the injector and cylinder from which it was removed. Each of these injectors is encoded by the manufacturer with information relating to its specific fuel flow rate, so it must be installed in the same cylinder from which it was removed. Failure to do so might set a Diagnostic Trouble Code and could cause driveability problems.*

42   Remove and discard the old injector copper compression washer and O-ring.

43   If the copper compression washer doesn't come out with the injector, remove it now and discard it.

Caution: *Never re-use an old compression washer. Always install a new one.*

Installation

44   If you're planning to install an old injector, before installing it, clean and inspect it as follows: Use a soft-bristle non-metallic brush and engine cleaner to remove any deposits from the nozzle tip and the area that seats on the copper sealing washer. When the injector is clean, inspect the injector nozzle tip for any signs of discoloration - dark yellow, tan or blue - caused by excessive heat. If there are any signs of discoloration, replace the injector.

45   Install a new compression washer and new injector O-rings **(see illustration 12.8b)**, then insert the injector into its bore. Install the injector bracket and tighten the bolt to the torque listed in this Chapter's Specifications.

46   Inspect the fuel high pressure pipe(s) for excessive corrosion or damaged sealing surfaces. If there is evidence of either of these conditions, replace the high pressure pipe(s) (see Section 10).

47   Installation is otherwise the reverse of removal. Be sure to tighten all fuel pipe fittings to the torque listed in this Chapter's Specifications. Refill the cooling system (see Chapter 1).

LMM
Removal

Note: *To remove a fuel injector you will need to obtain a special fuel injector puller (GM #J46594) or a suitable equivalent from an aftermar-*

ket tool manufacturer. You might not be able to remove an injector without this special tool

48   Disconnect the cables from the negative battery terminals (see Chapter 5). Drain the cooling system (see Chapter 1).

49   Unscrew the threaded fittings and disconnect the fuel feed pipes between the fuel rail(s) and the fuel injector(s) (see Section 10).

50   Remove the clips that secure the fuel return line to each fuel injector, then disconnect the fuel return line from the fuel injectors.

51   If you're removing an injector, or injectors, on the left cylinder head, cut the tie strap that secures the fuel return line to the engine wiring harness.

52   If you're removing an injector, or injectors, on the right cylinder head, disconnect the fuel return line from the fuel feed manifold.

53   Disconnect and remove the fuel return line from the fuel return pipe.

54   Clearly label the injector electrical connectors, then disconnect the electrical connectors from the injectors.

55   Remove the fuel injector bracket bolts.

56   Install the special injector puller tool on the injector mounting bracket (see **Note** above).

57   Install a flare-nut wrench on the injector puller and remove the injector by prying *away from the injector.* Alternatively, carefully pry the injector from its bore, being very careful not to damage the valve cover.

Caution: *When removing more than one fuel injector, make sure that you clearly mark the injector and cylinder from which it was removed. Each of these injectors is encoded by the manufacturer with information relating to its specific fuel flow rate, so it must be installed in the same cylinder from which it was removed. Failure to do so will set Diagnostic Trouble Codes and will cause drivability problems.*

58   Remove and discard the old injector copper compression washer and O-ring.

59   If the copper compression washer doesn't come out with the injector, remove it now and discard it.

Caution: *Never re-use an old compression washer. Always install a new one.*

Installation

60   If you're planning to install an old injector, before installing it, clean and inspect it as follows: Use a soft bristle non-metallic brush and engine cleaner to remove any deposits from the nozzle tip and the area that seats on the copper sealing washer. When the injector is clean, inspect the injector nozzle tip for any signs of discoloration - dark yellow, tan or blue - caused by excessive heat. If there are any signs of discoloration, replace the injector.

61   Install a new compression washer and new injector O-rings **(see illustration 12.8b)**, then insert the injector into its bore. Install the injector bracket and tighten the bolt to the torque listed in this Chapter's Specifications.
62   Inspect the fuel high pressure pipe(s) for excessive corrosion or damaged sealing surfaces. If there is evidence of either of these conditions, replace the high pressure pipe(s) (see Section 10).
63   Installation is otherwise the reverse of removal. Be sure to tighten all fuel pipe fittings to the torque listed in this Chapter's Specifications. Refill the cooling system (see Chapter 1).

LGH/LML

Note: *GM recommends a special tool (GM #EN 49774) to remove the fuel injectors on these engines. Note that this is not the same tool recommended for injector removal on earlier engines. You might be able to obtain a suitable equivalent tool from an aftermarket specialty tool manufacturer such as Snap-On. The injectors on these models do not have the same shape as earlier injectors, so you might not be able to use a prybar to remove the injector(s) as you could on early engines.*
64   Drain the cooling system (see Chapter 1).
65   Remove the fuel injector feed pipes (see Section 10).
66   Remove the fuel injector bracket bolts. Install the special injector removal tool on the fuel injector bracket. Using a wrench on the special tool, pull back (away from) the injector to pry it up and out of its bore in the cylinder head.
Caution: *When removing more than one fuel injector, make sure that you clearly mark the injector and cylinder from which it was removed. Each of these injectors is encoded by the manufacturer with information relating to its specific fuel flow rate, so it must be installed in the same cylinder from which it was removed. Failure to do so will set Diagnostic Trouble Codes and will cause drivability problems.*
67   Remove and discard the old injector copper compression washer and O-ring.
68   If the copper compression washer doesn't come out with the injector, remove it now and discard it.
Caution: *Never re-use an old compression washer. Always install a new one.*

Installation

69   If you're planning to install an old injector, before installing it, clean and inspect it as follows: Use a soft bristle non-metallic brush and engine cleaner to remove any deposits from the nozzle tip and the area that seats on the copper sealing washer. When the injector is clean, inspect the injector nozzle tip for any signs of discoloration - dark yellow, tan or blue - caused by excessive heat. If there are any signs of discoloration, replace the injector.
70   Install a new compression washer and new injector O-rings **(see illustration 12.8b)**, then insert the injector into its bore. Install the injector bracket and tighten the bolt to the torque listed in this Chapter's Specifications.
71   Inspect the fuel high pressure pipe(s) for excessive corrosion or damaged sealing surfaces. If there is evidence of either of these, replace the high pressure pipe(s) (see Section 10).
72   Installation is otherwise the reverse of removal. Be sure to tighten all fuel pipe fittings to the torque listed in this Chapter's Specifications.
73   Refill the cooling system (see Chapter 1).

L5P

Removal

74   Drain the cooling system (see Chapter 1).
75   Remove the fuel rail(s) (see Section 10).
75   Remove the sound reducing panel lower section.
76   Remove the injector bracket bolts. Install the injector puller into the bracket bolt hole.
77   Using the puller, work the injector out of the head.
Caution: *When removing more than one fuel injector, make sure that you clearly mark the injector and cylinder from which it was removed. Each of these injectors is encoded by the manufacturer with information*

13.4 Fuel injector return pipe banjo bolts (LB7)

relating to its specific fuel flow rate, so it must be installed in the same cylinder from which it was removed. Failure to do so will set Diagnostic Trouble Codes and will cause drivability problems.
Note: *A slide hammer with an M6 x 1.0 thread can be installed for any injectors that are extremely stuck in place. In such cases, ensure all the leverage force is directed straight upwards on the injector with no side-to-side motion. This will prevent any damage to the injector or engine.*
Note: *With the injector removed, inspect the nozzle tip of the injector and make sure the entire injector was removed from the engine. Inspect the fuel injector nozzle tip for any cracks, dents, or other damage. A dark yellow, tan or blue discoloration is sign of excessive heat buildup in the combustion chamber. Replace the fuel injector if any damage is found.*
78   Remove and discard the old injector copper compression washer and O-ring.
79   If the copper compression washer doesn't come out with the injector, remove it now and discard it.
Caution: *Never re-use an old compression washer. Always install a new one.*
80   Repeat the steps for the remaining injectors.

Installation

81   If you're planning to install an old injector, before installing it, clean and inspect it as follows: Use a soft bristle non-metallic brush and engine cleaner to remove any deposits from the nozzle tip and the area that seats on the copper sealing washer. When the injector is clean, inspect the injector nozzle tip for any signs of discoloration - dark yellow, tan or blue - caused by excessive heat. If there are any signs of discoloration, replace the injector.
82   Install a new compression washer and new injector O-rings (see illustration 12.8b), then insert the injector into its bore. Install the injector retainer and tighten the bolt to the torque listed in this Chapter's Specifications.
83   Installation is otherwise the reverse of removal. Be sure to tighten all fasteners and fittings to the torque values listed in this Chapter's Specifications.

13   Fuel return pipe - removal and installation

Warning: *Diesel fuel is flammable, so take extra precautions when you work on any part of the fuel system. See the Warning in Section 1.*
Warning: *Wait until the engine is completely cool before beginning this procedure.*

LB7

Refer to illustration 13.4

1   Disconnect the cables from the negative battery terminals (see Chapter 5). Drain the cooling system (see Chapter 1).

2   Remove the upper and lower valve covers from the cylinder on which you intend to remove the fuel injector return pipe (see Chapter 7).
3   Disconnect the electrical connectors from the fuel injectors on the fuel return pipe you are working on **(see illustration 12.4)**.
4   Remove the fuel injector return pipe bolts **(see illustration)**, then remove the return pipe.
5   Remove and discard the old copper return pipe gaskets.
6   Using new copper gaskets, install the return pipe, then install the return pipe bolts and tighten them to the torque listed in this Chapter's Specifications.
7   Installation is otherwise the reverse of removal. Refill the cooling system (see Chapter 1).
8   When you're done, prime the fuel system (see Chapter 1, Section 11), then start the engine. If the engine stalls, prime the fuel system again. Once the engine starts, inspect for fuel leaks.

LLY

9   Disconnect the cables from the negative battery terminals (see Chapter 5).
10   Drain the cooling system (see Chapter 1).
11   Remove the air filter housing outlet duct.
12   Remove the charge air cooler inlet and outlet ducts from the turbocharger (see Chapter 4).
13   Remove the engine wiring harness.
14   Remove the fuel feed front pipe bracket retaining nut, then remove the fuel feed front pipe.
15   Loosen the hose clamp, then disconnect and remove the fuel injection fuel feed front hose.
16   Remove the glow plug controller (see Chapter 5).
17   Remove the fuel return pipe rear banjo bolt from the cylinder head.
18   Remove the fuel return pipe retaining bracket bolt and remove the bracket.
19   Remove the banjo bolt from the other end of the fuel return pipe and remove the return pipe.
20   When installing the fuel return pipe, ALWAYS use new copper gaskets, and be sure to tighten the banjo bolts to the torque listed in this Chapter's Specifications.
21   Installation is otherwise the reverse of removal. Refill the cooling system (see Chapter 1).
22   When you're done, prime the fuel system (see Chapter 1, Section 11), then start the engine. If the engine stalls, prime the fuel system again. Once the engine starts, inspect for fuel leaks.

LBZ

23   Disconnect the cables from the negative battery terminals (see Chapter 5). Drain the cooling system (see Chapter 1).
24   Remove the engine wiring harness. Remove the coolant outlet tube.
25   Remove the Exhaust Gas Recirculation (EGR) cooler tube (see Chapter 6).
26   Loosen the hose clamp and disconnect the fuel return lines hoses from the return line.
27   Remove the fuel return line clamp bolts.
28   Loosen the return line hose clamp at the fuel rail, then remove the fuel return line.
29   Installation is the reverse of removal. Refill the cooling system (see Chapter 1).
30   When you're done, prime the fuel system (see Chapter 1, Section 11), then start the engine. If the engine stalls, prime the fuel system again. Once the engine starts, inspect for fuel leaks.

LMM

31   Remove the intake manifold cover.
32   Drain the cooling system (see Chapter 1).
33   Remove the radiator inlet hose.
34   Loosen the hose clamp and disconnect the coolant inlet hose from the turbocharger bypass valve (see Chapter 4).
35   Unscrew and remove the turbocharger coolant bypass valve.

36   Remove the wiring harness bracket bolts at the thermostat housing and set the bracket and harness aside.
37   Disconnect the main engine harness electrical connectors.
Note: *Lift up on the latches to disconnect the connectors.*
38   Open the clip that secures the main engine harness.
39   Disconnect the electrical connector from the turbocharger vane position sensor (see Chapter 4).
40   Unclip and detach the main engine harness electrical connectors from the connector harness bracket.
41   Remove the bolts that secure the main electrical connector harness bracket, then remove the harness bracket and set the harness aside.
42   Detach the electrical connector for the manifold intake temperature sensor from the coolant tube bracket.
43   Remove the coolant outlet retaining bolts and remove the coolant outlet tube. Remove and discard the old tube O-ring seal.
44   Remove the intake manifold tube (see Chapter 7).
45   Remove the glow plug control module and mounting bracket (see Chapter 5).
46   Remove the fuel temperature sensor (see Chapter 6).
47   Loosen the hose clamp that secures the fuel hose to the return pipe and disconnect the fuel hose.
48   Loosen the hose clamp that secures the fuel return hose to the fuel return pipe.
49   Remove the fuel return pipe clip retaining bolt and remove the clip.
50   Remove the fuel return pipe clamp bolt and remove the bracket.
51   Loosen the fuel return hose clamp at the return pipe and disconnect the fuel return hose from the return pipe.
52   Remove the fuel return pipe clamp retaining bolt and remove the clamp.
53   Disconnect the fuel injection feed pipe from the fuel return pipe.
54   Note the routing of the fuel return pipe, then disconnect and remove it from the fuel return hose.
55   Installation is the reverse of removal. Refill the cooling system (see Chapter 1).
Note: *Be sure to use a new O-ring seal when installing the coolant tube.*

LML/LGH

56   Drain the cooling system (see Chapter 1).
57   Remove the turbocharger (see Chapter 4).
58   To disconnect the fuel return line, pull up on the cylindrical locking sleeve.
59   Disconnect the fuel return line from each fuel injector.
60   Remove the fuel return line assembly.
61   Installation is the reverse of removal.

L5P

62   Drain the cooling system (see Chapter 1).

Right-side return pipe

63   Remove the top front fuel injector insulator.
64   Disconnect the quick-connect fitting on the return line, then remove the return pipe retainer.
65   Remove the bolts and insulating washers securing the return line at the valve cover (obtain new washers for installation).
66   Remove the pipe by working it loose.
67   Installation is the reverse of removal. Refill the cooling system (see Chapter 1).

Left side return pipe

68   Remove the left-side sound reducing panels.
69   Remove the fuel return pipe clip bolt.
70   Remove the bolts and insulating washers securing the return line at the valve cover (obtain new washers for installation).
71   Disconnect the hose clamps to the fuel return hose.
72   Disconnect the fuel return hose.
73   Remove the line by working it out of the engine area.
74   Installation is the reverse of removal. Refill the cooling system (see Chapter 1).

14 Fuel cooler - removal and installation

Note: *The fuel cooler is simply a small heat exchanger (it looks like a small radiator) that helps cool fuel on its way back to the fuel tank. The high operating pressure of the fuel delivery system raises the temperature of the fuel. On LB7 and LLY models, fuel also absorbs heat as it passes through and cools off the Fuel Injection Control Module (FICM). Not all later models have a fuel cooler. If your vehicle is equipped with a fuel cooler, it will be located in the return line just ahead of the fuel tank.*

1   Remove the fuel filler neck cap to relieve fuel tank pressure.
2   Raise the vehicle and place it securely on jackstands.
3   Disconnect the fuel pipes from the fuel cooler.
Note: *If you're not yet familiar with quick-connect metal collar fittings, refer to Section 3.*
4   Remove the fuel cooler mounting bolts and remove the fuel cooler.
5   If you're replacing the cooler, remove the bracket from the old cooler and install it on the new unit.
6   Installation is the reverse of removal.

15 Fuel filter head/priming pump/fuel heater - removal and installationn

Refer to illustration 15.2

Warning: *Diesel fuel is flammable, so take extra precautions when you work on any part of the fuel system. See the Warning in Section 1.*
Note: *The fuel heater element is an integral component of the fuel filter housing (not the fuel filter itself).*
Note: *This procedure applies to 2016 and earlier truck models only.*
1   Drain the fuel from the fuel filter (see Chapter 1, Section 11). On models where it would interfere with access, remove the passenger's side intercooler tube.
2   Locate the electrical terminals on top of the fuel filter/fuel heater element housing for the heater's 12-volt power supply and ground **(see illustration)**, and the electrical lead on the underside of the fuel filter element for the water-in-fuel sensor. Trace the wiring harnesses for both electrical leads to their electrical connectors and disconnect them.
3   Loosen the hose clamps and disconnect the fuel hoses from the fuel filter/heater element housing **(see illustration 15.2)**.
4   Disconnect the electrical connectors and vacuum lines from the Exhaust Gas Recirculation (EGR) valve vent solenoid, the EGR valve vacuum sensor and the EGR valve solenoid (see Chapter 6).
5   Remove the fuel filter/heater element housing mounting bolts **(see illustration 15.2),** and remove the fuel filter/heater element housing and filter as a single assembly.
6   If you're planning to reuse the old filter with the new fuel filter/fuel heater element housing, unscrew and remove the fuel filter from the housing and install it on the new unit.

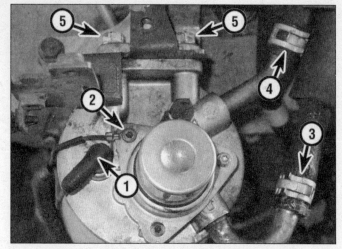

15.2 Fuel filter/fuel heater element housing details:

1   *12-volt power supply terminal*
2   *Ground terminal*
3   *Hose clamp for fuel inlet hose*
4   *Hose clamp for fuel outlet hose*
5   *Fuel filter/fuel heater element housing mounting bolts*

7   Installation is the reverse of removal. Be sure to tighten the fuel filter/fuel heater element housing mounting bolts to the torque listed in this Chapter's Specifications.

16 Fuel filter head/priming pump/fuel heater - overhaul

Warning: *Diesel fuel is flammable, so take extra precautions when you work on any part of the fuel system. See the Warning in Section 1.*
Note: *This procedure applies to 2016 and earlier truck models only.*
Note: *The fuel filter head/priming pump is also referred to as the Diesel Fuel Conditioning Module (DFCM). On 2016 and earlier truck models, it's located on the right side of the engine. On van models it's located under the vehicle, attached to the frame rail forward of the fuel tank. On van models the priming pump is electric; On truck models it's a manually operated pump.*
Note: *2017 and later model trucks use an in-tank transfer pump which is part of the fuel level sending unit, eliminating the need for a priming pump.*
1   Disconnect the cables from the negative battery terminals (see Chapter 5).
2   Drain the fuel filter (see Chapter 1, Section 11).

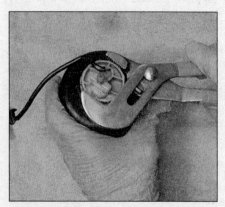

16.4 Unscrew the water-in-fuel sensor from the bottom of the filter

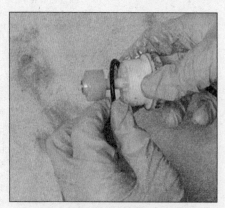

16.5 Remove the O-ring from the water-in-fuel sensor

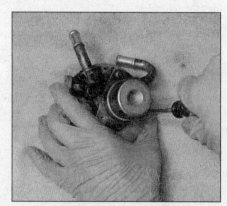

16.6a Remove the screws from the plunger housing . . . .

16.6b ... then remove the housing, plunger and spring

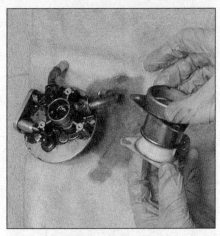

16.7a Remove the plunger cap retainer ...

16.7b ... then remove the cap from the pump head

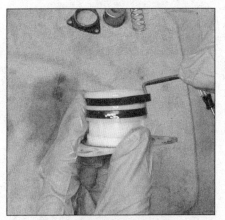

16.8a Remove the outer ...

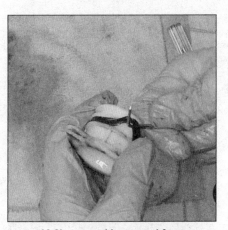

16.8b ... and inner seal from the pump head

16.9 Remove the O-ring from the filter head

3   Remove the fuel filter head/priming pump/fuel heater assembly (see Section 15).

4   Remove the filter from the filter head, then unscrew the water-in-fuel sensor **(see illustration)**.

5   Remove the O-ring from the water-in-fuel sensor **(see illustration)**.

6   Remove the screws and detach the pump assembly from the filter head **(see illustrations)**.

7   Separate the retainer and plunger cap from the pump head **(see illustrations)**.

8   Remove the seals from the pump head **(see illustrations)**.

9   Remove the O-ring from the filter head **(see illustration)**.

10   Remove the screws and detach the fuel heater from the filter head **(see illustrations)**.

16.10a Remove the two screws ...

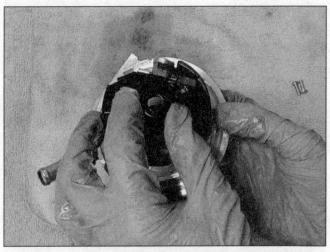

16.10b ... and separate the fuel heater from the filter head

16.11a Remove the check ball . . .

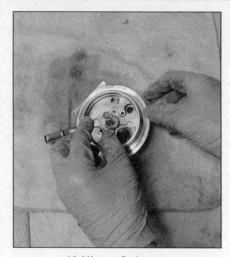

16.11b . . . O-ring . . .

16.11c . . . and spring

11   Remove the check ball, O-ring and spring **(see illustrations)**.
12   Remove the O-ring from the fuel heater **(see illustration)**.
13   Remove the bleeder screw from the filter head **(see illustrations)**.

14   Thoroughly clean the filter head, especially all of the orifices and O-ring seal areas **(see illustration)**.
15   Install a new O-ring to the fuel heater **(see illustration)**.

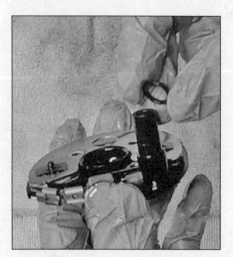

16.12 Remove the O-ring from the fuel heater

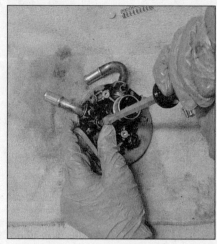

16.13a Remove the bleeder screw . . .

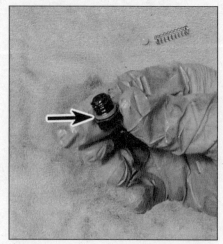

16.13b . . . then remove the O-ring

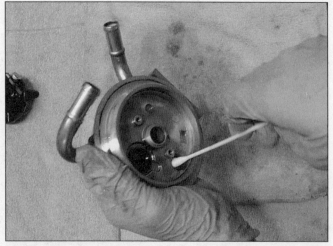

16.14 Clean the filter head with brake system cleaner. A cotton swab works well for cleaning recessed areas

16.15 Install a new O-ring on the fuel heater

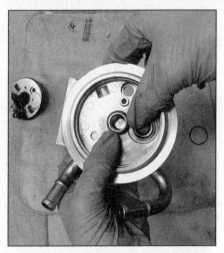

16.16 Install a new O-ring around the center boss of the filter head

16.17a Install the check ball spring . . .

16.17b . . . and the check ball

16   Install a new O-ring to the center of the filter head **(see illustration)**.
17   Install the check ball spring and check ball **(see illustrations)**.
18   Install the fuel heater, being careful not to disturb the check ball **(see illustrations)**.

19   Install the new lip seals to the pump head, making sure the lips of the seals face away from each other **(see illustrations)**.
20   Install the new O-ring to the top of the filter head **(see illustration)**.

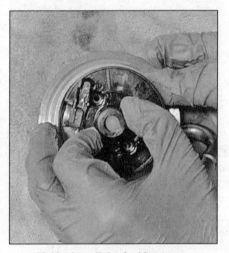

16.18a Install the fuel heater . . .

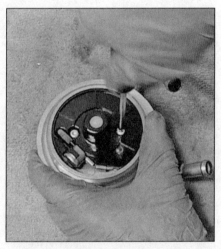

16.18b . . . and secure it with the screws, tightening them securely

16.19a Install the inner lip seal . . .

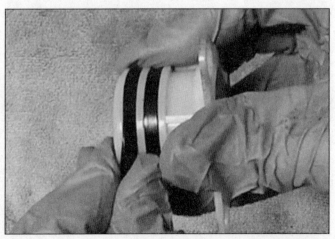

16.19b . . . and the outer lip seal. The lips of the seals must face away from each other

16.20 Install a new O-ring to the top of the filter head

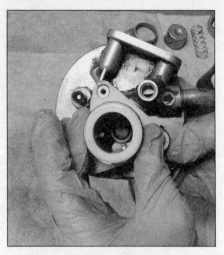

16.21a Place the pump head onto
the filter head

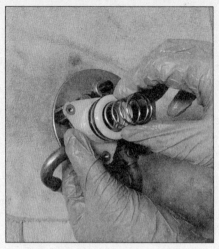

16.21b Install the plunger spring

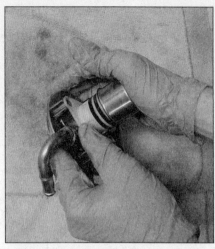

16.21c Lubricate the lip seals with clean
engine oil, then install the plunger cap

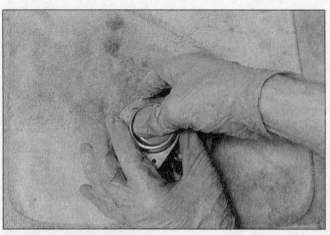

16.21d Install the plunger cap retainer, then depress the
plunger cap and install the retainer screws . . .

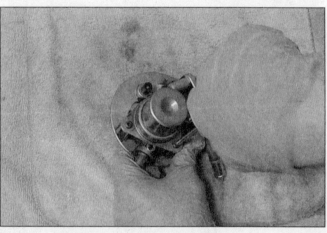

16.21e . . . tightening them securely. Note: *Don't install the screw
that secures the ground wire at this time*

21 Assemble the pump head, plunger cap and retainer to the filter head **(see illustrations)**.
Note: *Lubricate the lip seals with clean engine oil prior to installing the plunger cap.*
22 Install a new O-ring to the bleeder screw, then install the

bleeder screw to the filter head.
23 Test the priming pump by placing a thumb over the pump inlet and cycling the plunger. If it has been assembled correctly, a suction should develop at the inlet port **(see illustration)**.
24 Install new O-rings on the new filter and on the water-in-fuel

16.22a Install a new O-ring to the bleeder screw . . .

16.22b . . . then install the bleeder screw, tightening it securely
(but be careful not to overtighten it)

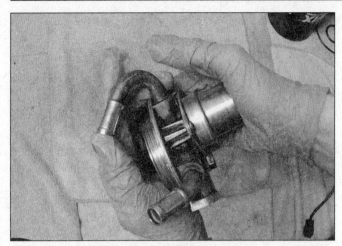

16.23 A suction should be created at the pump inlet port while operating the pump plunger

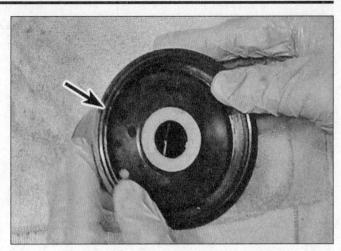

16.24a Install a new O-ring onto the new filter

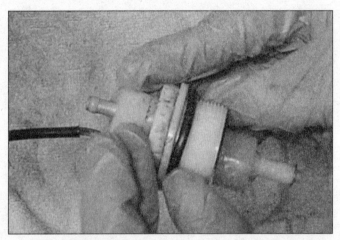

16.24b Install a new O-ring onto the water-in-fuel sensor

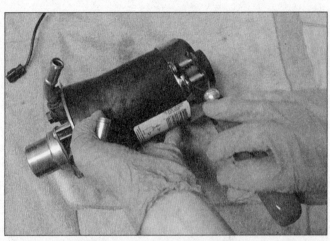

16.24c Install the new filter to the filter head, then tighten it snugly using an oil filter wrench

sensor. Install the fuel filter to the pump head, then install the sensor to the bottom of the filter (see illustrations).

25 Install the assembly by reversing the removal procedure, making sure to tighten the mounting fasteners to the torque listed in this

Chapter's Specifications.

26 Prime and bleed the system as described in Chapter 1, Section 11, Step 20.

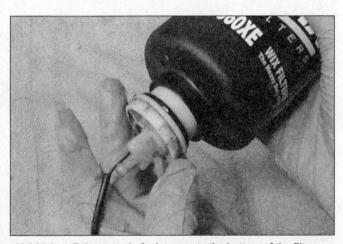

16.24d Install the water-in-fuel sensor to the bottom of the filter . . .

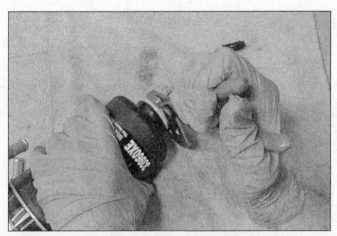

16.24e . . . and tighten it securely

Notes

Chapter 4
Turbocharger and charge air cooler

Contents

Specifications

General
Turbocharger
  Axial play .... 0.0043 inch (0.11 mm)
  Radial play .... 0.0079 inch (0.20 mm)

Torque specifications

Note: *One foot-pound (ft-lb) of torque is equivalent to 12 inch-pounds (in-lbs) of torque. Torque values below approximately 15 ft-lbs are expressed in inch-pounds, because most foot-pound torque wrenches are not accurate at these smaller values.*

	Ft-lbs (unless otherwise indicated)	Nm
Hood hinge bolts	18	25
Exhaust pipe clamp		
Lower clamp	30	40
Turbocharger outlet pipe bolts		
2010 and earlier models	132 in-lbs	15
2011 and later models	89 in-lbs	10
Transmission fill tube-to-bellhousing nuts	156 in-lbs	18
Exhaust heat shield bolts		
2006 and earlier models	71 in-lbs	8
2007 and later models	89 in-lbs	10
Exhaust manifold-to-turbocharger pipe bolts	39	53

Torque specifications (continued)

	Ft-lbs (unless otherwise indicated)	Nm

Note: One foot-pound (ft-lb) of torque is equivalent to 12 inch-pounds (in-lbs) of torque. Torque values below approximately 15 ft-lbs are expressed in inch-pounds, because most foot-pound torque wrenches are not accurate at these smaller values.

	Ft-lbs	Nm
Turbocharger pipe-to-turbocharger bolts		
All except LGH models	39	53
LGH models	18	25
Exhaust pipe-to-EGR cooler fasteners	18	25
Turbocharger heat shield bolts		
2006 and earlier models	80 in-lbs	9
2007 and later models	89 in-lbs	10
Turbocharger oil feed banjo bolt		
2010 and earlier models	25	34
2011 and later models	37	50
Turbocharger oil return pipe-to-turbocharger bolts		
2016 and later models	15	20
2017 and later models	84 in-lbs	10
Turbocharger oil return pipe-to-flywheel housing nuts	18	25
Turbocharger mounting bolts		
2010 and earlier models	80	108
2011 through 2016 models	58	78
2017 and later models	43	58
Turbocharger coolant outlet banjo bolt		
All except LGH models	19	26
LGH models	26	35
EGR valve cooler bolts		
2004 and earlier LB7 models	15	20
2004 LLY through 2006 models		
Front	37	50
Rear	15	20
2007 through 2010 models		
Front	37	50
Rear	39	53
2011 and later models	Not available	
EGR pipe-to-cooler nuts	18	25

1　General information

A turbocharger is a small turbine that forces compressed air into the combustion chambers, which creates more power. The power is produced by the additional amounts of fuel that can be combusted because of the additional compressed air. The turbocharger is made up of two separate housings: a turbine on one side and compressor wheel on the other side, connected by a shaft. The turbine is spun by the exhaust gas as it flows out of the engine and is directed over the turbine blades. As the turbine is spun, the compressor wheel is turned at the other end of the turbine shaft, which forces more air into the intake system.

On LB7 models, a wastegate is used to limit boost pressure. Once a predetermined amount of boost is achieved, the wastegate opens and bleeds exhaust out the turbocharger downpipe so excessive pressure is not created in the intake system.

LLY and later engines are not equipped with a wastegate. Instead, a variable-vane system is used inside the turbo, controlled by the Engine Control Module (ECM). By controlling the opening position of the vanes, the ECM can control the amount of boost pressure regardless of the actual engine speed and can also be used to create additional pressure and temperature during idle.

Before you get started, read through the procedures you're planning to perform, familiarize yourself with the steps and gather up all the parts and tools you'll need. If it looks like you might run into problems during a particular job, seek advice from a mechanic or an experienced do-it-yourselfer.

2　Turbocharger - removal and installation

Warning: *Wait until the engine is completely cool before beginning this procedure.*

Caution: *If your turbocharger has failed, clean any debris or excessive oil from the charge air cooler system before installing a new turbocharger. If the components are not cleaned, there is a good chance that the debris or excessive oil will cause severe damage to the engine and new turbo-*

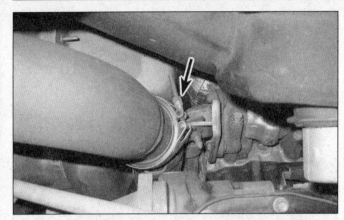

2.6 Loosen the exhaust pipe clamp and slide the clamp down

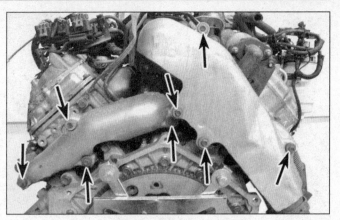

2.8 Heat shield fastener locations

charger upon startup. If the excess oil is not cleaned from the charge air cooler and ducts, it can cause the engine to accelerate uncontrollably or "runaway" when started, which will cause extreme engine damage.

Note: Although it is possible, this is a **very** difficult and time consuming job to perform with the engine in the vehicle. The exhaust fasteners are difficult to access and are very tight. Much of the procedure is done by feel, since you will not be able to see them. Many mechanics share the opinion that it is actually easier to remove the engine from the vehicle first, then remove the turbocharger.

Note: There are many 12-point, 12 mm-head bolts used on the turbocharger pipes.

Note: Apply penetrating oil to all turbocharger and exhaust fasteners before attempting to remove them.

Removal

2016 and earlier models

Refer to illustrations 2.6, 2.8, 2.9, 2.12, 2.18, 2.19, 2.24, 2.25, 2.26, 2.27, 2.28a, 2.28b, 2.28c and 2.28d

1   Disconnect the negative battery cables (see Chapter 5).

2   Open the hood and place rags or covers over the windshield and fenders to protect them during this procedure.

3   Have an assistant support the hood, then remove the hinge-to-hood bolt on each side. Once the bolts have been removed, raise the hood until the hinge and bolts can be installed in the next lower position on the hood which is the "service position," then tighten the bolts securely.

4   Loosen the front wheel lug nuts. Raise the front of the vehicle and support it securely on jackstands, remove the wheels, then remove the inner fender splash shields. Drain the cooling system (see Chapter 1).

5   If you're working on a 2007 through 2016 truck model, remove the transmission (see the Haynes manual for your particular vehicle for details).

6   Loosen the exhaust pipe clamp and slide the clamp down onto the exhaust pipe **(see illustration)**.

7   Remove the automatic transmission fill tube mounting nuts from the top of the bellhousing and maneuver it to the side of the vehicle.

Note: It is not necessary to remove the tube from the transmission.

8   Remove the left and right side exhaust shield fasteners and move the shields enough to access the turbo inlet pipe-to-exhaust manifold bolts **(see illustration)**.

Note: Do not try to remove the exhaust heat shield from the vehicle at this time, not all of the heat shield bolts can be removed until the turbocharger heat shield is removed (see Step 18).

9   Remove the turbocharger exhaust outlet lower retaining bolts **(see illustration)**.

10   Remove the left-side manifold-to-turbocharger pipe bolts and discard the gaskets.

Caution: During the removal of the exhaust system the exhaust can easily be damaged if the exhaust pipe(s) are bent at the expansion areas.

11   Lower the vehicle.

12   Remove the air intake resonator **(see illustration)**.

Warning: Once all the ducts to the turbocharger are removed, cover the openings with tape or rags to prevent anything from falling into the openings.

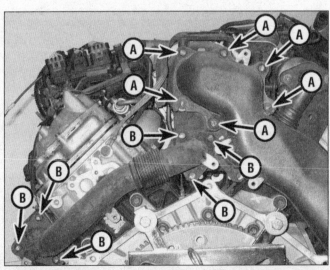

2.9 Turbocharger exhaust outlet fasteners (A) and left-side manifold-to-turbocharger pipe fasteners (B)

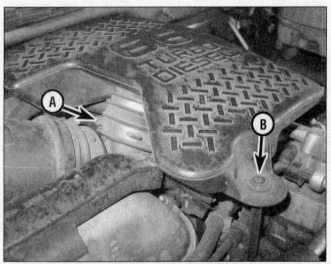

2.12 Loosen the hose clamp (A), then unscrew the bolt (B) and remove the resonator

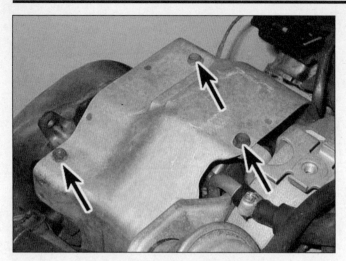

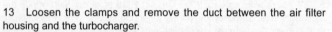

2.18 Turbocharger heat shield fasteners

2.19 Loosen the hose clamps and detach the turbocharger inlet and outlet coolant hoses

13   Loosen the clamps and remove the duct between the air filter housing and the turbocharger.
14   Loosen the charge air cooler inlet and outlet duct to intake hose clamps and remove the ducts.
15   Disconnect the air conditioning compressor clutch and cut-out switch electrical connectors.
16   Remove the drivebelt (see Chapter 1).
17   Remove the air conditioning compressor bolts and move the air conditioning compressor, with the hoses attached, to the right side of the engine compartment.
Warning: *Do not disconnect the refrigerant lines from the air conditioning compressor.*
18   Remove the turbocharger heat shield bolts **(see illustration)** and the heat shield.
19   Remove the turbocharger inlet and outlet coolant hoses **(see illustration)** from the turbocharger.
20   On LMM, LGH and LML models, remove the EGR cooler pipe, adapter brackets and hook brackets (see Chapter 6). Also, disconnect the electrical connectors for the vane position sensor and control solenoid.
21   Disconnect the Positive Crankcase Ventilation (PCV) hose from the left valve cover (see Chapter 6) and move the hose out of the way.
22   Remove the electrical connector from the intake heater and (if equipped), remove the intake air heater relay (see Chapter 6).

23   Remove the remaining exhaust heat shield bolts and heat shields.
24   Move the turbocharger exhaust outlet out of the way, remove the right-side manifold-to-turbocharger pipe bolts and discard the gaskets **(see illustration)**.
Note: *It is not necessary to completely remove the exhaust outlet to remove the turbocharger.*
25   Remove the turbocharger oil feed pipe bolt and washers **(see illustration)** and move the oil feed pipe out of the way.
Caution: *Do not twist or bend the turbocharger oil feed pipe or the internal plastic coating will be damaged and possibly cause the turbocharger to fail.*
26   Remove the turbocharger oil return pipe mounting nuts located at the flywheel housing **(see illustration)**.
27   Remove the turbocharger inlet elbow **(see illustration)**.
28   Remove the turbocharger bolts and remove the turbocharger **(see illustrations)**.
Caution: *If the turbocharger failed or you think it failed due to lack of oil, the No.4 camshaft bearing should be checked **(see illustration)**. Oil is supplied from the No.4 camshaft bearing through the oil supply pipe to the turbocharger. If this camshaft bearing has spun in its bore, the turbocharger will be starved for oil and fail. The camshaft bearing will have to be checked before a new turbocharger is installed or the new unit(s) will fail as well.*

2.24 Right-side manifold-to-turbocharger pipe fasteners

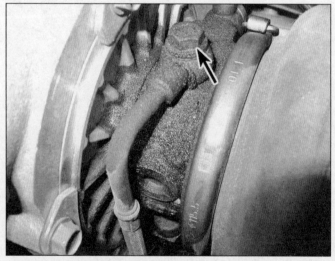

2.25 Remove the turbocharger oil feed pipe bolt and washers

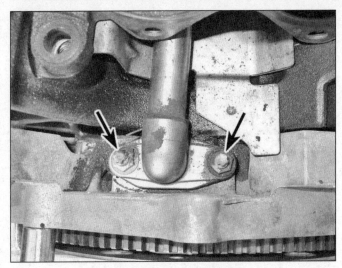

2.26 Oil return pipe nuts

2.27 Use a 1/4-inch drive swivel socket and extension to access the turbocharger inlet elbow bolts (one of three shown)

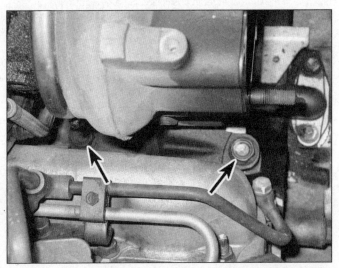

2.28a Left-side turbocharger mounting bolts

2.28b Right-side turbocharger mounting bolt

2.28c Make sure everything is disconnected and positioned out of the way, then carefully remove the turbocharger

2.28d Make sure the No. 4 camshaft bearing has not spun in its bore (the turbocharger bearing is supplied with oil from this point; if the bearing has spun, the new turbocharger will fail)

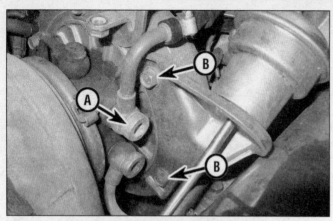

**3.4 Turbocharger upper coolant fitting bolt (A)
and wastegate actuator bolts (B)**

**3.5 Wastegate actuator rod retaining clip
(turbocharger removed for clarity)**

2017 and later models

29   Have the air conditioning system discharged by a licensed air conditioning technician.

30   Drain the cooling system (see Chapter 1).

31   Disconnect the cables from the negative battery terminals (see Chapter 5).

32   Remove the alternator.

33   Remove the air conditioning compressor. Cap the lines to prevent the entry of moisture and contamination.

34   Loosen the right-front wheel lug nuts. Raise the front of the vehicle and support it securely on jackstands, then remove the wheel and the inner fender splash shield.

35   Remove the charge air cooler (intercooler) outlet hose.

36   Remove the EGR recirculation pipe.

37   Move the air inlet adapter out of the way.

Note: *The turbocharger air inlet adapters contain a tamper-proof type band clamp which connects to the PCV hose. Do NOT destroy these clamps when repositioning the turbocharger air inlet adapter. When you're making repairs in that area, just reposition the turbocharger air inlet adapter and PCV hose out of the way without disturbing the clamps.*

38   Disconnect the hose clamp to the radiator inlet hose and remove the hose.

39   Remove the charge air cooler (intercooler) inlet hose.

40   Disconnect the turbo valve solenoid and sensor electrical connections.

41   Remove the coolant expansion tank inlet hose.

42   Remove the upper intake manifold.

43   Remove the oil feed pipe bolts from the turbocharger and position the feed pipe out of the way.

44   Remove the EGR manifold coolant return pipe.

45   Remove the transmission filler tube and seal.

46   Remove the exhaust temperature sensor from the turbocharger outlet.

47   Remove the turbocharger heat shields.

48   Remove the EGR cooler.

49   Remove the turbocharger coolant return pipe.

50   Remove the bolts and reposition the turbocharger coolant feed pipe out of the way.

51   Remove the bolts securing the oil return pipe to the engine.

52   Remove the exhaust bracket from the rear of the right cylinder head.

53   Loosen the band clamp at the turbocharger outlet.

54   Remove the turbocharger mounting bolts and maneuver the turbocharger from the engine compartment.

Installation

55   Carefully clean the mating surfaces of the turbocharger, exhaust manifolds and pipes.

Caution: *Check for any debris in the intake and exhaust systems. Even very small debris can destroy a turbocharger.*

56   Place the turbocharger in position, using a new gasket.

57   Apply anti-seize compound to the turbocharger bolts. Tighten the bolts to the torque listed in this Chapter's Specifications.

58   The remainder of the installation is the reverse of removal.

59   Change the engine oil and filter, and refill the cooling system (see Chapter 1).

60   Perform the turbocharger learn procedure (see Section 4).

---

3   Wastegate actuator (LB7 models) - replacement

Refer to illustrations 3.4 and 3.5

Warning: *Wait until the engine is completely cool before beginning this procedure.*

1   Remove the shield from the turbocharger **(see illustration 2.18)**.

2   Partially drain the cooling system (see Chapter 1).

3   Detach the hose from the actuator.

4   Remove the bolt from the turbocharger upper coolant fitting, and remove and discard the sealing washers **(see illustration)**.

5   Remove the clip that retains the wastegate actuator rod to the wastegate arm on the turbocharger **(see illustration)**.

Note: *If you have trouble accessing this clip, remove the EGR cooler (see Chapter 6).*

6   Remove the wastegate actuator mounting bolts and detach the actuator.

7   Installation is the reverse of the removal procedure. Be sure to use new sealing washers on the coolant fitting.

8   Refill the cooling system (see Chapter 1).

---

4   Turbocharger learn procedure

Note: *This procedure applies to all except LB7 models.*

Note: *This procedure requires a Tech II scan tool or equivalent. If you don't have access to this tool, have the procedure performed by a dealer service technician or other qualified repair shop.*

General information

1   The turbocharger automatically learns the vane positions every time the engine is started. The Engine Control Module (ECM) automatically performs the turbocharger learn procedure when the engine is started, the air conditioning is turned off, the engine is allowed to idle and the engine coolant reaches 104-degrees F (40-degrees C).

2   If the turbocharger vane position control solenoid valve, vane position sensor, the Engine Control Module (ECM) or turbocharger itself is removed or replaced, the turbocharger learn procedure must be performed.

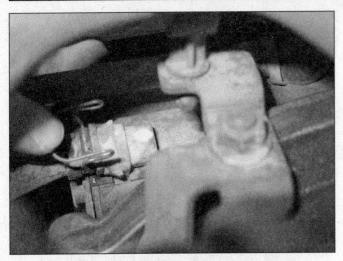

5.4 Disconnect the vane position control solenoid electrical connector from the solenoid

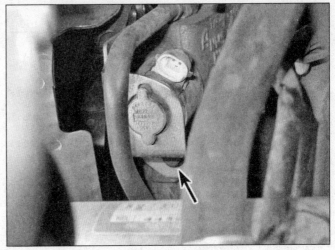

5.5 Remove the control solenoid retaining bracket bolt

3   The ECM will use the old learned values if not allowed to re-learn. If a new component has been installed, the ECM will use preprogrammed data. If either of these situations occur the "CHECK ENGINE" light will come on and the ECM will set trouble codes.

Procedure

4   Connect a TECH II scan tool or equivalent to the 16-pin Data Link connector located under the instrument panel.
Caution: *Once the four conditions have been met, the throttle must remain at idle. Do not touch the brake pedal during this procedure or the Accelerator Pedal Position (APP) sensor will give a false reading.*

  a) *Turn the air conditioning controls to the OFF position.*
  b) *Place the vehicle in Park or Neutral.*
  c) *Start and allow the engine to idle.*
  d) *Using the scan tool, verify that the engine coolant is more than 104-degrees F (40-degrees C).*

5   After the four conditions have been met and the engine idle is normal, follow the turbocharger learn output function from the scanner menu. Once in this menu you will have to select the vane position sensor to ON function for at least 5-seconds, then select the OFF function.
6   If the system has learned the new positions, the menu will display "turbocharger learned" or the menu box moved from No to Yes.

5   Vane position control solenoid (LLY, LBZ, LMM, LGH and LML models) - replacement

Refer to illustrations 5.4 and 5.5

Warning: *Wait until the engine is completely cool before beginning this procedure.*
Note: *The vane position control solenoid is located on the right side of the turbocharger.*
1   Remove the air intake resonator **(see illustration 2.12).**
2   Remove the EGR valve cooler (see Chapter 6).
3   Remove the turbocharger oil feed pipe, banjo bolt and washers (see Section 2), and move the pipe back without bending the pipe.
4   Disconnect the control solenoid electrical connector **(see illustration)**.
5   Remove the solenoid retaining bracket bolt and bracket **(see illustration)**.
6   Clean the area around the solenoid, then pull it out from the turbocharger.
7   Installation is the reverse of removal, making sure to tighten the mounting bracket bolt securely.
8   If a new vane position control solenoid is installed, the turbocharger learn procedure must be performed (see Section 4).

6.4 Remove the vane position sensor from the turbocharger

6   Vane position sensor (LLY, LBZ, LMM, LGH and LML models) - replacement

Refer to illustration 6.4

Note: *The vane position sensor is located on top of the turbocharger.*
1   Remove the air intake resonator **(see illustration 2.12).**
2   Follow the harness from the sensor to the electrical connector, then unplug the connector.
Note: *Before disconnecting the harness connector, make a note or take a picture of how the harness is routed.*
3   Detach the connector from its bracket.
4   Unscrew the vane position sensor from the turbocharger **(see illustration)**.
Note: *On later models, the heat shielding tape may have to be removed to access the sensor.*
5   Installation is the reverse of removal.
6   If a new vane position sensor is installed, the turbocharger learn procedure must be performed (see Section 3).

7   Charge air cooler - removal and installation

Refer to illustration 7.3

1   Detach the charge air cooler ducts from the charge air cooler (see Section 2).

2   Remove the radiator (see Chapter 2) and the left side support and bottom mounts.

3   Remove the charge air cooler-to-radiator support mounting bolts **(see illustration)**.

4   Lift the right side of the cooler up slightly first, and keep it an angle, then rotate the cooler and remove it from the engine compartment.

Caution: *Take care not to damage the cooler fins when removing the cooler for the engine compartment.*

5   If the charge air cooler is being reused, clean the cooler with mild soapy water and rinse it with a garden hose, taking care not to get any water inside of it.

Caution: *The charge air cooler is easily damaged; do not pressure wash or steam clean the cooler.*

6   Installation is the reverse of removal.

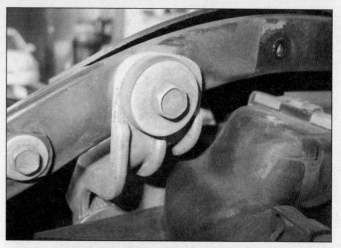

**7.3 Typical charge air cooler mounting bolt
(LLY model, left side shown)**

Chapter 5
Engine electrical systems

Contents

Specifications

General
Battery open-circuit voltage .... At least 12.6 volts
Cylinder numbering
    Bank 1 (right side) 1-3-5-7
    Bank 2 (left side) 2-4-6-8

Torque specifications

Ft-lbs (unless otherwise indicated)   **Nm**

Note: *One foot-pound (ft-lb) of torque is equivalent to 12 inch-pounds (in-lbs) of torque. Torque values below approximately 15 ft-lbs are expressed in inch-pounds, because most foot-pound torque wrenches are not accurate at these smaller values.*

	Ft-lbs	Nm
Alternator mounting bolts	37	50
Glow plugs	156 in-lbs	18
Glow plug buss bar nuts (LB7 engines with Federal emissions)	156 in-lbs	18
Glow plug nuts	18 in-lbs	2
Starter mounting bolts		
2006 and earlier models	58	78
2007 and later models	63	85

1 General information, precautions and battery disconnection

Glow plug system

The glow plugs are individual heaters screwed into each of the cylinders. When voltage is applied to the glow plugs, they heat up and aid in the starting of the engine. Diesel engines compress air in the cylinders, then fuel is sprayed and combustion occurs due to the heat that is generated during compression. The glow plugs are used to aid in this process, especially when the engine is cold.

The glow plug controller is a solid state unit that controls the amount of voltage to the glow plugs, the length of time voltage is applied and when the voltage is applied or the glow plugs are used.

Precautions

Always observe the following precautions when working on the electrical system:

a) *Be extremely careful when servicing engine electrical components. They are easily damaged if checked, connected or handled improperly.*
b) *Never leave the ignition switched on for long periods of time when the engine is not running.*
c) *Never disconnect the battery cables while the engine is running.*
d) *Maintain correct polarity when connecting battery cables from another vehicle during jump starting - see the "Booster battery (jump) starting" Section at the front of this manual.*
e) *Always disconnect the negative cables from the batteries before working on the electrical system, but read the following battery disconnection procedure first.*

It's also a good idea to review the safety-related information regarding the engine electrical systems located in the "Safety first!" Section at the front of this manual before beginning any operation included in this Chapter.

Battery disconnection

Warning: *On models with OnStar, make absolutely sure the ignition key is in the Off position and Retained Accessory Power (RAP) has been depleted before disconnecting the cables from the negative battery terminals. Also, never remove the OnStar fuse with the ignition key in any position other than Off. If these precautions are not taken, the OnStar system's back-up battery will be activated, and remain activated, until it goes dead. If this happens, the OnStar system will not function as it should in the event that the main vehicle battery power is cut off (as might happen during a collision).*

Note: *To disconnect the batteries for service procedures requiring power to be cut from the vehicle, first open the driver's door to disable Retained Accessory Power (RAP), then loosen the cable end bolts and disconnect the cables from the negative battery terminals. Isolate the cable ends to prevent them from coming into accidental contact with the battery terminals.*

The batteries are located in the engine compartment on all vehicles covered by this manual. To disconnect a battery for service procedures that require battery disconnection, simply disconnect the cable from each negative battery terminal. Make sure that you isolate the cables to prevent them from coming into contact with the battery negative terminals.

Some vehicle systems (radio, alarm system, power door locks, etc.) require battery power all the time, either to enable their operation or to maintain control unit memory (Powertrain Control Module, Transmission Control Module, etc.), which would be lost if the battery were to be disconnected. So before you disconnect the batteries, note the following points:

a) *Before connecting or disconnecting the cables from the negative terminals of the batteries, make sure that you turn the ignition key and the lighting switch to their OFF positions. Failure to do so could damage semiconductor components.*
b) *On a vehicle with power door locks, it is a wise precaution to remove the key from the ignition and to keep it with you, so that it does not get locked inside if the power door locks should engage accidentally when the batteries are reconnected!*
c) *After the batteries have been disconnected, then reconnected (or a new battery has been installed), the Transmission Control Module (TCM) will need some time to relearn its adaptive strategy. As a result, shifting might feel firmer than usual. This is a normal condition and will not adversely affect the operation or service life of the transmission. Eventually, the TCM will complete its adaptive learning process and the shift feel of the transmission will return to normal.*
d) *The engine management system's PCM has some learning capabilities that allow it to adapt or make corrections in response to minor variations in the fuel system in order to optimize drivability and idle characteristics. However, the PCM might lose some or all of this information when the batteries are disconnected. The PCM must go through a relearning process before it can regain its former drivability and performance characteristics. Until it relearns this lost data, you might notice a difference in drivability, idle and/ or shift feel.*

Memory savers

Devices known as "memory savers" (typically, small 9-volt batteries) can be used to avoid some of the above problems. A memory saver is usually plugged into the cigarette lighter, then you can disconnect the batteries from the electrical system. The memory saver will deliver sufficient current to maintain security alarm codes and maybe PCM memory. It will also run unswitched (always on) circuits such as the clock and radio memory, while isolating the vehicle batteries in the event that a short circuit occurs while the vehicle is being serviced.

Warning: *If you're going to work around any airbag system components, disconnect the batteries and do not use a memory saver. If you do, the airbag could accidentally deploy and cause personal injury.*

Caution: *Because memory savers deliver current to operate unswitched circuits when the batteries are disconnected, make sure that the circuit that you're going to service is actually open before working on it!*

2 Glow plug system - component check and replacement

Glow plug system normal operation check

2004 and earlier models with LB7 engine code

1   With the engine at room temperature or cold, turn the ignition key to the "ON" position with the engine OFF.

2   The glow plugs should turn ON and stay on between 1 and 16 seconds.

3   If the engine is cranked during or after Steps 1 and 2, the glow plugs may cycle ON and OFF after the key switch is returned from the crank position, whether the engine was started or not.

Note: *The initial glow plug "ON" time will vary based on the system voltage, engine internal temperature and outside temperature. Lower temperatures cause longer ON times which is controlled by the Engine Control Module (ECM).*

All other models

4   With the engine at room temperature or cold, turn the ignition key to the "ON" position and the engine OFF.

5   The glow plugs should turn ON and be fully heated up in two seconds, then they should pulse modulate for two more seconds.

Note: *During Pulse-Width Modulation (PWM), the Engine Control Module (ECM) is turning the power to the glow plugs on and off very fast with very little power loss.*

6   The glow plug wait lamp on the instrument panel should be illuminated for one full second on cold start.

Note: *The glow plug wait lamp may not illuminate during a warm engine start.*

7   If the engine is cranked during or after Steps 4, 5 and 6, the glow plugs may cycle ON and OFF after the key switch is returned from the crank position, whether the engine starts or not.

Note: *The initial glow plug "ON" time will vary based on the system voltage, engine internal temperature and outside temperature. Lower temperatures cause longer ON times which is controlled by the Engine Control Module (ECM).*

8   After a cold engine is started, the ECM will initiate the glow plugs again, once the key switch is returned from the "START" position from the "RUN" position to help clean up excessive white smoke and improve the engine idle quality after starting.

Glow plug system troubleshooting

9   Connect a scan tool to the diagnostic connector and retrieve any codes. See Chapter 6 for code details and definitions.

Glow plugs

Caution: *If at all possible, apply penetrating oil to the glow plug threads and let it sit overnight before attempting to remove them. Sometimes the glow plugs can break off in the head if the threads become corroded.*

Caution: *Whenever a glow plug is removed on 2017 and later models, it must be replaced with a new one. Do not reuse the glow plugs on these models.*

Note: *It's a good idea to replace all of the glow plugs at once even if only one fails.*

Removal

Refer to illustrations 2.15, 2.17a and 2.17b

10   Disconnect the cables from the negative terminals of the batteries (see Section 1).

11   To remove the passenger's side (BANK 1) glow plugs, loosen the wheel lug nuts for the right front wheel, raise the front of the vehicle and support it securely on jackstands. Remove the right front wheel and the right front wheelwell splash shield **(see illustration 8.3)**.

12   To remove the driver's side (BANK 2) glow plugs, loosen the wheel lug nuts for the left front wheel, raise the front of the vehicle and support it securely on jackstands. Remove the left front wheel and the left front wheelwell splash shield **(see illustration 8.3)**.

13   Remove the engine cover mounting bolt and lift the cover off the top of the engine.

14   On 2004 and earlier LB7 models where it would interfere, remove the air cleaner assembly and disconnect the inlet and outlet ducts (see Chapter 1).

15   Remove the glow plug electrical connector nuts **(see illustration)** and harness from the glow plug(s).

16   On 2004 and earlier LB7 models with Federal emission systems, remove the buss bar from the glow plugs.

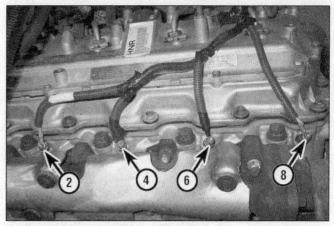

2.15 Glow plug electrical connector nuts, bank 2 (LB7 engine shown, other models similar)

17   Using a deep socket, loosen and remove the glow plugs from the cylinder head **(see illustrations)**.

Caution: *Inspect the glow plug once it is removed from the cylinder head. If the tip of the plug is burned off, chipped or missing, the cylinder head must be removed and cleaned.*

Installation

18   Install the glow plug(s) and tighten the glow plug(s) to the torque listed in this Chapter's Specifications.

19   On 2004 and earlier LB7 engine models, install the buss bar to the glow plug(s), if equipped.

20   Install the glow plug electrical nut(s) and tighten them to the torque listed in this Chapter's Specifications.

21   The remaining installation is the reverse of removal.

Glow plug learn procedure (E12-type glow plugs, 2017 and later models)

Note: *A learn procedure is required when E12-type glow plugs have been replaced. This procedure is accomplished with a scan tool. It will trigger the glow plug control module to learn the new values of the E12 glow plugs. Failure to perform this procedure may result in poor system performance and a Diagnostic Trouble Code (DTC) being set.*

Note: *The proper type of professional-grade scan tool capable of performing this procedure is generally not readily available to the DIYer. We recommend seeking out a professional repair facility to perform this task.*

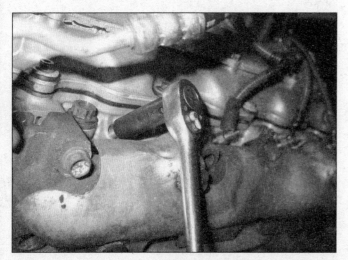

2.17a Use a deep socket and ratchet to loosen the glow plug . . .

2.17b . . . then remove the glow plug from the cylinder head

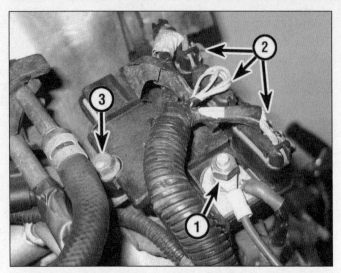

2.30a Glow plug controller - 2004 and earlier models with CA emission models and LB7 engine code

1   Battery supply cable   3   Mounting bolt
2   Electrical connectors

Glow plug controller

Note: *The glow plug controller is mounted on a bracket at the rear of the left cylinder bank.*

Removal

22   Disconnect the batteries (see Section 1).

2004 and earlier models with Federal emission (49 state vehicle) and LB7 engine code

23   Loosen and disconnect the outlet duct clamp and duct from the engine cover, then remove the engine cover and position the duct out of the way.

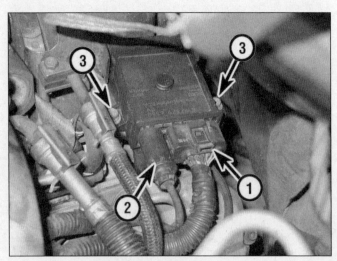

2.33 Glow plug controller details - 2004 models with LLY engine code and all 2005 through 2010 models

1   Electrical connector (squeeze the table to unlock the connector)
2   Battery supply cable (dislodge the ertainers with a small screwdriver)
3   Mounting bolts

2.30b To disconnect the electrical connectors, lift up the locking tabs and pull the connector from the controller

24   Use a flat bladed screwdriver to disengage the glow plug controller cover clips and remove the controller cover.
Note: *The glow plug controller is actually a relay on all Federal emission system and California emission system models.*
25   Mark the glow plug relay terminal wires then loosen and remove the wire mounting nuts **(see illustrations 2.30a and 2.30b)**. Lift the wires from the relay.
26   Remove the glow plug controller mounting nuts and remove the glow plug controller off of the studs.
27   Insert a small screwdriver between the controller housing and the top of the relay to disengage the relay to controller mounting clip then slide the relay off of the controller.
28   Using a small screwdriver, disengage the wiring harness clip from the relay and unplug the relay from the harness.

2004 and earlier models with CA emission models and LB7 engine code

Refer to illustrations 2.30a and 2.30b

29   Loosen and disconnect the outlet duct clamp and duct from the engine cover, then remove the engine cover and position the duct out of the way.
30   Using a small socket and ratchet, remove the battery supply cable nut, then remove the cable from the glow plug relay battery post **(see illustration)**.
31   Disconnect the glow plug electrical connectors from the glow plug relay.
32   Remove the glow plug relay mounting bolt and remove the glow plug relay from the bracket.

2004 models with LLY engine code and all 2005 through 2010 models

Refer to illustration 2.33

33   Disconnect the glow plug controller multi-wire electrical connector and place the harness out of the way **(see illustration)**.
34   Disconnect the single battery feed wire connector from the controller.
35   Remove the glow plug controller mounting screws and remove the glow plug control module from the bracket.

2011 through 2016 models

36   Disconnect the glow plug controller multi-wire electrical connector and place the harness out of the way.

37   Disconnect the single battery feed wire connector from the controller.
38   Remove the glow plug controller mounting nuts and remove the glow plug control module from the bracket.

2017 and later models

Note: *The glow plug control module is located at the front of the engine near the drivebelt tensioner.*

39   Remove the air filter assembly.
40   Disconnect the electrical connector from the glow plug control module.
41   Remove the fasteners securing the glow plug control module to the engine and remove the module.
42   Installation is the reverse of removal.

Installation

2004 and earlier models with Federal emission (49 state vehicle) and LB7 engine code

43   Connect the relay to the harness, then engage the relay onto the controller housing.
44   Place the assembly onto the studs and install the nuts then tighten them securely.
45   Snap the controller cover into place
46   The remaining installation is the reverse of removal.

2004 and earlier models with CA emission models and LB7 engine code

47   Place the glow plug relay onto the mounting bracket, then install the mounting bolt and tighten it securely.
48   Connect the electrical connector to the relay then place the battery supply cable onto the terminal. Install the cable mounting nut and tighten the nut securely.
49   The remaining installation is the reverse of removal.

2004 models with LLY engine code and all 2005 through 2010 models

50   Place the control module on the mounting bracket and install and tighten the mounting screws securely.
51   Connect the electrical connectors to the controller; the remaining installation is the reverse of removal.

2011 and later models

Note: *The glow plug control module will have to be programmed to the vehicle with the proper type of scan tool. The proper type of professional-grade scan tool capable of performing this procedure is generally not readily available to the DIYer. We recommend seeking out a professional repair facility to perform this task.*

52   Install the control module, tightening the mounting fasteners securely.
53   Connect the electrical connectors to the module.
54   The remainder of installation is the reverse of removal.
55   Have the glow plug controller programmed.

3   Charging system - general information and precautions

The charging system includes the alternator(s), an internal voltage regulator, a charge indicator, the batteries, a fusible link and the wire between all the components. The charging system supplies electrical power for the glow plug system, the lights, the radio, etc. The alternator(s) is driven by a drivebelt at the front of the engine.

The purpose of the voltage regulator is to limit the alternator's voltage to a preset value. This prevents power surges, circuit overloads, etc., during peak voltage output.

The fusible link is a short length of insulated wire integral with the engine compartment wiring harness. The link is four wire gauges smaller in diameter than the circuit it protects. Production fusible links and their identification flags are identified by the flag color.

The charging system doesn't ordinarily require periodic maintenance. However, the drivebelt, batteries, wires and connections should be inspected at the intervals outlined in Chapter 1.

The dashboard warning light should come on when the ignition key is turned to Start, then go off immediately. If it remains on, there's a malfunction in the charging system (see Section 4). Some vehicles are also equipped with a voltmeter. If the voltmeter indicates abnormally high or low voltage, check the charging system.

Be very careful when making electrical circuit connections to a vehicle equipped with an alternator and note the following:

a) *When reconnecting wires to the alternator from the battery, note the polarity.*
b) *Before using arc welding equipment on the vehicle, disconnect the wires from the alternator and the battery terminals.*
c) *Never start the engine with a battery charger connected.*
d) *Always disconnect all battery cables before using a battery charger.*
e) *The alternator is turned by an engine drivebelt, which could cause serious injury if your hands, hair or clothes become entangled in it with the engine running.*
f) *Since the alternator is connected directly to the batteries, it could arc or cause a fire if overloaded or shorted out.*
g) *Wrap a plastic bag over the alternator and secure it with rubber bands before steam cleaning the engine.*

4   Charging system - check

Refer to illustration 4.2

1   If a charging system malfunction occurs, don't immediately assume the alternator is causing the problem. First check the following items:

a) *Check the drivebelt tension and condition. Replace it if it's worn or deteriorated.*
b) *Make sure the alternator mounting and adjustment bolts are tight.*
c) *Inspect the alternator wiring harness and the connectors at the alternator and voltage regulator. They must be in good condition and tight.*
d) *Check the fusible link (if equipped) located between the starter solenoid and the alternator. If it's burned, determine the cause, repair the circuit and replace the link (the engine won't start and/or the accessories won't work if the fusible link blows). Sometimes a fusible link may look good, but still be bad. If in doubt, remove it and check for continuity.*
e) *Start the engine and check the alternator for abnormal noises (a shrieking or squealing sound indicates a bad bearing).*
f) *Check the specific gravity of the battery electrolyte. If it's low, charge the batteries (doesn't apply to maintenance free batteries).*
g) *Make sure the batteries are fully charged (one bad cell in a battery can cause overcharging by the alternator).*
h) *Disconnect the battery cables (negative first, then positive) from each battery. Inspect the battery terminals and the cable ends for corrosion. Clean them thoroughly if necessary. Reconnect the cables to the positive terminals.*
i) *With the key off, connect a test light between the negative battery post and the disconnected negative cable clamp.*
   1) *If the test light does not come on, reattach the clamp and proceed to the next step.*
   2) *If the test light comes on, there is a short (drain) in the electrical system of the vehicle. The short must be repaired before the charging system can be checked.*
   3) *Disconnect the alternator wiring harness.*
      (a) *If the light goes out, the alternator is bad.*
      (b) *If the light stays on, pull each fuse until the light goes out (this will tell you which component is shorted).*

4.2 To check the open-circuit voltage of the battery, connect the voltmeter leads to the terminals of the battery; if the battery is fully charged, the voltmeter should read at least 12.6 volts (depending on ambient temperature)

5.3 Disconnect the electrical connectors from the back of the alternator

Note: *On 2011 and later models, remove the upper half of the fan shroud (see Chapter 2).*

3   Disconnect the wires from the back side of the alternator **(see illustration)**.

4   Remove the mounting bolts and separate the alternator from the engine **(see illustration)**.

5   If you're replacing the alternator, take the old one with you when purchasing the replacement. Make sure the new/rebuilt unit looks identical to the old one. Look at the terminals - they should be the same in number, size and location as the terminals on the old alternator. Finally, look at the identification numbers stamped into the housing or printed on a tag attached to the housing. Make sure the numbers are the same on both alternators.

6   Some new/rebuilt alternators DO NOT have a pulley installed, so you may have to switch the pulley from the old unit to the new/rebuilt one. When buying an alternator, find out the shop's policy regarding pulleys - some shops will perform this service free of charge.

7   Installation is the reverse of removal.

5.4 Alternator mounting bolts

2   Using a voltmeter, check the battery voltage with the engine off. It should be at least 12.6-volts **(see illustration)**.

3   Start the engine and check the battery voltage again. It should now be approximately 14 to 15 volts.

4   Turn on the headlights. The voltage should drop, and then come back up, if the charging system is working properly.

5   If the voltage reading is more than specified, the voltage regulator is faulty. If the voltage is less, the alternator diodes, stator or rectifier may be bad or the voltage regulator may be malfunctioning.

5   Alternator(s) - removal and installation

Refer to illustrations 5.3 and 5.4

Note: *All years and models have an option for an auxiliary alternator which is checked, removed and installed in the same manner as the primary alternator.*

1   Disconnect the cables from the negative battery terminals (see Section 1).

2   Remove the drivebelt (see Chapter 1).

6   Starting system - general information and precautions

The solenoid/starter motor assembly is installed on the lower part of the engine, next to the transmission bellhousing.

The starting system consists of the batteries, the starter motor, the starter solenoid and the wires connecting them. The solenoid is mounted directly on the starter motor.

When the ignition key is turned to the Start position, the starter solenoid is actuated through the starter control circuit. The starter solenoid then connects the batteries to the starter. The batteries supply the electrical energy to the starter motor, which does the actual work of cranking the engine.

The starter motor can only be operated when the shift lever is in Park or Neutral.

Always observe the following precautions when working on the starting system:

a) *Excessive cranking of the starter motor can overheat it and cause serious damage. Never operate the starter motor for more than 15 seconds at a time without pausing to allow it to cool for at least two minutes.*

b) *The starter is connected directly to the batteries and could arc or cause a fire if mishandled, overloaded or shorted out.*

c) *Always detach the cables from the negative terminals of the batteries before working on the starting system.*

7 Starting system - check

Refer to illustrations 7.3 and 7.4

1   If a malfunction occurs in the starting circuit, do not immediately assume that the starter is causing the problem. First, check the following items:

  a) Make sure that the battery cable clamps are clean and tight where they connect to the batteries.

  b) Check the condition of the battery cables (see Section 4). Replace any defective battery cables.

  c) Test the condition of the batteries (see Section 4). If it does not pass all the tests, replace it.

  d) Check the starter solenoid wiring and connections. Refer to the wiring diagrams at the end of the manual, if necessary.

  e) Check the starter mounting bolts for tightness.

  f) Make sure that the shift lever is in PARK or NEUTRAL.

2   If the starter motor does not operate when the ignition switch is turned to the START position, check for battery voltage to the solenoid. Connect a test light or voltmeter to the starter solenoid switched terminal (the small wire) while an assistant turns the ignition switch to the START position. If voltage is not available, check the starting system circuit (see the wiring diagrams at the end of this manual). If voltage is available but the starter motor does not operate, remove the starter (see Section 8) and bench test it (see Step 4).

3   If the starter turns over slowly, check the starter cranking voltage and the current draw from the batteries. This test must be performed with the starter on the engine. Crank the engine over (for 10 seconds or less) and observe the battery voltage. It should not drop below 8.5 volts. Also, observe the current draw using an inductive type ammeter **(see illustration)**. It should not exceed 400 amps or drop below 250 amps.

Caution: *The battery cables might overheat because of the large amount of current being drawn from the batteries. Discontinue the testing until the starting system has cooled down.* If the starter motor cranking amp values are not within the correct range, replace it with a new unit. There are several conditions that may affect the starter cranking potential. The batteries must be in good condition and the battery cold-cranking rating must not be under-rated for the particular application. The battery terminals and cables must be clean and not corroded. Also, in cases of extreme cold temperatures, make sure the batteries and/or

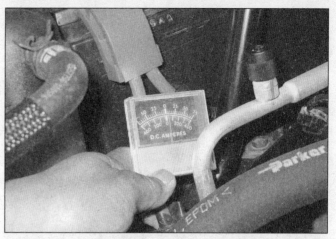

7.3 Use an inductive-type ammeter to measure the current draw. It can be placed directly on the positive or negative battery cable, whichever is easier to access (there's no reading on this ammeter because the engine is not being cranked) (typical)

engine block is warmed before performing the tests.

4   If the starter is receiving voltage but does not activate, remove and check the starter/solenoid assembly on the bench **(see illustration)**. Most likely the solenoid is defective. In some rare cases, the engine may be seized so be sure to try and rotate the crankshaft pulley (see Chapter 7) before proceeding. With the starter/solenoid assembly mounted in a vise on the bench, connect one jumper cable from the negative battery terminal to the body of the starter. Connect the other jumper cable from the positive battery terminal to the B+ terminal on the starter. Connect a starter switch and apply battery voltage to the solenoid S terminal (for 10 seconds or less) and see if the solenoid plunger, shift lever and overrunning clutch extends and rotates the pinion drive. If the pinion drive extends but does not rotate, the solenoid is operating but the starter motor is defective. If there is no movement but the solenoid clicks, the solenoid and/or the starter motor is defective. If the solenoid plunger extends and rotates the pinion drive, the starter/solenoid assembly is working properly.

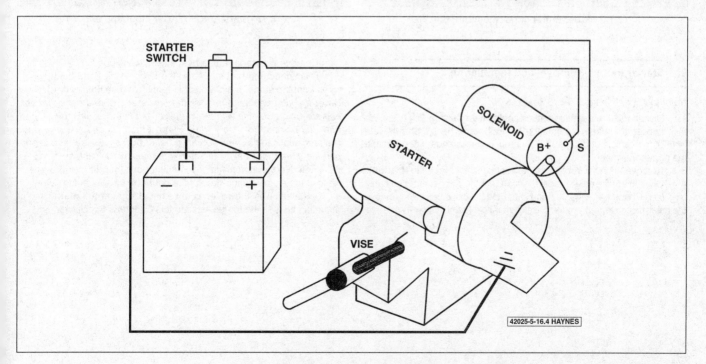

42025-5-16.4 HAYNES

7.4 Starter motor bench testing details

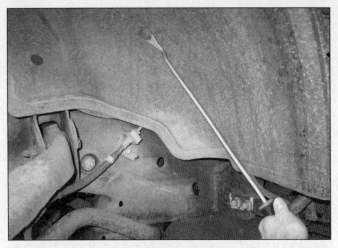

8.3 Remove the plastic fasteners, then remove the splash shield from the wheel well

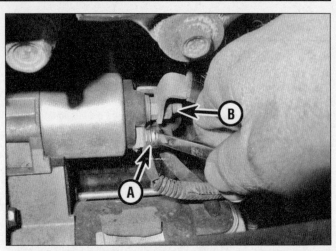

8.6 Remove the nut (A) and disconnect the cable from the starter solenoid terminal, then remove nut (B) and disconnect the battery cable from the starter

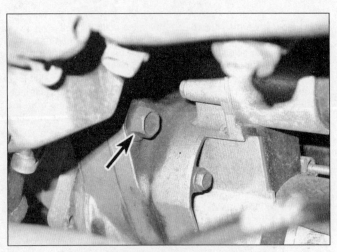

8.7a Starter motor upper mounting bolt

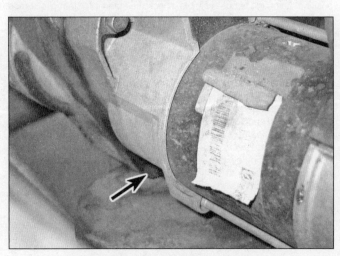

8.7b Starter motor lower mounting bolt

8   Starter motor - removal and installation

Refer to illustrations 8.3, 8.6, 8.7a and 8.7b

1   Disconnect the negative battery cables (see Section 1).
2   Loosen the wheel lug nuts for the right front wheel, then raise the front of the vehicle and support it securely on jackstands. Then remove the right front wheel.
3   Remove the right front wheel well splash shield **(see illustration)**.
4   On 2006 and earlier models, disconnect the turbocharger exhaust pipe (see Chapter 4). On 2007 and later models, disconnect and remove the catalytic converter from the exhaust manifold (see Chapter 6).

5   Remove the starter motor heat shield, if equipped.
6   Disconnect the battery cable (the larger cable) and the solenoid wires from the starter motor solenoid terminals **(see illustration)**.
Note: *If you're unable to remove the nuts that secure the starter cable and solenoid wire nuts with the starter bolted in place, skip this step for now and proceed to Step 7, then remove the nuts and disconnect the two electrical cables when you have better access. But be sure to support the starter; don't allow the starter to hang by the cables!*
7   Remove the starter motor mounting bolts **(see illustrations)** and remove the starter motor through the right wheelwell opening.
8   Installation is the reverse of removal. Tighten the starter motor mounting bolts to the torque listed in this Chapter's Specifications.

Chapter 6
Emissions and engine control systems

Contents

Specifications

Torque specifications

Note: *One foot-pound (ft-lb) of torque is equivalent to 12 inch-pounds (in-lbs) of torque. Torque values below approximately 15 ft-lbs are expressed in inch-pounds, since most foot-pound torque wrenches are not accurate at these smaller values.*

	Ft-lbs (unless otherwise indicated)	Nm
Camshaft Position (CMP) sensor mounting bolt		
2016 and earlier models	71 in-lbs	8
2017 and later models	89 in-lbs	10
Crankshaft Position (CKP) sensor mounting bolt		
2016 and earlier models	71 in-lbs	8
2017 and later models	89 in-lbs	10
Charge air temperature sensor		
Charge air outlet duct	168 in-lbs	19
Turbocharger	32	44
Engine Coolant Temperature (ECT) sensor		
2016 and earlier models	15	20
2017 and later models	24	33
Exhaust temperature sensors (LMM/LLGH/LML/L5P)	33	45
Intake Air Temperature (IAT) sensor		
Sensor 2 (LBZ and LMM)	18	24
L5P	14	19
Fuel temperature sensor	16	21
Fuel rail pressure sensor		
2016 and earlier models	52	70
2017 and later models		
Step 1	15	20
Step 2	Tighten an additional 15 degrees	
Oil level sensor		
2016 and earlier models	80 in-lbs	9
2017 and later models	89 in-lbs	10

Torque specifications (continued)

Ft-lbs (unless otherwise indicated)   **Nm**

Note: *One foot-pound (ft-lb) of torque is equivalent to 12 inch-pounds (in-lbs) of torque. Torque values below approximately 15 ft-lbs are expressed in inch-pounds, since most foot-pound torque wrenches are not accurate at these smaller values.*

	Ft-lbs	Nm
Exhaust Gas Recirculation (EGR) system (LB7)		
EGR assembly-to-EGR cooler tube bolts	15	20
EGR assembly-to-exhaust pipe nuts	15	20
EGR assembly-to-intake manifold nuts	168 in-lbs	19
EGR assembly-to-EGR bracket bolts	15	20
EGR valve solenoid mounting bolt	89 in-lbs	10
EGR valve throttle solenoid mounting bolt	89 in-lbs	10
EGR valve vacuum pump mounting bolts	16	21
Exhaust Gas Recirculation (EGR) system (LLY)		
EGR cooler tube bolts	37	50
EGR cooler tube rear bolts	15	20
EGR coolant pipe bolts	18	24
Air inlet tube nuts	18	24
Air inlet tube-to-intake manifold tube bolt and nut	89 in-lbs	10
Charged air cooler outlet duct-to-intake hose clamp	53 in-lbs	6
EGR valve/solenoid assembly mounting bolts	15	20
Exhaust Gas Recirculation (EGR) system (LBZ)		
EGR valve cooler tube front mounting bolts	37	50
EGR valve cooler tube rear mounting bolts	15	20
EGR coolant pipe bolts	18	24
Air inlet tube nuts	18	24
Air inlet tube-to-intake manifold tube bolt and nut	89 in-lbs	10
EGR valve/solenoid assembly mounting bolts	18	24
Exhaust Gas Recirculation (EGR) system (LMM)		
EGR valve-to-EGR valve cooler tube mounting bolts	15	20
EGR valve temperature sensors 1 and 2	32	43
EGR valve cooler tube bolts front mounting bolts	37	50
EGR valve cooler tube rear mounting bolts	18	24
Right exhaust pipe-to-EGR valve cooler tube mounting nuts	39	53
Exhaust Gas Recirculation (EGR) system (LML/LGH)		
EGR valve mounting bolts - tighten in following sequence		
1st: Four horizontally installed bolts	18	24
2nd: Two long vertically installed bolts	18	24
EGR bypass valve mounting bolts - tighten in following sequence		
1st: Two long vertically installed bolts	39	53
2nd: Exhaust manifold-to-EGR cooler bypass nuts and bolt	18	24
3rd: Two inner EGR cooler bypass valve mounting bolts	18	24
4th: Four outer EGR cooler bypass mounting bolts	18	24
EGR rear cooler		
EGR bracket bolts	18	24
EGR mounting bolts	39	53
EGR front cooler-to-rear cooler bolts	18	24
EGR bypass pipe center mounting bolt	89 in-lbs	10
EGR bypass pipe bolts	18	24
EGR front cooler		
EGR front cooler-to-rear cooler bolts	18	24
EGR front cooler mounting bolts		
Two longer, vertically installed, bolts at right end	18	24
Single longer, vertically installed bolt at left end	18	24
EGR valve mounting bolts (four horizontally installed bolts)	18	24
EGR valve temperature sensors	32	44
Exhaust Gas Recirculation EGR system (L5P)		
EGR cooler bolts	18	25
EGR valve mounting bolts		
Step 1	18	25
Step 2	Tighten an additional 60 degrees	
EGR valve nut	18	25
Exhaust pressure differential sensor pipe clamp nut	80 in lbs	9
Exhaust pressure differential sensor pipe nut	33	45

Torque specifications (continued)

	Ft-lbs (unless otherwise indicated)	Nm
Intake Air Heater (IAH)		
LB7	37	50
LBZ		
Air inlet tubes-to-IAH bolts and nuts	15	20
Air inlet tube-to-intake manifold tube bolt and nut	89 in-lbs	10
EGR motor-to-EGR valve mounting screws	18 in-lbs	2
EGR valve mounting bolts	18	24
LMM		
Air inlet tubes-to-IAH bolts and nuts (two bolts, two nuts)	15	20
Upper intake manifold brace bolts	18	24
LML/LGH		
Intake Air Heater (IAH) mounting bolt	89 in-lbs	10
Intake air valve/IAH mounting bolts	89 in-lbs	10
L5P		
Intake air heater bolts	89 in-lbs	10
Upper intake fasteners	18	25
Diesel Oxidation Catalyst (DOC)/exhaust pipe assembly		
Turbocharger-to-DOC/exhaust pipe clamp	106 in-lbs	12
DOC-to-particulate filter mounting flange nuts	33	45
Transmission support crossmember bolts	70	95
Transmission mount-to-transmission support nuts	30	40
Indirect fuel injector bracket bolt	80 in-lbs	9
Indirect fuel injector tube-to-exhaust pipe fitting nut	33	45
Throttle body mounting bolts (2011 and later models)	89 in-lbs	10
SCR/EPF housing/exhaust pipe		
Forward mounting flange nuts	33	45
EGT 1 and EGT 2 sensors	33	45
NOx 1 and NOx 2 sensors	33	45
Exhaust muffler-to-Exhaust Particulate Filter (EPF) mounting nuts	33	45
NOx sensors		
To exhaust	33	45
To firewall or frame	89 in-lbs	10

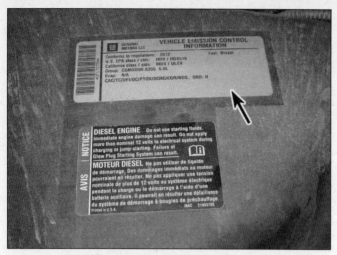

1.9 The Vehicle Emissions Control Information (VECI) label, located on the air filter housing, specifies what emission control systems are installed on the vehicle

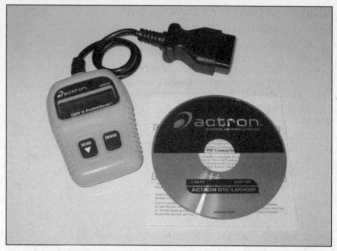

2.1a Simple code readers are an economical way to extract codes when the CHECK ENGINE light comes on

1   General information

Refer to illustration 1.9

1   The emission control systems and components are an integral part of the Duramax engine management system, which has Federal government-mandated diagnostic capabilities similar to On-Board Diagnostics II (OBD-II) systems employed on gasoline engines.

2   The engine management system is controlled by the Engine Control Module (ECM). The ECM uses a variety of *information sensors* to monitor all the important engine operating parameters (temperature, speed, load, etc.). The ECM also uses an array of *output actuators* (fuel injectors, EGR valve, various solenoids and relays, etc.) to alter these parameters as necessary to maintain optimal performance and fuel economy and to control emissions.

3   The principal emission control systems used on Duramax engines include:

•   Exhaust Gas Recirculation (EGR) system
•   Diesel Oxidation Catalyst (DOC) (LMM and later)
•   Diesel Particulate Filter (DPF) system (LMM and later)
•   Positive Crankcase Ventilation (PCV) system

4   Depending on the model year, the engine management system uses most or all of the following information sensors to monitor engine operating conditions and send this data to the ECM:

•   Accelerator Pedal Position (APP) sensor
•   Barometric pressure (BARO) sensor
•   Boost pressure sensor
•   Camshaft Position (CMP) sensor
•   Crankshaft Position (CKP) sensor
•   Engine Coolant Temperature (ECT) sensor(s)
•   Fuel Rail Pressure (FRP) sensor
•   Fuel temperature sensor
•   Intake Air Temperature (IAT) sensor(s)
•   Mass Air Flow (MAF) sensor
•   Oil level sensor
•   Vehicle Speed Sensor (VSS)

5   The sections in this Chapter include general descriptions and component replacement procedures for most of the information sensors and output actuators, as well as the important components that are part of the systems listed above. Refer to Chapter 3 for more information on the fuel system, to Chapter 4 for information on the turbocharger and charge air cooler (intercooler), or to Chapter 5 for information on the engine electrical system, including the glow plug system.

6   The procedures in this Chapter are practical, affordable and within the capabilities of the home mechanic. The diagnosis of most engine and emission control functions and drivability problems requires specialized tools, equipment and training. When servicing emission devices or systems becomes too difficult or requires special test equipment, consult a dealer service department or other qualified repair shop.

7   Although engine and emission control systems are quite sophisticated on Duramax engines, you can do most of the regular maintenance and even some servicing at home using common tune-up and hand tools and relatively inexpensive "generic" scan tools. Because of the Federally-mandated warranty that covers the emission control system, be sure to check with a dealer before trying to diagnose and/ or repair any emission-related system at home. After the warranty has expired, you might wish to tackle some of the component replacement procedures in this Chapter yourself to save money. Many emission and driveability problems are simply the result of a disconnected electrical connector or a broken wire. So always carefully inspect the electrical connections and the wiring harnesses first.

8   Pay close attention to any special precautions in this Chapter. Illustrations or photographs of various emission components or devices or systems might not exactly match those on the engine on which you're working because of production line changes made by the manufacturer or from one model year to another.

9   A Vehicle Emission Control Information (VECI) label **(see illustration)** is located in the engine compartment. The VECI label contains essential information like what emission control systems are installed on your vehicle.

2   On-Board Diagnostic (OBD) system and Diagnostic Trouble Codes (DTCs)

Scan tool information

Refer to illustrations 2.1a and 2.1b

1   Hand-held scanners **(see illustrations)** are necessary for analyzing the engine management systems used on late-model vehicles. Extracting the Diagnostic Trouble Codes (DTCs) from an engine management system is the first step in troubleshooting many computer-controlled systems and components, so even the most basic generic code readers are capable of accessing a computer's DTCs. More powerful scan tools can also perform many of the diagnostics once associated with expensive factory scan tools. If you're planning to purchase a scan

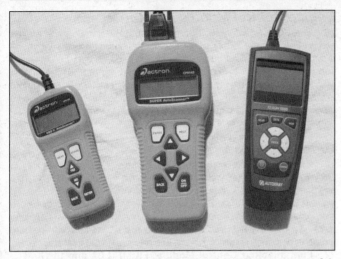

2.1b Scanners like these from Actron and AutoXray are powerful diagnostic aids - they can tell you just about anything that you want to know about your engine management system

tool for your vehicle, make sure that it's compatible with OBD-II systems. If you aren't planning on buying a scan tool and you don't have access to one, you can have the codes extracted by a dealer service department or by an independent repair shop (they will usually charge you for an hour of labor to do so).

OBD-II system general information

2   All engines covered by this manual are equipped with an OBD-II system, which consists of the Engine Control Module (ECM) and information sensors that monitor various functions of the engine and send a constant stream of data to the ECM during engine operation. Besides monitoring everything, storing DTCs and, when necessary, illuminating a Check Engine Light or Malfunction Indicator Light (MIL) when there's a problem, the ECM can also predict the probably imminent failure of systems and components when their output data starts to become suspicious.

3   Think of the ECM as the "brain" of the electronically controlled OBD-II system. It receives data from information sensors and switches monitoring various engine functions. The ECM processes this data and constantly alters engine operating conditions to optimize drivability, performance, emissions and fuel economy as necessary. It does so by controlling or by turning on and off various output actuators such as relays, solenoids, valves and other devices. The ECM is mounted in the left front corner of the engine compartment.

4   Virtually every fuel and emission control component in the OBD-II system is covered by a Federally-mandated extended warranty that is longer than the warranty coverage for the rest of the engine. You'll find the terms of this warranty in your owner's manual. It's not a good idea to try to repair anything in the engine management system while the emission controls are still protected by the extended warranty because if you damage the ECM, the sensors or the control devices or output actuators it might void the warranty. So as long as the extended warranty is still in effect, take the vehicle to a dealer service department if there's a problem.

Information sensors

5   **Accelerator Pedal Position (APP) sensor** - The APP sensor, which is an integral component of the accelerator pedal assembly, is part of the electronic throttle control system. None of the Duramax engines covered in this manual use a conventional accelerator cable. The APP sensor constantly monitors the angle of the accelerator pedal and sends this data to the ECM, which controls a couple of output actuators known as the Throttle Actuator Control (TAC) and (on LB7 and LLY engines) the Fuel Injection Control Module (FICM); on LBZ and later engines, the FICM is eliminated because the fuel injector driv-

ers formerly housed inside the FICM are instead located inside a new Bosch ECM that includes the injector drivers. The APP sensor actually consists of three identical sensors known as *potentiometers* (variable resistors), each of which has its own ground circuit, 5-volt reference circuit and a sensor signal circuit to the ECM that's proportional to the angle of the accelerator pedal. The ECM compares the signal outputs from all three sensors to assess the accuracy of the APP's signal.

6   **Barometric pressure (BARO) sensor** – The BARO sensor measures ambient air pressure. The ECM uses this measurement to calculate engine fuel and turbocharger requirements. It also uses it to determine altitude in order calculate the correct manifold pressure and air intake volume in relation to ambient pressure conditions.

7   **Boost pressure sensor** – The boost pressure sensor monitors the boost pressure of the turbocharger. It's located in the intake air stream, after the charge air cooler, so that it can measure the pressure inside the manifold produced by the turbocharger. The ECM compares the boost pressure to barometric pressure (outside, ambient pressure) to determine the difference so that it can calibrate for altitude. Intake pressure varies with respect to engine speed, load and the position of the turbocharger wastegate (LB7) or vane position (all others). The ECM uses boost sensor input as an engine load monitor so that it calculate fuel and timing requirements.

8   **Camshaft Position (CMP) sensor** - The CMP sensor is a device that produces a signal that the ECM uses to monitor the position of the camshaft. This data enables the CMP sensor to identify the number 1 cylinder so that it can time the firing sequence of the fuel injectors. The CMP sensor is located on the right side of the front engine cover, above the CKP sensor.

9   **Crankshaft Position (CKP) sensor** - The CKP sensor is a sensor which generates a signal to tell the ECM the sped and position of the crankshaft. The ECM uses data from the CKP sensor and from the CMP sensor to synchronize fuel injector firing. It also enables the ECM to calculate engine rpm, the rotational position of the crankshaft and variations in crank rotation speed, which the ECM interprets as misfire events. The crankshaft *reluctor*, or trigger wheel, is a toothed disc with 60 teeth and three missing teeth that provide a reference point. When the three-tooth gap passes by the CKP sensor, signal voltage is low; when any of the 60 teeth are passing the CKP sensor, signal voltage is high. If the CKP sensor fails, the engine won't start.

10   **Engine Coolant Temperature (ECT) sensor** - The ECT sensor is a *thermistor* (temperature-sensitive variable resistor) that sends a voltage signal to the ECM, which uses this data to determine the temperature of the engine coolant. The ECT sensor tells the ECM when the engine is sufficiently warmed up to go into closed loop, helps the ECM control the air/fuel mixture ratio and ignition timing, and also helps the ECM determine when to turn the Exhaust Gas Recirculation (EGR) system on and off. The ECT sensor is located in the thermostat housing, next to the two thermostats.

11   **Exhaust pressure differential sensor (LMM/LML/LGH)** - The exhaust pressure differential sensor measures the difference in pressure between the inlet and outlet of the Diesel Particulate Filter (DPF), which is located in the exhaust pipe just ahead of the catalyst. (You'll find the two pressure lines near the exhaust temperature sensors, fore and aft of the DPF.) When the difference in pressure exceeds a programmed threshold, the ECM determines that the filter is clogged or restricted (GM calls it "high particulate loading"). The ECM responds by initiating a "regeneration event" (like a self-cleaning oven turning up the heat to burn off deposits), as soon as the engine operating conditions are okay to do so. The exhaust pressure differential sensor works like a Manifold Absolute Pressure (MAP) sensor: It has a five-volt reference circuit, a sensor ground circuit and a sensor signal return circuit. Its signal voltage changes in relation to the difference in pressure between the two sensor ports.

12   **Exhaust Gas Temperature (EGT) sensors (LMM/LML/LGH)** - The EGT sensors monitor changes in temperature inside the DPF during regeneration, which must occur within a prescribed temperature range: if the DPF is too cool, regeneration will be inefficient or won't occur at all; if the DPF gets too hot (over 1472 degrees F, it will be damaged. If the ECM senses that the DPF is overheating during regeneration it cancels the regeneration process.

13   **Fuel level sensor** – The fuel level sensor is located at the lower end of the fuel level sending unit, which is located inside the fuel tank (you have to remove the fuel tank and then the fuel level sending unit to replace this sensor). The fuel level sensor is a variable resistor that changes its resistance in response to the fuel level. On LB7 engines, the fuel level sensor's resistance is between 40 ohms (empty) and 250 ohms (full). If the sensor "sticks," i.e. there is no variation over a period of time during normal operation, the ECM assumes a stuck sensor and sets a DTC for a stuck sensor; if the sensor or sensor circuit are open, the ECM commands the fuel gauge to indicate that the fuel level is full. On LLY and later engines, the resistance values are reversed, i.e. 40 ohms when full, 250 ohms when empty. This was done so that the fuel gauge reads low – instead of full - when a fuel level related DTC occurs.

14   **Fuel rail pressure sensor** - The fuel rail pressure sensor is screwed into the fuel junction block (LB7), the center of the right fuel rail (LLY), the back end of the right fuel rail (LBZ and LMM) or the back end of the left fuel rail (LML/LGH). The operating fuel pressure for Dura-max engines ranges from 23,000 psi (LB7 and LLY), to 26,000 psi (LBZ and LMM), to 30,000 psi (LML/LGH). Fuel rail pressure varies in accor-dance with changes in engine load and speed. The FRP sensor con-verts these changes to a linear voltage signal that it sends to the ECM, which adjusts the Fuel Rail Pressure Regulator (FRPR) as necessary in accordance with this signal, so the FRP sensor is a critical sensor for the ECM to verify that the FRPR is maintaining the correct fuel pressure.

15   **Fuel temperature sensor** – The ECM uses the fuel tempera-ture sensor, which is located on the fuel return line to the fuel tank, to measure the temperature of the fuel. Fuel temperature has little effect on engine management within a broad temperature range. But in cold weather the fuel can cool down and thicken, which affects its flow through the injectors. The ECM responds by fine-tuning fuel delivery. The fuel temperature sensor works the same way as an ECT sensor: it's a *thermistor* (temperature-sensitive variable resistor) that sends a voltage signal to the ECM.

16   **Intake Air Temperature sensor 2 (IAT2) (LBZ and LMM)** - The IAT2 sensor is located on the right side of the intake manifold. The ECM uses the IAT2 sensor to measure the temperature of air entering the cylinders. The IAT2 sensor helps the ECM to fine-tune fuel adjustment and reduce emissions. (The IAT2 sensor is used in conjunction with the newer style intake air heater introduced on LBZ engines – see *Output actuators*).

17   **Mass Air Flow/Intake Air Temperature (MAF/IAT) sensor** - The MAF sensor uses a hot wire sensing element to enable the ECM to measure the amount of intake air drawn into the engine. The wire is constantly maintained at a specified temperature above the ambi-ent temperature of the incoming air by electrical current. As intake air passes through the MAF sensor and over the hot wire, it cools the wire, and the control system immediately corrects the temperature back to its constant value. The current required to maintain the constant value is used by the ECM to determine the volume of air flowing through the MAF sensor. The MAF sensor also includes an integral **Intake Air Temperature (IAT) sensor**. Like the ECT sensor, the IAT sensor is a thermistor that monitors air temperature instead of coolant temperature. These two components cannot be serviced separately; if either sensor is defective, replace the MAF sensor. The MAF/IAT sensor is located between the air filter housing and the air intake duct that goes to the turbocharger.

18   **Oil level sensor** – The oil level sensor tells the ECM if the oil level is correct, or low. If it's low, the ECM illuminates the "**Check Eng Oil Level**" light in the instrument cluster. The oil level sensor is hard-wired into the instrument cluster, so if the engine oil level is getting to be a little low, the ECM will illuminate the Check Eng Oil Level light for about 60 seconds each time that you start the engine, to remind you to check the engine oil level. The oil level sensor is located on the left side of the oil pan.

19   **Vehicle Speed Sensor (VSS)** – The VSS, which is located on the transmission, tells the ECM the vehicle speed. The VSS is a *permanent magnet generator* that produces an alternating current (AC) voltage as long as the vehicle speed is over 3 mph. Its AC voltage output and num-ber of pulses increase with vehicle speed.

Engine Control Module (ECM)

20   The ECM, which is located at the left front corner of the engine compartment, is the "brain" of the engine management system. It moni-tors data input from all information sensors, processes this informa-tion by comparing it to the operational map (program) for the engine management system, then sends command decisions to the output actuators that execute those commands. These decisions are made so quickly (in milliseconds) that the entire process is virtually undetectable. As a result, drivability is smooth and seamless.

Output actuators

21   **Exhaust Gas Recirculation (EGR) valve** – LB7 engines sold in California (and in other states using California air emissions laws) are equipped with an EGR system. All LLY and later engines are equipped with an EGR system. The EGR systems used on Duramax engines are more complex than EGRs on gasoline engines, because diesel engines have no intake manifold vacuum (and because all Duramax engines are turbocharged, they usually have *positive pressure* in the intake system).

22   **Fuel Injection Control Module (FICM) (LB7 and LLY)** - The FICM houses *drivers* that operate the fuel injector solenoids. On LB7 engines, capacitors inside the FICM are charged by capturing the con-tinuous succession of voltage spikes generated by the collapse of the solenoids inside the injectors as they're turned off by the ECM at the end of each injection event. The ECM uses this current stored in the capacitors to operate the drivers that turn the injector solenoids on and off. Because the injector solenoids must open the injector nozzles against very high operating fuel pressures, it takes a lot of current, and very high voltage (93 volts), for the drivers to open and close the injec-tors, so the drivers generate a lot of heat. The FICM sheds this heat by running fuel through it as "coolant."

   Another important difference between LB7 and LLY engines is that the large capacitors the FICM uses to store injector voltage spikes on LB7 engines are replaced by *oscillators* on FICM units for LLY engines. An oscillator is an electronic circuit that produces a repetitive oscillat-ing electronic signal. Oscillators help the FICM on LLY engines control rapid cycling during the "hold" portion of each injector event (the period during which the injector nozzle must be held open), and they help build voltage to "fire" the next injector.

Note: *There is no FICM on LBZ and later engines. On these engines, the FICM was eliminated because the new Bosch ECM includes the high-current drivers for fuel injector control.*

23   **Fuel injectors** - The ECM-controlled fuel injectors spray a fine mist of fuel into the combustion chambers, where it mixes with incoming air. The injectors use solenoids (LB7, LLY, LBZ and LMM), or *piezo* crystal elements (LML/LGH), to open and close the injector nozzles in order to administer precise amounts of pressurized fuel, in firing order, to the cylinders. For more information about the injectors, see Chapter 4.

24   **Fuel Rail Pressure Regulator (FRPR)** – The FRPR is an ECM-controlled valve located on the upper rear part of the fuel injection pump. There are actually two pumps inside the fuel injection pump: the low-pressure supply pump and the high-pressure pump. The FRPR is installed between the outlet side of the low-pressure pump and the inlet-side of the high-pressure pump. Technically, "Fuel Rail *Pressure* Regulator" is a bit of a misnomer because the FRPR doesn't directly control fuel pressure; it controls the *volume* of fuel that is available to the high-pressure pump. The ECM controls an electromagnet inside the FRPR, which opens and closes an armature that controls the volume of fuel that can flow into the high-pressure pump.

25   **Glow plugs** – The glow plugs are 12-volt, high-current devices used to start a cold diesel engine; a glow plug is screwed into the cyl-inder head for each cylinder. When the engine has cooled off enough that it can't restart using heat and pressure alone, either because the outside air temperature is too cold and/or because the engine itself is simply too cold, the ECM turns on the glow plugs to get the engine started. The glow plugs are energized by the ECM when the ignition key is turned to ON or when cranking over the engine to start it. The ECM might continue to keep the glow plugs on for some time after the engine starts to speed up the phase during which the combustion chambers

are still coming up to temperature, which reduces the white smoke and poor idle that characterize a cold diesel engine. For more information about the glow plugs, see Chapter 5.

26 **Intake Air Heater (IAH)** – The IAH heats incoming air during cold ambient conditions, and during warm-ups and after long decelerations, to reduce white smoke. If your engine emits white smoke during a cold start, the IAH is the first thing to check. On LB7 engines, the IAH is a heater coil; on LBZ and later models, it's a heater grid, with much more surface area. LLY engines are not equipped with an IAH.

Obtaining and clearing Diagnostic Trouble Codes (DTCs)

27 All models covered by this manual are equipped with on-board diagnostics. When the ECM recognizes a malfunction in a monitored emission control system, component or circuit, it turns on the Malfunction Indicator Light (MIL) on the dash. The ECM will continue to display the MIL until the problem is fixed and the Diagnostic Trouble Code (DTC) is cleared from the ECM's memory. You'll need a scan tool to access any DTCs stored in the ECM.

28 Before outputting any DTCs stored in the ECM, thoroughly inspect ALL electrical connectors and hoses. Make sure that all electrical connections are tight, clean and free of corrosion. Make sure that all hoses are correctly connected, fit tightly and are in good condition (no cracks or tears).

Accessing the DTCs

Refer to illustration 2.29

29 On these models, all of which are equipped with On-Board Diagnostic II (OBD-II) systems, the Diagnostic Trouble Codes (DTCs) can only be accessed with a code reader or a scan tool **(see illustrations 2.1a and 2.1b)**. Simply plug the connector of the tool into the Data Link Connector (DLC) or diagnostic connector **(see illustration)**, which is located under the lower edge of the dash, just to the right of the steering column. Then follow the instructions included with the scan tool to extract the DTCs.

30 Once you have outputted all of the stored DTCs, look them up on the accompanying DTC chart.

31 After troubleshooting the source of each DTC, make any necessary repairs or replace the defective component(s).

2.29 The 16-pin Data Link Connector (DLC), also referred to as the diagnostic connector, is located under the left part of the dash

Clearing the DTCs

32 Clear the DTCs with the scan tool in accordance with the instructions provided by the scan tool's manufacturer.

Diagnostic Trouble Codes

33 The accompanying tables are a list of the Diagnostic Trouble Codes (DTCs) that can be accessed by a do-it-yourselfer working at home (there are many, many more DTCs available to dealerships with proprietary scan tools and software, but those codes cannot be accessed by a generic scan tool). If, after you have checked and repaired the electrical connectors, electrical wiring and vacuum hoses (if applicable) for an emission-related system, component or circuit, the problem persists, have the vehicle checked by a dealer service department or other qualified repair shop.

OBD-II Diagnostic Trouble Codes (DTCs)

Code	Probable cause
P0016	ECM detects Crankshaft Position (CKP) sensor and Camshaft Position (CMP) sensor signals not synchronized (more than 6 degrees difference of crank angle or more than 12 degrees difference of cam angle)
P003A	Turbocharger boost control position not learned (ECM doesn't detect valid learn in 45 seconds (up to 2006) or 30 seconds (2007 on)
P0045	ECM detects circuit failure in turbocharger vane control solenoid valve
P0046	ECM detects that commanded position of turbocharger vanes does not match actual position

OBD-II Diagnostic Trouble Codes (DTCs) (continued)

Code	Probable cause
P0047	Turbocharger boost control solenoid control circuit low voltage (commanded and actual driver states don't match for 4+ seconds)
P0048	Turbocharger boost control solenoid control circuit high voltage (commanded and actual driver states don't match for 4+ seconds)
P006E	Turbocharger boost control solenoid high control circuit low voltage (commanded and actual drives don't match for over 3 seconds)
P006F	Turbocharger boost control solenoid high control circuit high voltage
P007C	Charge air cooler temperature sensor circuit signal voltage less than 0.03 V (charge air warmer than 482 degrees F for 5+ seconds)
P007D	Charge air cooler temperature sensor circuit signal voltage more than 5.8 V (charge air colder than -63 degrees F for 5+ seconds)
P0087	Fuel rail pressure sensor indicates pressure lower than commanded fuel rail pressure (1595 psi or more below expected pressure)
P0088	Fuel rail pressure sensor indicates pressure higher than commanded fuel rail pressure (2900 psi or more above expected pressure)
P0089	Fuel rail pressure sensor indicates pressure more than 20 MPa greater than expected
P008F	Engine Coolant Temperature (ECT) sensor fuel temperature not plausible (ECM determines that absolute temperature difference between ECT sensor and fuel temperature sensor is more than 180 degrees F when cranking engine)
P0090	Fuel pressure regulator control circuit current outside expected range
P0091	Fuel pressure regulator solenoid 1 control circuit low voltage (for more than 1 second)
P0092	Fuel pressure regulator solenoid 1 control circuit high voltage (for more than 1 second)
P0097	Intake Air Temperature (IAT) sensor 2 circuit low voltage (equal to or less than 0.03 V on IAT sensor 2 signal circuit)
P0098	Intake Air Temperature (IAT) sensor 2 circuit high voltage (equal to or greater than 4.8 V on IAT sensor 2 signal circuit)
P009E	Fuel rail pressure relief valve performance (stored fuel pressure deviation values above calibrated limits)
P00C9	Fuel pressure regulator 1 high control circuit low voltage (for more than 1 second)
P00CA	Fuel pressure regulator 1 high control circuit high voltage (for more than 1 second)
P0101	Mass Air Flow (MAF) sensor voltage signal not within predetermined range of calculated MAF value
P0102	ECM detects that actual Mass Air Flow (MAF) sensor circuit voltage is lower than range of a normally operating sensor
P0103	ECM detects that actual Mass Air Flow (MAF) sensor circuit voltage is higher than range of a normally operating sensor
P0106	Manifold Absolute Pressure (MAP) sensor performance (BARO and MAP sensors disagree by more than 14 kPa, with ignition on, for more than 10 seconds)

Code	Probable cause
P0107	Manifold Absolute Pressure (MAP) sensor circuit low voltage
P0108	Manifold Absolute Pressure (MAP) sensor circuit high voltage
P0112	ECM detects excessively low Intake Air Temperature (IAT) sensor signal voltage (indicating high temperature)
P0113	ECM detects excessively high Intake Air Temperature (IAT) sensor signal voltage (indicating low temperature)
P0116	Engine Coolant Temperature (ECT) sensor performance (temperature difference outside calculated range)
P0117	Engine Coolant Temperature (ECT) sensor circuit, excessively low signal voltage (high temperature indication)
P0118	Engine Coolant Temperature (ECT) sensor circuit, excessively high signal voltage (low temperature indication)
P011A	Engine Coolant Temperature (ECT) sensor 1-2 correlation (ECM detects temperature difference between ECT sensor 1 and ECT sensor 2 of more than 41 degrees F.)
P0128	Engine coolant temperature fails to reach preset target temperature before calculated amount of fuel is burned
P0137	HO2S circuit low voltage sensor 2 (NOx sensor module tells ECM that HO2S signal is outside normal limit for 3+ seconds)
P0138	HO2S circuit high voltage sensor 2 (NOx sensor module tells ECM that HO2S signal is outside normal limit for 3+ seconds)
P0168	Engine fuel temperature too high (above 252 degrees F for more than five seconds)
P0181	Fuel temperature sensor performance (ECM detects irrational fuel, coolant and intake air temperatures)
P0182	Fuel temperature sensor 1 circuit, excessively low signal voltage (fuel temperature is more than 300 degrees F for 5 seconds)
P0183	Fuel temperature sensor 1 circuit, excessively high signal voltage (fuel temperature is less than -38 degrees F for 5 seconds)
P0187	Fuel temperature sensor 2 circuit low (fuel temperature is more than 300 degrees F for 5 seconds)
P0188	Fuel temperature sensor 2 circuit high (fuel temperature is less than -38 degrees F for 5 seconds)
P0191	Fuel Rail Pressure (FRP) sensor performance (FRP below 0 psi or above 112 psi with ignition ON and engine OFF; or FRP below 0 psi or above 112 psi within 70 seconds of ignition being turned OFF
P0192	Fuel Rail Pressure (FRP) sensor circuit, low signal voltage (pressure below sensor lower limit: less than .254 volt for over 1 second)
P0193	Fuel Rail Pressure (FRP) sensor circuit, high signal voltage (pressure above upper limit: more than 4.75 volts for over 1 second)
P0201	Injector no. 1/FICM circuit malfunction
P0202	Injector no. 2/FICM circuit malfunction
P0203	Injector no. 3/FICM circuit malfunction
P0204	Injector no. 4/FICM circuit malfunction
P0205	Injector no. 5/FICM circuit malfunction

OBD-II Diagnostic Trouble Codes (DTCs) (continued)

Code	Probable cause
P0206	Injector no. 6/FICM circuit malfunction
P0207	Injector no. 7/FICM circuit malfunction
P0208	Injector no. 8/FICM circuit malfunction
P0230	Fuel pump relay control circuit (ECM detects incorrect voltage on fuel pump relay control circuit for 1 second)
P0234	Turbocharger overboost (boost sensor signal voltage above predicted range)
P0236	Boost sensor signal voltage below predicted range
P0237	Boost sensor signal voltage excessively low
P0238	Boost sensor signal voltage excessively high
P0263	Cylinder 1 balance system, fuel injector balance correction is greater than calibrated limit
P0266	Cylinder 2 balance system, fuel injector balance correction is greater than calibrated limit
P0269	Cylinder 3 balance system, fuel injector balance correction is greater than calibrated limit
P0272	Cylinder 4 balance system, fuel injector balance correction is greater than calibrated limit
P0275	Cylinder 5 balance system, fuel injector balance correction is greater than calibrated limit
P0278	Cylinder 6 balance system, fuel injector balance correction is greater than calibrated limit
P0281	Cylinder 7 balance system, fuel injector balance correction is greater than calibrated limit
P0284	Cylinder 8 balance system, fuel injector balance correction is greater than calibrated limit
P0299	Turbocharger underboost (measured MAP pressure if more than 39 kPa below the expected range for 10 seconds)
P029D	Injector 1 leak
P02A1	Injector 2 leak
P02A5	Injector 3 leak
P02A9	Injector 4 leak
P02AD	Injector 5 leak
P02B1	Injector 6 leak
P02B5	Injector 7 leak
P02B9	Injector 8 leak

Code	Probable cause
P02E0	Intake Air (IA) Flow Valve control circuit: duty cycle greater than 10 percent and IA valve control circuit less than 25 mA; or ECM detects open circuit condition or over-temperature condition of throttle valve control circuit inside ECM for more than 3 seconds
P02E2	Intake Air (IA) Flow Valve control circuit low voltage: ECM detects throttle valve control circuit voltage is less than calibrated threshold for more than 3 seconds
P02E3	Intake Air (IA) Flow Valve control circuit high voltage: ECM detects throttle valve control circuit voltage is greater than a calibrated threshold for more than 3 seconds
P02EB	Intake Air (IA) Flow Valve control motor current performance: ECM detects short circuit condition in throttle valve motor control circuits for more than 2 seconds
P02E7	Intake Air (IA) Flow Valve position sensor performance: difference between expected and actual IA valve position more than 3 percent for 10 seconds
P02E8	Intake Air (IA) Flow Valve position sensor circuit low voltage (IA valve position less than 0.102 volt for 3 seconds)
P02E9	Intake Air (IA) Flow Valve position sensor circuit high voltage (IA valve position greater than 4.75 volts for 3 seconds)
P0300	ECM identifies cylinder misfire, or cylinders misfiring, requiring excessive amount of fuel to maintain correct crankshaft speed
P0301	Cylinder 1 misfire (ECM identifies cylinder 1 requiring excessive amount of fuel to maintain correct crankshaft speed)
P0302	Cylinder 2 misfire (ECM identifies cylinder 2 requiring excessive amount of fuel to maintain correct crankshaft speed)
P0303	Cylinder 3 misfire (ECM identifies cylinder 3 requiring excessive amount of fuel to maintain correct crankshaft speed)
P0304	Cylinder 4 misfire (ECM identifies cylinder 4 requiring excessive amount of fuel to maintain correct crankshaft speed)
P0305	Cylinder 5 misfire (ECM identifies cylinder 5 requiring excessive amount of fuel to maintain correct crankshaft speed)
P0306	Cylinder 6 misfire (ECM identifies cylinder 6 requiring excessive amount of fuel to maintain correct crankshaft speed)
P0307	Cylinder 7 misfire (ECM identifies cylinder 7 requiring excessive amount of fuel to maintain correct crankshaft speed)
P0308	Cylinder 8 misfire (ECM identifies cylinder 8 requiring excessive amount of fuel to maintain correct crankshaft speed)
P0315	Crankshaft Position (CKP) sensor system variation not learned: ECM detects that CKP reluctor wheel learn values are not stored in memory for accumulated time of more than 84 minutes
P0335	ECM determines no signal from Crankshaft Position (CKP) sensor signal for less than 8 seconds
P0336	ECM determines that Crankshaft Position (CKP) sensor signal voltage out of range for less than two seconds
P0340	ECM does not see Camshaft Position (CMP) sensor signal for more than 2 seconds
P0341	ECM determines that Camshaft Position (CMP) sensor signal is out of range for less than 2 seconds
P0370/P0374	FICM doesn't receive crank signal, but receives injection requests from ECM
P0370/P0374	FICM receives invalid crank signal from ECM

OBD-II Diagnostic Trouble Codes (DTCs) (continued)

Code	Probable cause
P0380 (FEDERAL)	ECM commands glow plugs ON and glow plug signal voltage is less than 4 volts
P0380 (FEDERAL)	ECM commands glow plugs OFF and glow plug signal voltage is more than 4 volts
P0380 (CALIF)	Glow plugs are commanded OFF and glow plug feedback is more than 2 volts
P0380 (CALIF)	Glow plugs are commanded ON and glow plug feedback is not between 5 volts and 6.2 volts
P0381	Wait-to-Start lamp control circuit: ECM detects open or short to voltage on Wait-to-Start indicator control circuit for over 1 second
P0400	Exhaust Gas Recirculation (EGR) flow incorrect: ECM detects that difference between desired mass air flow and actual mass air flow is greater than calibrated threshold for more than 15 seconds
P0401	ECM detects calibrated difference between expected Mass Air Flow (MAF) flow rate and actual MAF flow rate during EGR operation; or PCM detects no difference between expected EGR vacuum sensor signal and actual EGR vacuum sensor signal
P0402	EGR flow excessive (ECM-calculated air flow deviation, based on MAF sensor input during EGR operation, indicates excessive EGR flow for 15 seconds)
P0403	EGR solenoid control circuit (ECM detects electrical malfunction in EGR motor control circuit for more than 30 seconds))
P0404	EGR vacuum sensor signal lower than expected and MAF rate higher than expected, for more than 8 seconds
P0405	EGR vacuum sensor signal voltage too low (less than19 kPa) for more than 5 seconds
P0406	EGR vacuum sensor signal voltage too high (more than 158 kPa for more than 5 seconds)
P040C	EGR temperature sensor 1 circuit low voltage (ECM detects EGR temp sensor voltage is less than 0.26 volts for over 1 second)
P040D	EGR temperature sensor 1 circuit high voltage (ECM detects EGR temp sensor voltage is more than 4.9 volts for over 1 second)
P040F	EGR temperature sensor 1-2 correlation (ECM detects temperature difference greater than 50 degrees F between EGR temperature sensors 1 and 2)
P041C	EGR temperature sensor 2 circuit low voltage (ECM detects EGR temp sensor voltage less than 0.26 volt for more than 1 second)
P041D	EGR temperature sensor 2 circuit high voltage (ECM detects EGR temp sensor voltage more than 4.9 volts for more than 1 second)
P0420	Diesel Oxidation Catalyst (DOC) low efficiency (ECM determines DOC functionality has degraded below calibrated threshold, during a regeneration event, for more than 4.5 minutes
P046C	EGR position sensor performance (difference between actual EGR position and expected EGR position more than 3 percent for more than 5 seconds)
P0489	ECM detects low voltage condition on EGR valve solenoid control circuit for more than 2 seconds
P0490	ECM detects high voltage condition on EGR valve vacuum solenoid control circuit for more than 2 seconds

Code	Probable cause
P049D	Exhaust Gas Recirculation (EGR) position not learned
P0506	Idle speed low (ECM detects that idle speed is at least 100 rpm below expected idle speed for more than 19 seconds)
P0507	Idle speed high (ECM detects that idle speed is at least 200 rpm above expected idle speed for more than 19 seconds)
P0540	ECM detects voltage on Intake Air Heater (IAH) circuit with relay commanded OFF or incorrect voltage with relay commanded ON
P0543	ECM detects voltage not pulled low on IAH circuit when relay is OFF, or voltage not high with relay ON
P0545	Exhaust Gas Temperature sensor 1 (EGT-1) circuit low voltage (ECM detects EGT sensor is less than 0.32 volt for over 1 second)
P0546	Exhaust Gas Temperature sensor 1 (EGT-1) circuit high voltage (ECM detects EGT sensor more than 3.37 volts for over 1 second)
P0601	ECM Read-Only Memory (ROM) problem
P0602	ECM not programmed
P0603	ECM long-term memory reset
P0604	ECM Random-Access Memory (RAM)
P0606	ECM internal performance
P060B	ECM analog-to-digital performance
P0611	ECM senses a problem in FICM circuits and sends an error message to ECM
P0612	ECM senses excessive voltage on ignition relay control circuit
P061C	ECM engine speed performance
P062C	ECM vehicle speed performance
P062F	ECM long-term memory performance
P0640	Intake Air Heater (IAH) control circuit
P0641	ECM's 5-volt reference circuit to APP sensors 1 and 3, fuel rail pressure sensor and engine oil pressure sensor is out of tolerance
P0641	ECM's 5-volt reference 1 circuit voltage for engine oil pressure sensor, Fuel Rail Pressure (FRP) sensor, air conditioning refrigerant pressure sensor, exhaust pressure differential sensor and Camshaft Position (CMP) sensor
P0642	ECM detects 5-volt reference circuit voltage for oil pressure sensor, EGR valve, APP sensor and fuel rail pressure sensor is less than 4.7 volts for 2 seconds
P0643	ECM detects 5-volt reference circuit voltage for oil pressure sensor, EGR valve, APP sensor and fuel rail pressure sensor is more than 5.2 volts for longer than 2 seconds
P064C	Glow Plug Control Module (GPCM) performance (GPCM detects variation between main battery supply to GPCM and to ECM)

OBD-II Diagnostic Trouble Codes (DTCs) (continued)

Code	Probable cause
P0650	ECM detects improper voltage on Malfunction Indicator Light (MIL) control circuit
P0651	ECM's 5-volt reference circuit to boost sensor, APP sensor, EGR vacuum sensor and BARO sensor is out of tolerance
P0651	ECM's 5-volt reference 2 circuit for Accelerator Pedal Position (APP) sensor and Manifold Absolute Pressure (MAP) sensor
P0652	ECM detects 5-volt reference circuit for A/C refrigerant pressure sensor, APP sensor 2, BARO sensor and boost sensor is less than 4.7 volts for 2 seconds
P0653	ECM detects 5-volt reference circuit for A/C refrigerant pressure sensor, APP sensor 2, BARO sensor and boost sensor is more than 5.2 volts for 5 seconds
P0670	Glow plug controller detects an open to the main battery supply for glow plugs, or an open in all 8 glow plug circuits for less than 1 second
P0671	Glow plug controller detects an open or short to ground in glow plug 1 control circuit for less than 1 second
P0672	Glow plug controller detects an open or short to ground in glow plug 2 control circuit for less than 1 second
P0673	Glow plug controller detects an open or short to ground in glow plug 3 control circuit for less than 1 second
P0674	Glow plug controller detects an open or short to ground in glow plug 4 control circuit for less than 1 second
P0675	Glow plug controller detects an open or short to ground in glow plug 5 control circuit for less than 1 second
P0676	Glow plug controller detects an open or short to ground in glow plug 6 control circuit for less than 1 second
P0677	Glow plug controller detects an open or short to ground in glow plug 7 control circuit for less than 1 second
P0678	Glow plug controller detects an open or short to ground in glow plug 8 control circuit for less than 1 second
P0697	ECM's 5-volt reference 3 circuit for Intake Air (IA) flow valve position sensor and APP sensor
P0698	ECM detects 5-volt reference circuit for APP sensor 3 and CMP sensor is less than 4.7 volts for 2 seconds
P0699	ECM detects 5-volt reference circuit for APP sensor 3 and CMP sensor is more than 5.2 volts for 2 seconds
P06A3	ECM's 5-volt reference 4 circuit for EGR position sensor and EGR cooler bypass position sensor (LML only)
P06D6	ECM's 5-volt reference 5 circuit for CKP sensor, cooling fan speed sensor, diesel exhaust fluid pressure sensor and turbocharger vane position sensor
P0700	Transmission Control Module (TCM) is requesting MIL illumination, or MIL request circuit is shorted to ground
P0802	ECM detects an improper voltage level on the TCM MIL request circuit

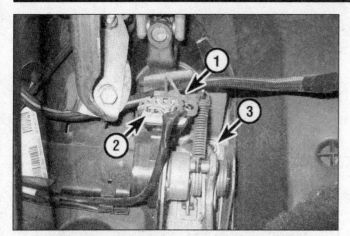

3.1 Typical Accelerator Pedal Position (APP) sensor details

1   Connector Position Assurance lock retainer
2   Electrical connector
3   Mounting nut (upper nut shown; to access lower nut, pull back upper edge of carpet)

3   Accelerator Pedal Position (APP) sensor - replacement

Refer to illustration 3.1

Note: *The APP sensor is located at the top of the accelerator pedal assembly. The APP sensor and the accelerator pedal are a one-piece assembly and are replaced as a unit.*

1   Locate the APP sensor at the top of the accelerator pedal assembly **(see illustration)**.
2   Remove the Connector Position Assurance (CPA) retainer, then disconnect the electrical connector from the APP sensor.
3   Pull back the carpet to access the lower APP sensor/accelerator pedal assembly mounting nut.
4   Remove the upper and lower mounting nuts and remove the APP sensor/accelerator pedal assembly.
5   Installation is the reverse of removal. Tighten the APP sensor assembly mounting nuts securely.

4   Camshaft Position (CMP) sensor - replacement

Refer to illustration 4.3

Note: *The CMP sensor is located on the engine front cover, above the CKP sensor, to the right of the crankshaft pulley.*

1   Disconnect the cables from the negative terminals of the batteries (see Chapter 5).
2   Remove the cooling fan pulley (see Chapter 2).
3   Disconnect the CMP sensor electrical connector **(see illustration)**.
4   Remove the CMP sensor retaining bolt and remove the CMP sensor.
5   Remove and discard the old CMP sensor O-ring. Install a new O-ring and lubricate it with clean engine oil.
6   Installation is the reverse of removal. Be sure to tighten the CMP sensor mounting bolt to the torque listed in this Chapter's Specifications.

5   Crankshaft Position (CKP) sensor - replacement

Refer to illustration 5.2

Note: *The CKP sensor is located at the lower right front corner of the engine, below the CMP sensor, to the right of the crankshaft pulley, on the right edge of the front engine cover.*

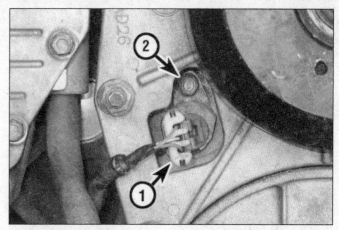

4.3 The Camshaft Position (CMP) sensor is located on the front of the engine front cover, above the CKP sensor

1   Electrical connector   2   Mounting bolt

1   Disconnect the cables from the negative terminals of the batteries (see Chapter 5).
2   Disconnect the electrical connector from the CKP sensor **(see illustration)**.
3   Remove the CKP sensor mounting bolt.
4   Remove and discard the old CKP sensor O-ring. Install a new O-ring and lubricate it with clean engine oil.
5   Installation is the reverse of removal. Be sure to tighten the CKP sensor mounting bolt to the torque listed in this Chapter's Specifications.

6   Engine Coolant Temperature (ECT) sensor - replacement

Refer to illustration 6.2

Warning: *Wait until the engine is completely cool before beginning this procedure.*

Note: *The ECT sensor is located on the upper front part of the engine, on the coolant crossover housing, behind the oil filler pipe, next to the thermostat housing.*

1   Drain the cooling system to a level that's below the level of the ECT sensor (see Chapter 1).

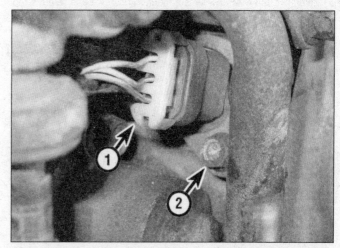

5.2 The Crankshaft Position (CKP) sensor is located at the right front corner of the engine front cover, below the CMP sensor, to the right of the crankshaft pulley

1   Electrical connector   2   Mounting bolt

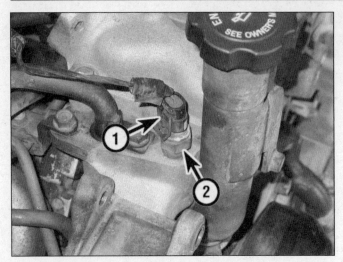

6.2 The ECT sensor is located on the coolant crossover, near the oil filler pipe

1   *Electrical connector*   2   *ECT sensor*

2   Disconnect the electrical connector from the ECT sensor **(see illustration)**.
3   Unscrew and remove the ECT sensor.
4   If you're installing the old sensor, wrap the threads of the sensor with Teflon tape. (The threads of a new sensor should already be coated with sealant; if not, then wrap them with Teflon tape.)
5   Installation is the reverse of removal. Be sure to tighten the ECT sensor to the torque listed in this Chapter's Specifications.
6   Refill the cooling system (see Chapter 1).

7   Mass Air Flow/Intake Air Temperature (MAF/IAT) sensor - replacement

Refer to illustration 7.1
Note: *The MAF/IAT sensor is located on the air intake duct near the air filter housing.*
1   Disconnect the electrical connector from the MAF/IAT sensor **(see illustration)**.
2   Remove the MAF/IAT sensor mounting screws and remove the MAF/IAT sensor.
3   Installation is the reverse of removal.

8   Intake Air Temperature sensor No. 2 (IAT2) (LBZ and LMM) - replacement

Note: *The IAT2 sensor is located on the center intake manifold.*
1   Remove the air intake pipe (see Chapter 4, Section 3).
2   Disconnect the electrical connector from the IAT 2 sensor.
3   Unscrew and remove the IAT 2 sensor.
4   Installation is the reverse of removal. Be sure to tighten the sensor to the torque listed in this Chapter's Specifications.

9   Barometric (BARO) pressure sensor - replacement

Refer to illustration 9.1
Note: *The BARO sensor is located on a small mounting bracket bolted to the top of the left valve cover.*
1   To disconnect the MAP sensor electrical connector **(see illustration)**, pry up the locking tab on top to disengage it from its lug, then pull off the connector.

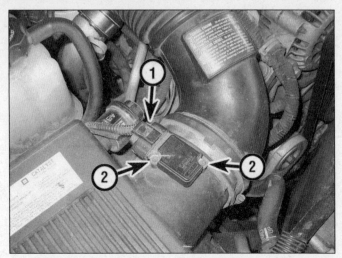

7.1 The Mass Air Flow/Intake Air Temperature (MAF/IAT) sensor is located on the air intake duct near the air filter housing

1   *Electrical connector*   2   *MAF/IAT sensor mounting screws*

2   To remove the BARO sensor from its mounting bracket, grasp it firmly and pull it straight down to disengage it from the two sensor bracket mounting tangs.
3   Installation is the reverse of removal.

10   Turbo boost sensor (LB7/LLY) - replacement

LB7
Federal
Note: *The turbo boost sensor is located on top of the air intake pipe. (It looks just like the boost sensor used on California models, shown in* **illustration 10.7***)*
1   Remove the air filter housing outlet duct.
2   Disconnect the electrical connector from the boost sensor.
3   Remove the nut that secures the boost sensor mounting bracket, lift the coolant tube off the stud and set it aside. Remove the boost sensor and mounting bracket.
4   Separate the boost sensor from the mounting bracket.
5   Installation is the reverse of removal.

California
Refer to illustration 10.7
Note: *The turbo boost sensor is located on top of the air intake pipe.*
6   Loosen the hose clamp that secures the outlet duct to the upper intake manifold cover and remove the upper intake manifold cover.
7   Disconnect the electrical connector from the boost sensor **(see illustration)**.
8   If a coolant hose bracket is attached to the boost sensor mounting bracket, remove the nut that secures this bracket to the boost sensor bracket. Then remove the boost sensor mounting bracket bolt and remove the boost sensor and mounting bracket.
9   Separate the boost sensor from its mounting bracket.
10   Installation is the reverse of removal.

LLY
Warning: *Wait until the engine is completely cool before beginning this procedure.*
Note: *The turbo boost sensor is located on a bracket above the left valve cover.*
11   Drain the engine coolant (see Chapter 1).
12   Remove the water outlet tube (see Chapter 2, Section 3).
13   Reposition the fuel feed pipe.

9.1 The barometric (BARO) sensor is located on this small bracket bolted to the top of the left valve cover:

1   *Electrical connector (pull up tab on top to unlock connector)*
2   *BARO sensor (pull down to disengage from two sensor bracket mounting tangs)*

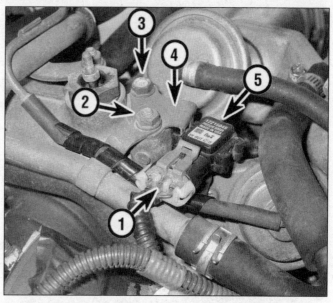

10.7 Turbo boost sensor (California model shown, Federal models use same sensor in a slightly different location)

1   *Electrical connector*
2   *Coolant hose bracket mounting nut (not on all models)*
3   *Boost sensor mounting bracket bolt*
4   *Boost sensor mounting bracket*
5   *Boost sensor*

14   Remove the bolt and detach the sensor and bracket, then separate the sensor from the bracket.
15   Installation is the reverse of removal. Refill the cooling system (see Chapter 1).

11 Exhaust pressure differential sensor (LMM/LML/LGH/L5P) - replacement

Refer to illustration 11.2
Note: *The exhaust pressure differential sensor is located under the vehicle attached to a bracket on the right-side frame rail, near the Diesel Particulate Filter (DPF).*
1   Raise the vehicle and place it securely on jackstands.
2   Disconnect the electrical connector from the exhaust pressure differential sensor.
3   Loosen the hose clamps that secure the two Diesel Particulate Filter (DPF) hoses to the pressure differential sensor and disconnect both hoses from the sensor.
4   Remove the two bolts that secure the pressure differential sensor to its mounting bracket and remove the sensor.
5   Installation is the reverse of removal.

12 Exhaust Gas Temperature (EGT) sensors (LMM/LML/LGH/L5P) - replacement

Refer to illustrations 12.2a, 12.2b,
Caution: *If you are replacing the exhaust gas temperature sensor, perform an exhaust gas temperature sensor reset using a scan tool capable of doing this. A code B131 (Exhaust Temperature Sensor) will indicate the need for the reset. Failure to perform this procedure after replacing one of the sensors may result in poor engine performance, and additional DTCs to be set. If necessary, have the procedure per-*

11.2 Location of the exhaust pressure differential sensor (LMM and later models)

formed by a dealer service department or other qualified repair facility.
Note: *On LMM models there are two exhaust temperature sensors: one sensor is located just downstream from the Diesel Oxidation Catalyst (DOC); the second sensor is located just downstream from the Exhaust Particulate Filter (EPF).*
Note: *On LML/LGH models there are four exhaust temperature sensors: the first sensor is just located just behind the turbocharger, ahead of the Diesel Oxidation Catalyst (DOC); the second sensor is just behind the DOC; the third sensor is located just downstream from the Selective Catalyst Reduction (SCR), which shares the same housing with the Diesel Particulate Filter (DPF), so the sensor, which is located on the housing, is actually behind the SCR and ahead of the DPF; the fourth sensor is located downstream in relation to the DPF.*
1   Raise the vehicle and place it securely on jackstands.

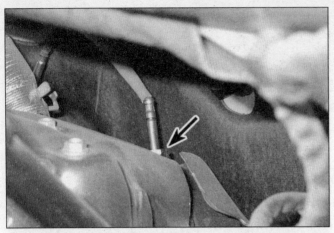

12.2a No. 1 exhaust temperature sensor (LML shown)

12.2b No. 2 exhaust temperature sensor (LML shown)

12.2c No. 3 exhaust temperature sensor (LML shown)

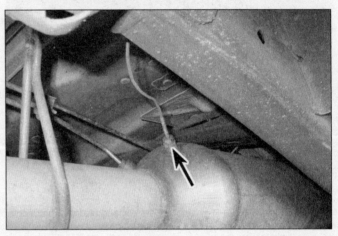

12.2d No. 4 exhaust temperature sensor (LML shown)

2   Locate the exhaust temperature sensor you wish to replace and trace its electrical lead from the sensor to the sensor electrical connector, then disconnect the sensor connector **(see illustrations)**.
3   Unscrew and remove the exhaust temperature sensor.
4   Installation is the reverse of removal. Be sure to tighten the sensor to the torque listed in this Chapter's Specifications.
Note: *If you're installing a new exhaust temperature sensor the threads will already be coated with anti-seize compound; if you're installing a used sensor, be sure to coat the threads with anti-seize compound.*

13   Fuel rail pressure sensor - replacement

LB7
Note: *On LB7 engines, the fuel rail pressure sensor is located on the junction block.*
1   Refer to Chapter 3, Section 8, *Fuel junction block – removal and installation.* That will get you to the fuel rail pressure sensor on an LB7 engine. In that section, you'll find the fuel rail pressure sensor in **illustration 8.14b.**
2   Disconnect the electrical connector from the fuel rail pressure sensor.
3   Before removing the fuel rail pressure sensor, be sure to thoroughly clean off the sensor and junction block with brake system cleaner, then use compressed air to blow dry the sensor and surrounding area.
4   Unscrew and remove the fuel rail pressure sensor. Remove and discard the old metal gasket.
5   Be sure to use a new metal gasket and tighten the fuel rail pressure sensor to the torque listed in this Chapter's Specifications.
6   Installation is otherwise the reverse of removal.

LLY
Note: *On LLY engines, the fuel rail pressure sensor is located on the center of the right fuel rail.*
7   Remove the air filter housing outlet duct.
8   Remove the Exhaust Gas Recirculation (EGR) cooler tube (see Section 21).
9   Disconnect the electrical connector from the fuel rail pressure sensor.
10   Before removing the fuel rail pressure sensor, be sure to thoroughly clean off the sensor and the fuel rail area near the sensor with brake system cleaner, then use compressed air to blow dry the sensor and surrounding area.
11   Unscrew and remove the fuel rail pressure sensor. Remove and discard the old metal gasket.
12   Be sure to use a new metal gasket and tighten the fuel rail pressure sensor to the torque listed in this Chapter's Specifications.
13   Installation is otherwise the reverse of removal.

LBZ and LMM
Note: *On LBZ and LMM engines, the fuel rail pressure sensor is located on the back end of the right fuel rail.*
14   Remove the Exhaust Gas Recirculation (EGR) valve cooler tube (see Section 22 [LBZ] or Section 23 [LMM]).
15   Remove the right exhaust manifold-to-turbocharger pipe (see Chapter 4, **illustration 2.24**).
16   Disconnect the engine wiring harness electrical connector from the fuel rail pressure sensor harness electrical connector and detach the fuel rail pressure sensor wiring harness clip from the wiring harness bracket.
17   Remove the EGR valve cooler tube rear mounting bracket bolts and remove the bracket.

18   Before removing the fuel rail pressure sensor, be sure to thoroughly clean off the sensor and the fuel rail area near the sensor with solvent, then use compressed air to blow dry the sensor and surrounding area.
19   Unscrew and remove the fuel rail pressure sensor. Remove and discard the old metal gasket.
20   Be sure to use a new metal gasket and tighten the fuel rail pressure sensor to the torque listed in this Chapter's Specifications.
21   Installation is otherwise the reverse of removal.

LML/LGH

Note: *On LML-LGH engines the fuel rail pressure sensor is located on the back end of the left fuel rail.*
22   Remove the bolts that secure the intake manifold shield to the left cylinder head and remove the shield.
23   Disconnect the electrical connector from the fuel pressure sensor.
24   Before removing the fuel pressure sensor, be sure to thoroughly clean off the sensor and fuel rail area near the sensor with brake system cleaner, then use compressed air to blow dry the sensor and surrounding area.
25   Unscrew and remove the fuel rail pressure sensor.
26   When installing a new fuel rail pressure sensor, be sure to tighten the sensor to the torque listed in this Chapter's Specifications.
27   Installation is other the reverse of removal.

L5P

Warning: *If the noise cancelling foam was exposed to any fluids, such as diesel fuel or coolant, the foam must be replaced. Failure to replace the foam may result in an engine fire. To help avoid this issue, wrap a shop towel around the fuel rail pressure sensor and any open fuel lines to absorb any fuel that may leak out.*
Note: *The fuel rail pressure sensor is located at the front of the right fuel rail.*
28   Disconnect the negative battery cables and insulate the ends from the battery terminals.
29   Remove the throttle body (see Section 35).
30   Disconnect the electrical connector from the sensor.
31   Remove the fuel rail pressure sensor and obtain a new one for installation. Do NOT reuse the sensor.
32   Installation is the reverse of removal. Tighten all fasteners to the torque values listed in this Chapter's Specifications.

14   Fuel temperature sensor - replacement

Note: *The fuel rail temperature sensor (LB7 and LLY) or simply fuel temperature (LMM/LML/LGH) is located on the fuel rail return line back to the fuel tank. Though its exact location varies somewhat depending on the engine, it's generally in the vicinity of the back part of the intake manifold. When you locate the fuel return line (the pipe with the smaller diameter of the two lines; the other slightly large diameter line is the fuel supply line from the tank) simply trace it back until you find the fuel temperature sensor screwed into it.*
Note: *On the L5P engine the fuel temperature sensor is located in the fuel filter assembly. The ECM monitors the fuel temperature through the fuel pump driver control module to determine the temperature of the fuel entering the fuel injection pump.*
1   Remove the upper intake manifold cover, if equipped. On LB7 engines, loosen the hose clamp that secures the outlet duct to the upper intake manifold cover, then remove the cover. On other engines, the upper intake manifold cover just comes off; it's connected to this outlet duct.
2   On most engines you'll have to loosen the hose clamp and disconnect the charge air cooler inlet pipe from the turbocharger to get to the fuel temperature sensor.
3   Disconnect the electrical connector from the fuel temperature sensor.

4   Unscrew and remove the fuel temperature sensor from the fuel return pipe.
5   Install the new fuel temperature sensor and tighten it to the torque listed in this Chapter's Specifications.
6   Installation is otherwise the reverse of removal.

15   Fuel level sensor - replacement

Note: *The fuel level sensor is located inside the fuel tank, at the lower end of the fuel level sending unit).*
1   Raise the vehicle and place it securely on jackstands.
2   Remove the fuel tank (refer to Haynes manual 24066 or 24067, as applicable).
3   Remove the fuel level sending unit (see Chapter 3).
4   Disconnect the fuel level sensor electrical connector from the underside of the fuel sender mounting flange.
5   Locate the fuel level sensor at the lower end of the fuel level sending unit and remove the sensor retaining clip.
Note: *On LML/LGH/L5P models, the redesigned fuel level sensor is not equipped with a retainer.*
6   Locate the two locking tangs on the lower part of the fuel level sensor, squeeze them together and remove the sensor.
Note: *On LML/LGH/L5P models, the redesigned fuel level sensor uses two plastic retaining tabs instead of the locking tangs used on earlier units.*
7   When installing the new fuel level sensor, make sure that the sensor tangs snap into place, and don't forget to install the sensor retainer.
8   Plug the fuel level sensor into its receptacle on the underside of the fuel sender assembly mounting flange.
9   Installation is otherwise the reverse of removal.
10   When you're done, start the engine and verify that the fuel level gauge is operating correctly.

16   Oil level sensor - replacement

Refer to illustrations 16.2 and 16.3
Note: *The oil level sensor is located on the side of the engine lower oil pan.*
1   Remove the engine lower oil pan (see Chapter 7) and place the pan on a workbench.
2   Remove the retainer clip that secures the sensor lead electrical terminal to the pan **(see illustration)**.

16.2 Slide off the retaining clip to free the oil level sensor electrical terminal from the oil pan

16.3 Oil level sensor mounting bolts

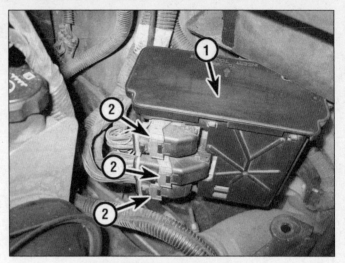

17.3 ECM details (LLY model shown)

1   Cover   2   Electrical connector latches

3   Remove the bolts that secure the oil level sensor to the pan and remove the sensor **(see illustration)**.
4   When installing the oil level sensor, be sure to tighten the sensor mounting bolt to the torque listed in this Chapter's Specifications.
5   Installation is otherwise the reverse of removal.

17   Engine Control Module (ECM) - removal and installation

Caution 1: *The procedures in this Section apply only to disconnecting, removing and installing the ECM that is already installed in your vehicle. If you need to* **replace** *the ECM, it must be programmed with new software and calibrations. This procedure requires the use of a GM scan tool to capture data from the old ECM and install it into the new ECM unit along with GM software updates, so you WILL NOT BE ABLE TO REPLACE THE ECM AT HOME.*
Caution 2: *To avoid electrostatic discharge damage to the ECM, handle the ECM only by its housing. Do not touch the electrical terminals during removal and installation. The best practice when handling the ECM is to ground yourself to the vehicle with an anti-static ground strap (available at computer supply stores)*
Note: *The ECM is mounted in the left front corner of the engine compartment next to the battery on all models.*

LB7 and LLY

Refer to illustration 17.2

1   Disconnect the cables from the negative terminals of the batteries (see Chapter 5).
2   Release the ECM cover mounting tabs, release the ECM cover from the mounting bracket and remove the ECM cover **(see illustration)**.
Note: *If the vehicle is equipped with an Allison transmission, there's an engine harness clip on the cover that must be removed before removing the cover.*
3   Loosen the ECM electrical connector retaining bolts (LB7) or flip open the latches (LLY) and disconnect the connectors from the ECM.
4   Release the spring latch from the ECM, release the ECM mounting tabs and remove the ECM.
5   Installation is the reverse of removal.

LBZ and LMM

6   Disconnect the cables from the negative terminals of the batteries (see Chapter 5).

7   Disconnect the ECM electrical connectors.
8   Release the two upper ECM retaining tabs and remove the ECM from its mounting bracket.
9   When installing the ECM, make sure that the lower edge of the ECM seats into the two retainers on the lower edge of the mounting bracket, then push the ECM toward the bracket until the upper edge of the ECM snaps into place.
10   Installation is otherwise the reverse of removal.

LML, LGH and L5P

Refer to illustration 17.12

11   Disconnect the cables from the negative terminals of the batteries (see Chapter 5).
12   Release the tab on the rear of the ECM cover and rotate the cover upward to remove it **(see illustration)**.
13   Disconnect the electrical connectors from the ECM.
14   Release the three tabs on the upper edge of the ECM mounting bracket and remove the ECM from its mounting bracket.
15   When installing the ECM into its mounting bracket, make sure that it snaps into place and is secured by all three tabs on the upper edge of the bracket.
16   Installation is otherwise the reverse of removal.

17.12 ECM details - LML/LGH models

1   Cover   2   Electrical connectors

18   Manual high-idle system - description

1   LLY and later engines are equipped with a high-idle system that shortens engine warm-up in cold weather. The high-idle system allows the ECM to increase idle speed above the normal idle speed by changing fuel injection timing and quantity, and by closing the turbocharger vanes.
2   The instrument panel indicates the high-idle system is active in one of two ways: On light-duty trucks, the Driver Information Center (DIC) indicates that the high-idle system is ON; on medium-duty trucks, an indicator lamp flashes to indicate that the high-idle system is ON.
3   To enable or disable the high-idle system, follow this procedure:
  a) *Turn the ignition ON, with the engine OFF*
  b) *Depress the accelerator pedal to the floor and hold it down*
  c) *While the accelerator pedal is depressed, depress the brake pedal three times in less than eight seconds*
  d) *Release the accelerator pedal*
  e) *Start the engine*
The engine idle speed will slowly increase to the calibrated high-idle speed, which is 1200 rpm (light-duty trucks) or 1500 (medium-duty trucks).
4   Idle speed will return to its normal speed if any of the following conditions occur:
•   Brake, clutch or throttle input from the driver
•   The automatic transmission is shifted out of PARK or NEUTRAL
•   The air temperature is more than 32-degrees F
•   The engine coolant temperature is more than 154-degrees F
5   The high-idle system will reactivate automatically when the following conditions occur:
•   The engine has been idling for more than 30 seconds
•   The transmission is placed in PARK or NEUTRAL
•   The vehicle speed is 0 mph
•   The ambient air temperature is less than 32-degrees F
•   The engine coolant temperature is less than 154-degrees F
•   The brake, clutch and throttle pedals are not depressed

19   Intake Air Heater (IAH) - description and replacement

Description
1   An ECM-controlled heater coil in the air intake heats incoming air during cold weather and during certain other operating conditions. The Intake Air Heater (IAH) helps to reduce white smoke during warm-up and after long decelerations. So if the vehicle suddenly begins to emit white smoke during a cold weather engine start-up or at the end of a long deceleration in cool weather, the intake air heater might be the cause.
Warning: *Do NOT use ether or any flammable starting aid into the intake for a cold weather start or a hard-to-start situation. The IAH can ignite most flammable liquids.*
2   On LB7 models, a heater-coil type IAH is used in the intake elbow attached to the center intake manifold. There is no IAH on LLY engines.
3   On LBZ, LMM and LML engines, the IAH is a heated grid instead of a heater coil. It's much more effective than a coil because it has much more surface area.

Replacement
LB7
Refer to illustration 19.7
4   Disconnect the cables from the negative terminals of the batteries (see Chapter 5).
5   Loosen the hose clamp that secures the outlet duct to the upper intake manifold cover, then disconnect the outlet duct from the upper intake manifold cover.
6   Remove the upper intake manifold cover.

19.7 On LB7 models the Intake Air Heater (IAH) is located inside the intake elbow attached to the center intake manifold. Remove the nut that secures the power feed lead to the terminal stud on top (power lead already disconnected in this photo), then use a wrench or big socket to unscrew the IAH

7   Remove the nut that secures the power lead to the IAH **(see illustration)**, then disconnect the power lead from the IAH terminal.
8   Unscrew and remove the IAH.
9   When installing the IAH, be sure to tighten it to the torque listed in this Chapter's Specifications.
10   Installation is otherwise the reverse of removal.

LBZ
11   Disconnect the cables from the negative terminals of the batteries (see Chapter 5).
12   Remove the intake manifold cover.
13   Loosen the hose clamps and remove the air filter housing outlet duct and remove the air filter housing (see Chapter 1, Section 13).
14   Remove the bolts that secure the electrical harness to the intake manifold tube and position the harness out of the way.
15   Remove the nut that secures the engine harness power lead to the Intake Air Heater (IAH) stud and disconnect the power lead from the stud.
16   Remove the bolt and nut that secure the air inlet tube to the intake manifold tube.
17   Disconnect the electrical connector from the Intake Air Heater (IAH).
18   Disconnect the electrical connector from the Manifold Absolute Pressure (MAP) sensor.
19   Detach the engine harness clip from the air inlet tube.
20   Remove the EGR valve motor from the EGR valve (see Section 22).
21   Remove the air inlet tube.
22   Remove the two bolts and two nuts that secure the IAH to the air inlet tube and remove the longer half of the air inlet tube.
23   Separate the IAH from the shorter half of the air inlet tube.
24   Remove and discard the old IAH gasket.
25   Installation is the reverse of removal. Be sure to use a new IAH gasket and tighten all fasteners to the torque listed in this Chapter's Specifications.

LMM
26   Disconnect the cables from the negative terminals of the batteries (see Chapter 5).
27   Remove the air filter housing.
28   Remove the Exhaust Gas Recirculation (EGR) valve motor (see Section 23).
29   Remove the upper intake manifold brace bolts and remove the brace.
30   Detach the engine wiring harness clip from the intake manifold tube.

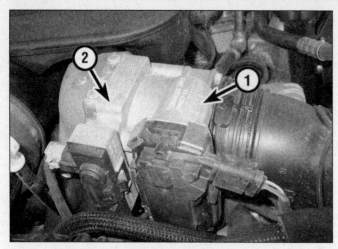

**19.44 Intake air heater and intake air valve details
(LML/LGH models)**

1   Intake Air Valve   *2   Intake Air Heater (IAH)*

31   Remove the bolt that secures the engine wiring harness clip to the intake manifold tube.
32   Disconnect the electrical connector from the Intake Air Heater (IAH).
33   Disconnect the electrical connector from the Manifold Absolute Pressure (MAP) sensor.
34   Place the wiring harness out of the way.
35   Open the harness lead cover on top of the IAH, remove the nut that secures the wiring harness lead and disconnect the lead from the IAH stud.
36   Remove the two bolts and two nuts that secure the IAH between the two parts of the air inlet tube and remove the IAH and the front air inlet tube.
37   Separate the IAH from the front air inlet tube.
38   Remove and discard the old IAH gasket.
39   Installation is the reverse of removal. Be sure to use a new IAH gasket and tighten all fasteners to the torque listed in this Chapter's Specifications.

LML/LGH/L5P

Refer to illustration 19.44

40   Remove the air filter housing.
41   Disconnect the cables from the negative terminals of the batteries (see Chapter 5). Raise the vehicle and place it securely on jackstands.
42   Remove the right wheel house liner.
43   The charge air cooler duct is secured at its upper and lower ends by locking rings. Rotate each locking ring counterclockwise until it stops and hold it in that position to disconnect each end of the charge air cooler outlet duct.
44   Disconnect the electrical connector from the intake air valve and the IAH **(see illustration)**.
45   Remove the four intake air valve mounting bolts and remove the intake air valve assembly. Remove and discard the old intake air valve gasket.
46   Remove the nut that secures the positive junction block cable to the terminal stud on the Intake Air Heater (IAH) and remove the nut that secures the other end of this cable to the junction block on top of the battery. Remove the positive junction block cable.
47   Remove the IAH bolt (lower left corner).
Note: *The other four bolts that secure the IAH are the four long through-bolts that secure the intake air valve to the intake manifold and go through the IAH.*
48   Remove the IAH and disconnect any remaining electrical connectors that you were unable to disconnect while it was still installed.
49   Installation is the reverse of removal. Be sure to use a new intake air valve gasket and tighten all fasteners to the torque listed in this Chapter's Specifications.

20   Exhaust Gas Recirculation (EGR) system (LB7) – description and component replacement

Description

1   LB7 engines sold in California (and in other states using California air emissions laws) are equipped with an EGR system. (All LLY and later engines are equipped with an EGR system.) The EGR systems used on Duramax diesel engines are more complex than EGR systems on gasoline engines because diesel engines have no intake manifold vacuum, and because all Duramax engines are turbocharged they often have *positive pressure* inside the intake system.
2   When combustion chamber pressures reach 2500 degrees F, nitrogen oxide (NOx) emissions are produced. Because diesel engines use high compression to ignite the air/fuel mixture, they generally produce higher combustion chamber temperatures than gasoline engines. The EGR system reduces NOx emissions by recirculating small amounts of exhaust gases back into the combustion chambers. This already-once-burned gas doesn't contribute anything to the combustion process, but it soaks up some of the thermal energy produced by combustion and decreases the temperature inside the combustion chambers and in exhaust gases, which helps to reduce NOx emissions. And the exhaust gases that are introduced into the combustion chamber displace some of the oxygen that would be there instead if there were no EGR system; so removing some of the oxygen from the combustion process also lowers the combustion chamber temperature.
3   The vacuum-operated **EGR valve** redirects exhaust gases from the exhaust system into the intake manifold where they are recirculated via the combustion process.
4   A belt-driven mechanical **vacuum pump** produces vacuum to operate the EGR system. The vacuum pump is always operating when the engine is running.
5   The ECM-controlled **EGR valve vacuum control solenoid**, which is located in the EGR control system between the vacuum pump and the EGR vacuum vent solenoid, directs vacuum from the pump to the EGR valve, which allows the EGR valve to open. The vacuum control solenoid is normally closed; it's opened by the ECM, which uses pulse width modulation to control the ground path of the solenoid.
6   The ECM-controlled **EGR vacuum vent solenoid**, which is located between the EGR valve vacuum control solenoid and the EGR vacuum sensor, is normally open to allow vacuum from the EGR vacuum control solenoid to reach the EGR valve. When energized by the ECM, the vent solenoid dumps vacuum to the atmosphere, which causes the EGR valve to close very quickly.
7   The **EGR throttle valve vacuum control solenoid** is located in the EGR control system between the vacuum pump and the **EGR throttle valve**. When the ECM opens the EGR throttle valve vacuum control solenoid, it allows vacuum from the vacuum pump to close the EGR throttle valve, which restricts incoming air in order to produce enough engine vacuum to pull EGR gases into the combustion chambers.
8   The **EGR vacuum sensor**, which is located in the EGR vacuum control system between the EGR vacuum vent solenoid and the EGR valve, monitors the amount of vacuum available to the EGR valve. The ECM uses this information to adjust the EGR vacuum control system as necessary to achieve the appropriate EGR valve position.
9   The **Mass Air Flow (MAF) sensor**, which is located in the air intake system between the air filter and EGR valve out-take port, monitors the EGR flow into the intake manifold. The ECM uses the signal from the MAF sensor to determine the actual amount of EGR flow and control it as necessary.
10   The **EGR valve cooler**, a stainless steel cooling element, is mounted on the right intake manifold between the EGR valve and the exhaust pipe. Engine coolant flows through the cooler to lower the temperature of the exhaust gases passing through the cooler. As exhaust gases from the exhaust pipe pass through the cooler, some of their heat is transferred to the cooler before they pass through the EGR valve and then into the intake manifold.

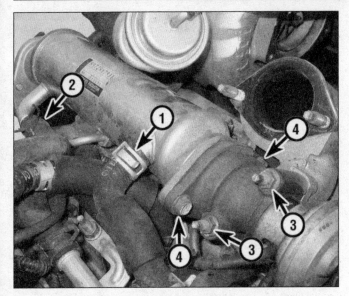

20.15 EGR valve cooler tube details - front (LB7)

1   Coolant inlet hose
2   Coolant outlet hose
3   EGR valve/cooler tube assembly-to-intake manifold nuts
4   EGR valve-to-cooler tube bolts

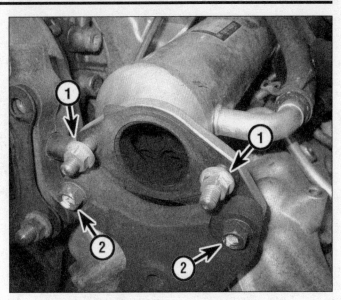

20.17 EGR valve cooler tube details - rear (LB7)

1   Cooler tube-to-exhaust pipe nuts (exhaust pipe already removed)
2   Cooler tube bracket nuts

11   The **ECM** calculates the amount of EGR needed based on the inputs it receives from the following information sensors:
•   Accelerator Pedal Position (APP) sensor
•   Barometric pressure (BARO) sensor
•   Boost sensor
•   Engine Coolant Temperature (ECT) sensor
•   Exhaust Gas Recirculation (EGR) vacuum sensor
•   Intake Air Temperature (IAT) sensor
•   Mass Air Flow (MAF) sensor
•   Vehicle Speed Sensor (VSS)
•   Engine speed

Component replacement

Note: *Anytime you remove and install, rather than replace, EGR system components, always inspect them for damage and wear. If they're clogged up then clean them thoroughly with carburetor cleaner or injector cleaner, then blow them out with compressed air. See Section 25 for more information about cleaning the EGR system components.*

12   Disconnect the cables from the negative battery terminals (see Chapter 5).

EGR valve cooler tube

Refer to illustrations 20.15 and 20.17

13   Drain the cooling system (see Chapter 1).
14   Remove the air filter housing outlet duct. Remove the intake manifold tube (see Chapter 7).
15   Disconnect the EGR inlet cooling hose from the cooler tube **(see illustration)**.
16   Remove the EGR outlet cooling hose from the cooler tube.
17   Remove the EGR assembly-to-exhaust pipe nuts **(see illustration)**
18   Remove the EGR assembly-to-bracket mounting nuts and remove the EGR assembly.
19   Remove the EGR assembly-to-EGR cooler tube bolts and remove the cooler tube.
20   Installation is the reverse of removal. Be sure to tighten all fasteners to the torque listed in this Chapter's Specifications. Refill the cooling system (see Chapter 1).

EGR valve

21   Drain the cooling system (see Chapter 1).
22   Remove the air filter housing outlet duct.
23   Remove the turbocharger boost sensor bracket bolt.
24   Remove the intake heater and gasket.
25   Remove the upper intake manifold tube mounting nuts and remove the upper intake manifold tube.
26   Disconnect the EGR valve vacuum hose.
27   Remove the EGR inlet cooling hose from the cooler tube **(see illustration 20.15)**.
28   Remove the EGR outlet cooling hose from the cooler tube.
29   Remove the EGR assembly-to-intake manifold mounting nuts **(see illustration 20.17)**.
30   Remove the EGR assembly-to-exhaust pipe mounting nuts.
31   Remove the EGR assembly.
32   Remove the EGR valve-to-EGR cooler tube mounting bolts and separate the EGR valve from the cooler tube.
33   Installation is the reverse of removal. Be sure to tighten all fasteners to the torque listed in this Chapter's Specifications.

EGR valve solenoid

34   Disconnect the EGR valve solenoid electrical connector.
35   Disconnect the EGR valve solenoid vacuum lines.
36   Remove the EGR valve solenoid mounting bolt and remove the solenoid.
37   Installation is the reverse of removal.

EGR valve throttle solenoid

38   Loosen the charge air cooler outlet duct clamp and remove the charge air cooler outlet duct.
39   Disconnect the EGR throttle valve solenoid electrical connector.
40   Disconnect the EGR throttle valve solenoid vacuum lines.
41   Remove the solenoid mounting bolt and remove the solenoid.
42   Installation is the reverse of removal.

EGR valve vacuum pump

Refer to illustration 20.47

43   Remove the air filter housing (see Chapter 1, Section 13).

20.47 Access the vacuum pump mounting nuts through the holes in the pulley

44   Loosen the charge air cooler outlet duct clamp and remove the charged air cooler outlet duct.
45   Remove the vacuum line from the EGR valve vacuum pump.
46   Remove the drivebelt (see Chapter 1).
47   Remove the vacuum pump mounting nuts and remove the vacuum pump **(see illustration)**.
48   Installation is the reverse of removal. Be sure to tighten all fasteners to the torque listed in this Chapter's Specifications.

EGR valve vacuum sensor
49   Disconnect the vacuum line from the EGR valve vacuum sensor.
50   Remove the EGR valve vacuum sensor from its bracket.
51   Installation is the reverse of removal.

EGR valve vent solenoid
52   Disconnect the electrical connector from the EGR valve vent solenoid.
53   Disconnect the vacuum lines from the EGR valve vent solenoid.
54   Remove the EGR valve vent solenoid mounting bolt and remove the vent solenoid.
55   Installation is the reverse of removal.

---

21   Exhaust Gas Recirculation (EGR) system (LLY) – description and component replacement

Description
1   Read the first two steps of the Description in Section 20.
2   Because it's vacuum-operated (and because a diesel engine has no intake manifold vacuum), the EGR system on LB7 engines is fairly complex. The EGR system used on all LLY and later engines is considerably simpler because it dispenses with the complicated vacuum system and instead uses a direct current (DC) *stepper* motor with a worm gear that, when the motor is energized by the ECM, extends from the motor to push the EGR valve stem open, directing spent exhaust gases into the intake manifolds. The worm gear is not connected to the EGR valve stem; it can only push the valve open. When the stepper motor is de-energized, a return spring forces the valve to close.
3   The ECM uses a Mass Air Flow (MAF) sensor to monitor EGR flow. The MAF sensor performs one flow test per ignition cycle. The ECM closes the EGR valve for five seconds, then opens the EGR valve to 100 percent for five seconds, then uses the MAF sensor data to calculate the difference so that it can determine whether the EGR flow is correct or not.

Note: *On Duramax engines, there is no separate MAF sensor; it's an integral component of the Mass Air Flow/Intake Air Temperature (MAF/IAT) sensor.*

Component replacement
Note: *Anytime you remove and install, rather than replace, EGR system components, always inspect them for damage and wear. If they're clogged up then clean them thoroughly with carburetor cleaner or injector cleaner, then blow them out with compressed air. See Section 25 for more information about cleaning the EGR system components.*

EGR valve cooler tube
4   Remove the intake manifold cover.
5   Remove the air filter housing outlet duct.
6   Loosen the hose clamp that secures the charged air cooler outlet duct to the intake hose duct and remove the charged air cooler outlet duct.
7   Drain the cooling system (see Chapter 1).
8   Remove the Positive Crankcase Ventilation (PCV) hose/pipe (see Section 26).
9   Remove the electrical harness cable tie, if necessary.
10   Remove the nut and bolt that secure the air inlet tube to the intake manifold tube, remove the air inlet tube mounting nuts and remove the air inlet tube.
11   Disconnect the electrical connector from the EGR valve.
12   Disconnect the EGR cooler tube heater hose.
13   Remove the EGR coolant pipe bolts and remove the EGR coolant pipe.
14   Remove the front and rear EGR cooler tube bolts and remove the EGR cooler tube.
15   Installation is the reverse of removal. Be sure to tighten all fasteners to the torque listed in this Chapter's Specifications. Refill the cooling system (see Chapter 1).

EGR valve
Note: *On LBZ and later engines, the EGR valve motor can be removed and replaced separately from the EGR valve assembly. If you just need to replace the motor itself, check with your GM dealer and/or an aftermarket auto parts store and/or online to see whether you can obtain a motor for the EGR valve on an LLY engine.*
16   Remove the EGR valve cooler tube (see Steps 4 through 14).
17   Remove the EGR valve mounting bolts and remove the EGR valve/solenoid assembly.
18   Remove and discard the old EGR valve/solenoid gasket.
19   Use a new gasket when installing the EGR valve.
20   Installation is otherwise the reverse of removal. Be sure to tighten all fasteners to the torque listed in this Chapter's Specifications. Refill the cooling system (see Chapter 1).

---

22   Exhaust Gas Recirculation (EGR) system (LBZ) - description and component replacement

Description
1   Read the first two steps of the Description in Section 20.
2   The EGR system on an LBZ engine is very similar to the EGR system used on LLY engines (see Section 21). One significant difference between the EGR system used on LBZ engines and the one used on LLY engines is that the cooler tube is both larger and has been reshaped to improve its ability to cool off incoming exhaust gases. Also, you can replace the EGR valve *motor* separately from the EGR assembly.

Component replacement
Note: *Anytime you remove and install, rather than replace, EGR system components, always inspect them for damage and wear. If they're clogged up then clean them thoroughly with carburetor cleaner or injector cleaner, then blow them out with compressed air. See Section 25 for more information about cleaning the EGR system components.*

EGR valve motor

3   Remove the air filter housing outlet duct.

4   Disconnect the electrical connector from the EGR valve motor.

5   Remove the four EGR valve motor mounting screws and remove the motor.

6   If there is a thin metal spacer between the motor and the EGR valve, remove it and save it; you'll need to install it when you install the new motor. (The spacer was used to correct for production variances on some EGR valves, and should be reinstalled with the new motor.)

7   When installing the motor, if the old motor used a spacer, make sure that you install the spacer, then the new motor. (If the old motor did not have a spacer, there is no need to add one.)

8   Be sure to tighten the motor mounting screws to the torque listed in this Chapter's Specifications. Installation is otherwise the reverse of removal.

EGR valve cooler tube

9   Remove the intake manifold cover.

10   Remove the air filter housing outlet duct.

11   Using a pick or a small flat-blade screwdriver, remove and discard the quick-connect fitting clip that secures the charged air cooler outlet duct to the intake and remove the charged air cooler outlet duct.

12   Drain the cooling system (see Chapter 1).

13   Remove the Positive Crankcase Ventilation (PCV) hose/pipe (see Section 26).

14   Remove the alternator (see Chapter 5).

15   Remove the bolts that secure the electrical harness.

16   Remove the nut that secures the engine harness power lead to the intake air heater stud and disconnect the power lead from the stud.

17   Disconnect the electrical connector from the Intake Air Heater (IAH).

18   Disconnect the electrical connector from the Manifold Absolute Pressure (MAP) sensor electrical connector.

19   Remove the engine wiring harness clip from the side of the air inlet tube.

20   Remove the bolt and nut that secure the air inlet tube to the intake manifold, remove the four air inlet tube mounting nuts and remove the inlet tube.

21   Disconnect the electrical connector from the Exhaust Gas Recirculation (EGR) valve.

22   Disconnect the heater hose from the EGR cooler tube.

23   Remove the two bolts that secure the EGR coolant pipe and remove the coolant pipe.

24   Remove the front and rear EGR cooler tube bolts and remove the EGR cooler tube.

25   Installation is the reverse of removal. Be sure to tighten all fasteners to the torque listed in this Chapter's Specifications. Refill the cooling system (see Chapter 1).

EGR valve

26   Remove the EGR valve cooler tube (see Steps 9 through 24).

27   Remove the EGR valve mounting bolts and remove the EGR valve/solenoid assembly.

28   Remove and discard the old EGR valve/solenoid gasket.

29   Use a new gasket when installing the EGR valve.

30   Installation is otherwise the reverse of removal. Be sure to tighten all fasteners to the torque listed in this Chapter's Specifications. Refill the cooling system (see Chapter 1).

23   Exhaust Gas Recirculation (EGR) system (LMM) – description and component replacement

Description

1   Read the first two steps of the Description in Section 20.

2   The EGR system on LMM engines is essentially the same system as the one used on LLY and LBZ engines.

Component replacement

Note: *Anytime you remove and install, rather than replace, EGR system components, always inspect them for damage and wear. If they're clogged up then clean them thoroughly with carburetor cleaner or injector cleaner, then blow them out with compressed air. See Section 25 for more information about cleaning the EGR system components.*

EGR valve motor

3   See Section 22, Steps 3 through 8.

EGR valve cooler tube

4   Remove the intake manifold cover.

5   Drain the cooling system (see Chapter 1).

6   Loosen the hose clamps that secure the air filter housing outlet duct to the air filter housing and to the turbocharger and remove the air filter housing outlet duct.

7   Loosen the hose clamps that secure the air filter housing outlet duct and to the turbocharger and remove the air filter housing outlet duct.

8   Remove the air filter housing.

9   Using a pick or a small flat-blade screwdriver, remove and discard the quick-connect fitting clip that secures the charge air cooler outlet duct to the Intake Air Heater (IAH) and detach the charge air cooler outlet duct from the IAH.

10   Working through the wheel well, use a pick or a small flat-blade screwdriver to remove and discard the quick-connect fitting clip that secures the charge air cooler outlet tube to the charge air cooler, detach the charge air cooler outlet tube from the charge air cooler and remove the charge air cooler outlet tube.

11   Loosen the hose clamp that secures the Positive Crankcase Ventilation (PCV) hose to the air inlet pipe and remove the PCV hose from the air inlet pipe. Detach the PCV hose clip located on top of the turbocharger. Remove the left and right PCV hose/pipe bolts and remove the PCV hose/pipe from the air intake pipe.

12   Disconnect the electrical connector from the turbocharger control solenoid valve, detach the wiring harness clip from the bracket on the turbocharger and set the turbocharger control solenoid valve wiring harness aside.

13   Loosen the hose clamp that secures the air intake pipe to the turbocharger (the clamp uses reverse threads), disconnect the air intake pipe from the turbocharger and remove the air intake pipe.

14   Disconnect the electrical connector from the intake air valve.

15   Remove the bolts that secure the upper intake manifold brace and remove the brace.

16   Remove the two bolts and two nuts that secure the intake air valve and remove the intake air valve.

17   Remove the two bolts that secure the electrical harness clips to the intake manifold tube and reposition the harness out of the way.

18   Remove the bolt and nut that secure the air inlet tube to the intake manifold tube and remove the air inlet tube.

19   Disconnect the electrical connectors from the Intake Air Heater (IAH) and the Manifold Absolute Pressure (MAP) sensor (the boost sensor).

20   Detach the engine wiring harness clip from the air inlet tube, remove the three nuts and single bolt that secure the air inlet tube and remove the air inlet tube.

21   Remove the intake manifold tube (see Chapter 7). If necessary, remove, discard and, before reassembly, replace the two tube O-ring seals.

22   Loosen the heater inlet hose clamp at the EGR valve cooler tube, disconnect the heater inlet hose from the cooler tube and place the hose out of the way.

23   Remove the nut that secures the coolant hose clip to the EGR valve cooler tube, remove the coolant hose from the EGR valve cooler tube and place the hose out of the way.

24   Remove the two nuts that secure the right exhaust pipe to the EGR valve cooler tube.

25   Remove the two rear EGR valve cooler tube mounting bolts and the two front EGR valve cooler tube mounting bolts.

24.5 EGR valve electrical connector (LML/LGH)

26   Disconnect the electrical connectors for the two EGR temperature sensors, then unscrew and remove both temperature sensors.
27   Remove the EGR valve cooler tube and remove and discard the cooler tube gasket.
28   Installation is the reverse of removal. Be sure to replace all gaskets and tighten all fasteners to the torque listed in this Chapter's Specifications. Refill the cooling system (see Chapter 1).

EGR valve

29   Remove the EGR valve cooler tube and EGR valve as a single assembly (refer to Steps 4 through 27).
30   Loosen the hose clamp that secures the EGR valve cooler hose to the EGR valve cooler tube and remove the hose from the cooler tube.
31   Remove the two EGR valve mounting bolts and separate the EGR valve from the EGR valve cooler tube.
32   Remove and discard the two EGR valve gaskets.
33   Installation is the reverse of removal. Be sure to use new EGR valve gaskets and tighten the EGR valve mounting bolts to the torque listed in this Chapter's Specifications.
34   When the EGR valve is reattached to the EGR valve cooler tube, install them in the reverse order in which you removed the cooler tube/EGR valve assembly (see Steps 4 through 28).
35   Refill the cooling system (see Chapter 1).

EGR valve temperature sensors

Note: *There are two EGR valve temperature sensors; sensor No. 1 is located at the rear of the EGR valve cooler tube, and sensor No. 2 is located at the front of the EGR valve cooler tube. This procedure applies to either sensor.*
36   Remove the air filter outlet duct.
37   Locate the sensor, then follow the harness to the electrical connector and unplug the connector.
38   Unscrew the sensor from the EGR valve cooler tube.
39   Installation is the reverse of removal. Tighten the sensor to the torque listed in this Chapter's Specifications.

---

24   Exhaust Gas Recirculation (EGR) system (LML/LGH/L5P) - description and component replacement

---

Description

1   Read the first two steps of the Description in Section 20.
2   The EGR system used on LML engines differs significantly from previous EGR systems. It uses *two* EGR valve coolers instead of a single cooler tube like earlier systems. An EGR cooler bypass valve routes exhaust gases through both cooler tubes, in series, under normal to high engine load and temperature conditions. Under light-load or idle

conditions the bypass valve routes exhaust gases directly to the EGR valve to prevent fouling of the two cooler tubes.
3   Unlike previous EGR valves - which use a stepper motor with a worm gear drive to open the valve stem and a spring to close it - both the EGR valve and the EGR cooler bypass valve use DC motors with a multi-stage gear drive system connected to the valve stem. There is no return spring inside either of these new units; the multi-stage gear drive system opens and closes the valve. An integral position sensor inside each unit tells the ECM the exact position of the EGR valve and the EGR cooler bypass valve, which improves the ECM's ability to control EGR flow more effectively.

Component replacement

Note: *Anytime you remove and install, rather than replace, EGR system components, always inspect them for damage and wear. If they're clogged up then clean them thoroughly with carburetor cleaner or injector cleaner, then blow them out with compressed air. See Section 25 for more information about cleaning the EGR system components.*

LML/LGH

EGR valve

Refer to illustration 24.5
Note: *The EGR valve is located on the left side of the engine, behind the air conditioning compressor.*
4   Unbolt the air conditioning compressor, reposition it so that it's out of the way and support it. Do not disconnect the A/C hoses.
5   Disconnect the electrical connector from the EGR valve **(see illustration)**.
6   Remove the four front EGR valve mounting bolts and the two upper mounting bolts and remove the EGR valve.
7   Remove and discard the old upper and lower EGR valve gaskets.
8   Installation is the reverse of removal. Be sure to use new gaskets and tighten all EGR valve mounting bolts to the torque listed in this Chapter's Specifications.

EGR cooler bypass valve

Note: *The EGR cooler bypass valve is located on the right rear side of the engine.*
9   Remove the turbocharger exhaust pipe (see Chapter 4).
10   Remove the two upper EGR cooler bypass valve mounting bolts.
11   Remove the bolt and two nuts that secure the exhaust manifold to the EGR cooler bypass valve.
12   Remove all six EGR bypass valve mounting bolts (two on the inner side and four on the outer side) and remove the bypass valve.
13   Remove and discard the exhaust manifold gasket and the two EGR cooler bypass valve gaskets.
14   Installation is the reverse of removal. Be sure to use all new gaskets and tighten all fasteners to the torque listed in this Chapter's Specifications.

EGR valve coolers

Note: *There are two EGR valve coolers on LML/LGH engines. They can be removed and installed, or replaced, independently of one another.*
15   Remove the alternator (see Chapter 5).
16   Raise the vehicle and support it securely on jackstands.
17   Drain the cooling system (see Chapter 1).

Rear EGR valve cooler

Note: *The rear EGR cooler is located on the right rear side of the engine*
18   Remove the right exhaust manifold-to-turbocharger pipe (see Chapter 4).
19   Remove the intake manifold tube bolts (three at the left end and two at the right end) and remove the intake manifold tube.
20   Remove the left, center and right EGR bypass pipe mounting bolts and remove the EGR bypass pipe.
21   Remove the turbocharger air inlet adapter (see Chapter 4).
22   Remove the rear EGR cooler-to-front EGR cooler bolts.
23   Disconnect and remove the two cooling feed hoses, the heater coolant bypass hose and the heater inlet hose.

Note: *If you're not sure you'll remember how to correctly install these four hoses during reassembly, clearly label where each end is supposed to be connected, take a photo or make a sketch.*

24   Note how the EGR bracket is oriented, then remove the rear EGR mounting bolts.

25   Disconnect the electrical connector from the EGR bypass valve.

26   Remove the rear EGR cooler and discard the old gasket.

27   When installing the rear EGR cooler, start by loosely installing the rear EGR mounting bolt to the EGR bracket. Make sure that the bracket is oriented correctly.

28   Position the rear EGR cooler, with a new gasket, on top of the engine, rotate the bracket into place and loosely tighten the rear EGR mounting bolts.

29   Install the rear EGR bracket bolts and tighten them to the torque listed in this Chapter's Specifications.

30   Lower the vehicle.

31   Installation is otherwise the reverse of removal. Be sure to use new gaskets and tighten all fasteners to the torque listed in this Chapter's Specifications.

32   Install the alternator (see Chapter 5).

33   When you're done with reassembly, refill the cooling system (see Chapter 1). Then start the engine and check for coolant leaks.

Front EGR valve cooler

Note: *The front EGR cooler is located on the front part of the engine, behind the oil filler tube*

34   Unbolt and reposition the air conditioning compressor so that it's out of the way. Do not disconnect the A/C hoses.

35   Remove the turbocharger coolant feed hose (see Chapter 4).

36   Remove the intake manifold tube bolts (three at the left end and two at the right end) and remove the intake manifold tube.

37   Remove the left, center and right EGR bypass pipe mounting bolts and remove the EGR bypass pipe.

38   Disconnect the electrical connector from the EGR valve and remove the EGR valve mounting bolts.

39   Remove the EGR manifold coolant return hose and the front EGR cooler mounting bolt (at the front left corner of the front EGR cooler).

40   Remove the four front EGR cooler-to-rear EGR cooler bolts (the four shorter bolts that secure the mounting flanges of the two coolers).

41   Remove the two front EGR cooler mounting bolts (the two longer vertically installed bolts).

42   Remove the front EGR cooler and remove and discard the old gasket.

43   Installation is the reverse of removal. Be sure to use new gaskets for the EGR valve, intake manifold and front EGR cooler. And tighten all fasteners to the torque listed in this Chapter's Specifications.

44   Install the alternator (see Chapter 5, Section 5).

45   When you're done with reassembly, refill the cooling system (see Chapter 1). Start the engine and check for coolant leaks.

L5P

EGR pipe shielding - removal and installation

46   Remove the right-front inner fender liner.

47   Drain the cooling system (see Chapter 1).

48   Remove the bolts to the EGR heat shield.

49   Remove the upper EGR heat shield section.

50   Disconnect the heater outlet hose and pipe.

51   Remove the EGR pipe heat shield lower bolt.

52   Remove the lower EGR pipe shield.

53   Installation is the reverse of removal.

EGR valve - removal and installation

Note: *Read the first two steps in the description in Section 20.*

54   Drain the cooling system (see Chapter 1).

56   Remove the EGR pipe heat shielding.

57   Remove the EGR pipe.

58   Remove the EGR coolant bypass hose.

59   Remove the EGR coolant feed hose.

60   Remove the right-hand rear fuel injector noise reducing panel.

61   Disconnect the electrical connections at the EGR.

24.49 Location of the EGR valve temperature sensor No. 2

61   Remove the EGR bolts and nuts, then remove the valve.

62   Discard the valve gasket.

63   Installation is the reverse of removal. Tighten all fasteners to the torque values listed in this Chapter's Specifications. Refill the cooling system (see Chapter 1).

EGR valve temperature sensors

Sensor No. 1

Note: *This sensor is located at the right rear end of the engine.*

64   Locate the sensor, then follow the harness to the electrical connector and unplug the connector.

65   Unscrew the sensor from the exhaust pipe.

66   Installation is the reverse of removal. Tighten the sensor to the torque listed in this Chapter's Specifications.

Sensor No. 2

Refer to illustration 24.49

Note: *This sensor is located at theleft side of the engine, between the EGR valve and the charge air duct.*

67   Locate the sensor **(see illustration)**, then follow the harness to the electrical connector and unplug the connector.

68   Unscrew the sensor.

69   Installation is the reverse of removal. Tighten the sensor to the torque listed in this Chapter's Specifications.

---

25   Exhaust Gas Recirculation (EGR) system - cleaning

1   Remove the EGR valve (see appropriate Section for LB7, LLY, LBZ, LMM or LML/LGH/L5P).

2   Depress the pintle valve several times with a pencil eraser or some other similarly soft object. The pintle should move smoothly in and out. If the pintle valve has a tendency to stick, replace the EGR valve.

3   Try to rotate or wiggle the EGR valve housing for the electrical connector. Then try the same thing with the coil housing. If either is loose, replace the EGR valve.

4   Inspect the EGR valve pintle and seat for carbon deposits. Use a soft cloth, clean shop rag to wipe off the deposits. Make sure that all loose particles are removed. If some of the deposits are impossible to remove from the pintle and the surface area on which it seats, replace the EGR valve.

Caution: *Do not use solvents, sharp tools, wire brushes or sand blasting to clean the powdered metal EGR valve base, all of which can damage it.*

5   Clean the passages with a wire brush. Remove all loose particles.

6   Install the EGR valve (see appropriate Section for LB7, LLY, LBZ, LMM or LML/LGH/L5P).

26.2 There is a PCV valve located in each valve cover on all models except LML/LGH engines (which only have one on the left valve cover) (left side on LB7 shown)

26.3 PCV oil separator (LB7 only)

26   Positive Crankcase Ventilation (PCV) system – description and troubleshooting

Description

Refer to illustration 26.2

1   All Positive Crankcase Ventilation (PCV) systems used on Dura-max engines - except for LB7 systems - reduce hydrocarbon emissions by scavenging crankcase vapors and burning them along with the air-fuel mixture.

2   All systems use spring-loaded diaphragm, (or a pair of spring-loaded diaphragms) valve cover, to control venting of crankcase vapors **(see illustration)**. Each of these diaphragm assemblies consists of a spring, the diaphragm, a metal plate and four screws. Each diaphragm prevents crankcase vapors from escaping until crankcase pressure exceeds spring pressure, at which point the diaphragm opens and allows crankcase vapors to escape through a hose.

LB7

Refer to illustration 26.3

3   On LB7 engines, crankcase vapors from each diaphragm travel through a hose leading to an oil separator **(see illustration)**. The oil separator collects the oil mist from the crankcase vapors and sends the oil back to the crankcase via a hose connected to the bottom of the separator. After the oil mist is separated, the remaining crankcase vapors are vented to the atmosphere. GM doesn't specify any routine maintenance for LB7 PCV systems.

LLY, LBZ and LMM

4   LLY, LBZ and LMM engines are equipped with a PCV system similar to LB7 engines, except that it's a closed system. Instead of going to the oil

separator (which is eliminated on these engines) and then into the atmo-sphere, crankcase vapors are routed to the intake system, where they are vented into the intake stream on the inlet side of the turbocharger.

5   On these engines, it's not unusual to see some oil residue on the inner walls of the intake ducts. GM doesn't specify any routine mainte-nance for LLY, LBZ or LMM PCV systems.

LML/LGH/L5P

6   On LML/LGH/L5P engines, an oil separator is mounted on top of the left valve cover in the same place as the diaphragm used on LLY, LBZ and LMM engines. (The other diaphragm, on the right valve cover, used on previous engines is also eliminated.) Crankcase vapors enter the separator where they flow through both fixed and variable nozzles inside the separator to separate the oil from the vapors.

7   Vapors exit through the larger hose on the upper side of the sepa-rator and go to a Crankcase Depression Regulator (CDR) valve. The CDR limits crankcase vacuum at higher engine speeds.

8   The oil that is removed from the vapors inside the separator flows through a tube on the lower side of the separator, down to a check valve on the lower left side of the engine front cover. The check valve allows oil to drain into the engine front cover when crankcase pressure is low enough, but prevents high crankcase pressure from pushing oil back up through the drain tube.

9   It's not unusual to find oil residue on the turbocharger compressor wheel and inside the charge air cooler, pipes and hoses. GM doesn't specify any routine maintenance for LML/LGH/L5P PCV systems.

Troubleshooting

10   Even though the PCV system doesn't require any routine mainte-nance, it's not a bad idea to inspect the PCV hoses once in a while for cracks. If you see oil leaking from a hose, replace the hose immediately. Here's a simple troubleshooting guide:

Symptom	Possible cause
Oil leak	Damaged hose or component, or restriction in one of the PCV hoses Diaphragm cover screw(s) loose Oil separator drain hose loose or damaged (LB7 only) Blow-by caused by excessive crankcase pressure Oil level too high
Noise	Cracked vent hose
Smoke	Engine damage
Fuel leaking out of PCV system	Check for leaking injector(s) or leaking injector return line(s)

27   Diesel Oxidation Catalyst (DOC) (LMM/LML/LGH) - description, removal and installation

Note: *Because of a Federally-mandated extended warranty which covers emission-related components such as the catalytic converter, check with a dealer service department before replacing the converter at your own expense.*

Description

Diesel Oxidation Catalyst (DOC)

1   The Diesel Oxidation Catalyst (DOC) was first installed on LB7 engines sold in the California market, and on LB7 engines sold in those northeastern states that also used California air laws. All LLY and later engines are equipped with a DOC.
2   The DOC reduces two exhaust emissions - non-methane hydrocarbons (NMHC) and carbon monoxide (CO) - by converting them into carbon dioxide (CO_2) and water vapor. (Carbon monoxide is one the six so-called *criteria pollutants*, each of which is so dangerous to human health that its acceptable emission levels must be set and monitored by the Federal government).
Caution: *All Duramax-powered vehicles since 2007 are equipped with stickers that specify Ultra Low Sulfur Diesel (ULSD) fuel (15 ppm sulfur). The DOC cannot operate optimally on any other fuel. Failure to use ULSD fuel will reduce catalyst efficiency and will eventually cause poor driveability and set Diagnostic Trouble Codes (DTCs).*
3   On LMM, LML and LGH models, the DOC also helps to start each *regeneration event*. Regeneration is the process of removing particulates captured by the Exhaust Particulate Filter (EPF) in LMM systems, or the Diesel Particulate Filter (DPF) in LML systems (different names, but essentially the same components). For more information about the EPF or DPF, or regeneration, see Section 30).

Exhaust Gas Temperature (EGT) sensors

Note: *Because regeneration must occur within a specific temperature range, Exhaust Gas Temperature (EGT) sensors are employed to monitor the temperature of various locations in the exhaust stream. LMM systems are equipped with either two (LMM) or four (LML) Exhaust Gas Temperature (EGT) sensors. See Section 12 for more information on the EGT sensors.*
4   On LMM systems, there are two EGT sensors. EGT 1 is located right behind the DOC, and EGT 2 is located right behind the Exhaust Particulate Filter (EPF).
5   On LML/LGH/L5P systems, there are four EGT sensors. EGT 1 is located just ahead of the DOC; EGT 2 is located just behind the DOC; EGT 3 is located on the housing for the Selective Catalyst Reduction (SCR) and the Diesel Particulate Filter (DPF); EGT 4 is located just behind the housing for the SCRR and DPF.

Removal and installation

Diesel Oxidation Catalyst (DOC)

6   Disconnect the cables from the negative battery terminals (see Chapter 5).
7   Raise the vehicle and place it securely on jackstands.
8   Support the transmission with a suitable jack.
9   Remove the transmission mount-to-transmission support crossmember nuts.
10   Raise the transmission off the support crossmember and remove the crossmember.
11   If the vehicle is equipped with an Exhaust Gas Temperature (EGT) sensor just behind the catalyst, disconnect the EGT sensor electrical connector.
12   If you're replacing the DOC/exhaust pipe assembly, unscrew and remove the EGT sensor.
13   Remove the Diesel Oxidation Catalyst (DOC)-to-particulate filter flange nuts.

14   Loosen the clamp that secures the turbocharger exhaust pipe to the DOC/exhaust pipe assembly and slide the clamp up onto the turbocharger exhaust pipe.
15   Remove the DOC/exhaust pipe assembly.
16   Installation is the reverse of removal. Be sure to tighten all fasteners to the torque listed in this Chapter's Specifications.

Exhaust Gas Temperature (EGT) sensors

Refer to Section 12 for the EGT sensor replacement procedures.

28   Selective Catalyst Reduction (SCR) (LML/LGH/L5P) – description, removal and installation

Description

1   A Diesel Oxidation Catalyst (DOC) (see previous Section) removes hydrocarbons (HC) and carbon monoxide (CO) from the exhaust. On an LML model, think of the DOC as "Stage One" and the Selective Catalyst Reduction (SCR) as "Stage Two" of emissions reduction. Diesel engines are more fuel efficient, and produce less hydrocarbons (HC) and carbon monoxide (CO), than gasoline engines, but generate much higher levels of nitrogen oxide (NOx). To comply with tighter state and Federal NOx limits, GM added the SCR to LML/LGH systems to convert NOx into nitrogen gas (N2), carbon dioxide (CO_2) and water (H_2O).
2   Diesel Exhaust Fluid (see next Section) is injected into the exhaust system upstream from the SCR. Once inside the SCR, exhaust heat converts the urea in the DEF into ammonia (NH_3), which reacts with NOx to form nitrogen, CO_2 and water vapor.
3   Optimum NOx reduction occurs when the temperature inside the SCR is above 480 degrees F. If the temperature is below 480 degrees F. the incomplete conversion of urea forms sulfates that can ruin the catalyst. To prevent this from happening, the ECM suspends DEF injection when exhaust temperature inside the SCR falls below the calibrated limit.

Removal and installation

Note: *The SCR and the Diesel Particulate Filter (DPF)/Exhaust Particulate Filter (EPF) are both located inside the same housing, so they can only be replaced as a single assembly.*
4   Disconnect the cable from the negative battery terminal (see Chapter 5).
5   Raise the vehicle and place it securely on jackstands.
6   Disconnect the two rubber hoses that connect the pressure differential sensor to the two pipes that are connected to the housing for the SCR and the DPF.
7   Unscrew the threaded fittings that connect the two metal pipes to the housing for the SCR and the DPF and remove the two pipes.
8   Locate the two Exhaust Gas Temperature (EGT) sensors (EGT 3 and EGT 4) on the housing for the SCR and the DPF, then trace their electrical leads back to their respective electrical connectors and disconnect them.
9   Unscrew and remove the two EGT sensors.
10   Locate the two Nitrogen Oxide (NOx) sensors: NOx 1 is installed on the front end of the exhaust pipe, near the firewall, and can be accessed from inside the back part of the engine compartment. NOx 2 is installed on the housing for the SCR and the DPF, next to the EGT 3 sensor. Once you've located the two NOx sensors, trace their electrical leads back to their respective electrical connectors and disconnect them.
11   Once all the sensor leads are disconnected and all sensors are removed, remove the four nuts that secure the front end of the exhaust pipe at the front end of the housing for the SCR and the DPF.
12   Remove the three exhaust system rubber insulators and remove the SCR/DPF housing/exhaust pipe assembly.
13   Installation is the reverse of removal. Be sure to tighten all fasteners and sensors to the torque listed in this Chapter's Specifications.

29   Diesel Exhaust Fluid (DEF) system (LML/LGH) - description

Note: *GM refers to each component of the DEF system as a "reductant (component)," i.e. reductant reservoir, reductant pump, reductant injector valve, etc. If you buy a part for this system from a dealer, its parts department might use this terminology when referring to the DEF system.*

1   Diesel Exhaust Fluid (DEF) is a mixture of 66 percent *deionized* (demineralized) water and 34 percent *urea* (a colorless, odorless liquid that, as its name suggests, is a substance found in mammal urine!). When DEF is injected into the SCR, exhaust heat converts the urea into ammonia ($NH3$), which reacts with NOx to form nitrogen, $CO2$ and water vapor.

2   The DEF system consists of an under-vehicle tank, a heater, a pressure sensor, a level/temperature sensor, a purge valve, a pump and an injector.

3   The DEF tank holds about five gallons of DEF. An ECM-controlled pump inside the DEF tank supplies pressurized DEF to the SCR via an injector located between the DOC and the SCR.

4   Refer to your owner's manual for the DEF refill procedure.

30   Exhaust Particulate Filter (EPF)/Diesel Particulate Filter (DPF) (LMM/LML/LGH) – description, removal and installation

Description

Note: *On LMM systems, this component is referred to as the Exhaust Particulate Filter (EPF); on LML/LGH systems, it's referred to as the Diesel Particulate Filter (DPF). These two names are interchangeable, because functionally they both work exactly the same way.*

1   The EPF/DPF captures diesel exhaust particulates, commonly referred to as soot, to prevent them from being released into the atmosphere. It does so by routing the exhaust through a filter substrate consisting of thousands of porous cells. Half of the cells are open at the filter inlet but are capped at the filter outlet. The other half of the cells are capped at the filter inlet but open at the filter outlet. When the particulate-heavy exhaust gases are forced through the porous walls of the inlet cells into the adjacent outlet walls, they're trapped. The EPF/DPF is so effective that it traps about 90 percent of the particulate matter in the exhaust gases.

2   But over time, so much soot becomes trapped on the cell walls that it begins to restrict exhaust gases flowing through the EPF/DPF, which causes backpressure inside the EPF/DPF. This backpressure increases as the trapped soot builds up inside the cells of the EPF/DPF. Eventually, the backpressure affects the performance of the EPF/DPF, and it affects vehicle driveability.

3   A Differential Pressure Sensor (DPS) monitors this growing pressure drop and sends a voltage signal to the ECM that's proportional to the backpressure. When the signal reaches a calibrated threshold, the ECM commands a regeneration event in order to burn off the accumulated soot particles trapped in the substrate.

Removal and installation

4   Disconnect the cables from the negative battery terminals (see Chapter 5).

5   Raise the vehicle and place it securely on jackstands.

LMM

6   Remove the Diesel Oxidation Catalyst (DOC) (see Section 27).

7   Locate the two Exhaust Gas Temperature (EGT) sensors, trace their electrical leads to their electrical connectors, disconnect the connectors, then unscrew and remove the EGT 1 and EGT 2 sensors (see Section 27).

8   Loosen the two hose clamps and disconnect the two rubber hoses that connect the pressure differential sensor to the two pipes that are connected to the DPF and disconnect the hoses from the pipes.

9   Unscrew the threaded fittings that connect the exhaust pressure differential sensor pipes to the EPF and remove the two pipes.

10   Remove the two nuts that secure the muffler to the rear exhaust pipe that's part of the EPF and remove the muffler.

11   Remove the EPF insulators from the exhaust hangers and remove the EPF.

12   Remove and discard the EPF-to-muffler gasket.

13   Installation is the reverse of removal. Be sure to use new gaskets and tighten all fasteners to the torque listed in this Chapter's Specifications.

LML/LGH/L5P

Note: *The DPF and the SCR share the same housing. If you need to replace either the DPF or the SCR, you must replace both components.*

14   See Section 28.

31   Intake air valve (LMM/LML/LGH/L5P) - description, removal and installation

Description

1   The intake air valve, which is located upstream in relation to the Intake Air Heater (IAH), is normally open. When the ECM initiates a regeneration event to incinerate the accumulated particulates inside the Exhaust Particulate Filter (EPF) or the Diesel Particulate Filter (DPF), the intake air valve closes so that the ECM can precisely control combustion temperature inside the EPF or DPF.

Removal and installation

2   Refer to Section 19, *Intake Air Heater (IAH) – description and replacement.* The intake air valve is located just upstream in relation to the IAH, and must be removed to remove or replace the IAH.

32   Nitrogen oxide (NOx) sensors (LML/LGH/L5P) - replacement

Sensor 1

Refer to illustrations 32.1 and 32.3

Note: *The NOx sensor 1 module is located under the hood, on the left side of the firewall.*

1   Disconnect the electrical connectors from the NOx sensor module **(see illustration)**.

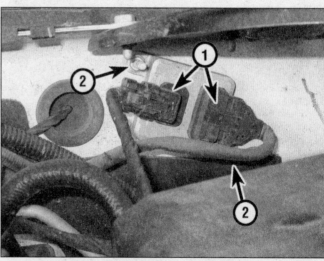

32.1 NOx sensor 1 module details

1   *Electrical connectors*   2   *Mounting nuts*

32.3 Unscrew the NOx sensor from the left side of the turbocharger exhaust pipe

2   Remove the nuts and detach the sensor module from the firewall.

3   Unscrew the sensor from the turbocharger exhaust pipe **(see illustration)**.

4   Installation is the reverse of the removal procedure. If you're installing the old sensor, coat its threads with anti-seize compound (a new sensor should already be coated; if not, apply some to it).

5   Operate the engine, at normal operating temperature and at 20 to 30 mph (32 to 48 kmh) until the DEF light on the instrument panel turns off.

Sensor 2

Refer to illustration 32.6

Note: *The NOx sensor 2 is located under the vehicle, mounted to the outside of the left frame rail to the rear of the DEF tank.*

6   Disconnect the electrical connectors from the NOx sensor module **(see illustration)**.

7   Remove the nuts and detach the sensor module from the frame rail.

8   Unscrew the sensor from the Diesel Particulate Filter.

9   Installation is the reverse of the removal procedure. If you're installing the old sensor, coat its threads with anti-seize compound (a new sensor should already be coated; if not, apply some to it).

10   Operate the engine, at normal operating temperature and at 20 to 30 mph (32 to 48 km/h) until the DEF light on the instrument panel turns off.

33   Manifold Absolute Pressure (MAP) sensor (LBZ and later models) - replacement

Refer to illustration 33.1

1   Disconnect the electrical connector from the sensor **(see illustration)**.

33.1 Location of the MAP sensor (LBZ and later models)

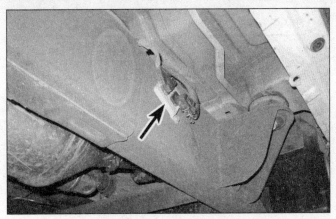

32.6 Location of the NOx sensor 2 module

2   Remove the bolt and pull the sensor from the air intake tube.

3   Installation is the reverse of removal.

34   Charge air temperature sensor (LML/LGH/L5P) - replacement

Charge air outlet duct sensor

Refer to illustration 34.1

1   Locate the sensor on the duct connected to the intake air valve, then follow the harness to the electrical connector and unplug the connector **(see illustration)**.

2   Unscrew the sensor from the duct.

3   Installation is the reverse of removal. Tighten the sensor to the torque listed in this Chapter's Specifications.

Turbocharger sensor

Note: *This sensor is located on the turbocharger compressor outlet.*

4   Locate the sensor on the turbocharger outlet, follow the harness to the electrical connector, then unplug the connector.

5   Unscrew the sensor from the turbocharger.

6   Installation is the reverse of removal. Tighten the sensor to the torque listed in this Chapter's Specifications.

34.1 Charge air outlet duct sensor details

1   *Electrical connector*   2   *Sensor*

35 Throttle body - removal and installation

1   Disconnect the cables from the negative battery terminals (see Chapter 5).

2   Loosen the clamp and detach the air intake duct from the throttle body.

3   Disconnect the electrical connector from the throttle body.

4   Remove the throttle body mounting bolts and detach the throttle body from the center intake manifold.

5   Clean the mating surfaces of all gasket material.

6   Install the throttle body to the center intake manifold using a new gasket. Install the bolts and tighten them to the torque listed in this Chapter's Specifications.

7   The remainder of installation is the reverse of removal.

Chapter 7 Engine
In-vehicle repair procedures

Contents

Specifications

General

Firing order	1-2-7-8-4-5-6-3
Valve clearance adjustment (engine cold)	
Intake	0.012 inch (0.03 mm)
Exhaust	0.012 inch (0.03 mm)
Valve stem seal installed height - measured from the top of the cylinder head to the bottom of the valve stem seal	0.2382 inch (6.05 mm)

Cylinder head warpage limits (all machined surfaces) .... 0.0039 inch (0.1 mm)

Camshaft

Endplay (service limit)	0.0079 inch (0.2 mm)
Lobe lift (standard)	
Intake	0.2863 inch (7.273 mm)
Exhaust	0.2326 inch (5.907 mm)
Journal diameter	
Standard	2.3990 to 2.4001 inches (60.932 to 60.962 mm)
Service limit	2.3984 inches (60.92 mm)
Camshaft bearing inside diameter	
Standard	2.4016 to 2.4028 inches (61.00 to 61.03 mm)
Service limit	2.4043 inches (61.07 mm)
Runout (service limit)	0.0020 inch (0.05 mm)

10331-1-specs HAYNES

Cylinder numbering

Rocker arms

Rocker arm ratio
  Intake 1.36:1
  Exhaust 1.69:1
Rocker shaft outside diameter
  Standard.. 0.8653 to 0.8661 inch (21.979 to 22.000 mm)
  Service limit.. 0.8602 inch (21.85 mm)
Rocker inside diameter (standard) .... 0.8665 to 0.8675 inch (22.010 to 22.035 mm)
Rocker arm bore-to-shaft - production value.............................. 0.0004 to 0.0022 inch (0.010 to 0.056 mm)
Rocker arm bore-to-shaft - service limit..................................... 0.0079 inch (0.20 mm)

Torque specifications

Note: *One foot-pound (ft-lb) of torque is equivalent to 12 inch-pounds (in-lbs) of torque. Torque values below approximately 15 ft-lbs are expressed in inch-pounds, because most foot-pound torque wrenches are not accurate at these smaller values.*

	Ft-lbs (unless otherwise indicated)	Nm
Air conditioning compressor bolts.....................................	37	50
Alternator bracket fasteners	37	50
Alternator mounting bolts..	See Chapter 5	
Camshaft gear bolt*..	173	234
Camshaft reluctor ring bolts		
2010 and earlier models..	80 in-lbs	9
2011 and later models..	106 in-lbs	12
Camshaft thrust plate bolts		
2002 and earlier models..	19	26
2003 and later models..	16	22
Crankshaft balancer bolt		
2002 and earlier models..	278	363
2003 and later models		
Step 1	74	100
Step 2		
2010 and earlier models..	Tighten an additional 105-degrees	
2011 and later models..	Tighten an additional 90-degrees	
Crossmember bolts	74	100
Cylinder head bolts (in sequence - **see illustration 9.23**)		
M12 bolts (bolts 1 through 18)*		
Step 1	37	50
Step 2	59	80
Step 3	Tighten an additional 60-degrees	
Step 4	Tighten an additional 60-degrees	
M8 bolts (bolts 19 through 22)		
2016 and earlier models...	18	25
2017 and later models...	24	32
Drivebelt tensioner pulley bolt	See Chapter 1	
Engine front cover bolts		
LB7..	15	21
LLY and later versions..	18	25
Engine mount-to-block bolts		
2011 and earlier models..	43	58
2012 models..	37	50
Engine mount-to-frame through-bolt (LLY).........................	55	75
Engine mount-to-frame bolt		
2011 and earlier models..	48	65
2012 models..	52	70
Exhaust manifold bolt/nut		
2005 and earlier models..	28	38
2006 and later models..	42	57
Exhaust manifold stud (2011 and later models)	89 in-lbs	10
Exhaust manifold heat shield bolts		
LB7..	71 in-lbs	8
LLY and later versions..	89 in-lbs	10
Exhaust heat shield at firewall nuts		
LB7..	80 in-lbs	9
LLY and later versions..	89 in-lbs	10
Exhaust outlet pipe clamp		
Lower clamp..	30	40
Turbo outlet		
2011 models..	89 in-lbs	10
All other models...	132 in-lbs	15
Exhaust outlet heat shield bolts		
LB7..	71 in-lbs	8
LLY and later versions..	89 in-lbs	10

*Use new bolt(s)

Torque specifications (continued)

	Ft-lbs (unless otherwise indicated)	Nm
Exhaust outlet pipe bolt	39	53
Exhaust pipe bolt	39	53
Exhaust pipe bracket bolt (LB7)	25	34
Exhaust pipe bracket nut (LLY and later)	39	53
Exhaust pipe-to-EGR cooler bolts/nuts	18	25
Exhaust pipe heat shield bolts		
LB7 models	71 in-lbs	8
2004 LLY to 2010 models	89 in-lbs	10
2011 and later models	53 in-lbs	6
Fan pulley bracket bolt		
LB7	34	46
LLY and later versions	37	50
Flywheel bolts*		
Step 1	58	79
Step 2	Tighten an additional 60-degrees	
Step 3	Tighten an additional 60-degrees	
Flywheel housing-to-block bolt		
2005 and earlier	60	80
2006 and later	70	95
Flywheel housing-to-upper oil pan bolt	37	50
Hood hinge bolts	18	25
Idler pulley bolt		
LB7	27	37
LLY and later versions	37	50
Intake manifold bolts/nuts		
LB7	15	21
LLY and later versions	18	25
Intake manifold tube bolts/nuts		
All except 2011	80 in-lbs	9
2011 only	18	25
Intake manifold bolt/nut - lower (2011 and later models)	18	25
Intake manifold bolt/nut - center (2011 and later models)	89 in-lbs	10
Intake manifold brace bolt - upper (2011 and later models)	18	25
Intake manifold heat shield bolt	18	25
Intake manifold stud		
2011	71 in-lbs	8
2012	53 in-lbs	6
Oil cooler adapter bolts		
LB7	15	21
LLY and later versions	18	25
Oil cooler adapter nuts	18	25
Oil cooler assembly bolts	18	25
Oil cooler adapter stud		
2010 and earlier models	89 in-lbs	10
2011 and later models	71 in-lbs	8
Oil drain plug	See Chapter 1	
Oil fill tube bolt		
LB7	15	21
LLY and later versions	18	25
Oil dipstick tube bolt		
2010 and earlier models	15	21
2011 and later models	18	25
Oil dipstick tube stud (2011 and later models)	89 in-lbs	10
Oil pan bolts		
Lower	89 in-lbs	10
Upper	15	20
Oil pan skid plate bolts	15	20
Oil pressure sensor adapter eye bolt	28	38
Oil pressure sensor unit		
LB7	22	30
LLY and later versions	36	49
Oil pressure relief valve	29	39
Oil pump bolts		
2011 models only	18	25
All other models	15	21
Oil pump driven gear nut	74	100
Oil pump cover screws	15	21

*Use new bolt(s)

Torque specifications

Ft-lbs (unless otherwise indicated)   **Nm**

Note: *One foot-pound (ft-lb) of torque is equivalent to 12 inch-pounds (in-lbs) of torque. Torque values below approximately 15 ft-lbs are expressed in inch-pounds, because most foot-pound torque wrenches are not accurate at these smaller values.*

	Ft-lbs	Nm
Oil strainer bolts/nuts	18	25
Positive Crankcase Ventilation (PCV) oil separator bracket/fuel bleed valve nuts	18	25
Positive Crankcase Ventilation (PCV) cover screws	35 in-lbs	4
Power steering pump bolts	37	50
Power steering pump stud (2011 and later models)	89 in-lbs	10
Power steering pump bracket bolt		
LB7	34	46
LLY and later versions	37	50
Rocker arm shaft bolts	30	41
Rocker arm oil deflector bolt (2011 and later models)	89 in-lbs	10
Starter motor bolt	See Chapter 5	
Transmission fluid fill tube nuts	156 in-lbs	18
Transmission-to-engine fasteners	37	50
Upper oil pan-to-flywheel housing screws	15	20
Vacuum pump nuts (California emissions models)	16	22
Valve adjusting screw nut	16	22
Valve lifter retainer hold-down bracket bolt	97 in-lbs	11
Valve cover bolt		
Lower	89 in-lbs	10
Upper		
2010 and earlier models	71 in-lbs (2 times)	8 (2 times)
2011 and later models	89 in-lbs	10

1   General information

This Chapter is devoted to in-vehicle repair procedures. These engines utilize induction-hardened cast-iron blocks with eight cylinders arranged in a "V" shape at a 90-degree angle between the two banks. The crankshaft is hardened steel design using five main bearings for strength, and endplay is controlled by the upper and lower thrust bearings on the No.5 main bearing cap. The connecting rods are made from one-piece forged steel. The connecting rods and caps are "fractured" (split) to increase strength and longevity. The small end of the connecting rod has been tapered to make it lighter and also increase its strength. The pistons are full floating design with a long skirt to improve strength.

The aluminum cylinder heads utilize an overhead valve arrangement with four valves per cylinder with high swirl ports for better combustion and have rapid heat dissipation. Mechanical roller lifters actuate the valves through tubular pushrods and rocker arms. One rocker arm moves two valves at the same time using a valve bridge.

The oil pump is mounted at the front of the engine, and is driven directly by the crankshaft.

To positively identify these engines, locate the Vehicle Identification Number (VIN) on the left front corner of the instrument panel. The VIN is visible from the outside of the vehicle through the windshield. The eighth character in the sequence is the engine designation:

1 = 6.6L, LB7 engine
2 = 6.6L, LLY engine
D = 6.6L LBZ engine
6 = 6.6L, LMM engine
8 = 6.6L, LML engine
L = 6.6L, LGH engine

Information concerning engine removal and installation and engine overhaul can be found in Chapter 8. The following repair procedures are based on the assumption that the engine is installed in the vehicle. If the engine has been removed from the vehicle and mounted on a stand, many of the steps outlined in this Chapter will not apply.

Please note that, due to the confinement of the engine compartment, many of our photographs were taken with the engine removed for clarity.

2   Repair operations possible with the engine in the vehicle

Many major repair operations can be accomplished without removing the engine from the vehicle.

Clean the engine compartment and the exterior of the engine with some type of pressure washer before any work is done. A clean engine will make the job easier and will help keep dirt out of the internal areas of the engine.

Caution: *Do not spray the Fuel Injection Control Module (FICM) with a pressure washer (see Chapter 3 for more information on the FICM).*

Depending on the components involved, it may be a good idea to remove the hood or place it in the "service position" to improve access to the engine as repairs are performed.

If oil or coolant leaks develop, indicating a need for gasket or seal replacement, the repairs can generally be made with the engine in the vehicle. The oil pan gasket, the cylinder head gaskets, intake and exhaust manifold gaskets, engine front cover gaskets and the crankshaft oil seals are all accessible with the engine in place.

Exterior engine components, such as the water pump, the starter motor, the alternator and the fuel injection components, as well as the intake and exhaust manifolds, can be removed for repair with the engine in place.

Since the cylinder heads can be removed without removing the engine, valve component servicing can also be accomplished with the engine in the vehicle.

Replacement of, repairs to or inspection of the timing gears, camshaft and the oil pump are all possible with the engine in place.

3   Valve covers - removal and installation

Warning: *Wait until the engine is completely cool before beginning this procedure.*

Upper valve covers
Removal
1   Disconnect the cables from the negative terminals of the batteries (see Chapter 5).
2   Remove the engine cover fasteners (if equipped) and lift the cover from the engine.
3   Drain the cooling system (see Chapter 1).
4   Disconnect and remove the charge air cooler ducts (see Chapter 4) and cover the turbocharger opening.
5   Disconnect the battery cables from the alternator(s) (see Chapter 5), then remove the cable(s) harness, mounting brackets and set the cable(s) out of the way.
6   Disconnect the interfering engine wiring harnesses and move them aside.

Left side upper cover
7   Remove the glow plug control module mounting bracket bolts and bracket.
8   Remove the auxiliary alternator if equipped (see Chapter 5).
9   Remove the harness main electrical connector bracket.

Right side upper cover
10   Disconnect the fuel line to the fuel filter.
11   Remove the fuel filter bracket bolts and filter assembly (see Chapter 3).
12   Disconnect the electrical connectors to the Fuel Injection Control Module (FICM), then remove the module (if equipped) (see Chapter 3).
13   Remove the EGR cooler tube, if equipped (see Chapter 6).

Both upper covers
14   Remove the fuel injector pipes (see Chapter 3).
Note: *Clean the area around the fuel injectors before disconnecting the fuel lines, and spray lithium grease around the fittings to trap any remaining debris.*
Tag the pipes with pieces of numbered tape so they can be returned to their original locations.
15   Disconnect the PCV hose from the valve cover.
16   Remove the upper valve cover bolts, then detach the cover from the lower cover **(see illustrations 3.18 and 3.19)**.
Note: *If the upper cover is stuck to the lower cover, bump one end with a block of wood and a hammer to jar it loose. If that doesn't work, try to slip a flexible putty knife between the two covers to break the gasket seal. Don't pry at the cover-to-cover joint or damage to the sealing surfaces may occur (leading to oil leaks in the future).*

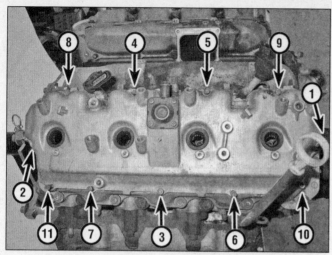

3.18 Upper valve cover bolt tightening sequence - LB7 engines

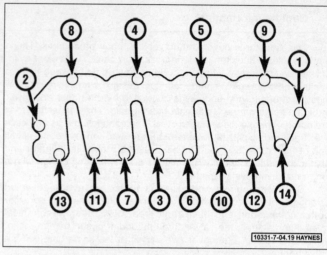

3.19 Upper valve cover bolt tightening sequence - LLY, LBZ, LMM, LML and LGH engines

Installation

Refer to illustrations 3.18 and 3.19

17   The mating surfaces of each upper and lower cover must be perfectly clean when the covers are installed. Use a gasket scraper to remove all traces of sealant and old gasket material, then clean the mating surfaces with brake system cleaner. If there's sealant or oil on the mating surfaces when the cover is installed, oil leaks may develop.

18   On LB7 engines, remove the grommets from the upper cover that seal around the injectors and insert new ones. Apply a 1/8-inch wide by 1/16-inch high bead of RTV sealant to the sealing surfaces of the upper cover then install the cover and tighten the upper cover-to-lower bolts in sequence **(see illustration)** to the torque listed in this Chapter's Specifications.

Note: *Bolts in the 1 and 2 positions of the sequence are used to align the cover.*

19   On all other engine models, position the gasket inside the cover lip. If the gasket will not stay in place in the cover lip, apply a thin coat of RTV sealant to the cover flange, then allow the sealant to set up so the gasket adheres to the cover. Tighten the bolts in sequence **(see illustration)** to the torque listed in this Chapter's Specifications.

20   The remainder of installation is the reverse of removal. Use non-hardening thread-locking compound on the glow plug control module bracket fasteners.

21   Refill the cooling system (see Chapter 1). Start the engine and check carefully for oil leaks as the engine warms up.

Lower valve covers

Removal

Refer to illustrations 3.24a and 3.24b

22   Remove the upper covers as previously described in this Section.

23   Disconnect the electrical connectors and move the harness. On all models except LB7 engines, remove the fuel injectors (see Chapter 3).

24   Remove the lower valve cover bolts, then detach the cover from the cylinder head **(see illustrations)**.

Note: *If the cover is stuck to the cylinder head, bump one end with a block of wood and a hammer to jar it loose. If that doesn't work, try to slip a flexible putty knife between the cylinder head and cover to break the gasket seal. Don't pry at the cover-to-head joint or damage to the sealing surfaces may occur (leading to oil leaks in the future).*

3.24a Remove the lower valve cover mounting bolts (left side shown) . . .

3.24b . . . then the washers with seals and the cover - LB7 engines

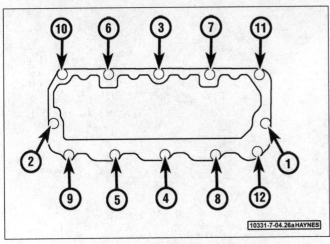

3.26a Lower valve cover bolt tightening sequence - LB7 engines

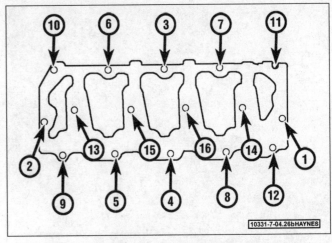

3.26b Lower valve cover bolt tightening sequence - LLY, LBZ, LMM, LML, LGH engines

Installation

Refer to illustrations 3.26a and 3.26b

25   The mating surfaces of the cylinder head and lower cover must be perfectly clean when the covers are installed. Use a gasket scraper to remove all traces of sealant and old gasket material, then clean the mating surfaces with brake system cleaner. If there's sealant or oil on the mating surfaces when the cover is installed, oil leaks may develop.

26   Position the gasket inside the cover lip. If the gasket will not stay in place in the cover lip, apply a thin coat of RTV sealant to the cover flange, then allow the sealant to set up so the gasket adheres to the cover. Tighten the bolts in sequence **(see illustrations)** to the torque listed in this Chapter's Specifications.

Note: *On LB7 engines, replace the bolt seals before installing the bolts.*

27   The remainder of installation is the reverse of removal. Use non-hardening thread-locking compound on the glow plug control module bracket fasteners.

28   Start the engine and check carefully for oil leaks as the engine warms up.

4   Rocker arms and pushrods - removal, inspection and installation

Removal

Refer to illustrations 4.2, 4.3, 4.4a, 4.4b and 4.5

Note: *Keep track of the component positions, since they must be returned to the same locations. Store each set of components separately in a marked container to ensure that they're reinstalled in their original locations. This includes the rocker arms, bridges, bridge pins and the shaft.*

1   Remove the valve covers from the cylinder heads (see Section 3).

2   Loosen all the valve adjuster lock nuts and back off the valve adjuster screws **(see illustration)**.

3   Loosen the rocker arm shaft mounting bolts a little at a time in sequence **(see illustration)**, then remove the shaft as an assembly.

Note: *The rocker arm shaft bolts hold the rocker arms in place; If the bolts are removed, the rockers will slide off the shaft.*

4.2 Loosen the adjuster locknut (A), then loosen the adjuster screw (B) on each rocker arm

4.3 Rocker arm shaft loosening sequence

4.4a Remove the bridge pins from the bridge . . .

4.4b . . . then remove the valve bridge from the tops of the valve stems

4   Remove the valve bridge pins and the bridges **(see illustrations)**.
5   Remove the pushrods **(see illustration)** and store them in order to make sure they don't get mixed up during installation.

Inspection

6   Check each rocker arm and bridge for wear, cracks and other damage, especially where the pushrods and valve stems contact the rocker arm and bridge.
7   Check the pivot points on the rocker arm shaft for wear and roughness.
8   Make sure the hole at the pushrod end of each rocker arm is open.
9   Inspect the pushrods for cracks and excessive wear at the ends. Also check that the oil hole running through each pushrod is not clogged. Roll each pushrod across a piece of plate glass to see if it's bent (if it wobbles, it's bent).

Installation

Refer to illustration 4.12

10   Lubricate the lower end of each pushrod with clean engine oil or engine assembly lube and install them in their original locations. Make sure each pushrod seats completely in the lifter socket.

11   Apply engine assembly lube to the ends of the valve stems and to the upper ends of the pushrods to prevent damage to the mating surfaces on initial start-up. Install the valve bridges in their original locations, then coat the bridge pins with engine oil and install the pins to the bridges.
12   Apply clean engine oil to the rocker arm shaft at each of the rocker arms and install the rocker shaft assembly with the valve adjusters loosely in their original locations. Tighten the rocker arm shaft bolts a little at a time in sequence **(see illustration)**, to the torque listed in this Chapter's Specifications.
13   Check and adjust the valve clearances (see Section 6).
14   Refer to Section 3 and install the valve covers. Start the engine, listen for unusual valve train noses and check for oil leaks at the valve cover gaskets.

---

5   Valve springs, retainers and seals - replacement

Refer to illustrations 5.9, 5.10, 5.11 and 5.16
Note: *Broken valve springs and defective valve stem seals can be replaced without removing the cylinder head. Two special tools and a compressed air source are normally required to perform this operation,*

4.5 Remove the push rods from each lifter, making sure to keep them in order

4.12 Rocker arm shaft tightening sequence

5.9 The lever-type spring compressor is the best type of compressor to use when replacing the valve stem seals while the cylinder head is still on

5.10 Once the spring is depressed, the keepers can be removed with a small magnet or needle-nose pliers (a magnet is preferred to prevent dropping the keepers)

so read through this Section carefully and rent or buy the tools before beginning the job.

1   Remove the upper and lower fan shroud (see Chapter 2).

2   Remove the glow plugs (see Chapter 1).

3   Remove the valve covers (see Section 3).

4   Rotate the crankshaft until the piston in the cylinder you're working on is at the bottom of the stroke.

5   Loosen the valve adjuster lock nuts for each arm, then loosen the adjusting screw to relieve the tension on each rocker arm. Remove the rocker arm shaft mounting bolts in sequence. Remove the rocker arm assembly, then the valve bridge pins and valve bridges (see Section 4).

6   Thread an adapter into the glow plug hole and connect an air hose from a compressed air source to it (see Chapter 8, **illustration 4.5**). Most auto parts stores can supply the air hose adapter.

Note: *Many cylinder compression gauges utilize a screw-in fitting that may work with your air hose quick-disconnect fitting. If a cylinder compression gauge fitting is used, it will be necessary to remove the Schrader valve from the end of the fitting before using it in this procedure.*

7   Apply compressed air to the cylinder. The valves should be held in place by the air pressure.

Warning: *If the cylinder isn't exactly at bottom of the stroke, air pressure may force the piston down, causing the engine to quickly rotate. DO NOT leave a wrench on the crankshaft balancer bolt or you may be injured by the tool.*

8   Using a socket and a hammer, gently tap on the top of each valve spring retainer several times (this will break the seal between the valve keeper and the spring retainer and allow the keeper to separate from the valve spring retainer as the valve spring is compressed).

9   Bolt the spring compressor to the cylinder head **(see illustration)**.

10   Compress the springs on the valve with a spring compressor and remove the keepers **(see illustration)**. Carefully release the valve spring compressor and remove the upper spring seat and spring.

Note: *Several different types of tools are available for compressing the valve springs with the head in place. One type grips the lower spring coils and presses on the retainer as the knob is turned, while the lever-type shown in **illustration 5.9** utilizes a lever arm, pivot shaft and bridge for leverage. Both types work very well, although the lever type is usually the easiest and fastest to use.*

5.11 Use a pair of needle-nose pliers to remove the valve stem seals

11   Remove the old valve stem seals and lower spring seats **(see illustration)**.

Note: *If air pressure fails to retain the valve in the closed position during this operation, the valve face or seat may be damaged. If so, the cylinder head will have to be removed for repair.*

12   Wrap a rubber band or tape around the top of the valve stem so the valve won't fall into the combustion chamber, then release the air pressure.

13   Inspect the valve stem for damage. Rotate the valve in the guide and check the end for eccentric movement, which would indicate that the valve is bent.

14   Move the valve up-and-down in the guide and make sure it does not bind. If the valve stem binds, either the valve is bent or the guide is damaged. In either case, the head will have to be removed for repair.

15   Reapply air pressure to the cylinder to retain the valve in the closed position, then remove the tape or rubber band from the valve stem.

5.16 Using a seal driver or a deep socket of the appropriate size, carefully tap the valve stem seal onto the valve guide

6.8 Rotate the crankshaft balancer until the mark on the balancer (A) is aligned with the mark (B) on the front cover

16   Install the lower spring seat, then the new valve stem seal on the valve stem and down over the valve guide **(see illustration)**. Drive the seal onto the guide until the distance between the bottom of the seal and the cylinder head is as listed in this Chapter's Specifications.
17   Install the spring and upper spring seat in position over the valve.
18   Compress the valve spring assembly only enough to install the keepers in the valve stem.
19   Position the keepers in the valve stem groove. Apply a small dab of grease to the inside of each keeper to hold it in place if necessary. Remove the pressure from the spring tool and make sure the keepers are seated.
20   Disconnect the air hose and remove the adapter from the glow plug hole.
21   Repeat the above procedure on the remaining cylinders, following the firing order sequence (see this Chapter's Specifications). Bring each piston to the bottom of the stroke before applying air pressure.
22   Reinstall the rocker arm assemblies and the valve covers (see Sections 3 and 4).
23   Start the engine, then check for oil leaks and unusual sounds coming from the valve cover area. Allow the engine to idle for at least five minutes before revving it up.

---

6   Valve clearance - check and adjustment

Locating Top Dead Center (TDC)

Refer to illustration 6.8

1   Top Dead Center (TDC) is the highest point in the cylinder that each piston reaches as it travels up the cylinder bore. Each piston reaches TDC on the compression stroke and again on the exhaust stroke, but TDC generally refers to piston position on the compression stroke.
2   Before beginning this procedure, be sure to place the transmission in Neutral or Park and apply the parking brake or block the rear wheels.
3   Disconnect the cables from the negative terminals of the batteries (see Chapter 5).
4   Clean the area around the glow plugs before you remove them (compressed air should be used, if available, otherwise a small brush or even a bicycle tire pump will work). The idea is to prevent dirt from getting into the cylinders once a glow plug is removed.
5   Remove all of the glow plugs from the engine (see Chapter 5).
6   Install a compression gauge in the No. 1 glow plug hole. It should be a gauge with a screw-in type fitting and a hose at least six inches long.

6.10a Check the clearance of each valve with a feeler gauge of the specified thickness - if the clearance is correct, you should feel a slight drag on the gauge as you pull it out

7   Turn the crankshaft with a socket and ratchet attached to the crankshaft balancer bolt. Turn the bolt in a clockwise direction while observing for pressure on the compression gauge. The moment the gauge shows pressure indicates that the No. 1 cylinder has begun the compression stroke.
8   To bring the piston to the top of the cylinder, slowly rotate the crankshaft until the notch on the crankshaft balancer aligns with the mark on the front cover **(see illustration)**.
Note: *If you go past TDC, rotate the crankshaft counterclockwise until the piston is approximately one inch below TDC, then slowly rotate the crankshaft clockwise again until TDC is reached.*

Valve clearance

Refer to illustrations 6.10a, 6.10b, 6.10c, 6.11a, 6.11b and 6.13

9   Remove the valve covers (see Section 3).
10   Rotate the engine to bring the No.1 cylinder to TDC on the compression stroke (see Steps 1 through 8) and measure the clearances of the indicated valves with feeler gauges **(see illustrations)**.
11   Rotate the engine one revolution and realign the marks on the crankshaft balancer and engine front cover to bring the No.1 cylinder to TDC exhaust stroke, then measure the clearances of the indicated valves with feeler gauges **(see illustrations)**.

6.10b With the No. 1 piston at TDC on the compression stroke,
check the indicated valves for cylinders 1, 3, 5 and 7

6.10c With the No. 1 piston at TDC on the compression stroke,
check the indicated valves for cylinders 2, 6 and 8

6.11a With the No. 1 piston at TDC on the exhaust stroke,
check the indicated valves for cylinders 3, 5 and 7

6.11b With the No. 1 piston at TDC on the exhaust stroke,
check the indicated valves for cylinders 2, 4, 6 and 8

12   To adjust the valves, loosen the valve adjuster lock nut, then loosen the valve adjuster screw (see illustration 4.2).
13   Tighten the valve adjuster until there is a slight drag on the feeler gauge, then tighten the lock nut to the torque listed in this Chapter's Specifications (see illustration).
13   Repeat this procedure until all the valves which are out of adjustment are corrected.
14   Reinstall the valve cover and any other components which were removed.

7   Intake manifold(s) - removal and installation

Warning: *Wait until the engine is completely cool before starting this procedure.*

Intake manifold tube

1   Disconnect the cables from the negative terminals of the batteries (see Chapter 5). Drain the cooling system (see Chapter 1).

6.13 Once the adjustment is correct, hold the adjuster from
turning and tighten the adjuster lock nut

7.6a Remove the mounting nuts and bolts . . .

7.6b . . . from each side of the intake manifold tube

LB7 and LLY engines

Removal

Refer to illustrations 7.6a and 7.6b

Note: *On LB7 engines the intake manifold tube is one piece. On LLY engines, the intake manifold tube is two pieces - the intake tube and the center manifold. On the LLY engines the intake tube can be unbolted from the center manifold.*

2   Remove the turbocharger boost sensor and bracket.

3   Remove the EGR valve and cooler (see Chapter 6), if equipped.

4   Remove the intake air heater from the manifold tube.

5   Remove the fuel lines, Fuel Injection Control Module (FICM) and the left side fuel rail (see Chapter 4).

Note: *If removing both intake manifolds, the right side fuel rail will also need to be removed.*

6   On LB7 engines, remove the intake manifold tube mounting fasteners and remove the tube from the intake manifolds (see illustrations).

7   On LLY engines, remove the intake manifold tube mounting fasteners and remove the tube from the center manifold, then remove the center manifold fasteners and manifold from the intake manifolds.

Installation

Refer to illustration 7.9

8   Note that the intake manifold tube/center manifold are made of aluminum, therefore aggressive scraping is not suggested and will damage the sealing surfaces. After the surfaces are cleaned and free of

7.9 Install a new gasket into each of the grooves of the intake manifold tube

any debris, wipe the mating surfaces with a cloth saturated with brake system cleaner. Use a vacuum cleaner to remove any gasket material that falls into the manifolds.

9   Position the new gaskets on the intake manifold tube (see illustration).

10   Carefully set the manifold tube in place on the intake manifold studs.

11   Install the nuts/bolts and tighten them to the torque listed in this Chapter's Specifications. Do not overtighten the nuts/bolts or gasket leaks may develop.

12   The remainder of installation is the reverse of removal. Refill the cooling system as described in Chapter 1.

LBZ and LMM engines

Removal

13   Remove the engine cover fasteners and remove the cover.

14   Disconnect and remove the intake heater wire connection at the heater.

15   Disconnect the Manifold Absolute Pressure (MAP) sensor electrical connector.

16   Remove the wiring harness clips and move the harness out of the way.

17   Disconnect the air inlet tube ducts.

18   Remove the air inlet tube mounting fasteners and remove the inlet tube.

19   Remove the intake manifold tube from the center manifold by slightly twisting the tube while pulling it out of the center manifold.

Installation

20   Replace the O-rings on the intake manifold tube and insert the tube into the center manifold.

21   The remainder of installation is the reverse of removal.

LML and LGH/L5P engines

Removal

22   Remove the engine cover fasteners and remove the cover.

23   Disconnect and remove the air cleaner outlet duct and charge air cooler ducts.

24   Disconnect the electrical connectors to the throttle body.

25   Remove the mounting bolts and lift the intake manifold tube off of the center manifold.

Installation

26   Position the new gaskets on the intake manifold tube.

27   Carefully set the manifold tube in place on the center manifold.

28   Install the bolts and tighten them to the torque listed in this Chapter's Specifications.

29   The remainder of installation is the reverse of removal.

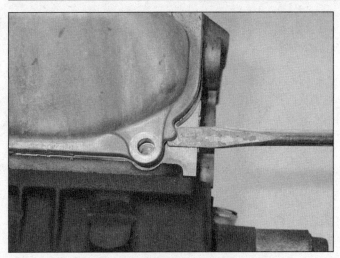

7.44 To break the manifold-to-cylinder head seal, pry only on the manifold at the tabs

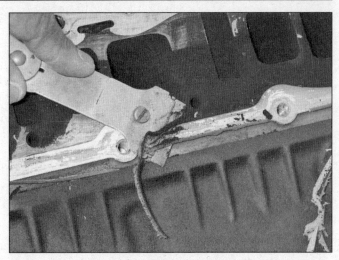

7.45 Carefully scrape the gasket sealant from the cylinder head and intake manifold sealing surfaces

Center intake manifold (LMM, LML and LGH/L5P engines)

Removal

30 Remove the intake manifold tube (see earlier in this Section).

31 Remove the water outlet tube (see Chapter 2).

32 Remove the turbocharger (see Chapter 4).

33 Remove the EGR valve and cooler (see Chapter 6), if equipped.

34 Disconnect and remove the Intake Air Temperature (IAT) sensor no. 2 (see Chapter 6).

35 Remove the center manifold mounting fasteners and manifold from the intake manifolds.

Installation

36 Position the new gaskets on the center intake manifold.

37 Carefully set the manifold in place on the intake manifold studs.

38 Install the nuts/bolts and tighten them to the torque listed in this Chapter's Specifications.

39 The remainder of installation is the reverse of removal.

Intake manifolds

Removal

Refer to illustration 7.44

40 Remove the EGR valve and cooler (see Chapter 6), if equipped.

41 Remove the turbocharger, boost sensor and bracket (see Chapter 4).

42 Remove the fuel lines, fuel control module and the left side fuel rail (see Chapter 4).

Note: *If removing both intake manifolds, the right side fuel rail will also need to be removed.*

43 Remove the intake manifold tube and/or the center manifold, as previously described in this Section.

44 Remove the intake manifold mounting fasteners and remove the manifold(s) from the cylinder heads **(see illustration 7.46a and 7.46b)**. To dislodge the manifold seal, place a long screwdriver between the outer edge of the manifold and cylinder head and carefully pry the manifold up **(see illustration)**.

Installation

Refer to illustrations 7.45, 7.46a and 7.46b

45 Note that the intake manifold and cylinder head are made of aluminum; carefully clean all the old sealant from the sealing surfaces **(see illustration)**. After the surfaces are cleaned and free of any debris, wipe the mating surfaces with a cloth saturated with brake system cleaner. Use a vacuum cleaner to remove any sealant material that falls into the cylinder head ports.

46 Apply a 1/8-inch wide by 1/16-inch high bead of RTV sealant to the sealing surface of the intake manifolds. Install the manifolds and tighten the bolts in sequence **(see illustrations)** to the torque listed in this Chapter's Specifications.

47 The remainder of installation is the reverse of removal.

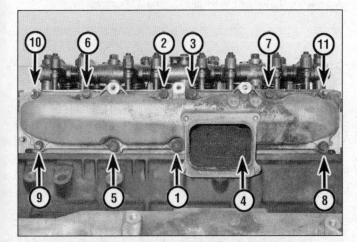

7.46a Left side intake manifold tightening sequence - LB7 engine shown, other models identical

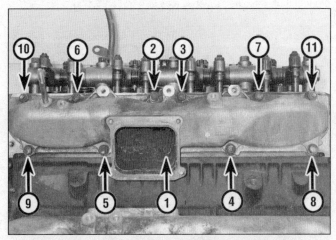

7.46b Right side intake manifold tightening sequence - LB7 engine shown, other models identical

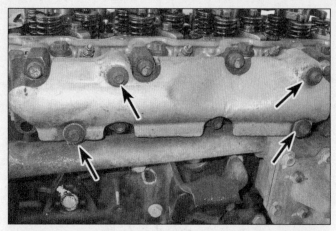

8.7a Typical left side exhaust manifold heat shield bolt locations

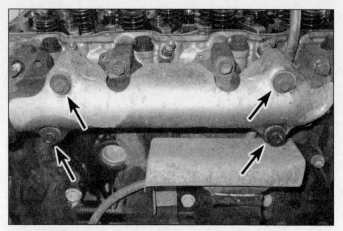

8.7b Typical right side exhaust manifold heat shield bolt locations

8   Exhaust manifolds - removal and installation

Removal

Refer to illustrations 8.7a and 8.7b

Warning: *Use caution when working around the exhaust manifolds - the sheetmetal heat shields can be sharp on the edges. Also, the engine should be cold when this procedure is followed.*

1   Disconnect the cables from the negative terminals of the batteries (see Chapter 5).

2   Loosen the front wheel lug nuts. Raise the vehicle and support it securely on jackstands. Remove the front wheel(s).

3   Remove the inner fender splash shield fasteners and splash shield from the side(s) you're working on.

4   Working under the vehicle, apply penetrating oil to the exhaust pipe-to-manifold studs and nuts (they're usually rusty).

5   Remove the manifold-to-turbocharger pipe bolts **(see illustrations 2.9 and 2.24 in Chapter 4)**.

Note: *Don't remove the turbocharger pipe; just remove the bolts that connect it to the manifold.*

6   Remove the charge air cooler inlet and outlet ducts, as necessary.

7   Working through the wheelwell, remove the exhaust manifold heat shield mounting bolts **(see illustration)** and shield.

Left side

8   Remove the exhaust manifold mounting nuts/bolts in the reverse order of the tightening sequence **(see illustration 8.17a)**.

9   Slide the manifold off the studs and out the bottom, working around the oil filter.

10   Remove and discard the gasket.

Right side

11   Remove the exhaust manifold mounting nuts/bolts in the reverse order of the tightening sequence **(see illustration 8.17b)**.

12   Slide the manifold off the studs and out the bottom of the vehicle.

13   Remove the oil dipstick tube bracket mounting bolt. Remove and discard the exhaust manifold gasket.

Installation

Refer to illustrations 8.17a and 8.17b

14   Check the manifold for cracks and make sure the bolt threads are clean and undamaged. The manifold and cylinder head mating surfaces must be clean before the manifolds are reinstalled - use a gasket scraper to remove all carbon deposits and gasket material.

Note: *The cylinder heads are made of aluminum, therefore aggressive scraping is not suggested and will damage the sealing surfaces.*

15   Install the gasket onto the cylinder head using the two studs to center the gasket.

16   Place the manifold on the cylinder head and install the mounting bolts finger tight. Insert a new gasket between the manifold and the turbocharger pipe.

Note: *There should be two washers on each bolt or stud. The flat washer goes against the manifold followed by the waved or concaved washer.*

17   Tighten the mounting bolts in sequence **(see illustrations)**, and in two steps to the torque listed in this Chapter's Specifications.

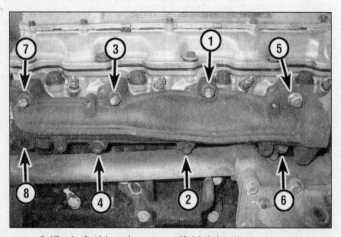

8.17a Left side exhaust manifold tightening sequence

8.17b Right side exhaust manifold tightening sequence

18   Install the heat shield.
19   The remainder of installation is the reverse of removal.
20   Start the engine and check for exhaust leaks.

9   Cylinder heads - removal and installation

Warning: *Wait until the engine is completely cool before beginning this procedure.*
Note: *It will be necessary to purchase a new set of cylinder head bolts for this procedure.*

Removal

Refer to illustration 9.12

1   Disconnect the cables from the negative terminals of the batteries (see Chapter 5) and drain the cooling system (see Chapter 1).
2   Remove the intake manifolds (see Section 7) and the coolant pipe.
3   Remove the thermostat housing crossover (see Chapter 2).
4   Detach the exhaust manifold(s) from the cylinder head(s) (see Section 8).
5   Remove the valve cover(s) (see Section 3).
6   Remove the rocker arms and pushrods (see Section 4).
Caution: *Again, as mentioned in Section 4, keep all the parts in order so they can be reinstalled in the same locations.*
7   Remove the coolant air bleed pipe.
8   Remove the alternator(s), bracket(s) and glow plugs (see Chapter 5).
9   Remove the fuel injectors (see Chapter 3).
10   On the right side cylinder head, remove the dipstick tube mounting bolt and move the tube aside.
11   Loosen the head bolts in 1/4-turn increments, in the reverse order of the tightening sequence **(see illustration 9.23),** until they can be removed by hand.
12   Lift the head(s) off the engine. If resistance is felt, do not pry between the head and block sealing surface, as damage to the mating surfaces will result. To dislodge the head, place a prybar or long screwdriver between the outer edge of the block and cylinder head boss and carefully pry the head off the engine **(see illustration).**
13   Store the heads on blocks of wood to prevent damage to the gasket sealing surfaces.

Installation

Refer to illustrations 9.19a, 9.19b, 9.19c, 9.20 and 9.23

14   The mating surfaces of the cylinder heads and block must be perfectly clean when the heads are installed. Gasket removal solvents are available at auto parts stores and may prove helpful.
15   Use a gasket scraper to remove all traces of carbon and old gasket material, then wipe the mating surfaces with a cloth saturated with brake system cleaner.
Note: *The cylinder heads are made of aluminum, therefore aggres-*

9.12 Pry only between the engine block and the boss on the cylinder head - do not use excessive force or damage to the head may result

sive scraping is not suggested and will damage the sealing surfaces. If there is oil on the mating surfaces when the heads are installed, the gaskets may not seal correctly and leaks may develop. When working on the block, use a vacuum cleaner to remove any debris that falls into the cylinders.
16   Check the block and head mating surfaces for nicks, deep scratches and other damage. If damage is slight, it can be removed with emery cloth. If it is excessive, machining may be the only alternative.
17   Use a tap of the correct size to chase the threads in the head bolt holes in the block. If a tap is not available, spray a liberal amount of brake cleaner into each hole. Use compressed air (if available) to remove the debris from the holes.
Warning: *Wear safety glasses or a face shield to protect your eyes when using compressed air.* All cylinder head bolts should be replaced with new bolts.
18   Position the new gaskets over the dowels in the block. If the dowels are not present in the block, they are stuck to the cylinder head; remove them and install them in their proper holes in the block.
Note: *There are several different head gaskets available; check to make sure the new gaskets match the ones you removed.*
Caution: *If the engine is being rebuilt, be sure to check the protrusion of each piston to determine the required gasket thickness (see Step 20). Failure to do so can result in engine damage.*

2001 and 2002 models

Gasket grade	Piston protrusion	Gasket thickness (compressed)
Grade A = No hole in gasket edge	0.0088 to 0.0108 inch (0.223 to 0.274 mm)	0.0354 to 0.0394 inch (0.90 to 1.00 mm)
Grade B = One hole in gasket edge	0.0108 to 0.0128 inch (0.274 to 0.325 mm)	0.0374 to 0.0413 inch (0.95 to 1.05 mm)
Grade C = Two holes in gasket edge	0.0128 to 0.0148 inch (0.325 to 0.376 mm)	0.0394 to 0.0433 inch (1.00 to 1.10 mm)

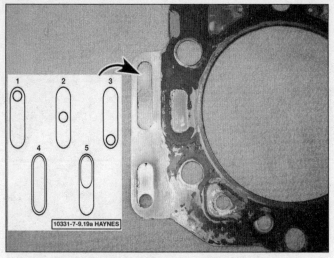

**9.19a Head gasket thickness details - 2003 and later models
(first design)**

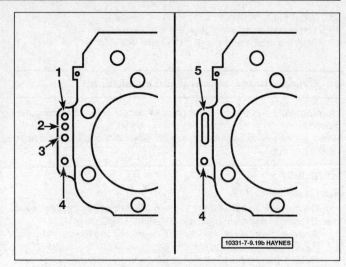

**9.19b Head gasket thickness details - 2003 and later models
(second design)**

1	Grade A	4	Over-bored cylinder block
2	Grade B	5	Over-bored and deck-milled block
3	Grade C		

1	Grade A	4	Right cylinder bank
2	Grade B	5	Over-bored cylinder block
3	Grade C		

19   The position and shape of the hole(s) at the end of the gasket identifies the thickness of the gasket required, based on the amount of piston protrusion **(see illustrations)**.

2003 and later models

Gasket grade	Piston protrusion	Gasket thickness (compressed)
Grade A	0.0088 to 0.0108 inch (0.223 to 0.274 mm)	0.0354 to 0.0394 inch (0.90 to 1.00 mm)
Grade B	0.0108 to 0.0128 inch (0.274 to 0.325 mm)	0.0374 to 0.0413 inch (0.95 to 1.05 mm)
Grade C	0.0128 to 0.0148 inch (0.325 to 0.376 mm)	0.0394 to 0.0433 inch (1.00 to 1.10 mm)
Block over-bored 0.010 to 0.030 inch	0.0088 to 0.0148 inch (0.223 to 0.376 mm)	0.0394 to 0.0433 inch (1.00 to 1.10 mm)
Block over-bored 0.010 to 0.030 inch and deck milled 0.008 inch (0.203 mm)	0.0168 to 0.0228 inch (0.4257 to 0.5777 mm)	0.0492 to 0.0532 inch (1.25 to 1.35 mm)

Checking piston protrusion

20   With the piston at Top Dead Center (TDC), use a precision straight-edge and a feeler gauge to measure the amount of piston protrusion above the cylinder block deck **(see illustration)**. Be sure to rotate the crankshaft back and forth a little to ensure your measurement is taken when the piston is at its highest point. Do this for all cylinders on each cylinder bank, and use the greatest measurement to determine what grade of head gasket is required for each bank.
21   Carefully position the heads on the block without disturbing the gaskets.

22   Install the 8mm head bolts (bolts 19 through 22), but don't tighten them yet.
23   Install **NEW** cylinder head bolts (bolts 1 through 18) and tighten them finger tight. Following the recommended sequence **(see illustration)**, tighten the bolts in four steps to the torque listed in this Chapter's Specifications.
Caution: *DO NOT reuse the large head bolts - always replace them with new ones.*
Caution: *The cylinder head bolts come with a pre-applied molybdenum disulfide coating on the threads. Do not remove the coating or apply*

9.19c Stamped into the other end of the gasket will be an L or R (left or right). When installed, the letter will be upright. The left and right side gaskets are NOT interchangeable

9.20 Measuring piston protrusion with a straightedge and feeler gauge

oil to the threads or cylinder block bolt holes. If oil or any other type of lubricant is applied, a false tightening torque will be obtained, resulting in engine damage.

24   The remainder of installation is the reverse of removal.

25   Add coolant and change the engine oil and filter (see Chapter 1). Start the engine and check for proper operation and coolant or oil leaks.

10   Crankshaft balancer - removal and installation

Refer to illustrations 10.5a and 10.5b

1   Disconnect the cables from the negative terminals of the batteries (see Chapter 5).

2   Raise the front of the vehicle and support it securely on jackstands. Apply the parking brake.

3   Remove the drivebelt. Remove the cooling fan and shroud assembly (see Chapter 2).

4   Working under the vehicle, remove the stone shield from below the engine (if equipped).

5   Remove the starter motor (see Chapter 5). Install a flywheel locking tool or wedge a punch or prybar through the one of the non-

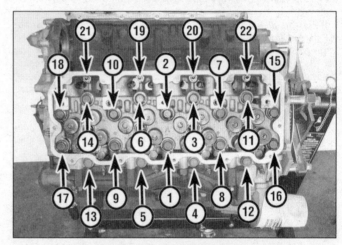

9.23 Cylinder head bolt tightening sequence

threaded holes in the flywheel **(see illustration)**, then loosen the crankshaft pulley center bolt **(see illustration)**.

Note: *Flywheel holding tools are available from specialty tool manufac-*

10.5a With the starter removed, insert a punch through one of the non-threaded holes in the flywheel to prevent the engine from turning

10.5b Using a socket on a breaker bar, loosen the balancer bolt and slide the balancer off the crankshaft (engine removed for clarity)

11.3 Carefully drill a hole in the metal side of the seal

11.4 Thread the screw and washer into the hole drilled in the seal

turers that attach to the bellhousing so the starter does not have to be removed.

Note: *This bolt is extremely tight. At the very least, a long breaker bar will be required. Soak the area around the bolt head and around the large washer with penetrating oil and let it soak in for awhile. If you can't loosen the bolt with the breaker bar, try pounding on the breaker bar with a hammer as force is applied to it. If it just won't break loose, you'll have to use an impact wrench, which, in most cases, will require removal of the radiator for clearance.*

6   Pull the balancer off the crankshaft.

7   Lubricate the internal hub of the balancer with engine oil, then position the crankshaft pulley/balancer on the crankshaft and slide it on as far as it will go.

Note: *The slot in the hub of the balancer hub must align with the pin on the nose of the crankshaft.*

8   Lubricate the balancer bolt with engine oil, then install the bolt and tighten it to the torque and angle of rotation listed in this Chapter's Specifications.

9   The remainder of installation is the reverse of removal.

11 Crankshaft front oil seal - removal and installation

Refer to illustrations 11.3, 11.4, 11.5 and 11.8

1   Remove the crankshaft balancer (see Section 10).

2   Note how the seal is installed - the new one must be installed to the same depth and facing the same way.

3   Using a drill, carefully drill a hole in the metal side of the seal **(see illustration)**.

4   Place a washer on to a screw then thread the screw into the hole drilled in the seal **(see illustration)**.

5   Connect a puller or equivalent around the screw and carefully pull the seal out from the housing **(see illustration)**.

6   Once the seal is removed, clean the crankshaft and front cover surfaces.

7   Lubricate the crankshaft seal journal and the lip of the new seal with multi-purpose grease.

8   Evenly drive the new seal into the retainer with a seal driver or a wood block and a section of pipe slightly smaller in diameter than the outside diameter of the seal **(see illustration)**. The new seal should be approximately flush with the surface of the front cover or the depth measured in Step 2.

9   Lubricate the balancer hub with clean engine oil and reinstall the crankshaft balancer (see Section 10).

10   The remainder of installation is the reverse of removal.

12 Engine front cover - removal and installation

Removal

Refer to illustrations 12.8, 12.9a, 12.9b and 12.10

1   Disconnect the cables from the negative terminals of the batteries (see Chapter 5).

11.5 Connect a puller to the screw and pull the seal from the housing

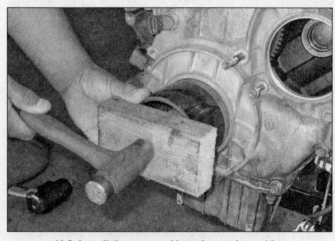

11.8 Install the new seal into the retainer with a wood block and a section of pipe

12.8 Upper oil pan-to-front cover mounting bolt locations

12.9a Front cover mounting bolt locations

12.9b Carefully pry the front cover at the tab, making sure not to damage the sealing surfaces of the cover

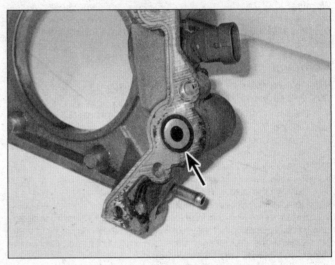

12.10 Check the pressure relief valve O-ring and replace it if necessary

2 Raise the vehicle and support it securely on jackstands. Drain the engine oil and remove the oil filter (see Chapter 1).
3 Remove the oil pan skid plate and splash shield, if equipped.
4 Remove the crankshaft balancer (see Section 10).
5 Remove the water pump (see Chapter 2).
6 Remove the crankshaft front oil seal from the cover (see Section 11).
7 Disconnect the electrical connectors the Crankshaft Position (CKP) sensor and the Camshaft Position (CMP) sensor, then remove the sensors (see Chapter 6).
Note: *On some models, it may be necessary to remove the right side inner fender well splash shield to access the CKP sensor.*
8 Remove the upper oil pan-to-front cover bolts **(see illustration)**.
9 Remove the front cover mounting bolts and carefully remove the cover from the cylinder block **(see illustrations)**.
Caution: *Do not bend or distort the turbocharger coolant pipe.*
10 If necessary, remove and discard the pressure relief valve O-ring from the back of the cover **(see illustration)**.

Installation
11 Thoroughly clean the mounting surfaces of the front cover, cylinder block and upper oil pan old gasket material and sealant. Wipe the gasket surfaces clean with a rag soaked in brake system cleaner.
12 Install a new pressure relief valve O-ring to the back of the cover, if it was removed.
13 Apply a 1/8-inch wide by 1/16-inch high bead of RTV sealant to the sealing surfaces of the front cover (engine block and oil pan), then install the cover and tighten the cover-to-engine block bolts to the torque listed in this Chapter's Specifications.
14 Install the oil pan-to-cover mounting bolts and tighten the bolts to the torque listed in this Chapter's Specifications.
15 Install a new front crankshaft seal (see Section 11).
16 The remainder of installation is the reverse of removal.
17 Refill the cooling system and add the proper type and quantity of oil (see Chapter 1), start the engine and check for leaks before placing the vehicle back in service.

13.9a Remove the lifter retainer hold-down bracket bolts . . .

13.9b . . . then remove the hold-down brackets and bolts from the block

13 Camshaft and lifters - removal and installation

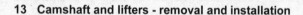

Warning: *Wait until the engine is completely cool before beginning this procedure.*
Caution: *If the camshaft is being replaced, always install new lifters as well. Do not use old lifters on a new camshaft.*

Removal

Refer to illustrations 13.9a, 13.9b, 13.10a, 13.10b, 13.12, 13.13, 13.14, 13.15, 13.16 and 13.17

1   Disconnect the cables from the negative terminals of the batteries (see Chapter 5).
2   Refer to Chapter 8, Section 6 and follow steps 2 through 24.
3   Remove the valve covers (see Section 3).
4   Remove the intake manifolds (see Section 7).
5   Remove the rocker arms and pushrods (see Section 4).
6   Remove the front cover (see Section 12).
7   Remove the cylinder heads (see Section 9).
8   Before removing the lifters, arrange to store them in a clearly labeled box to ensure that they're reinstalled in their original locations.
9   Remove the lifter retainer hold-down bracket bolts and remove the hold-down brackets **(see illustrations)**.
10   Remove the retainers and lifters and store them where they won't get dirty **(see illustrations)**. DO NOT attempt to withdraw the camshaft with the lifters in place.

11   Remove the oil pump drive gear, crankshaft reluctor ring and driven gear (see Section 15).
12   Mount a dial indicator to the engine and check the camshaft endplay **(see illustration)**. Compare the camshaft endplay readings with this Chapter's Specifications; if the endplay exceeds the limits, the cam-

13.10a The roller lifters are held in place by the retainers - remove the retainer (using a pair of needle-nose pliers) . . .

13.10b . . . and the lifters (without pliers). Note that each retainer houses two individual lifters and they must be installed back in their original locations if they're going to be reused

13.12 Mount a dial indicator the engine as shown and measure the camshaft endplay from the front of the camshaft

13.13 Camshaft reluctor ring fasteners

13.14 Use a large breaker bar and socket to loosen
the camshaft gear bolt

shaft thrust plate or camshaft gear must be replaced.

13 Remove the camshaft reluctor ring fasteners and remove the reluctor ring **(see illustration)**. On engines with two-piece camshaft gears, use a punch or screwdriver to align the two camshaft gears. Once the gears are aligned, a bolt can be installed through the outer gear, threaded into the inner gear and tightened to secure the spring tension.

Caution: *The two-piece cam gear must be bolted together to prevent the spring tension from unloading upon removal. The two-piece cam gear must remain bolted together until the camshaft is installed and aligned with the crankshaft gear. If the bolt is removed, the gear will spin and cause personal injury.*

14 Prevent the engine from rotating **(see illustration 10.5a)**, then loosen the camshaft gear bolt **(see illustration)**.

15 Remove the camshaft thrust plate bolts **(see illustration)**, noting which direction the trust plate faces.

16 Carefully and slowly pull the camshaft out. Support the cam near the block so the lobes don't nick or gouge the bearings as it's withdrawn **(see illustration)**.

17 Remove and discard the camshaft gear bolt, then slide the gear and thrust plate from the camshaft **(see illustration)**.

13.15 Remove the thrust plate bolts through the
openings in the camshaft gear

13.16 As the camshaft is removed, it must be supported

13.17 Remove the camshaft gear (A) and the thrust plate (B),
noting which side of the thrust plate faces the block

13.18a Lobe lift can be obtained by measuring camshaft lobe height . . .

13.18b . . . and by measuring the camshaft base circle - the difference between the two measurements equals lobe lift

Inspection

Camshaft lobe lift check

Refer to illustrations 13.18a and 13.18b

18   Measure the camshaft lobe height and the base circle (see illustrations). The difference between the two measurements is the lobe lift (lobe height - base circle = lobe lift). Record this figure for future reference and repeat the check on the remaining camshaft lobes.

19   After the lobe lift check is complete, compare the results to the values listed in this Chapter's Specifications.

20   If the lobe lift is 0.002 inch less than specified, cam lobe wear has occurred and a new camshaft should be installed.

Camshaft bearing journals, lobes and bearings

Refer to illustration 13.22

21   After the camshaft has been removed from the engine, cleaned with solvent and dried, inspect the bearing journals for uneven wear, pitting and evidence of seizure. If the journals are damaged, the bearing inserts in the block are probably damaged as well. Both the camshaft and bearings will have to be replaced. Also check the number 4 camshaft bearing to make sure it has not spun in its bore (see illustration 2.28d in Chapter 4). If it has, the turbocharger will be starved of oil.

Note: *Camshaft bearing replacement requires special tools and expertise that place it beyond the scope of the average home mechanic. The tools for bearing removal and installation are available at stores that carry automotive tools, possibly even found at a tool rental business. It is advisable though, if the bearings are bad and the procedure is beyond your ability, take the engine block to an automotive machine shop to ensure that the job is done correctly.*

22   Measure the bearing journals with a micrometer to determine if they are excessively worn or out-of-round (see illustration).

23   Check the camshaft lobes for heat discoloration, score marks, chipped areas, pitting and uneven wear. If the lobes are in good condition and if the lobe lift measurements recorded earlier are as specified, the camshaft can be reused.

Lifters

Refer to illustrations 13.24 and 13.25

24   Clean the lifters with solvent and dry them thoroughly without mixing them up. Check each lifter wall and pushrod seat for score marks and uneven wear (see illustration). If the lifter walls are damaged or worn (which is not very likely), inspect the lifter bores in the engine block as well. If the pushrod seats are worn, check the pushrod ends.

25   Check the rollers carefully for wear and damage and make sure

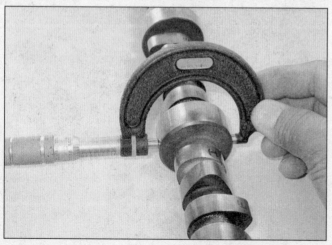

13.22 Check the diameter of each camshaft bearing journal to pinpoint excessive wear and out-of-round conditions

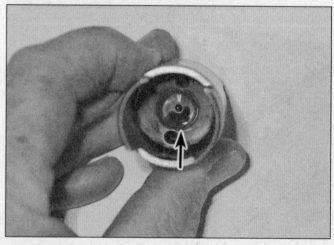

13.24 Check the pushrod seat in the top of each lifter for wear

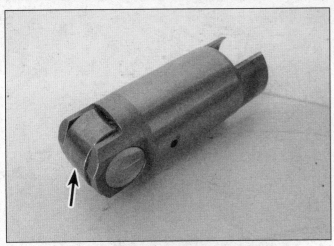

**13.25 The rollers on the lifters must turn freely -
check for wear and excessive play as well**

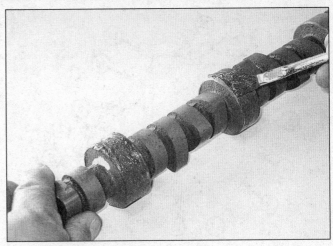

**13.27 Apply camshaft assembly lube to the cam lobes and
bearing journals before installing the camshaft**

they turn freely without excessive play **(see illustration)**.

26   Used roller lifters cannot be reinstalled with a new camshaft, but the original camshaft can be used if new lifters are installed. Always use new lifters when installing a new camshaft.

Installation

Refer to illustrations 13.27, 13.28 and 13.30

27   Install the thrust plate (facing the correct direction), then the camshaft gear and hand tighten the NEW camshaft gear bolt. Lubricate the camshaft bearing journals and cam lobes with camshaft and lifter assembly lube **(see illustration)**.

28   Slide the camshaft into the engine. Support the cam near the block and be careful not to scrape or nick the bearings. As the camshaft is installed, mesh the camshaft gear with the crankshaft gear, aligning the timing marks **(see illustration)**.

29   Install the thrust plate bolts and tighten them to the torque listed in this Chapter's Specifications. On models with a two-piece camshaft gear, remove the bolt holding the two camshaft gears together.

30   Align the pins on the camshaft gear with the reluctor **(see illustration)**, then install the mounting fasteners and tighten the fasteners to the torque listed in this Chapter's Specifications.

31   Hold the engine from rotating **(see illustration 10.5a)**, and tighten the camshaft gear mounting bolt to the torque listed in this Chapter's Specifications.

32   Mount a dial indicator to the engine and recheck the camshaft endplay **(see illustration 13.13)**. Compare the camshaft endplay readings with this Chapter's Specifications; if the endplay exceeds the limits, the camshaft thrust plate or camshaft gear must be replaced.

33   Install the oil pump drive gear, crankshaft reluctor and oil pump driven gear (see Section 15).

34   Lubricate the lifters with clean engine oil and install them in the lifter retainers. Align the flats on the lifters with the flats in the lifter retainers. Install the retainer and lifters into the engine block. If the original lifters are being reinstalled, be sure to return them to their original locations. If a new camshaft is being installed, install new lifters as well. Install the lifter retainers and retainer hold-down brackets, tightening the bolts to the torque listed in this Chapter's Specifications.

35   The remainder of installation is the reverse of removal.

36   Before starting and running the engine, refill the cooling system, change the engine oil and install a new oil filter (see Chapter 1).

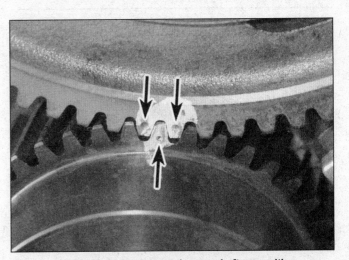

**13.28 Align the dots on the camshaft gear with
the dot on the crankshaft gear**

**13.30 The camshaft reluctor must line up with
the pins of the camshaft gear**

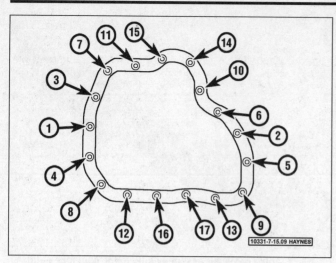

14.9 Lower oil pan tightening sequence

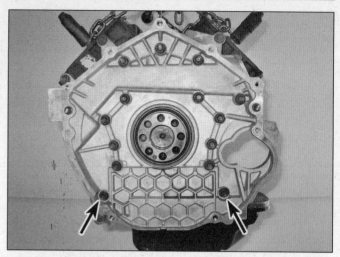

14.18 Remove the two flywheel housing-to-upper oil pan bolts

14   Oil pans - removal and installation

1   Disconnect the cables from the negative terminals of the batteries (see Chapter 5).
2   Raise the vehicle and support it securely on jackstands. Drain the engine oil and remove the oil filter (see Chapter 1).
3   Remove the oil pan skid plate and splash shield, if equipped.

Lower pan

Removal

4   Remove the crossmember mounting bolts/nuts and remove the crossmember.
5   Disconnect the electrical connector to the oil level sensor.
6   Remove all the oil pan bolts, then lower the pan from the upper pan. The pan will probably stick to the engine, so strike the pan with a rubber mallet until it breaks the gasket seal.
Caution: *Before using force on the oil pan, be sure all the bolts have been removed. Carefully slide the oil pan down and out, to the rear.*

Installation

Refer to illustration 14.9

7   Thoroughly clean the mounting surfaces of the oil pan and upper oil pan of old gasket material and sealant. Wipe the gasket surfaces clean with a rag soaked in brake system cleaner.
8   Apply a 1/8-inch wide by 1/16-inch high, bead of RTV sealant to the sealing surface of the pan, install the pan and tighten the bolts finger-tight.

9   Tighten the bolts in sequence **(see illustration)** to the torque listed in this Chapter's Specifications.
10   The remainder of installation is the reverse of removal.
11   Add the proper type and quantity of oil (see Chapter 1), start the engine and check for leaks before placing the vehicle back in service.

Upper pan

Removal

Refer to illustrations 14.18, 14.19 and 14.20

12   Remove the engine oil dipstick tube bracket bolt and pull the tube from the oil pan. Discard the O-ring.
13   Disconnect the relay rod from the Pitman arm and idler arm, and move it out of the way.
14   On 4WD models, unbolt and disconnect the driveaxles from the front differential. Disconnect the electrical connector and vent hose from the carrier. Remove the front driveshaft mounting bolts and remove the front driveshaft. Support the differential with a floor jack and remove the mounting bolts and nuts. Slowly lower the differential from the vehicle.
15   Remove the lower oil pan as previously described in this Section.
16   Remove the transmission and flywheel (see Section 17).
17   Remove the harness and cable bracket nuts.
18   Remove the flywheel housing-to-upper oil pan bolts **(see illustration)**.
19   Remove the oil pan bolts **(see illustration)**.

14.19 Remove the six internal pan bolts, then the external bolts

14.20 Carefully pry the pan down from the right front corner, then the rear; make sure you have all 24 bolts removed before trying to pry the pan off

15.2a Insert a hex socket into the secondary oil pump shaft (A), then loosen the driven gear nut (B) from the oil pump shaft . . .

15.2b . . . and slide the driven gear off of the oil pump shaft

20 Lower the upper pan from the engine. The pan will probably stick to the engine, so carefully pry the pan from the corners **(see illustration)** until it breaks the gasket seal.
Caution: *Before using force on the oil pan, be sure all the bolts have been removed. Carefully slide the oil pan down and out, to the rear.*

Installation

21 Thoroughly clean the mounting surfaces of the upper pan and engine block of old sealant. Wipe the gasket surfaces clean with a rag soaked in brake system cleaner.
22 Apply a 1/8-inch wide by 1/16-inch high, bead of RTV sealant to the sealing surface of the pan, install the pan and tighten the bolts finger-tight.
23 Tighten the bolts in a circular pattern starting from the middle working your way outwards to the torque listed in this Chapter's Specifications.
24 The remainder of installation is the reverse of removal.
25 Add the proper type and quantity of oil (see Chapter 1), start the engine and check for leaks before placing the vehicle back in service.

15.4 Remove the nuts and bolts securing the oil pick-up tube to the oil pump and cylinder block then remove the pick-up tube from the engine

---

15 Oil pump - removal and installation

Removal

Refer to illustrations 15.2a, 15.2b, 15.4, 15.5 and 15.6

1 Remove the engine front cover (see Section 12).
2 Prevent the engine from rotating **(see illustration 10.5a)**. Insert a hex socket into the secondary oil pump shaft to prevent it from turning while the oil pump driven gear nut is removed **(see illustrations)**.
Note: *Some models have left-hand threaded drive gear nuts. If the end of the oil pump shaft is stamped with an "L" the nut must removed by turning it clockwise.*
3 Remove the engine upper oil pan (see Section 14).
4 Remove the oil pump pick-up tube mounting nuts/bolts, then lower the pick-up tube and screen assembly from the engine **(see illustration)**. Discard the old pick up tube gasket.
5 Remove the oil pump drive gear and crankshaft reluctor from the crankshaft **(see illustration)** but do not remove the reluctor-to-drive gear bolts.
Note: *It may be necessary to tap off the drive gear with a brass drift or punch to remove it. Make sure to tap it as close to the center as possible to prevent damage to the reluctor ring outer edges.*

15.5 Remove the oil pump drive gear and reluctor ring assembly from the crankshaft

15.6 Oil pump mounting fasteners

15.8 Always install a new O-ring into the groove of the oil pump body

6   Remove the oil pump mounting fasteners and remove the pump from the engine **(see illustration)**.
7   Remove and discard the oil pump O-ring.

Installation

Refer to illustration 15.8

8   Install a new oil pump O-ring to the oil pump **(see illustration)**.
9   Install the oil pump to the engine block and tighten the fasteners to the torque listed in this Chapter's Specifications.
10   Slide the oil pump drive gear and reluctor ring onto the crankshaft, making sure to align the notch in the gear with the pins on the crankshaft.
Note: *Replace the pins on the crankshaft if they are worn.*
11   Install the driven gear to the oil pump shaft and tighten the nut while holding the secondary oil pump shaft **(see illustration 15.2a)**.
12   Install a new oil pump pick up tube gasket onto the studs on the oil pump. Slide the pickup tube onto the studs and install the bolts and nuts. Tighten the nuts and bolts to the torque listed in this Chapter's Specifications.
Caution: *Be absolutely certain that the pick-up tube-to-oil pump nuts are properly tightened so that no air can be sucked into the oiling system at this connection.*
13   Install the front cover, then install the oil pan (see Sections 12 and 14).
14   The remainder of installation is the reverse of removal.
15   Add oil as necessary. Run the engine and check for oil leaks. Also check the oil pressure (see Chapter 8).

16   Oil filter adapter/engine oil cooler - removal and installation

Warning: *The engine must be completely cool before beginning this procedure.*

Removal

Refer to illustrations 16.9, 16.11, 16.13a, 16.13b, 16.14, 16.15 and 16.16

1   Disconnect the cables from the negative terminals of the batteries (see Chapter 5).
2   Loosen the left front wheel lug nuts. Raise the vehicle and support it securely on jackstands. Drain the engine oil and remove the oil filter (see Chapter 1).
3   Remove the oil pan skid plate and splash shield, if equipped.
4   Drain the engine coolant (see Chapter 1).
5   Remove the four crossmember mounting bolts/nuts and remove the crossmember.
6   Remove the oil filter (see Chapter 1).
7   Remove the left front wheel, then remove the inner fender splash shield fasteners and splash shield.
8   Remove the water pump outlet pipe nuts (see Chapter 2).
9   Remove the two nuts that mount the flywheel housing-to-oil cooler assembly adapter **(see illustration)**.
10   Remove the oil filter adapter/engine cooler mounting bolts **(see illustration 16.9)** and remove the assembly with the water pump outlet pipe attached.
11   Remove and discard the oil filter adapter O-rings **(see illustration)**.

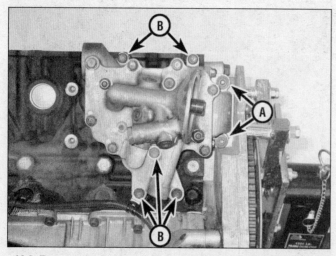

16.9 Remove the flywheel housing-to-oil cooler adapter nuts (A), remove the oil filter housing-to-cylinder block bolts (B), and remove the housing

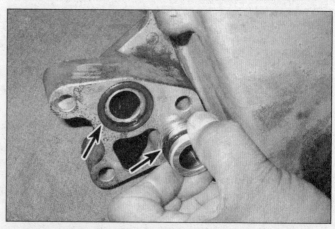

16.11 Remove the O-ring from the oil filter adapter housing

16.13a Remove the flywheel housing-to-oil cooler assembly adapter bolts . . .

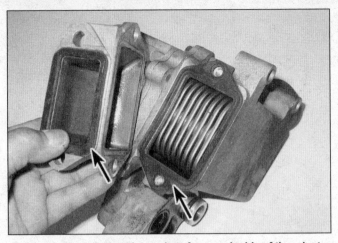

16.13b . . . then remove the gaskets from each side of the adapter

12   Remove the water pump outlet tube from the oil cooler and discard the O-ring.
13   Remove the flywheel housing-to-oil cooler assembly adapter bolts and remove the adapter and gaskets **(see illustrations)**.
14   Remove the oil filter adapter-to-oil cooler bolts **(see illustration)**.
15   Separate the oil filter adapter with heat exchanger from the oil cooler housing **(see illustration)**.
16   Remove the heat exchanger mounting nuts, then separate the exchanger from the adapter **(see illustration)**.

Installation

17   Clean the adapter, heat exchanger and cooler gasket surface areas and inspect the surface areas for cracks.
18   Install new gaskets to the heat exchanger and mount the exchanger to the oil filter adapter, then tighten the nuts to the torque listed in this Chapter's Specifications.
19   Place a new gasket onto the oil cooler housing and assemble the oil cooler to the oil filter adapter. Install the bolts and tighten them to the torque listed in this Chapter's Specifications.
20   Install a new O-ring to the water pump outlet tube and insert the tube into the oil filter housing.
21   Place a new gasket onto both sides of the flywheel housing-to-oil cooler adapter, then install the bolts and tighten them to the torque listed in this Chapter's Specifications.
22   Clean the cylinder block and oil filter adapter housing, then install the new O-ring to the oil filter adapter.
23   Install the oil filter adapter/engine oil cooler assembly to the cyl-

16.14 Remove the oil cooler housing-to-oil filter housing bolts

inder block and tighten the bolts to the torque listed in this Chapter's Specifications.
24   Install the flywheel housing adapter nuts and tighten the nuts to the torque listed in this Chapter's Specifications.
25   The remainder of installation is the reverse of the removal procedure. Replace the oil filter and refill the engine oil and cooling system.

16.15 Lift the oil filter housing with heat exchanger from the oil cooler

16.16 Separate the heat exchanger from the oil filter housing, then replace the gaskets

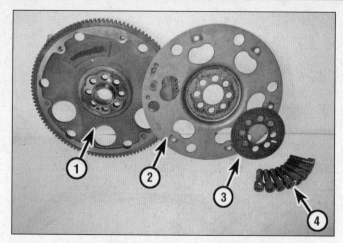

**17.14 Typical flywheel assembly details –
automatic transmission models**

1	Flywheel	3	Flywheel washer
2	Flywheel plate	4	Flywheel bolts

17   Flywheel - removal and installation

Removal

Refer to illustration 17.14

1   Disconnect the cables from the negative terminals of the batteries (see Chapter 5).
2   Raise the vehicle and support it securely on jackstands.
3   Disconnect the exhaust pipes from the engine.
4   Disconnect the shift linkage (manual models) or the shift cable (automatic models) from the transmission.
5   Remove the starter motor (see Chapter 5).
6   Disconnect the electrical connectors to the transmission.
7   Disconnect the rear driveshaft and, on 4WD models, disconnect the front driveshaft from the transfer case.
8   Using a transmission jack support the transmission, then remove the rear transmission mount nuts and bolts.
9   Raise the transmission slightly and remove the transmission mount.
10   Place a jack with a block of wood under the rear of the engine to support it.
11   Remove the transmission-to-engine mounting bolts and remove the transmission.
12   Make alignment marks on the flywheel and crankshaft to ensure correct alignment during reinstallation. On manual transmission models, unbolt the clutch pressure plate and disc.
13   Remove and discard the bolts securing the flywheel to the crankshaft. If the crankshaft turns, prevent the flywheel from turning using one of the methods described in Section 10.
Note: *These bolts are VERY tight. A 3/4-inch drive breaker bar is recommended. We also found it necessary to apply heat to the bolts before they would break loose.*
14   On automatic transmission models, remove the flywheel washer and plate **(see illustration)**. Remove the flywheel from the crankshaft. Since the flywheel is fairly heavy, be sure to support it while removing the last bolt.
Warning: *The ring-gear teeth may be sharp, so wear gloves to protect your hands.*

Installation

15   Clean the flywheel to remove grease and oil. On manual transmission models, inspect the surface for cracks, rivet grooves, burned areas and score marks. Light scoring can be removed with emery cloth.

18.13 Carefully drill a hole in the metal side of the seal

Check for cracked or broken ring gear teeth. Lay the flywheel on a flat surface and use a straightedge to check for warpage.
16   On manual transmission models, check the pilot bearing, if doesn't turn or feels rough when turning the bearing, remove the bearing from the flywheel and replace it.
17   Clean and inspect the mating surfaces of the flywheel and the crankshaft. If the crankshaft rear seal is leaking, replace it before reinstalling the flywheel (see Section 18).
18   Position the flywheel against the crankshaft. Align the marks made during removal. Note that some engines have an alignment dowel or staggered bolt holes to ensure correct installation. Before installing the new bolts, apply thread-locking compound to the threads.
19   On automatic transmission models, install the flywheel plate then the washer **(see illustration 17.14)**.
20   Wedge a screwdriver in the ring gear teeth to keep the flywheel from turning and tighten the bolts to the torque listed in this Chapter's Specifications, using a criss-cross pattern.
21   The remainder of installation is the reverse of the removal procedure.

18   Rear main oil seal - replacement

Refer to illustrations 18.13, 18.14, 18.15 and 18.18
1   Disconnect the cables from the negative terminals of the batteries (see Chapter 5).
2   Raise the vehicle and support it securely on jackstands.
3   Disconnect the exhaust pipes from the engine.
4   Disconnect the shift linkage (manual models) or the shift cable (automatic models) from the transmission.
5   Remove the starter motor (see Chapter 5).
6   Disconnect the electrical connectors to the transmission.
7   Disconnect the rear driveshaft and, on 4WD models, disconnect the front driveshaft from the transfer case.
8   Using a transmission jack support the transmission, then remove the rear transmission mount nuts and bolts.
9   Raise the transmission slightly and remove the transmission mount.
10   Place a jack with a block of wood under the rear of the engine to support it.
11   Remove the transmission-to-engine mounting bolts and remove the transmission.
12   Remove the flywheel (see Section 17).
13   Using a drill, carefully drill a hole in the metal side of the seal **(see illustration)**.
14   Place a washer onto a screw, then thread the screw into the hole drilled in the seal **(see illustration)**.
15   Connect a puller or equivalent around the screw and carefully pull the seal out from the housing **(see illustration)**.

18.14 Thread the screw and washer into the hole drilled in the seal

18.15 Connect a puller to the screw and pull the seal from the housing

16   Once the seal is removed, clean the crankshaft and housing surfaces.

17   Lubricate the crankshaft seal journal and the lip of the new seal with multi-purpose grease.

18   Evenly drive the new seal into the retainer with a seal driver or a wood block and a section of pipe slightly smaller in diameter than the outside diameter of the seal **(see illustration)**. The new seal should be approximately flush with the surface of the housing or the depth measured in Step 2.

19   The remainder of installation is the reverse of removal.

19   Flywheel housing – removal and installation

Removal

Refer to illustrations 19.8 19.9, and 19.10

1   Disconnect the cables from the negative terminals of the batteries (see Chapter 5).

2   Raise the vehicle and support it securely on jackstands.

3   Drain the cooling system (see Chapter 1).

4   Remove the transmission and rear main oil seal (see Section 18).

5   Remove the turbocharger oil return line mounting nuts from the top of the housing and make sure the line is clear of the housing.

6   Remove the oil filter (see Chapter 1), then remove the oil cooler adapter nuts from the flywheel housing and the mounting studs.

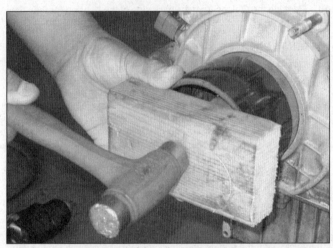

18.18 Install the new seal into the retainer with a wood block and a section of pipe

7   Remove the upper and lower oil pans (see Section 14).

8   Remove the flywheel housing bolts **(see illustration)**.

9   Remove the flywheel housing from the engine **(see illustration)**.

19.8 Flywheel housing bolt locations

19.9 Remove the flywheel housing from the cylinder block

**19.10 Remove the O-rings from the housing
or from the engine block**

10   Remove the O-rings from the back side of the housing (or they may be stuck to the cylinder block) **(see illustration)** and replace them.

Installation

Refer to illustration 19.13

11   Thoroughly clean the mounting surfaces of the flywheel housing, oil pan and engine block of old gasket material and sealant. Wipe the gasket surfaces clean with a rag soaked in brake system cleaner.
12   Install the O-rings to the flywheel housing.
13   Install a new oil cooler adapter gasket to each side of the adapter, then install the adapter to the flywheel housing.
14   Apply a 1/8-inch wide by 1/16-inch high bead of RTV sealant along the sealing surface of the flywheel housing **(see illustration)**. Install the housing to the cylinder block and tighten the bolts to the torque listed in this Chapter's Specifications.
15   Install a new rear main oil seal (see Section 18).
16   The remainder of installation is the reverse of removal.
17   Replace the oil filter, add the proper type and quantity of oil (see Chapter 1), start the engine and check for leaks before placing the vehicle back in service.

---

20   Engine mounts - check and replacement

1   Engine mounts seldom require attention, but broken or deteriorated mounts should be replaced immediately or the added strain placed on the driveline components may cause damage.

Check

2   During the check, the engine must be raised slightly to remove the weight from the mounts.
3   Raise the vehicle and support it securely on jackstands. Remove the skid plate and lower engine splash shield fasteners, then remove the plate and splash shield.
4   Check the mounts to see if the rubber is cracked, hardened or separated from the metal plates. Sometimes the rubber will split right down the center.
5   Check for relative movement between the mount plates and the engine or frame (use a large prybar to attempt to move the engine away from the mounts). If movement is noted, check the tightness of the mount fasteners first before condemning the mounts. Usually when engine mounts are broken, they are very obvious, as the engine will easily move away from the mount when pried or under load.

Replacement

Engine mounts

Refer to illustrations 20.13a and 20.13b

6   Disconnect the cables from the negative terminals of the batteries (see Chapter 5), then raise the vehicle and support it securely on jackstands. Remove the front wheels.
7   Remove the skid plate and lower engine splash shield fasteners, then remove the plate and splash shield.
8   Remove the inner fender splash shield and the exhaust manifold heat shield from the side you're working on.
9   On 4WD models, the driveaxle may need to be moved depending on the model year. Remove the driveaxle-to-differential bolts and lower the front part of the driveaxle out of the way.
10   Working through the wheel well, remove the engine mount-to-frame bracket bolts. There are three bolts on each side securing the mounts to the frame bracket.
11   On 4WD models, attach an engine hoist to the top of the engine for lifting; do not use a jack under the oil pan to support the entire weight of the engine or the oil pump pick-up could be damaged. On 2WD models, the hoist can be used or a jack placed under the large ground wire bolt bosses on each side of the engine block to support the weight of the engine while the engine mounts are being replaced.
12   Raise the engine far enough to remove the mount from between the engine and the frame, then unbolt the mount from the engine block. **Caution:** *Raise the engine only enough to remove the mount, if the engine is raised too much, the fan shroud and engine exhaust can be damaged.*
13   Remove the mount through-bolts **(see illustrations)** then remove the mount frame bracket and mount.
14   Installation is the reverse of removal. Use non-hardening thread-locking compound on the mount bolts and tighten them to the torque listed in this Chapter's Specifications.

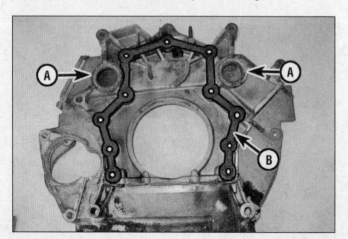

**19.13 Install the O-rings (A) to the housing, then apply a bead of
sealant to the flywheel housing sealing surface (B) area**

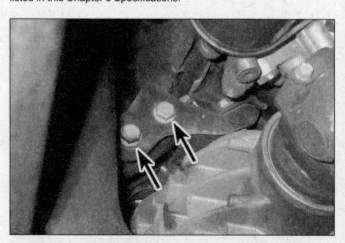

20.13a Location of the left side engine mount through-bolts

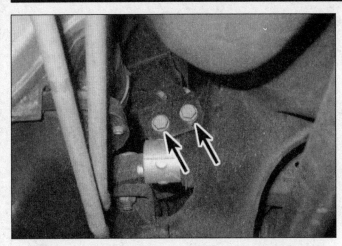

20.13b Location of the right side engine mount through-bolts

Transmission mount

15 Disconnect the cables from the negative battery terminals. Raise the vehicle and support it securely on jackstands, then remove the front wheels.

16 Support the engine with a transmission jack or good floor jack.

17 Remove the transmission mount-to-crossmember nuts.

18 Remove the transmission mount-to-transmission or transfer case adapter bolts.

19 Raise the transmission far enough to remove the mount from between the crossmember and the transmission or transfer case adapter and remove the mount.

Caution: *Raise the transmission only enough to remove the mount, if the transmission is raised too much, the shift linkage and engine exhaust can be damaged.*

20 Installation is the reverse of removal. Use non-hardening thread-locking compound on the mount bolts and tighten them to the torque listed in this Chapter's Specifications.

Notes

Chapter 8
Engine overhaul procedures

Contents

Specifications

Note: *Refer to Chapter 7 for additional specifications.*

General

Engine type	90 degree V8
Displacement	402 cubic inches (6.6 liters)
Idle speed	
2001 models	600 rpm
2002 and later models	680 rpm
Compression ratio	
2001 through 2005 models	17.5:1
2006 through 2016 models	16.8:1
2017 and later models	16.0:1
Compression pressure	
Standard	458 psi (3158 kPa)
Minimum	300 psi (2069 kPa)
Oil pressure (engine warm)	
2009 and earlier models	
At idle	14 psi (96 kPa)
At 1800 rpm	42 psi (298 kPa)
2010 through 2016 models	
At idle	7 psi (48 kPa)
At 1800 rpm	28 psi (193 kPa)
2017 and later models	
At 1000 rpm	25 psi (172 kPa)
At 2000 rpm	29 psi (200 kPa)
Bore diameter	
Standard	4.0550 to 4.0560 inches (102.997 to 103.023 mm)
Service limit	4.0594 inches (103.11 mm)
Stroke	3.8976 inches (99 mm)
Firing order	1-2-7-8-4-5-6-3

Cylinder numbering

Connecting rods

Length center-to-center	
2016 and earlier models	6.42 inches (163.0 mm)
2017 and later models	6.43 inches (163.25 mm)
Connecting rod bearing oil clearance	
2016 and earlier models	
Standard	0.0014 to 0.0030 inch (0.036 to 0.077 mm)
Service limit	0.0039 inch (0.10 mm)
2017 and later models	
Standard	0.0018 to 0.0033 inch (0.045 to 0.085 mm)
Service limit	0.0039 inch (0.10 mm)
Connecting rod side clearance	
2016 and earlier models	
Standard	0.0122 to 0.0193 inch (0.031 to 0.49 mm)
Service limit	0.0213 inch (0.54 mm)
2017 and later models	
Standard	0.0283 to 0.0425 inch (0.72 to 1.08 mm)
Service limit	0.0445 inch (1.13 mm)

Connecting rods (continued)
Small end inside diameter
    2016 and earlier models
        Standard .... 1.3587 to 1.3591 inches (34.512 to 34.522 mm)
        Service limit .... 1.3594 inches (34.53 mm)
    2017 and later models
        Standard .... 1.4181 to 1.4185 inches (36.019 to 36.029 mm)
        Service limit .... 1.4188 inches (36.037 mm)
Connecting rod bearing end inside diameter (standard)
    2016 and earlier models.. 2.4789 to 2.4795 inches (62.958 to 62.979 mm)
    2017 and later models... 2.6678 to 2.6793 inches (68.016 to 68.056 mm)

Crankshaft
Crankshaft bearing oil clearance
    2016 and earlier models
        Standard .... 0.0015 to 0.0028 inch (0.039 to 0.070 mm)
        Service limit .... 0.0055 inch (0.014 mm)
    2017 and later models
        Standard .... 0.0016 to 0.0031 inch (0.041 to 0.079 mm)
        Service limit .... 0.0055 inch (0.014 mm)
Crankshaft endplay
    2016 and earlier models
        Standard .... 0.0016 to 0.0081 inch (0.040 to 0.205 mm)
        Service limit .... 0.0213 inch (0.54 mm)
    2017 and later models
        Standard .... 0.0041 to 0.0140 inch (0.104 to 0.358 mm)
        Service limit .... 0.0213 inch (0.54 mm)
Crankshaft journal diameter
    Mains
        Standard .... 3.1459 to 3.1466 inches (79.905 to 79.925 mm)
        Service limit .... 3.1453 inches (79.89 mm)
    Connecting rods (crankpins)
        2016 and earlier models
            Standard.. 2.4764 to 2.4772 inches (62.902 to 62.922 mm)
            Service limit .... 2.4756 inches (62.88 mm)
        2017 and later models
            Standard.. 2.6768 to 2.6775 inches (67.992 to 68.008 mm)
            Service limit .... 2.6760 inches (67.97 mm)
Crankshaft runout
    2016 and earlier models
        Standard .... 0.0020 inch (0.05 mm)
        Service limit .... 0.0173 inch (0.44 mm)
    2017 and later models.. 0.0016 inch (0.04 mm)

Pistons
Piston diameter (standard).. 4.0510 to 4.0516 inches (102.898 to 102.910 mm)
Piston-to-bore clearance (standard)
    2016 and earlier models.. 0.0035 to 0.0047 inch (0.090 to 0.120 mm)
    2017 and later models... 0.0023 to 0.0037 inch (0.058 to 0.094 mm)
Piston outside diameter - at 7/8-inch (22 mm)
    from piston bottom (standard)... 4.0531 to 4.0535 inches (102.948 to 102.960 mm)
Piston pin bore inside diameter (standard)
    2016 and earlier models.. 1.3584 to 1.3587 inches (34.504 to 34.512 mm)
    2017 and later models... 1.4176 to 1.4178 inches (35.008 to 36.013 mm)

Piston pins
Pin diameter
    2016 and earlier models
        Standard .... 1.3581 to 1.3583 inches (34.495 to 34.5 mm)
        Service limit .... 1.3563 inches (34.45 mm)
    2017 and later models
        Standard .... 1.4170 to 1.4173 inches (35.994 to 36.000 mm)
        Service limit .... 1.41535 inches (35.950 mm)
Clearance in piston
    Standard.. 0.0002 to 0.0007 inch (0.004 to 0.017 mm)
    Service limit... 0.0007 inch (0.017 mm)

Piston rings
Compression ring end gap
    2016 and earlier models
        Standard .... 0.0118 to 0.0177 inch (0.3 to 0.45 mm)
        Service limit .... 0.0539 inch (1.37 mm)
    2017 and later models (standard) .... 0.0098 to 0.0138 inch (0.25 to 0.35 mm)
2nd ring end gap
    2016 and earlier models
        Standard .... 0.0197 to 0.0256 inch (0.50 to 0.65 mm)
        Service limit .... 0.0531 inch (1.35 mm)
    2017 and later models (standard) .... 0.0138 to 0.0177 inch (0.35 to 0.45 mm)
Oil ring end gap
    Standard.. 0.0059 to 0.0138 inch (0.15 to 0.35 mm)
    Service limit... 0.0472 inch (1.20 mm)

Piston rings (continued)
Piston ring-to-groove (side) clearance
  Compression ring
    2016 and earlier models
      Standard.. 0.0030 to 0.0067 inch (0.08 to 0.17 mm)
      Service limit... 0.0102 inch (0.26 mm)
    2017 and later models (standard)............................. 0.0030 to 0.0043 inch (0.08 to 0.11 mm)
  2nd ring
    2016 and earlier models
      Standard.. 0.0004 to 0.0012 inch (0.01 to 0.03 mm)
      Service limit... 0.0039 inch (0.10 mm)
    2017 and later models (standard)............................. 0.0020 to 0.0035 inch (0.05 to 0.09 mm)
  Oil ring
    2016 and earlier models
      Standard.. 0.0004 to 0.0012 inch (0.01 to 0.03 mm)
      Service limit... 0.0047 inch (0.12 mm)
    2017 and later models (standard)............................. 0.0012 to 0.0028 inch (0.03 to 0.07 mm)

Camshaft ..... See Chapter 7
Rocker arms ..... See Chapter 7

Valves and related components

Valves, intake
Valve stem outside diameter (standard)......................... 0.28 inch (7.0 mm)
Valve stem-to-guide clearance
  Standard.. 0.0012 to 0.0025 inch (0.030 to 0.063 mm)
  Service limit... 0.0079 inch (0.20 mm)

Valves, exhaust
Valve stem outside diameter (standard)......................... 0.28 inch (7.0 mm)
Valve stem-to-guide clearance
  Standard.. 0.0015 to 0.0028 inch (0.038 to 0.071 mm)
  Service limit... 0.0079 inch (0.20 mm)

Valve springs
Valve spring free length (standard)............................... 2.2283 inches (56.6 mm)
Valve spring installed height, intake and exhaust (standard) ... 1.6142 inches (41 mm)
Valve spring tension - intake
  Standard.. 71.0 to 81.6 lbs at 1.61 inches (315 to 363 N at 41 mm)
  Service limit... 68.8 lbs at 1.61 inches (306 N at 41 mm)
Valve spring tension - exhaust
  Standard.. 71.0 to 81.6 lbs at 1.61 inches (315 to 363 N at 41 mm)
  Service limit... 61.8 lbs at 1.61 inches (275 N at 41 mm)

Oil pump
Gear teeth-to-housing clearance
  Standard.. 0.0049 to 0.0087 inch (0.125 to 0.221 mm)
  Service limit... 0.0087 inch (0.22 mm)
Gear-to-cover clearance
  Standard.. 0.0025 to 0.0043 inch (0.064 to 0.109 mm)
  Service limit... 0.0043 inch (0.109 mm)
Gear shaft-to-bushing clearance (service limit)............... 0.0055 inch (0.14 mm)
Drive gear shaft outside diameter
  Standard.. 0.7853 to 0.7858 inch (19.947 to 19.960 mm)
  Service limit... 0.7819 inch (19.86 mm)
Driven gear shaft outside diameter
  Standard.. 0.7853 to 0.7858 inch (19.947 to 19.960 mm)
  Service limit... 0.7819 inch (19.86 mm)

Torque specifications

	Ft-lbs (unless otherwise indicated)	Nm

Note: *One foot-pound (ft-lb) of torque is equivalent to 12 inch-pounds (in-lbs) of torque. Torque values below approximately 15 ft-lbs are expressed in inch-pounds, because most foot-pound torque wrenches are not accurate at these smaller values.*

Connecting rod cap bolts*
  2016 and earlier models
    Step 1 ..... 47 64
    Step 2 ..... Tighten an additional 30-degrees
    Step 3 ..... Tighten an additional 30-degrees
  2017 and later models
    Step 1 ..... 26 35
    Step 2 ..... Tighten an additional 30-degrees
    Step 3 ..... Tighten an additional 30-degrees
    Step 4 ..... Tighten an additional 30-degrees
Main bearing cap bolts*
  Step 1 ..... 72 98
  Step 2 ..... 97 132
  Step 3 ..... Tighten an additional 60-degrees
Main bearing cap side bolts 52 70
Piston cooling nozzle bolts 15 21
Torque converter bolts 44 60
Transmission-to-engine fasteners 37 50

*Use new bolts

1   General information and diagnosis

General information

Included in this Chapter are the general overhaul procedures for the cylinder head(s) and internal engine components.

The information ranges from advice concerning preparation for an overhaul and the purchase of replacement parts to detailed, step-by-step procedures covering removal and installation of internal engine components and the inspection of parts.

The following Sections have been written based on the assumption that the engine has been removed from the vehicle. For information concerning in-vehicle engine repair, as well as removal and installation of the external components necessary for the overhaul, see the pertinent Chapters of this manual.

Diagnosis

Correct diagnosis is an essential part of every repair; without it you can only cure the problem by accident.

Sometimes a simple service item will cause symptoms similar to a worn out or defective engine. Be sure the engine is serviced to manufacturer's specifications (see Chapter 1) before you begin with the following diagnosis procedures.

If you are concerned about the condition of your engine because of decreased performance or fuel economy, perform a compression test. If the engine is making unusual noises, perform an oil pressure test and noise diagnosis. Also, the engine should be checked with a scan tool to eliminate that system as the source of the problem (this is normally done by a dealer service department or other qualified repair shop).

One of the more common reasons people rebuild their engines is because of oil consumption. Before you decide that the engine needs an overhaul based on oil consumption, make sure that oil leaks aren't responsible. If you park the vehicle in the same place every day on pavement, look for oil stains or puddles of oil. To check more accurately, place a large piece of cardboard under the engine overnight. Compare the color and feel of the oil on the dipstick to the fluids found under the vehicle to verify that it's oil (transmission fluid is slightly red).

If any drips are evident, raise the vehicle and support it securely on jackstands and carefully inspect the underside. Sometimes leaks will only occur when the engine is hot, under load or on an incline, so look for signs of leakage as well as active drips. If a significant oil leak is found, correct it before you take oil consumption measurements.

Excessive oil consumption is an indication that cylinders, pistons, rings, valve stems, seals and/or valve guides may be worn. A clogged crankcase ventilation system can also cause this problem.

Every engine uses oil at a different rate. However, if an engine uses a quart of oil in 700 miles or less, or has visible blue exhaust smoke, it definitely needs repair.

To measure oil consumption accurately, park the vehicle on a level surface and shut off the engine. Wait about 5 minutes to allow the oil to drain down into the sump. Wipe the dipstick and insert it into the dipstick tube until it hits the stop. Then withdraw it carefully and read the level before the oil has a chance to flow. Fill the sump exactly to the full mark with the correct grade and viscosity of oil and write down the mileage shown on the odometer. Then monitor the oil level, using this same checking procedure until one quart of oil has been consumed and note the mileage.

Every moving part in the vehicle can make noise. Owners frequently blame the engine for a noise that is actually in the transmission or driveline.

Set the parking brake and place the transmission in Neutral (manual) or Park (automatic). Start the engine with the hood open and determine if the noise is actually coming from the engine. Rev the engine slightly; does the noise increase directly with engine speed? If the noise sounds like it's coming from the engine and it varies with engine speed, it probably is an engine or flywheel/torque converter noise (automatic transmissions only).

What kind of noise is it? If it's a squealing sound, check drivebelt tension. Spray some belt dressing (available at auto parts stores) on the belt; if the noise goes away, the belt might be worn out or the tensioner could be defective. Sometimes it's necessary to remove the drivebelt briefly to eliminate the engine accessories as a source of noise. With the belt removed and the engine off, turn each accessory by hand and listen for sounds. Then run the engine briefly and listen for the noise.

Knocking or ticking noises are the most common types of internal engine noises. Noises that occur at crankshaft speed are usually caused by crankshaft, connecting rod and bearing problems, so begin your search on the lower part of the engine. Noises that occur at half of crankshaft speed usually involve the camshaft, lifters, rocker arms, valves, springs and mechanical fuel pump pushrod. Listen for these sounds near the top of the engine.

To pinpoint the source of the noise, a mechanic's stethoscope is best. If you don't have one, improvise with a length of hose held to your ear. You can also hold the handle of a large screwdriver to your ear and touch the tip to the suspected areas.

Move the listening device around until the sound is loudest. Think about which components are in the area of the noise and which part could produce this sound.

If the noise is in the lower portion of the engine, check for piston slap, piston pin, connecting rod, main bearing and piston ring noises.

Piston slap is loudest on a cold engine and quiets down as the engine warms up. Listen for a dull, hollow sound in the cylinder wall just below the head. If you suspect that a piston has a hole in it, remove the dipstick and listen in the opening. Hold a piece of rubber hose between your ear and the tube. You should be able to hear and feel combustion gasses escaping if the piston has a hole or is cracked.

Main bearing knocks have a low-pitched knock deep within the engine that will sound loudest when the engine is first started. It will also be quite noticeable under heavy load.

Connecting rod bearings knock loudest when the accelerator is pressed briefly and then quickly released. The noise is usually caused by excessive bearing wear or insufficient oil pressure.

Piston rings that are loose in their grooves or broken make a chattering noise that is loudest during acceleration. This should be confirmed by a dealership service department or other qualified repair shop. A compression check will tell you what mechanical condition the upper end (pistons, rings, valves, head gaskets) of your engine is in. Specifically, it can tell you if the compression is down due to leakage caused by worn piston rings, defective valves and seats or a blown head gasket.

Note: *The engine must be at normal operating temperature and the battery must be fully charged for this check. Refer to Section 4 for more information.*

Engine oil pressure provides a fairly good indication of bearing condition in an engine. As bearing surfaces wear, oil clearances increase. This increased clearance allows the oil to flow through the bearings more readily, which results in lower oil pressure. Oil pumps also wear, which causes an additional loss of pressure.

Check the oil pressure with a gauge installed in place of the oil pressure sending unit (see Section 3). Allow the engine to reach normal operating temperature before performing the test. If the pressure is extremely low, the bearings and/or oil pump are probably worn out.

Worn camshaft lobes are fairly common on high-mileage engines. If the engine is low on power, runs rough and/or backfires constantly through the intake or exhaust, suspect a worn camshaft.

To check for worn camshaft lobes, remove the valve covers. Then remove the rocker arms.

Mount a dial indicator so it bears on the end of the pushrod. Using a socket and ratchet on the crankshaft balancer bolt, slowly turn the crankshaft clockwise through two full rotations (720-degrees) while observing the dial indicator. Note the high and low readings and subtract the low from the high to obtain the lift. Record the measurements for each cylinder and note whether it was for exhaust or intake.

Compare the measurements of all the intake lobes; they should be within 0.002 inch of each other. Repeat this check for the exhaust lobes as well.

When the surface hardening wears off of a camshaft lobe, the metal below it scuffs away rapidly. Usually, worn lobes will be several tenths of an inch below the good ones.

If one or more lobes are worn, replace the camshaft and lifters as an assembly. Never use old lifters on a new camshaft.

A cracked block or cylinder head and/or a blown head gasket will cause a loss of power, overheating and a host of other problems. These problems are usually brought on by severe overheating or freezing due to insufficient antifreeze.

If you suspect internal engine leakage, check the oil on the dipstick for contamination of the oil by coolant. The oil level may increase and the oil will appear milky in color. Sometimes, oil will also get into the radiator; it will usually float on the top of the coolant. Occasionally steam and coolant will come out of the exhaust pipe, even when the engine is warmed up, because of a leaking head gasket.

Note: *Don't confuse this with the condensation vapor normally present when an engine is warming up in cool weather.*

The cooling system and engine may be checked for leaks with a pressure tester. Follow the instructions provided by the tool manufacturer. Correct any external leaks in the hoses, water pump and radiator, etc. If no external leaks are found, look and listen for signs of leakage on the engine.

Note: *A leaking heater core will cause a hidden pressure loss. Clamp off the hoses going to it at the firewall to eliminate this source of leakage.*

Another device that is useful for determining if there is a crack in the engine or a blown head gasket is a combustion leak detector. Combustion leak detectors use a blue colored fluid to test for combustion gases in the cooling system, which indicates a compression leak from a cylinder into the coolant. Be sure to follow the instructions included with the tester. A sample of gasses present in the top of the radiator is drawn into the tester. If any combustion gases are present in the sample taken, the test fluid will change color to yellow. Leak detectors and extra test fluid are readily available from most auto parts stores.

If the engine is overheating but testing indicates no cracks, blown gaskets or other internal problems, carefully inspect the cooling system for problems and correct as necessary. Frequently, partially clogged radiators, stuck thermostats and defective water pumps cause overheating.

When an internal coolant leak is found, the cylinder heads should be removed for a thorough inspection. If a gasket has blown, have an automotive machine shop check for warpage on both heads and resurface as necessary. If no warpage is found, have both cylinder heads checked for cracks. If tests indicate internal leakage, but the heads check out OK, have the block checked.

Correct the cause of the failure, such as a clogged radiator, before the vehicle is put back in service. Otherwise, the problem will likely reoccur.

2   Engine overhaul - general information

It's not always easy to determine when, or if, an engine should be completely overhauled, as a number of factors must be considered.

High mileage is not necessarily an indication that an overhaul is needed, while low mileage doesn't preclude the need for an overhaul. Frequency of servicing is probably the most important consideration. An engine that's had regular and frequent oil and filter changes, as well as other required maintenance, will most likely give many thousands of miles of reliable service. Conversely, a neglected engine may require an overhaul very early in its life.

Before beginning any work, perform the diagnostic checks in Section 1. Excessive oil consumption is an indication that piston rings, valve seals and/or valve guides are in need of attention. Make sure that oil leaks aren't responsible before deciding that the rings and/or guides are bad. Perform a cylinder compression check to determine the extent of the work required (see Section 4).

Check the oil pressure with a gauge installed in place of the oil pressure sending unit (see Section 3) and compare it to this Chapter's Specifications. If it's extremely low, the bearings and/or oil pump are probably worn out.

Loss of power, rough running, knocking or metallic engine noises, excessive valve train noise and high fuel consumption rates may also point to the need for an overhaul, especially if they're all present at the same time. If a complete service doesn't remedy the situation, major mechanical work is the only solution.

An engine overhaul involves restoring the internal parts to the specifications of a new engine. During an overhaul, the piston rings are replaced and the cylinder walls are reconditioned (rebored and/or honed). If a rebore is done by an automotive machine shop, new oversize pistons will also be installed.

Note: *Consult an automotive machine shop as to whether or not they recommend re-boring. Some claim that the engine block must be replaced if any dimensions are out of specification.*

The main bearings, connecting rod bearings and camshaft bearings are generally replaced with new ones and, if necessary, the crankshaft may be reground to restore the journals. Generally, the valves are serviced as well, since they're usually in less-than-perfect condition at this point. While the engine is being overhauled, other components, such as the starter and alternator can be rebuilt as well. The end result should be a like-new engine that will give many trouble-free miles.

Note: *Critical cooling system components such as the hoses, drivebelt, thermostat and water pump MUST be replaced with new parts when an engine is overhauled. The radiator should be checked carefully to ensure that it isn't clogged or leaking. Also, we don't recommend overhauling the oil pump - always install a new one when an engine is rebuilt.*

Before beginning the engine overhaul, read through the entire procedure to familiarize yourself with the scope and requirements of the job. Check on availability of parts and make sure that any necessary special tools and equipment are obtained in advance. Most work can be done with typical hand tools, although a number of precision measuring tools are required for inspecting parts to determine if they must be replaced. Often an automotive machine shop will handle the inspection of parts and offer advice concerning reconditioning and replacement.

Note: *Always wait until the engine has been completely disassembled and all components, especially the engine block, have been inspected before deciding what service and repair operations must be performed by an automotive machine shop. Since the block's condition will be the major factor to consider when determining whether to overhaul the original engine or buy a rebuilt one, never purchase parts or have machine work done on other components until the block has been thoroughly inspected.*

As a final note, to ensure maximum life and minimum trouble from a rebuilt engine, everything must be assembled with care in a spotlessly clean environment.

3.2a The oil pressure sending unit on LB7 engines is mounted to an adapter on the left front side of the engine

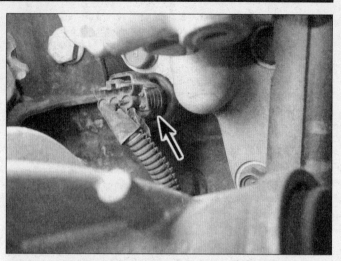

3.2b The oil pressure sending unit on all except LB7 engines is located at the left rear of the engine, near the oil filter adapter/oil cooler

3   Oil pressure check

Refer to illustrations 3.2a and 3.2b

1   Low engine oil pressure can be a sign of an engine in need of rebuilding. A low oil pressure indicator (often called an "idiot light") is not a test of the oiling system. Such indicators only come on when the oil pressure is dangerously low. Even a factory oil pressure gauge in the instrument panel is only a relative indication, although much better for driver information than a warning light. A better test is with a mechanical (not electrical) oil pressure gauge.

2   Locate the oil pressure indicator sending unit on the side of the engine block **(see illustrations)** and disconnect the electrical connector.

3   Unscrew and remove the oil pressure sending unit, then screw in the hose for your oil pressure gauge. If necessary, install an adapter fitting. Use Teflon tape or thread sealant on the threads of the adapter and/or the fitting on the end of your gauge's hose.

4   Connect an accurate tachometer to the engine, according to the tachometer manufacturer's instructions.

5   Check the oil pressure with the engine running (normal operating temperature) at the specified engine speed, and compare it to this Chapter's Specifications. If it's extremely low, the bearings and/or oil pump are probably worn out.

Caution: *Make sure the hose from the gauge is clear of any moving parts.*

4   Compression check

Refer to illustrations 4.4 and 4.5

Warning: *Due to the extremely high cylinder pressures created by a diesel engine, a compression gauge made specifically for use with diesel engines must be used.*

Caution: *Do not add oil to any cylinder during a compression check on a diesel engine; this will cause extensive internal engine damage.*

Note: *It is normal for cylinder to cylinder variations to be higher on engines with less than 12,000 miles (20,000 km).*

1   A compression check will tell you what mechanical condition the upper end (pistons, rings, valves, head gaskets) of your engine is in. Specifically, it can tell you if the compression is down due to leakage caused by worn piston rings, defective valves and seats or a blown head gasket.

Note: *Make sure the engine is fully warmed up. In order to receive an accurate compression reading, the battery must have an adequate charge and the engine must crank at approximately 200 rpm.*

2   Begin by cleaning the area around the glow plugs before you remove them (compressed air should be used, if available). The idea is to prevent dirt from getting into the cylinders as the compression check is being done.

3   Remove all of the glow plugs from the engine (see Chapter 5).

4   Connect a remote starter switch (available from most auto parts stores) to the starter **(see illustration)**.

Caution: *Do not crank the engine with the ignition key switch; the glow plug circuit and fuel injectors will be energized, potentially causing engine damage when the engine is cranked.*

5   Install the compression gauge in the number one glow plug hole **(see illustration)**.

6   Crank the engine over at least six compression strokes (or "puffs") and watch the gauge. The compression should build up quickly in a healthy engine. Low compression on the first stroke, followed by gradually increasing pressure on successive strokes, indicates worn piston rings. A low compression reading on the first stroke, which doesn't build up during successive strokes, indicates leaking valves or a blown head gasket (a cracked head could also be the cause). Deposits on the undersides of the valve heads can also cause low compression. Record the highest gauge reading obtained.

7   Repeat the procedure for the remaining cylinders and compare the results to this Chapter's Specifications.

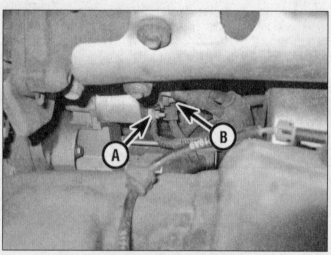

4.4 Connect a remote starter to the S terminal (A) and the battery terminal (B) of the starter

4.5 Install a special adapter into the glow plug hole and couple the compression gauge onto the adapter

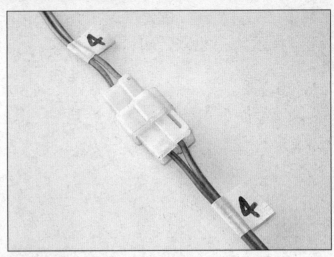

6.6 Label each wire before unplugging the connector

8   If two adjacent cylinders have equally low compression, there's a strong possibility that the head gasket between them is blown. The appearance of coolant in the combustion chambers or the crankcase would verify this condition.

9   There should not be more than a 50 psi difference between the average overall compression results and any one cylinder.

10   The results are normal when the compression for each cylinder builds up quickly and evenly to the compression listed in this Chapter's Specifications.

11   If the compression is low on the first stroke and builds up with after more cranking, but does not reach the specified pressure, the piston rings are most likely leaking.

12   If the compression is low on the first stroke and does not build up after more cranking, the valves are most likely leaking.

13   If compression is way down or varies greatly between cylinders, it would be a good idea to have a crankcase pressure test performed by an automotive repair shop. This test will pinpoint exactly where the leakage is occurring and how severe it is.

5   Engine removal - methods and precautions

If you've decided that an engine must be removed for overhaul or major repair work, several preliminary steps should be taken.

Locating a suitable place to work is extremely important. Adequate work space, along with storage space for the vehicle, will be needed. If a shop or garage isn't available, at the very least a flat, level, clean work surface made of concrete or asphalt is required.

Cleaning the engine compartment and engine before beginning the removal procedure will help keep tools clean and organized.

An engine hoist or A-frame will also be necessary. Make sure the equipment is rated in excess of the combined weight of the engine and accessories. Safety is of primary importance, considering the potential hazards involved in lifting the engine out of the vehicle.

If the engine is being removed by a novice, a helper should be available. Advice and aid from someone more experienced would also be helpful. There are many instances when one person cannot simultaneously perform all of the operations required when lifting the engine out of the vehicle.

Plan the operation ahead of time. Arrange for or obtain all of the tools and equipment you'll need prior to beginning the job. Some of the equipment necessary to perform engine removal and installation safely and with relative ease are (in addition to an engine hoist) a heavy duty floor jack, complete sets of wrenches and sockets as described in the front of this manual, wooden blocks and plenty of rags and cleaning solvent for mopping up spilled oil, coolant and fuel. If the engine hoist must

be rented, make sure that you arrange for it in advance and perform all of the operations possible without it beforehand. This will save you money and time.

Plan for the vehicle to be out of use for quite a while. A machine shop will be required to perform some of the work which the do-it-yourselfer can't accomplish without special equipment. These shops often have a busy schedule, so it would be a good idea to consult them before removing the engine in order to accurately estimate the amount of time required to rebuild or repair components that may need work.

Always be extremely careful when removing and installing the engine. Serious injury can result from careless actions. Plan ahead, take your time and a job of this nature, although major, can be accomplished successfully.

6   Engine - removal and installation

Warning: *The air conditioning system is under high pressure! Have a dealer service department or service station discharge the system before disconnecting any air conditioning system hoses or fittings.*
Warning: *The engine must be completely cool before beginning this procedure.*

Removal

Refer to illustrations 6.6, 6.17, 6.18a, 6.18b, 6.18c, 6.19, 6.20, 6.22 and 6.23

1   Disconnect the negative cables from the batteries (see Chapter 5).

2   Cover the fenders and cowl and remove the hood or place it in the service position. Special pads are available to protect the fenders, but an old bedspread or blanket will also work.

3   Remove the air filter housing and air intake duct.

4   Drain the engine oil (Chapter 1).

5   Drain the cooling system (see Chapter 1).

6   Label all hoses, electrical connectors, ground straps and fuel lines, to ensure correct reinstallation, then detach them. Pieces of masking tape with numbers or letters written on them work well **(see illustration)**. If there's any possibility of confusion, make a sketch of the engine compartment and clearly label the lines, hoses and wires.

7   Raise the front of the vehicle and place it securely on jackstands. Remove the oil pan skid plate and splash shield from under the vehicle.

8   Remove both front wheels, then the inner fender splash shields.

Note: *Depending on the engine hoist type and overhead clearances, the front wheels may need to be reinstalled and the vehicle lowered.*

9   Remove the charge air cooler pipes.

10   Remove the drivebelt (see Chapter 1) and the alternator (see Chapter 5).

**6.17 Disconnect the hoses from the compressor,
then remove the mounting bolts**

11   Label and detach all coolant hoses from the engine.
12   Remove the radiator expansion tank, fan shroud, cooling fan and radiator (see Chapter 2).
Note: *On Kodiak/Topkick models, the radiator support and radiator is removed as a single unit using an engine hoist.*
13   Remove the tie bar mounting bolts and nuts and separate it from the radiator support.
14   Disconnect and plug the refrigerant lines to the condenser, then unbolt and remove the condenser. Plug or cap all open fittings/lines.
15   Unbolt the radiator support from the front of the vehicle.
16   Disconnect the fuel lines running from the engine to the chassis. Plug or cap all open fittings/lines.
17   On air-conditioned models, disconnect the hoses from the compressor, then unbolt the compressor **(see illustration)** and remove it. Plug or cap all open fittings.
18   Unbolt the power steering pump brackets and disconnect the hoses from the back of the pump **(see illustrations)**. If the pump is going to be serviced while the engine is being overhauled, remove the power steering pump pulley using a puller **(see illustration)**, then unbolt the pump and the bracket from the engine.
19   Remove the air conditioning compressor and power steering pump bracket bolts and bracket **(see illustration)**.

6.18a Remove the power steering pump front mounting bolts . . .

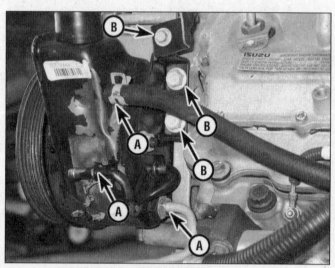

**6.18b . . . then disconnect the hoses (A) and
remove the rear mounting bolts (B)**

**6.18c If necessary, use a power steering pump pulley remover
tool to pull the pulley from the pump shaft**

**6.19 A/C compressor/power steering pump bracket mounting bolt
locations - LB7 model shown, other models similar**

20   Remove the idler pulleys and the drivebelt tensioner pulley from the alternator mounting bracket **(see illustration)**.

21   Remove the fuel service port mounting nuts and remove the port and PCV oil separator from the alternator bracket.

22   On models so equipped, rotate the vacuum pump pulley until the mounting nuts can be seen **(see illustration),** then remove the pump mounting nuts and the pump.

23   Remove the alternator bracket mounting bolts and remove the bracket **(see illustration)**.

24   Remove the engine electrical harness bracket mounting fasteners and work your way around the engine to remove the brackets and place the harness out of the way.

25   On 4WD models, remove the driveaxles and the front differential from the vehicle.

26   Unbolt the exhaust system from the engine.

27   Remove the starter motor.

28   On Kodiak/TopKick models, remove the driveshaft and parking brake cable actuator.

29   If you're working on a vehicle with an automatic transmission, remove the torque converter-to-flywheel fasteners. Remove the transmission oil line bracket retaining nut and the nuts securing the transmission dipstick tube to the top of engine. Once the tube is removed, make note of the stud locations and remove them.

30   Remove the EGR cooling pipe from the rear of the driver's side cylinder head and attach a lifting bracket with a suitable bolt to the cylinder head.

31   Install a lifting bracket with a suitable bolt to the cylinder head on the front passenger's side.

32   Attach an engine sling or a length of chain to the lifting brackets.

33   Roll the hoist into position and connect the sling to it. Take up the slack in the sling or chain, but don't lift the engine.

Warning: *DO NOT place any part of your body under the engine when it's supported only by a hoist or other lifting device.*

34   Support the transmission with a jack. Position a block of wood between them to prevent damage to the transmission. Special transmission jacks with safety chains are available - use one if possible.

35   Remove the transmission-to-engine bolts.

36   Working through the wheel wells, remove the engine mount-to-frame bolts from each side.

37   Recheck to be sure nothing is still connecting the engine to the transmission or vehicle. Disconnect anything still remaining.

38   Raise the engine slightly and remove the mounts. Carefully work the engine forward to separate it from the transmission. If you're working on a vehicle with an automatic transmission, be sure the torque converter stays in the transmission (clamp a pair of vise-grips to the housing to keep the converter from sliding out). If you're working on a

6.20 Remove the tensioner and idler pulley mounting bolts and detach the pulleys from the alternator bracket

vehicle with a manual transmission, the input shaft must be completely disengaged from the clutch before raising the engine.

39   Slowly raise the engine out of the engine compartment. Check carefully to make sure nothing is hanging up.

Note: *The engine will have to be placed at an angle to remove it from the vehicle.*

40   Remove the flywheel, turbocharger exhaust outlet, upper oil pan and flywheel housing (see Chapter 7) and mount the engine on an engine stand.

Installation

Caution: *If you're replacing an engine that failed, clean any engine oil that may have collected in the charge air cooler before installing the new engine. If the oil is not cleaned out of the charge air cooler and pipes when the engine is started, a condition called "runaway" can occur. This condition causes the engine to accelerate uncontrollably, causing severe engine damage and possibly personal injury.*

41   Check the engine and transmission mounts. If they're worn or damaged, replace them.

42   If you're working on a manual transmission equipped vehicle, install the clutch and pressure plate. Now is a good time to install a new clutch.

6.22 Rotate the vacuum pump pulley until the mounting nuts can be seen, then remove the nuts - LB7 model shown

6.23 Alternator bracket mounting bolt locations - LB7 model shown, other models similar

43   Carefully lower the engine into the engine compartment - make sure the engine mounts line up.
44   If you're working on a manual transmission equipped vehicle, apply a dab of high-temperature grease to the input shaft and guide it into the crankshaft pilot bearing until the bellhousing is flush with the engine block.
45   Install the transmission-to-engine bolts and tighten them securely. **Caution:** *DO NOT use the bolts to force the transmission and engine together!*
If you're working on an automatic transmission-equipped vehicle, install the torque converter-to-flywheel bolts, tightening them to the torque listed in this Chapters Specifications.
46   Reinstall the remaining components in the reverse order of removal.
47   Add coolant, oil, power steering and transmission fluid as needed.
48   Run the engine and check for leaks and proper operation of all accessories, then install the hood and test drive the vehicle.
49   Have the air conditioning system recharged and leak tested by the shop that discharged it.

7   Engine rebuilding alternatives

The do-it-yourselfer is faced with a number of options when performing an engine overhaul. The decision to replace the engine block, piston/connecting rod assemblies and crankshaft depends on a number of factors, with the number one consideration being the condition of the block. Other considerations are cost, access to machine shop facilities, parts availability, time required to complete the project and the extent of prior mechanical experience on the part of the do-it-yourselfer.
Some of the rebuilding alternatives include:
Individual parts - If the inspection procedures reveal that the engine block and most engine components are in reusable condition, purchasing individual parts may be the most economical alternative. The block, crankshaft and piston/connecting rod assemblies should all be inspected carefully. Even if the block shows little wear, the cylinder bores should be surface honed.
Short block - A short block consists of an engine block with a crankshaft and piston/connecting rod assemblies already installed. All new bearings are incorporated and all clearances will be correct. The existing camshaft, valve train components, cylinder head(s) and external parts can be bolted to the short block with little or no machine shop work necessary.
Long block - A long block consists of a short block plus an oil pump, oil pan, cylinder head(s), valve cover(s), camshaft and valve train components, timing gears and front cover. All components are installed with new bearings, seals and gaskets incorporated throughout. The installation of manifolds and external parts is all that's necessary.
Give careful thought to which alternative is best for you and discuss the situation with local automotive machine shops, auto parts dealers and experienced rebuilders before ordering or purchasing replacement parts.

8   Engine overhaul - disassembly sequence

1   It's much easier to disassemble and work on the engine if it's mounted on a portable engine stand. A heavy duty stand can often be rented quite cheaply from an equipment rental yard. Before the engine is mounted on a stand, the flywheel/driveplate should be removed from the engine.
2   If you're going to obtain a rebuilt engine, all external components must come off first, to be transferred to the replacement engine, just as they will if you're doing a complete engine overhaul yourself. These include:

Alternator and brackets
Emissions control components
Fuel injection pump
Thermostat and housing cover
Water pump
Fuel lines and clamps

Intake/exhaust manifolds
Oil filter
Oil cooler
Engine mounts
Clutch and flywheel
Flywheel housing
Front timing gear cover
Engine rear plate

Note: *When removing the external components from the engine, pay close attention to details that may be helpful or important during installation. Note the installed position of gaskets, seals, spacers, pins, brackets, washers, bolts and other small items.*
3   If you're obtaining a short block, which consists of the engine block, crankshaft, pistons and connecting rods all assembled, then the cylinder head(s), oil pans and oil pump will have to be removed as well. See *Engine rebuilding alternatives* for additional information regarding the different possibilities to be considered.
4   If you're planning a complete overhaul, the engine must be disassembled and the internal components removed in the following order:

Valve covers
Intake and exhaust manifolds
Rocker arms and pushrods
Valve lifters
Cylinder head(s)
Engine front cover
Timing gears
Camshaft
Upper and lower oil pans
Oil pump
Piston/connecting rod assemblies
Crankshaft and main bearings

5   Before beginning the disassembly and overhaul procedures, make sure the following items are available. Also, refer to *Engine overhaul - reassembly sequence* for a list of tools and materials needed for engine reassembly.

Common hand tools
Small cardboard boxes or plastic bags for storing parts
Gasket scraper
Ridge reamer
Micrometers
Telescoping gauges
Dial indicator set
Valve spring compressor
Cylinder surfacing hone
Piston ring groove cleaning tool
Electric drill motor
Tap and die set
Wire brushes
Oil gallery brushes
Cleaning solvent

9   Cylinder head - disassembly

Refer to illustrations 9.2, 9.3a, 9.3b and 9.4
Warning: *Use extreme care when removing the cylinder head bolts from the engine. Failure to remove the cylinder head bolts in the correct order can cause the head to warp, or in extreme cases the head will crack and/or the cylinder bores can become distorted. Refer to Chapter 7 for cylinder head removal.*
Note: *New and rebuilt cylinder heads are commonly available for most engines. Due to the fact that some specialized tools are necessary for the disassembly and inspection procedures, and replacement parts may not be readily available, it may be more practical and economical for the home mechanic to purchase replacement heads rather than taking the time to disassemble, inspect and recondition the originals.*
1   Cylinder head disassembly involves removal of the intake and exhaust valves and related components. Remove the valve bridge pins

9.2 A small plastic bag, with an appropriate label, can be used to store the valve train components so they can be kept together and reinstalled in the original location

9.3a Use a valve spring compressor to compress the spring, remove the keepers from the valve stem . . .

9.3b . . . then remove the retainer, spring and spring seat

9.4 If the valve won't pull through the guide, deburr the edge of the stem end and the area around the top of the keeper groove with a file or whetstone

and valve bridges (see Chapter 7). Label the parts or store them separately so they can be reinstalled in their original locations.

2   Before the valves are removed, arrange to label and store them, along with their related components, so they can be kept separate and reinstalled in the same valve guides they are removed from **(see illustration)**.

3   Compress the springs on the first valve with a spring compressor and remove the keepers **(see illustration)**. Carefully release the valve spring compressor and remove the retainer **(see illustration)**, the spring and the spring seat.

4   Pull the valve out of the head, then remove the oil seal from the guide. If the valve binds in the guide (won't pull through), push it back into the head and deburr the area around the keeper groove with a fine file or whetstone **(see illustration)**.

5   Repeat the procedure for the remaining valves. Remember to keep all the parts for each valve together so they can be reinstalled in the same locations.

6   Once the valves and related components have been removed and stored in an organized manner, the head should be thoroughly cleaned and inspected. If a complete engine overhaul is being done, finish the engine disassembly procedures before beginning the cylinder head cleaning and inspection process.

10   Cylinder head - cleaning and inspection

1   Thorough cleaning of the cylinder head and related valve train components, followed by a detailed inspection, will enable you to decide how much valve service work must be done during the engine overhaul. **Note:** *If the engine was severely overheated, the cylinder head is probably warped (see Step 15).*

Cleaning

2   Scrape all traces of old gasket material and sealing compound off the head gasket, intake manifold and exhaust manifold sealing surfaces. Be very careful not to gouge the cylinder head.

3   Remove all built-up scale from the coolant passages.

4   Run a stiff wire brush through the various holes to remove deposits that may have formed in them.

5   Run an appropriate size tap into each of the threaded holes to remove corrosion and thread sealant that may be present. If compressed air is available, use it to clear the holes of debris produced by this operation.

Warning: *Wear eye protection when using compressed air!*

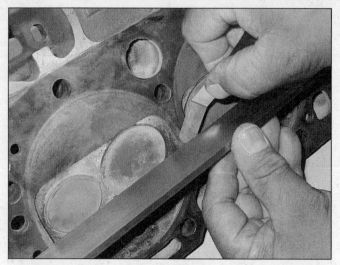

10.15 Check the cylinder head gasket surface for warpage, by trying to slip a feeler gauge under the straightedge (see this Chapter's Specifications for the allowed and use a feeler gauge of that thickness)

10.17 A dial indicator can be used to determine the valve stem-to-guide clearance (move the valve stem as indicated by the arrows)

6   Clean the rocker arm bolts and valve adjuster screw threads with a wire brush.

7   Clean the cylinder head with solvent and dry it thoroughly. Compressed air will speed the drying process and ensure that all holes and recessed areas are clean.

Note: *Decarbonizing chemicals are available and may prove very useful when cleaning cylinder heads and valve train components. They are very caustic and should be used with caution. Be sure to follow the instructions on the container.*

8   Clean the cylinder head gasket sealing surface and check for corrosion or pitting. If corrosion or pitting are found, use something very flat like a sanding block or equivalent and wrap it with 600-grit wet grade sandpaper.

Note: *The sanding block should be at least four inches by two inches. Using moisture displacing lubricant (Part #88900331, available from a GM parts department), wet sand the cylinder head surface to remove any remaining gasket material or corrosion.*

Caution: *Do not use any sandpaper coarser than 600 grit.*

Keep the sanding block parallel with the cylinder head and evenly sand the sealing surface.

Note: *When the surface is sanded the corrosion will leave a stain on the metal. Once you're to this point, do not continue to sand any further.*

9   Continually wipe the surface, with a clean rag, to prevent debris from building up and depositing in the oil or coolant cavities.

10   Once the sanding is completed clean the head gasket surfaces with brake system cleaner to remove any oil or debris.

11   Clean the rocker arms, rocker arm shafts and valve bridges and pushrods with solvent and dry them thoroughly (don't mix them up during the cleaning process). Compressed air will speed the drying process and can be used to clean out the oil passages.

12   Clean all the valve springs, spring seats, keepers and retainers (rotators) with solvent and dry them thoroughly. Do the components from one valve at a time to avoid mixing up the parts.

13   Scrape off any heavy deposits that may have formed on the valves, then use a motorized wire brush to remove deposits from the valve heads. Again, make sure the valves don't get mixed up.

Inspection

Refer to illustrations 10.15 and 10.17

Note: *Be sure to perform all of the following inspection procedures before concluding that machine shop work is required. Make a list of the items that need attention.*

14   Inspect the head very carefully for cracks, evidence of coolant leakage and other damage. If cracks are found, check with an automotive machine shop concerning repair. If repair isn't possible, a new cylinder head must be obtained.

15   Using a precision machinist's straightedge and feeler gauge, check the cylinder head gasket sealing surface for warpage **(see illustration)**. If the warpage exceeds the allowable limit listed in this Chapter's Specifications, replace the cylinder head. The manufacturer doesn't recommend resurfacing cylinder heads on these engines because there is danger of the valves colliding with the pistons if too much material is removed. Consult with a very experienced machine shop if considering cylinder head machining.

16   Examine the valve seats. If they're pitted, cracked or burned, the head will require valve service that's beyond the scope of the home mechanic.

17   Check the valve stem-to-guide clearance by measuring the lateral movement of the valve stem with a dial indicator attached securely to the head **(see illustration)** and the indicator tip contacting the valve stem about 0.4 inches (10 mm) up from the top of the guide. The valve must be in the guide and approximately 1/16-inch off the seat. The total valve stem movement indicated by the gauge needle must be divided by two to obtain the actual clearance. After this is done, if there's still some doubt regarding the condition of the valve guides, they should be checked by an automotive machine shop.

Note: *Excessive guide clearance prevents adequate cooling of the valve through the guide and allows the valve to tilt or tip. This can cause valve breakage at high engine speed. These conditions prevent the valve from seating properly and combustion leakage will occur. Diesel engines rely on extremely high pressures in the combustion chamber to heat the air that ignites the fuel. Any leakage of the pressure will severely affect the ignition of the fuel. If the leakage past the valve face is excessive, the fuel will not ignite. This is much more critical than in a gasoline engine because the air/fuel ratio would normally ignite even with leaky valves because it has a spark to set the fuel off.*

Valves

Refer to illustrations 10.18, 10.19, 10.20 and 10.21

18   Carefully inspect each valve face for uneven wear, deformation, cracks, pits and burned areas **(see illustration)**. Check the valve stem for scuffing and galling and the neck for cracks. Rotate the valve and check for any obvious indication that it's bent. Look for pits and excessive wear on the end of the stem. The presence of any of these conditions

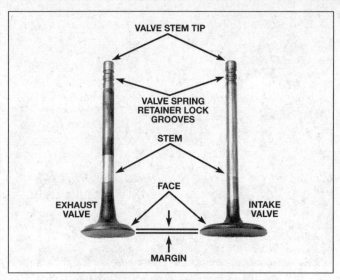

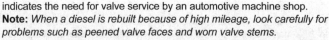

10.18 Inspect these areas on each valve

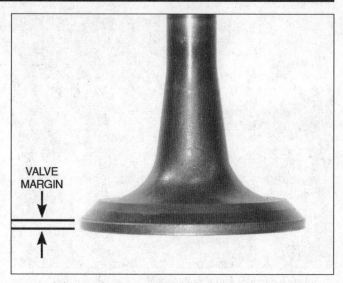

10.19 The valve margin width must not be less than specified - if it is, do not reuse the valve

indicates the need for valve service by an automotive machine shop.

Note: *When a diesel is rebuilt because of high mileage, look carefully for problems such as peened valve faces and worn valve stems.*

19   Measure the seat width and margin width on each valve **(see illustration)**. Any seat or valve out of specification will have to be replaced with a new one.

20   Check each valve spring for wear (on the ends) and pits. Measure the free length and compare it to the Specifications **(see illustration)**. Any springs that are shorter than specified have sagged and should not be reused. The tension of all springs should be checked with a special fixture before deciding that they're suitable for use in a rebuilt engine (take the springs to an automotive machine shop for this check).

21   Stand each spring on a flat surface and check it for squareness **(see illustration)**. If any of the springs are distorted or sagged, replace all of them with new parts.

22   Check the spring retainers and keepers for obvious wear and cracks. Any questionable parts should be replaced with new ones, as extensive damage will occur if they fail during engine operation.

23   Check the rocker arm faces (the areas that contact the pushrod ends and valve stems) for pits, wear, galling, score marks and rough spots. Check the rocker arm pivot contact areas on the shaft as well. Look for cracks in each rocker arm and bolt.

24   Inspect the pushrod ends for scuffing and excessive wear. Roll each pushrod on a flat surface, like a piece of plate glass, to determine if it's bent.

25   Check the valve adjuster screws for damaged threads.

26   Any damaged or excessively worn parts must be replaced with new ones.

27   If the inspection process indicates that the valve components are in generally poor condition and worn beyond the limits specified, which is usually the case in an engine that's being overhauled, reassemble the valves in the cylinder head and refer to Section 11 for valve servicing recommendations.

11 Valves - servicing

1   Because of the complex nature of the job and the special tools and equipment needed, servicing of the valves, the valve seats and the valve guides, commonly known as a valve job, should be done by a professional.

2   The home mechanic can remove and disassemble the head, do the initial cleaning and inspection, then reassemble and deliver it to a dealer service department or an automotive machine shop for the

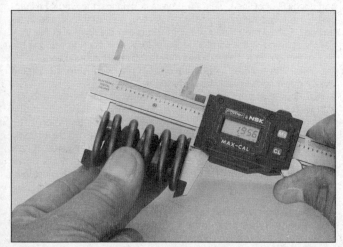

10.20 Measure the free length of each valve spring with a dial or vernier caliper

10.21 Check each valve spring for squareness

12.3 Use a hammer and a seal installer (or, as shown here, a deep socket) to drive the new seal onto the valve guide; tap the seal into place until it's completely seated on the guide

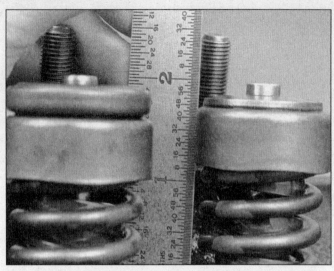

12.8 Be sure to check the valve spring installed height (the distance from the top of the seat/shims to the top of the spring or spring shield)

actual service work. Doing the inspection will enable you to see what condition the head and valvetrain components are in and will ensure that you know what work and new parts are required when dealing with an automotive machine shop.

3   The automotive machine shop will remove the valves and springs, recondition or replace the valves and valve seats, recondition the valve guides, check and replace the valve springs, spring retainers and keepers (as necessary), replace the valve seals with new ones, reassemble the valve components and make sure the installed spring height is correct. The cylinder head gasket surface will also be resurfaced if it's warped.

4   After the valve job has been performed by a professional, the head will be in like-new condition. When the head is returned, be sure to clean it again before installation on the engine to remove any metal particles and abrasive grit that may still be present from the valve service or head resurfacing operations. Use compressed air, if available, to blow out all the oil holes and passages.

12   Cylinder head - reassembly

Refer to illustrations 12.3 and 12.8

1   Regardless of whether or not the head was sent to an automotive machine shop for valve servicing, make sure it's clean before beginning reassembly.

2   If the head was sent out for valve servicing, the valves and related components will already be in place. Begin the reassembly procedure with Step 8.

3   Install new seals on each of the intake valve guides. Using a hammer and a deep socket or seal installation tool, gently tap each seal into place until it's completely seated on the guide **(see illustration)**. Don't twist or cock the seals during installation or they won't seal properly on the valve stems.

4   Beginning at one end of the head, lubricate and install the first valve. Apply clean engine oil to the valve stem.

5   Drop the spring seat or shim(s) over the valve guide and set the valve spring and retainer in place.

6   Compress the springs with a valve spring compressor and carefully install the keepers in the upper groove, then slowly release the compressor and make sure the keepers seat properly. Apply a small dab of grease to each keeper to hold it in place, if necessary.

7   Repeat the procedure for the remaining valves. Be sure to return the components to their original locations - don't mix them up!

8   Check the installed valve spring height with a ruler graduated in 1/32-inch increments or a dial caliper **(see illustration)**. If the head was sent out for service work, the installed height should be correct (but don't automatically assume that it is). If the height is greater than the figure listed in this Chapter's Specifications, shims can be added under the springs to correct it.

Caution: *Don't shim the springs to the point where the installed height is less than specified.*

9   Apply moly-base grease to the valve bridges, rocker arm faces and the shaft, then install the bridges, rocker arms, rocker arm shaft and any pivot points.

13   Pistons/connecting rods - removal

Refer to illustrations 13.1, 13.3 and 13.4

Note: *Prior to removing the piston/connecting rod assemblies, remove the cylinder head(s), the oil pans and the oil pump by referring to the appropriate Sections in Chapter 7.*

1   Use your fingernail to feel if a ridge has formed at the upper limit of ring travel (about 1/4-inch down from the top of each cylinder). If carbon deposits or cylinder wear have produced ridges, they must be completely removed with a scraper or, if severe, a special tool **(see illustration)**. Follow the manufacturer's instructions provided with the tool. Failure to remove the carbon ridges before attempting to remove the piston/connecting rod assemblies may result in piston breakage.

2   After the cylinder ridges have been removed, turn the engine upside-down so the crankshaft is facing up.

3   Before the connecting rods are removed, check the endplay with feeler gauges. Slide them between the first connecting rod and the crankshaft throw until the play is removed **(see illustration)**. The endplay is equal to the thickness of the feeler gauge(s). If the endplay exceeds the service limit, new connecting rods will be required. If new rods (or a new crankshaft) are installed, the endplay may fall under the specified minimum (if it does, the rods will have to be machined to restore it - consult an automotive machine shop for advice if necessary). Repeat the procedure for the remaining connecting rods.

4   Check the connecting rods and caps for identification marks **(see illustration)**. If they aren't plainly marked, use a small center-punch to make the appropriate number of indentations on each rod and cap (1, 2, 3, etc., depending on the engine type and cylinder they're associated with).

13.1 A ridge reamer might be required to remove the ridge from the top of each cylinder - do this before removing the pistons (if just heavy carbon deposits are present, a scraper can be used)

13.3 Check the connecting rod side clearance with a feeler gauge

Caution: *The connecting rods and rod bearing caps are not interchangeable; make sure they are marked before removing them. Also mark the piston crowns as to which cylinder they belong to* **(see illustration 25.8)**.

5   Loosen each of the connecting rod cap bolts 1/4-turn at a time until they can be removed by hand. Remove the number one connecting rod cap and bearing insert. Don't drop the bearing insert out of the cap.

6   Remove the bearing insert and push the connecting rod/piston assembly out through the top of the engine. Use a wooden hammer handle to push on the upper bearing surface in the connecting rod. If resistance is felt, double-check to make sure that all of the ridge was removed from the cylinder.

7   Repeat the procedure for the remaining cylinders.

8   After removal, reassemble the connecting rod caps and bearing inserts with their respective connecting rods and install the cap bolts finger tight. Leaving the old bearing inserts in place until reassembly will help prevent the connecting rod bearing surfaces from being accidentally nicked or gouged.

14 Crankshaft - removal

Refer to illustrations 14.2, 14.3, 14.4, 14.5, 14.6 and 14.8

Note: *The crankshaft can be removed only after the engine has been removed from the vehicle. It's assumed that the flywheel, vibration damper, camshaft, oil pans, flywheel housing, oil pump and piston/connecting rod assemblies have already been removed*

1   Before the crankshaft is removed, check the endplay. Mount a dial indicator in line with the crankshaft and touching the end **(see illustration)**.

2   Push the crankshaft all the way to the rear and zero the dial indicator. Next, pry the crankshaft to the front as far as possible and check the reading on the dial indicator. The distance that it moves is the endplay. If it's greater than the limit listed in this Chapter's Specifications, check the crankshaft thrust surfaces for wear. If no wear is evident, new main bearings should correct the endplay.

13.4 The connecting rods and caps should already be marked for the cylinder they go with. If they aren't marked, mark them in order from the front of the engine to the rear (one mark for the front cap, two for the second one and so on)

14.2 Checking crankshaft endplay with a dial indicator

14.3 Checking crankshaft endplay with a feeler gauge

14.4 The main bearing caps should already be numbered consecutively from the front of the engine to the rear (the numbers should be upright when the front of the crankshaft is on your left)

14.5 Remove the ten bearing cap side bolts - three of ten shown

3   If a dial indicator isn't available, feeler gauges can be used. Gently pry or push the crankshaft all the way to the front of the engine. Slip feeler gauges between the crankshaft and the front face of the thrust main bearing (the number 5 main bearing) to determine the clearance **(see illustration)**.
4   Check the main bearing caps to see if they're marked to indicate their locations. They should be numbered consecutively from the front of the engine to the rear **(see illustration)**. If not, you will have to mark which side points to the front of the engine with number stamping dies or a center-punch.
5   Remove the ten bearing cap side bolts from the side of the engine **(see illustration)**. Loosen the main bearing cap bolts 1/4-turn at a time each until they can be removed by hand.
6   Gently tap the caps with a soft-face hammer, then separate them from the engine block. If necessary, use the bolts as levers to remove the caps **(see illustration)**. Try not to drop the bearing inserts if they come out with the caps.
7   Carefully lift the crankshaft out of the engine. It may be a good idea to have an assistant available, since the crankshaft is quite heavy. Remove the thrust bearings, then with the remaining bearing inserts in place in the engine block and main bearing caps, return the caps to their respective locations on the engine block and tighten the bolts finger tight.
8   Remove the piston oil cooling nozzles **(see illustration)**.

14.6 Use the bolts as levers to help remove the caps

14.8 Unscrew the piston oil cooling nozzle bolts and remove the nozzles

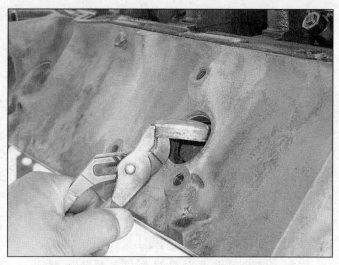

15.1 Pull the core plugs from the block with pliers

15.8 All bolt holes in the block - particularly the main bearing cap and head bolt holes - should be cleaned and restored with a tap (be sure to remove debris from, the holes after this is done)

15 Engine block - cleaning

Refer to illustrations 15.1, 15.8 and 15.10

Caution: *The core plugs (also known as freeze plugs or soft plugs) may be difficult or impossible to retrieve if they're driven into the block coolant passages.*

1   Using a large drift punch, tap the outer edges of the core plugs sideways in their bores. Then, using a pair of pliers, pull the core plugs from the engine block **(see illustration)**.

2   Using a gasket scraper, remove all traces of gasket material from the engine block. Be very careful not to nick or gouge the gasket sealing surfaces.

3   Remove the main bearing caps and separate the bearing inserts from the caps and the engine block. Tag the bearings, indicating which cylinder they were removed from and whether they were in the cap or the block, then set them aside.

4   Remove all of the threaded oil gallery plugs from the block. The plugs are usually very tight - they may have to be drilled out and the holes retapped. Use new plugs when the engine is reassembled.

5   If the engine is extremely dirty it should be taken to an automotive machine shop to be steam cleaned or hot tanked.

6   After the block is returned, clean all oil holes and oil galleries one more time. Brushes specifically designed for this purpose are available at most auto parts stores. Flush the passages with warm water until the water runs clear, dry the block thoroughly and wipe all machined surfaces with a light, rust preventive oil. If you have access to compressed air, use it to speed the drying process and to blow out all the oil holes and galleries.

Warning: *Wear eye protection when using compressed air!*

7   If the block isn't extremely dirty or sludged up, you can do an adequate cleaning job with hot soapy water and a stiff brush. Take plenty of time and do a thorough job. Regardless of the cleaning method used, be sure to clean all oil holes and galleries very thoroughly, dry the block completely and coat all machined surfaces with light oil.

8   The threaded holes in the block must be clean to ensure accurate torque readings during reassembly. Run the proper size tap into each of the holes to remove rust, corrosion, thread sealant or sludge and restore damaged threads **(see illustration)**. If possible, use compressed air to clear the holes of debris produced by this operation.

9   Reinstall the main bearing caps and tighten the bolts finger tight.

10   After coating the sealing surfaces of the new core plugs with core plug sealant, install them in the engine block **(see illustration)**. Make sure they're driven in straight and seated properly or leakage could

15.10 A large socket on an extension can be used to drive the new core plugs into the bores

result. Special tools are available for this purpose, but a large socket, with an outside diameter that will just slip into the core plug, a 1/2-inch drive extension and a hammer will work just as well.

11   Apply non-hardening sealant (such as Permatex no. 2 or Teflon pipe sealant) to the new oil gallery plugs and thread them into the holes in the block. Make sure they're tightened securely.

12   If the engine isn't going to be reassembled right away, cover it with a large plastic trash bag to keep it clean.

16 Engine block - inspection

Refer to illustrations 16.4a, 16.4b, 16.4c and 16.5

1   Before the block is inspected, it should be cleaned (see Section 15).

2   Check the block for cracks, rust and corrosion. Look for stripped threads in the threaded holes. It's also a good idea to have the block checked for hidden cracks by an automotive machine shop that has the special equipment to do this type of work. If defects are found, have the block repaired, if possible, or replaced.

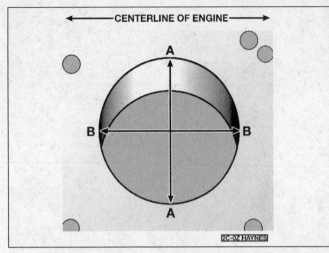

16.4a Measure the diameter of each cylinder at a right angle to
the engine centerline (A), and parallel to the engine centerline (B)
- out-of-round is the difference between A and B; taper is the
difference between A and B at the top of the cylinder and
A and B at the bottom of the cylinder

16.4b The ability to "feel" when the telescoping gauge is
at the correct point will be developed over time, so work
slowly and repeat the check until you're satisfied
the bore measurement is accurate

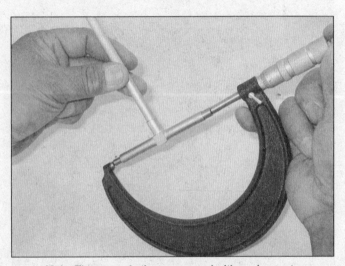

16.4c The gauge is then measured with a micrometer
to determine the bore size

16.5 Location of the stamping marks that indicate whether
the cylinder is standard or re-bored

3   Check the cylinder bores for scuffing and scoring.

4   Measure the diameter of each cylinder at the top (just under the ridge area), center and bottom of the cylinder bore, parallel to the crankshaft axis (see illustrations).

5   Next, measure each cylinder's diameter at the same three locations across the crankshaft axis. Compare the results to this Chapter's

Specifications. All remanufactured cylinder blocks have been stamped on both sides of the fuel pressure pump boss (see illustration). The stamp indicates whether the cylinder is standard or re-bored, and if the deck surface is standard or has been machined.

Note: *If there is no stamping then the cylinder bore and deck surface is standard.*

Block top deck (head surface)	Cylinder bore size	Stamping identification
Standard	Standard	SS
Standard	0.010 inches	01S
Standard	0.020 inches	02S
Standard	0.030 inches	03S
Machined	Standard	SM
Machined	0.010 inches	01M
Machined	0.020 inches	02M
Machined	0.030 inches	03M

6   If the required precision measuring tools aren't available, the piston-to-cylinder clearances can be obtained, though not quite as accurately, using feeler gauge stock. Feeler gauge stock comes in 12-inch lengths and various thicknesses and is generally available at auto parts stores.

7   To check the clearance, select a feeler gauge and slip it into the cylinder along with the matching piston. The piston must be positioned exactly as it normally would be. The feeler gauge must be between the piston and cylinder on one of the thrust faces (90-degrees to the piston pin bore).

8   The piston should slip through the cylinder (with the feeler gauge in place) with moderate pressure.

9   If it falls through or slides through easily, the clearance is excessive and a new piston will be required. If the piston binds at the lower end of the cylinder and is loose toward the top, the cylinder is tapered. If tight spots are encountered as the piston/feeler gauge is rotated in the cylinder, the cylinder is out-of-round.

10   Repeat the procedure for the remaining pistons and cylinders.

11   If the cylinder walls are badly scuffed or scored, or if they're out-of-round or tapered beyond the limits given in this Chapter's Specifications, have the engine block rebored and honed at an automotive machine shop. If a rebore is done, oversize pistons and rings will be required.

Note: *Consult an automotive machine shop as to whether or not they recommend re-boring. Some claim that the engine block must be replaced if any dimensions are out of specification.*

12   If the cylinders are in reasonably good condition and not worn to the outside of the limits, and if the piston-to-cylinder clearances can be maintained properly, then they don't have to be rebored. Honing is all that's necessary.

17   Cylinder honing

Refer to illustration 17.1

1   The engine block is induction hardened and honing is not needed. Light honing can be performed to remove any traces of carbon. If there is a scratch that can be felt with your fingernail the cylinder block must be replaced. It is normal for the cylinder walls to have spotting **(see illustration)** on the top third of the cylinder. If the spots appear bigger than a quarter, then the factory honing has been worn away and the cylinder block should be replaced.

2   If there is a question about the condition of the engine block, have it checked by an automotive machine shop to see if there are alternatives to cylinder block replacement.

3   Once the block has been cleaned and inspected, wrap the block in a plastic trash bag to keep it clean, and set it aside until reassembly.

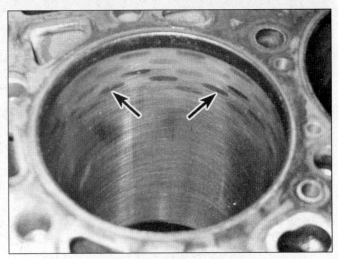

17.1 It is normal for the cylinder walls to have spotting on the top third of the cylinder

18   Pistons/connecting rods - inspection

Refer to illustrations 18.4a, 18.4b, 18.10, 18.13a, 18.13b, 18.14a and 18.14b

Note: *The connecting rods and rod bearing caps are not interchangeable; make sure they're properly marked to prevent mixing them up.*

1   Before the inspection process can be carried out, the piston/connecting rod assemblies must be cleaned and the original piston rings removed from the pistons.

Note: *Always use new piston rings when the engine is reassembled.*

2   Using a piston ring installation tool, carefully remove the rings from the pistons. Be careful not to nick or gouge the pistons in the process.

3   Scrape all traces of carbon from the top of the piston. A hand-held wire brush or a piece of fine emery cloth can be used once the majority of the deposits have been scraped away. Do not use a wire brush mounted in a drill motor to remove deposits from the pistons. The piston material is soft and may be eroded away by the wire brush.

4   Use a piston ring groove cleaning tool to remove carbon deposits from the ring grooves **(see illustration)**. If a tool isn't available, a piece broken off the old ring will do the job. Be very careful to remove only the carbon deposits - don't remove any metal and do not nick or scratch the sides of the ring grooves **(see illustration)**.

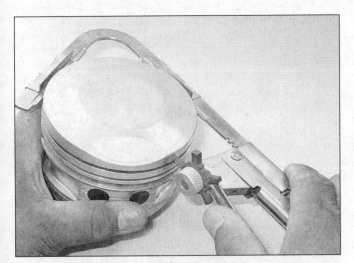

18.4a The piston ring grooves can be cleaned with a special tool, as shown here . . .

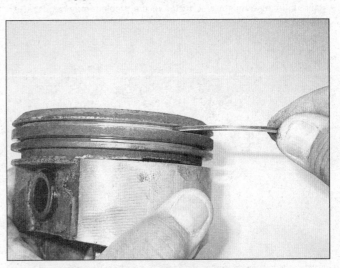

18.4b . . . or a section of a broken ring

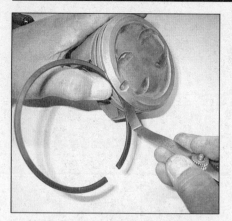

18.10 Check the ring side clearance with a feeler gauge at several points around the groove

18.13a Use a small pick to remove the piston pin circlip

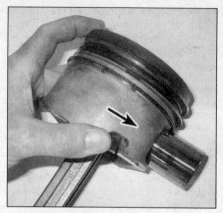

18.13b Push the piston pin out of the piston and connecting rod

5   Once the deposits have been removed, clean the piston/rod assemblies with solvent and dry them with compressed air (if available). Make sure the oil return holes in the back sides of the ring grooves are clear.

6   If the pistons and cylinder walls aren't damaged or worn excessively, and if the engine block is not rebored, new pistons won't be necessary. Normal piston wear appears as even vertical wear on the piston thrust surfaces and slight looseness of the top ring in its groove. New piston rings, however, should always be used when an engine is rebuilt.

7   Carefully inspect each piston for cracks around the skirt, at the pin bosses and at the ring lands.

8   Look for scoring and scuffing on the thrust faces of the skirt, holes in the piston crown and burned areas at the edge of the crown. If the skirt is scored or scuffed, the engine may have been suffering from overheating and/or abnormal combustion, which caused excessively high operating temperatures. The cooling and lubrication systems should be checked thoroughly. A hole in the piston crown is an indication that abnormal combustion (preignition) was occurring. If only one or two pistons show heavy scuffing, look for an improper piston-to-bore clearance. If any of the above problems exist, the causes must be corrected or the damage will occur again. The causes may include intake air leaks, head gasket leaks, improper clearances and EGR system malfunctions.

9   Corrosion of the piston, in the form of small pits, indicates that coolant is leaking into the combustion chamber and/or the crankcase. Again, the cause must be corrected or the problem may persist in the rebuilt engine.

10   Measure the piston ring side clearance by laying a new piston ring in each ring groove and slipping a feeler gauge in beside it **(see illustration)**. Check the clearance at three or four locations around each groove. Be sure to use the correct ring for each groove - they are different. If the side clearance is greater than the figure listed in this Chapter's Specifications, new pistons will have to be used.

11   Check the piston-to-bore clearance by measuring the bore (see Section 16) and the piston diameter. Make sure the pistons and bores are correctly matched. Measure the piston across the skirt, at a 90-degree angle with the piston pin. Subtract the piston diameter from the bore diameter to obtain the clearance. If it's greater than specified, the block will have to be rebored or replaced and new pistons and rings installed.

12   Check the piston-to-rod clearance by twisting the piston and rod in opposite directions. Any noticeable play indicates excessive wear, which must be corrected.

13   Using a pick, remove the spring steel circlip from each side of the piston pin **(see illustration)**. Push the piston pin out from the piston and separate the piston from the connecting rod **(see illustration)**.

Note: *The arrow or triangle on the piston crown faces the cylinder valley when installed, and the numbers on the connecting rods face outward when installed. Be sure to reassemble the rods and pistons like this.*

14   Check the connecting rod-to-piston pin clearance by measuring the rod bore and the piston pin diameter **(see illustrations)**. Subtract the piston pin diameter from the connecting rod inside diameter to obtain the clearance. If it's greater than specified, the connecting rod will have to be replaced.

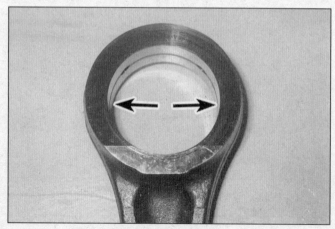

18.14a Measure the small end of the rod inside diameter . . .

18.14b . . . then measure the piston pin diameter at several points

19.1 The oil holes should be chamfered so sharp edges don't gouge or scratch the new bearings

19.2 Use a wire or stiff plastic bristle brush to clean the oil passages in the crankshaft

15   Check the connecting rods for damage. Temporarily remove the rod caps, lift out the old bearing inserts, wipe the rod and cap bearing surfaces clean and inspect them for nicks, gouges and scratches. After checking the rods, reinstall the old bearings, slip the caps into place and tighten the nuts finger tight.
Note: *If the engine is being rebuilt because of a connecting rod knock, be sure to install new rods.*

19   Crankshaft - inspection

Refer to illustrations 19.1, 19.2, 19.4 and 19.6

1   Remove all burrs from the crankshaft oil holes with a stone, file or scraper **(see illustration)**.
2   Clean the crankshaft with solvent and dry it with compressed air (if available). Be sure to clean the oil holes with a stiff brush **(see illustration)** and flush them with solvent.
3   Check the main and connecting rod bearing journals for uneven wear, scoring, pits and cracks.
4   Rub a penny across each journal several times **(see illustration)**. If a journal picks up copper from the penny, it's too rough and must be reground.
5   Check the rest of the crankshaft for cracks and other damage. It should be Magnafluxed to reveal hidden cracks - an automotive machine shop will handle the procedure.
6   Using a micrometer, measure the diameter of the main and connecting rod journals in four different sections and compare the results to this Chapter's Specifications **(see illustration)**. By measuring the diameter at a number of points around each journal's circumference, you'll be able to determine whether or not the journal is out-of-round. Take the measurement at each end of the journal, near the crank throws, to determine if the journal is tapered.
7   If the crankshaft journals are damaged, tapered, out-of-round or worn beyond the limits given in the Specifications, have the crankshaft reground by an automotive machine shop. Be sure to use the correct size bearing inserts if the crankshaft is reconditioned.
8   Check the oil seal journals at each end of the crankshaft for wear and damage. If the seal has worn a groove in the journal, or if it's nicked or scratched, the new seal may leak when the engine is reassembled. In some cases, an automotive machine shop may be able to repair the journal by pressing on a thin sleeve. If repair isn't feasible, a new or different crankshaft should be installed.
9   Refer to Section 20 and examine the main and rod bearing inserts.

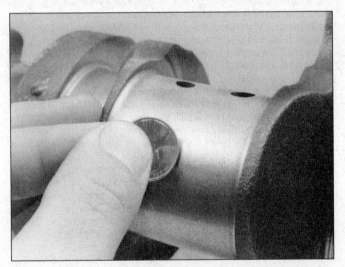

19.4 Rubbing a penny lengthwise on each journal will reveal its condition - if copper rubs off and is embedded in the crankshaft, the journals should be reground

19.6 Measure the diameter of each crankshaft journal at several points to detect taper and out-of-round conditions

20 Main and connecting rod bearings - inspection

1   Even though the main and connecting rod bearings should be replaced with new ones during the engine overhaul, the old bearings should be retained for close examination, as they may reveal valuable information about the condition of the engine.

2   Bearing failure occurs because of lack of lubrication, the presence of dirt or other foreign particles, overloading the engine and corrosion. Regardless of the cause of bearing failure, it must be corrected before the engine is reassembled to prevent it from happening again.

3   When examining the bearings, remove them from the engine block, the main bearing caps, the connecting rods and the rod caps and lay them out on a clean surface in the same general position as their location in the engine. This will enable you to match any bearing problems with the corresponding crankshaft journal.

4   Dirt and other foreign particles get into the engine in a variety of ways. It may be left in the engine during assembly, or it may pass through filters or the crankcase ventilation system. It may get into the oil, and from there into the bearings. Metal chips from machining operations and normal engine wear are often present. Abrasives are sometimes left in engine components after reconditioning, especially when parts are not thoroughly cleaned using the proper cleaning methods. Whatever the source, these foreign objects often end up embedded in the soft bearing material and are easily recognized. Large particles will not embed in the bearing and will score or gouge the bearing and journal. The best prevention for this cause of bearing failure is to clean all parts thoroughly and keep everything spotlessly clean during engine assembly. Frequent and regular engine oil and filter changes are also recommended.

5   Lack of lubrication (or lubrication breakdown) has a number of interrelated causes. Excessive heat (which thins the oil), overloading (which squeezes the oil from the bearing face) and oil leakage or throw-off (from excessive bearing clearances, worn oil pump or high engine speeds) all contribute to lubrication breakdown. Blocked oil passages, which usually are the result of misaligned oil holes in a bearing shell, will also oil-starve a bearing and destroy it. When lack of lubrication is the cause of bearing failure, the bearing material is wiped or extruded from the steel backing of the bearing. Temperatures may increase to the point where the steel backing turns blue from overheating.

6   Driving habits can have a definite effect on bearing life. Full throttle, low speed operation (lugging the engine) puts very high loads on bearings, which tends to squeeze out the oil film. These loads cause the bearings to flex, which produces fine cracks in the bearing face (fatigue failure). Eventually the bearing material will loosen in pieces and tear away from the steel backing. Short trip driving leads to corrosion of bearings because insufficient engine heat is produced to drive off the condensed water and corrosive gases. These products collect in the engine oil, forming acid and sludge. As the oil is carried to the engine bearings, the acid attacks and corrodes the bearing material.

7   Incorrect bearing installation during engine assembly will lead to bearing failure as well. Tight fitting bearings leave insufficient bearing oil clearance and will result in oil starvation. Dirt or foreign particles trapped behind a bearing insert result in high spots on the bearing which lead to failure.

8   There are two ways for selecting the proper size crankshaft bearings. The first one is to select the bearing by "grade" based on the cylinder block stampings and the crankshaft journal stampings. The second is using plastic gauge material to measure the actual clearance.
Note: *The grade stamping for the crankshaft main bearing journal is located on the back side of the rear counter weight of the crankshaft. The stamping for the connecting rod journal is stamped on the cylinder block where the high pressure fuel pump is mounted. The grade stamping for the crankshaft main and connecting rod journals are also on the first counterweight of the crankshaft. There are only two options: no stamp means the journals are Standard, and an M20 or R20 stamping means the crankshaft is 0.020-inch oversized.*

21 Engine overhaul - reassembly sequence

1   Before beginning engine reassembly, make sure you have all the necessary new parts, gaskets and seals as well as the following items on hand:

> *Common hand tools*
> *A 1/2-inch drive torque wrench*
> *Piston ring installation tool*
> *Piston ring compressor*
> *Vibration damper installation tool*
> *Short lengths of rubber or plastic hose to fit over connecting
>   rod bolts*
> *Plastigage*
> *Feeler gauges*
> *A fine-tooth file*
> *New engine oil*
> *Engine assembly lube or moly-base grease*
> *Gasket sealant*
> *Thread locking compound*

2   In order to save time and avoid problems, engine reassembly must be done in the following general order:

> *New camshaft bearings (must be done by automotive
>   machine shop)*
> *Piston rings*
> *Piston oil cooler nozzles*
> *Crankshaft and main bearings*
> *Piston/connecting rod assemblies*
> *Oil pump*
> *Camshaft and lifters*
> *Oil pans*
> *Timing gears*
> *Cylinder head(s), pushrods and rocker arms*
> *Timing cover*
> *Intake and exhaust manifolds*
> *Rocker arm cover(s)*
> *Engine rear plate*
> *Flywheel*

22 Crankshaft - installation and main bearing oil clearance check

1   Crankshaft installation is the first step in engine reassembly. It's assumed at this point that the engine block and crankshaft have been cleaned, inspected and, if necessary, reconditioned.

2   Position the engine with the bottom facing up and install the piston oil cooling nozzles, tightening the bolts to the torque listed in this Chapter's Specifications.

3   Remove the main bearing cap bolts and lift out the caps. Lay them out in the proper order to ensure correct installation.

4   If they're still in place, remove the original bearing inserts from the block and the main bearing caps. Wipe the bearing surfaces of the block and caps with a clean, lint-free cloth. They must be kept spotlessly clean.

Main bearing oil clearance check

Refer to illustrations 22.6, 22.11 and 22.15

5   Clean the back sides of the new main bearing inserts and lay one in each main bearing saddle in the block. If one of the bearing inserts from each set has a large groove in it, make sure the grooved insert is installed in the block. Lay the other bearing from each set in the corresponding main bearing cap. Make sure the tab on the bearing insert fits into the recess in the block or cap.
Caution: *The oil holes in the block must line up with the oil holes in the bearing insert. Do not hammer the bearing into place and don't nick or gouge the bearing faces. No lubrication should be used at this time.*

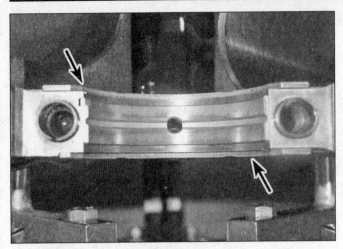

22.6 Location of the No.5 saddle (upper) thrust washers

22.11 Lay the Plastigage strips on the main bearing journals, parallel to the crankshaft centerline

6   There are three thrust bearings: One at the rear of the No.5 bearing cap (lower) and two in the No.5 bearing saddle (upper) **(see illustration)**.
Note: *The reliefs (or "grooves") in the thrust bearings must face away from the bearing saddle and cap.*
7   Clean the faces of the bearings in the block and the crankshaft main bearing journals with a clean, lint-free cloth.
8   Check or clean the oil holes in the crankshaft, as any dirt here can go only one way - straight through the new bearings.
9   Once you're certain the crankshaft is clean, carefully lay it in position in the main bearings.
10   Before the crankshaft can be permanently installed, the main bearing oil clearance must be checked.
11   Cut several pieces of the appropriate size Plastigage (they must be slightly shorter than the width of the main bearings) and place one piece on each crankshaft main bearing journal, parallel with the journal axis **(see illustration)**.
12   Clean the faces of the bearings in the caps and install the caps in their respective positions (don't mix them up), with the mark made in Section 14 pointing toward the front of the engine. Don't disturb the Plastigage.
13   Using the old crankshaft bolts, starting with the center main and working out toward the ends, tighten the main bearing cap bolts, in three steps, to the torque listed in this Chapter's Specifications. Then install the side bolts and, starting from the right side working in line around to the opposite side, tighten the bolts to the torque listed in this Chapter's Specifications. Don't rotate the crankshaft at any time during this operation.
14   Remove the bolts and carefully lift off the main bearing caps. Keep them in order. Don't disturb the Plastigage or rotate the crankshaft. If any of the main bearing caps are difficult to remove, tap them gently from side-to-side with a soft-face hammer to loosen them.
15   Compare the width of the crushed Plastigage on each journal to the scale printed on the Plastigage envelope to obtain the main bearing oil clearance **(see illustration)**. Check the Specifications to make sure it's correct.
16   If the clearance is not as specified, the bearing inserts may be the wrong size (which means different ones will be required). Before deciding that different inserts are needed, make sure that no dirt or oil was between the bearing inserts and the caps or block when the clearance was measured. If the Plastigage was wider at one end than the other, the journal may be tapered (see Section 19).
17   Carefully scrape all traces of the Plastigage material off the main bearing journals and/or the bearing faces. Use your fingernail or the edge of a credit card - don't nick or scratch the bearing faces.

Final crankshaft installation
Warning: *There are two different crankshaft bearing cap bolt lengths used over the years these engines have been in production. If the*

improper bolt is used, the bolt may bottom out before it is properly torqued. To identify the different bolts used, look at the bolt heads - one design has a raised circle and the other is unmarked or flat. Make sure you replace the bolts with the same type originally installed.
18   Carefully lift the crankshaft out of the engine.
19   Clean the bearing faces in the block, then apply a thin, uniform layer of moly-base grease or engine assembly lube to each of the bearing surfaces. Be sure to coat the thrust faces as well as the journal face of the thrust bearings.
20   Make sure the crankshaft journals are clean, then lay the crankshaft back in place in the block.
21   Clean the faces of the bearings in the caps, then apply lubricant to them.
22   Install the caps in their respective positions with the marks pointing toward the front of the engine.
23   Install **NEW** main bearing cap bolts.
Caution: *The main bearing cap bolts come with a preapplied molybdenum disulfide coating on the threads. Do not remove the coating or apply oil to the threads or cylinder block bolt bores. If oil or any other type of lubricant is applied, a false tightening torque will be obtained, resulting in engine damage.*

22.15 Compare the width of the crushed Plastigage to the scale on the envelope to determine the main bearing oil clearance (always take the measurement at the widest point of the Plastigage); be sure to use the correct scale - standard and metric ones are included

ENGINE BEARING ANALYSIS

Debris

Babbitt bearing embedded with debris from machinings

Microscopic detail of debris

Microscopic detail of gouges

Overplated copper alloy bearing gouged by cast iron debris

Aluminum bearing embedded with glass beads

Microscopic detail of glass beads

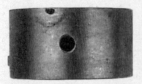

Damaged lining caused by dirt left on the bearing back

Misassembly

Result of a lower half assembled as an upper - blocking the oil flow

Excessive oil clearance is indicated by a short contact arc

Polished and oil-stained backs are a result of a poor fit in the housing bore

Result of a wrong, reversed, or shifted cap

Overloading

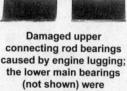

Damage from excessive idling which resulted in an oil film unable to support the load imposed

Damaged upper connecting rod bearings caused by engine lugging; the lower main bearings (not shown) were similarly affected

The damage shown in these upper and lower connecting rod bearings was caused by engine operation at a higher-than-rated speed under load

Misalignment

A warped crankshaft caused this pattern of severe wear in the center, diminishing toward the ends

A poorly finished crankshaft caused the equally spaced scoring shown

A tapered housing bore caused the damage along one edge of this pair

A bent connecting rod led to the damage in the "V" pattern

Lubrication

Result of dry start: The bearings on the left, farthest from the oil pump, show more damage

Result of a low oil supply or oil starvation

Severe wear as a result of inadequate oil clearance

Corrosion

Microscopic detail of corrosion

Corrosion is an acid attack on the bearing lining generally caused by inadequate maintenance, extremely hot or cold operation, or inferior oils or fuels

Microscopic detail of cavitation

Example of cavitation - a surface erosion caused by pressure changes in the oil film

Damage from excessive thrust or insufficient axial clearance

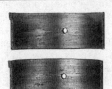

Bearing affected by oil dilution caused by excessive blow-by or a rich mixture

24.3 When checking piston ring end gap, the ring must be square in the cylinder bore (this is done by pushing the ring down with the top of a piston)

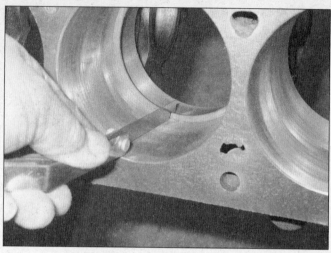

24.4 With the ring square in the cylinder, measure the end gap with a feeler gauge

24   Tighten all the bearing cap bolts to the specified torque (work from the center out and approach the final torque in three steps).

25   Install the crankshaft bearing cap side bolts and, starting from the right side, working in line around to the opposite side, tighten the bolts to the torque listed in this Chapter's Specifications.

26   Rotate the crankshaft a number of times by hand to check for any obvious binding.

27   The final step is to check the crankshaft endplay with a feeler gauge or a dial indicator (see Section 14). The endplay should be correct if the crankshaft thrust faces aren't worn or damaged and new bearings have been installed.

28   Bolt the flywheel housing to the block, then install a new rear main oil seal (see Chapter 7).

29   Install the oil pressure sending unit and tighten the sending unit to the torque listed in this Chapter's Specifications.

23   Rear main oil seal replacement

Refer to Chapter 7 for the rear main oil seal replacement procedure.

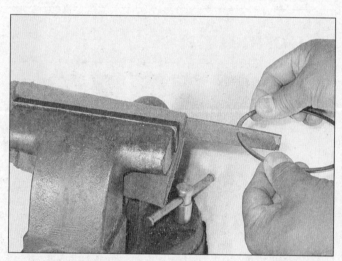

24.5 If the end gap is too small, clamp a file in a vise and file the ring ends (from the outside in only) to enlarge the gap slightly

24   Piston rings - installation

Refer to illustrations 24.3, 24.4, 24.5, 24.9a, 24.9b and 24.12

1   Before installing the new piston rings, the ring end gaps must be checked. It's assumed that the piston ring side clearance has been checked and verified correct (see Section 18).

2   Lay out the piston/connecting rod assemblies and the new ring sets so the ring sets will be matched with the same piston and cylinder during the end gap measurement and engine assembly.

3   Starting with the first compression ring (number one) insert the ring into the first cylinder and square it up with the cylinder walls by pushing it in with the top of the piston **(see illustration)**. The ring should be near the bottom of the cylinder, at the lower limit of ring travel.

4   To measure the end gap, slip feeler gauges between the ends of the ring until a gauge equal to the gap width is found **(see illustration)**. The feeler gauge should slide between the ring ends with a slight amount of drag. Compare the measurement to this Chapter's Specifications. If the gap is larger or smaller than specified, double-check to make sure you have the correct rings before proceeding.

5   If the gap is too small, it must be enlarged or the ring ends may come in contact with each other during engine operation, which can cause serious damage to the engine. The end gap can be increased by filing the ring ends very carefully with a fine file. Mount the file in a vise equipped with soft jaws, slip the ring over the file with the ends contacting the file face and slowly move the ring to remove material from the ends. When performing this operation, file only from the outside in **(see illustration)**.

6   Excess end gap isn't critical unless it's greater than 0.040-inch. Again, double-check to make sure you have the correct rings for your engine.

7   Repeat the procedure for each ring that will be installed in the first cylinder and for each ring in the remaining cylinders. Remember to keep rings, pistons and cylinders matched up.

8   Once the ring end gaps have been checked/corrected, the rings can be installed on the pistons.

9   The oil control ring (lowest one on the piston) is installed first. It's composed of two separate components. Slip the expander into the groove. Next, install the oil ring into the same groove over the expander **(see illustration)**.

10   After the two oil ring components have been installed, check to make sure that both components can be turned smoothly in the ring groove.

11   The number two (middle) ring is installed next. It's usually stamped with a mark "(2N)" which must face up, toward the top of the piston.

24.9a Install the oil ring expander . . .

24.9b . . . then the oil ring ("wind" it around the piston by hand - don't use a piston ring installation tool)

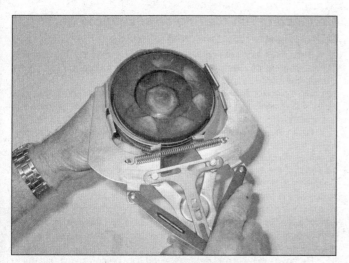

24.12 Installing the compression rings with a ring expander - the mark (2N) must face up

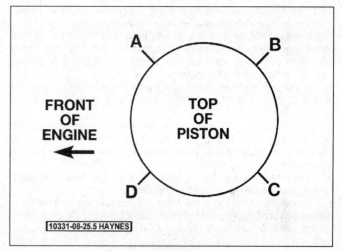

25.5 Piston ring spacing

A   Top compression ring gap
B   Oil expander ring gap
C   Second compression ring gap
D   Oil ring gap

Note: *Always follow the instructions printed on the ring package or box - different manufacturers may require different approaches. Do not mix up the top and middle rings, as they have different cross-sections.*

12   Use a piston ring installation tool and make sure the identification mark is facing the top of the piston, then slip the ring into the middle groove on the piston **(see illustration)**. Don't expand the ring any more than necessary to slide it over the piston.

Note: *The piston has a groove between the number two ring and the number one (top) ring to allow for expansion of blow-by; nothing should be installed in this groove.*

13   Install the number one (top) ring in the same manner. Be careful not to confuse the number one and number two rings.

14   Repeat the procedure for the remaining pistons and rings.

25 Pistons/connecting rods - installation and rod bearing oil clearance check

Refer to illustrations 25.5, 25.8 and 25.10

1   Before installing the piston/connecting rod assemblies, the cylinder walls must be perfectly clean, the top edge of each cylinder must be chamfered, and the crankshaft must be in place.

2   Remove the cap from the end of the number one connecting rod (refer to the marks made during removal). Remove the original bearing inserts and wipe the bearing surfaces of the connecting rod and cap with a clean, lint-free cloth. They must be kept spotlessly clean.

3   Clean the back side of the new upper bearing insert, then lay it in place in the connecting rod. Make sure the tab on the bearing fits into the recess in the rod. Don't hammer the bearing insert into place and be very careful not to nick or gouge the bearing face. Don't lubricate the bearing at this time.

Note: *There are two designs used: on the first design, the tabs are opposite each other, and on the second designs the tabs face each other.*

4   Clean the back side of the other bearing insert and install it in the rod cap. Again, make sure the tab on the bearing fits into the recess in the cap, and don't apply any lubricant. It's critically important that the mating surfaces of the bearing and connecting rod are perfectly clean and oil free when they're assembled.

5   Stagger the piston ring gaps around the piston **(see illustration)**. The two compression ring gaps should be spaced 180-degrees from each other. The inner oil expander ring gap should be 180-degrees

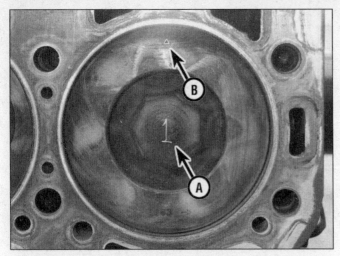

25.8 Install the piston/connecting rod with the mark you made (A) in the proper cylinder and the arrow on the piston (B) facing towards the valley of the engine block

25.10 Drive the piston gently into the cylinder bore with the end of a wooden or plastic hammer handle

from the oil rail ring gap. And once all the rings are on the piston all four ring gaps should 90-degrees apart from each other.

6   Lubricate the piston and rings with clean engine oil and attach a piston ring compressor to the piston. Leave the skirt protruding about 1/4-inch to guide the piston into the cylinder. The rings must be compressed until they're flush with the piston.

7   Rotate the crankshaft until the number one connecting rod journal is at BDC (bottom dead center) and apply a coat of engine oil to the cylinder walls.

8   With the mark on top of the piston **(see illustration)** facing the center of the engine block, gently insert the piston/connecting rod assembly into the number one cylinder bore and rest the bottom edge of the ring compressor on the engine block.

9   Tap the top edge of the ring compressor to make sure it's contacting the block around its entire circumference.

10   Gently tap on the top of the piston with the end of a wooden hammer handle **(see illustration)** while guiding the end of the connecting rod into place on the crankshaft journal. The piston rings may try to pop out of the ring compressor just before entering the cylinder bore, so keep some downward pressure on the ring compressor. Work slowly, and if any resistance is felt as the piston enters the cylinder, stop immediately. Find out what's hanging up and fix it before proceeding. Do not force the piston into the cylinder - you might break a ring and/or the piston.

25.12 Lay the Plastigage strips on each rod bearing journal, parallel to the crankshaft centerline

Connecting rod bearing oil clearance check

Refer to illustrations 25.12 and 25.16

11   Once the piston/connecting rod assembly is installed, the connecting rod bearing oil clearance must be checked before the rod cap is permanently bolted in place.

12   Cut a piece of the appropriate size Plastigage slightly shorter than the width of the connecting rod bearing and lay it in place on the number one connecting rod journal, parallel with the journal axis **(see illustration)**.

13   Clean the connecting rod cap bearing face and install the rod cap. Make sure the mating mark on the cap is on the same side as the mark on the connecting rod.

14   Install the old bolts and tighten them to the torque listed in this Chapter's Specifications.

Note: *Use a thin-wall socket to avoid erroneous torque readings that can result if the socket is wedged between the rod cap and bolt. If the socket tends to wedge itself between the bolt and the cap, lift up on it slightly until it no longer contacts the cap. Do not rotate the crankshaft at any time during this operation.*

15   Remove the bolts and detach the rod cap, being very careful not to disturb the Plastigage.

16   Compare the width of the crushed Plastigage to the scale printed on the Plastigage envelope to obtain the oil clearance **(see illustration)**. Compare it to the Specifications to make sure the clearance is correct.

17   If the clearance is not as specified, the bearing inserts may be the wrong size (which means different ones will be required). Before deciding that different inserts are needed, make sure that no dirt or oil was between the bearing inserts and the connecting rod or cap when the clearance was measured. Also, recheck the journal diameter. If the Plastigage was wider at one end than the other, the journal may be tapered (see Section 19).

Final connecting rod installation

18   Carefully scrape all traces of the Plastigage material off the rod journal and/or bearing face. Be very careful not to scratch the bearing - use your fingernail or the edge of a credit card.

19   Make sure the bearing faces are perfectly clean, then apply a uniform layer of clean moly-base grease or engine assembly lube to both of them. You'll have to push the piston into the cylinder to expose the face of the bearing insert in the connecting rod.

20   Slide the connecting rod back into place on the journal, install the rod cap and tighten the *NEW* bolts to the specified torque.

Caution: *The rod bolts come with a preapplied molybdenum disulfide coating on the threads. Do not remove the coating or apply oil to the threads or rod bolt bores. If oil or any other type of lubricant is applied, a false tightening torque will be obtained, resulting in engine damage.*

25.16 Measuring the width of the crushed Plastigage to determine the rod bearing oil clearance (be sure to use the correct scale - standard and metric ones are included)

21   Repeat the entire procedure for the remaining pistons/connecting rods.

22   The important points to remember are:

a)   *Keep the back sides of the bearing inserts and the insides of the connecting rods and caps perfectly clean when assembling them.*

b)   *Make sure you have the correct piston/rod assembly for each cylinder.*

c)   *The arrow or triangle mark on the piston must face the proper direction.*

d)   *Lubricate the cylinder walls with clean oil.*

e)   *Lubricate the bearing faces when installing the rod caps after the oil clearance has been checked.*

23   After all the piston/connecting rod assemblies have been properly installed, rotate the crankshaft a number of times by hand to check for any obvious binding.

24   As a final step, the connecting rod endplay must be checked as described in Section 13.

25   Compare the measured endplay to the Specifications to make sure

it's correct. If it was correct before disassembly and the original crankshaft and rods were reinstalled, it should still be right. If new rods or a new crankshaft were installed, the endplay may be inadequate. If so, the rods will have to be removed and taken to an automotive machine shop for resizing.

26   Initial start-up and break-in after overhaul

Warning: *Have a fire extinguisher handy when starting the engine for the first time.*

1   Once the engine has been installed in the vehicle, the oiling system will have to be prelubed just before the engine can be started.

2   Remove the oil filter and fill it with oil. Reinstall the filter (see Chapter 1).

3   Remove the oil pressure sending unit (see Section 3) and install an adapter that matches the threads of the oil pressure sending unit. Connect a hose from the adapter to a hand pump and insert the pump into a container of engine oil. Pump a minimum of one to two gallons of oil into the engine, then disconnect the hose and reinstall the oil pressure sending unit.

4   Double-check the engine oil and coolant levels, then crank the engine until oil pressure registers on the gauge or the light goes out.

5   Prime the fuel system (see Chapter 1, Section 11). Start the engine; it may take a few moments for the fuel system to build up pressure, but the engine should start without a great deal of effort.

6   After the engine starts, it should be allowed to warm up to normal operating temperature. While the engine is warming up, make a thorough check for fuel, oil and coolant leaks.

7   Shut the engine off and recheck the engine oil and coolant levels.

8   Drive the vehicle to an area with minimal traffic, accelerate at full throttle from 30 to 50 mph, then allow the vehicle to slow to 30 mph with the throttle closed. Repeat the procedure 10 or 12 times. This will load the piston rings and cause them to seat properly against the cylinder walls. Check again for oil and coolant leaks.

9   Drive the vehicle gently for the first 500 miles (no sustained high speeds) and keep a constant check on the oil level. It is not unusual for an engine to use oil during the break-in period.

10   At approximately 500 to 600 miles, change the oil and filter.

11   For the next few hundred miles, drive the vehicle normally. Do not pamper it or abuse it.

12   After 2000 miles, change the oil and filter again and consider the engine broken in.

COMMON ENGINE OVERHAUL TERMS

B

Backlash - The amount of play between two parts. Usually refers to how much one gear can be moved back and forth without moving the gear with which it's meshed.

Bearing Caps - The caps held in place by nuts or bolts which, in turn, hold the bearing surface. This space is for lubricating oil to enter.

Bearing clearance - The amount of space left between shaft and bearing surface. This space is for lubricating oil to enter.

Bearing crush - The additional height which is purposely manufactured into each bearing half to ensure complete contact of the bearing back with the housing bore when the engine is assembled.

Bearing knock - The noise created by movement of a part in a loose or worn bearing.

Blueprinting - Dismantling an engine and reassembling it to EXACT specifications.

Bore - An engine cylinder, or any cylindrical hole; also used to describe the process of enlarging or accurately refinishing a hole with a cutting tool, as to bore an engine cylinder. The bore size is the diameter of the hole.

Boring - Renewing the cylinders by cutting them out to a specified size. A boring bar is used to make the cut.

Bottom end - A term which refers collectively to the engine block, crankshaft, main bearings and the big ends of the connecting rods.

Break-in - The period of operation between installation of new or rebuilt parts and time in which parts are worn to the correct fit. Driving at reduced and varying speed for a specified mileage to permit parts to wear to the correct fit.

Bushing - A one-piece sleeve placed in a bore to serve as a bearing surface for shaft, piston pin, etc. Usually replaceable.

C

Camshaft - The shaft in the engine, on which a series of lobes are located for operating the valve mechanisms. The camshaft is driven by gears or sprockets and a timing chain. Usually referred to simply as the cam.

Carbon - Hard, or soft, black deposits found in combustion chamber, on plugs, under rings, on and under valve heads.

Cast iron - An alloy of iron and more than two percent carbon, used for engine blocks and heads because it's relatively inexpensive and easy to mold into complex shapes.

Chamfer - To bevel across (or a bevel on) the sharp edge of an object.

Chase - To repair damaged threads with a tap or die.

Combustion chamber - The space between the piston and the cylinder head, with the piston at top dead center, in which air-fuel mixture is burned.

Compression ratio - The relationship between cylinder volume (clearance volume) when the piston is at top dead center and cylinder volume when the piston is at bottom dead center.

Connecting rod - The rod that connects the crank on the crankshaft with the piston. Sometimes called a con rod.

Connecting rod cap - The part of the connecting rod assembly that attaches the rod to the crankpin.

Core plug - Soft metal plug used to plug the casting holes for the coolant passages in the block.

Crankcase - The lower part of the engine in which the crankshaft rotates; includes the lower section of the cylinder block and the oil pan.

Crank kit - A reground or reconditioned crankshaft and new main and connecting rod bearings.

Crankpin - The part of a crankshaft to which a connecting rod is attached.

Crankshaft - The main rotating member, or shaft, running the length of the crankcase, with offset throws to which the connecting rods are attached; changes the reciprocating motion of the pistons into rotating motion.

Cylinder sleeve - A replaceable sleeve, or liner, pressed into the cylinder block to form the cylinder bore.

D

Deburring - Removing the burrs (rough edges or areas) from a bearing.

Deglazer - A tool, rotated by an electric motor, used to remove glaze from cylinder walls so a new set of rings will seat.

E

Endplay - The amount of lengthwise movement between two parts. As applied to a crankshaft, the distance that the crankshaft can move forward and back in the cylinder block.

F

Face - A machinist's term that refers to removing metal from the end of a shaft or the face of a larger part, such as a flywheel.

Fatigue - A breakdown of material through a large number of loading and unloading cycles. The first signs are cracks followed shortly by breaks.

Feeler gauge - A thin strip of hardened steel, ground to an exact thickness, used to check clearances between parts.

Free height - The unloaded length or height of a spring.

Freeplay - The looseness in a linkage, or an assembly of parts, between the initial application of force and actual movement. Usually perceived as slop or slight delay.

Freeze plug - See Core plug.

G

Gallery - A large passage in the block that forms a reservoir for engine oil pressure.

Glaze - The very smooth, glassy finish that develops on cylinder walls while an engine is in service.

H

Heli-Coil - A rethreading device used when threads are worn or damaged. The device is installed in a retapped hole to reduce the thread size to the original size.

I

Installed height - The spring's measured length or height, as installed on the cylinder head. Installed height is measured from the spring seat to the underside of the spring retainer.

J

Journal - The surface of a rotating shaft which turns in a bearing.

K

Keeper - The split lock that holds the valve spring retainer in position on the valve stem.

Key - A small piece of metal inserted into matching grooves machined into two parts fitted together - such as a gear pressed onto a shaft - which prevents slippage between the two parts.

Knock - The heavy metallic engine sound, produced in the combustion chamber as a result of abnormal combustion - usually detonation. Knock is usually caused by a loose or worn bearing. Also referred to as detonation, pinging and spark knock. Connecting rod or main bearing knocks are created by too much oil clearance or insufficient lubrication.

L

Lands - The portions of metal between the piston ring grooves.

Lapping the valves - Grinding a valve face and its seat together with lapping compound.

Lash - The amount of free motion in a gear train, between gears, or in a mechanical assembly, that occurs before movement can begin. Usually refers to the lash in a valve train.

Lifter - The part that rides against the cam to transfer motion to the rest of the valve train.

M

Machining - The process of using a machine to remove metal from a metal part.

Main bearings - The plain, or babbit, bearings that support the crankshaft.

Main bearing caps - The cast iron caps, bolted to the bottom of the block, that support the main bearings.

O

O.D. - Outside diameter.

Oil gallery - A pipe or drilled passageway in the engine used to carry engine oil from one area to another.

Oil ring - The lower ring, or rings, of a piston; designed to prevent excessive amounts of oil from working up the cylinder walls and into the combustion chamber. Also called an oil-control ring.

Oil seal - A seal which keeps oil from leaking out of a compartment. Usually refers to a dynamic seal around a rotating shaft or other moving part.

O-ring - A type of sealing ring made of a special rubberlike material; in use, the O-ring is compressed into a groove to provide the sealing action.

Overhaul - To completely disassemble a unit, clean and inspect all parts, reassemble it with the original or new parts and make all adjustments necessary for proper operation.

P

Pilot bearing - A small bearing installed in the center of the flywheel (or the rear end of the crankshaft) to support the front end of the input shaft of the transmission.

Pip mark - A little dot or indentation which indicates the top side of a compression ring.

Piston - The cylindrical part, attached to the connecting rod, that moves up and down in the cylinder as the crankshaft rotates. When the fuel charge is fired, the piston transfers the force of the explosion to the connecting rod, then to the crankshaft.

Piston pin (or wrist pin) - The cylindrical and usually hollow steel pin that passes through the piston. The piston pin fastens the piston to the upper end of the connecting rod.

Piston ring - The split ring fitted to the groove in a piston. The ring contacts the sides of the ring groove and also rubs against the cylinder wall, thus sealing space between piston and wall. There are two types of rings: Compression rings seal the compression pressure in the combustion chamber; oil rings scrape excessive oil off the cylinder wall.

Piston ring groove - The slots or grooves cut in piston heads to hold piston rings in position.

Piston skirt - The portion of the piston below the rings and the piston pin hole.

Plastigage - A thin strip of plastic thread, available in different sizes, used for measuring clearances. For example, a strip of plastigage is laid across a bearing journal and mashed as parts are assembled. Then parts are disassembled and the width of the strip is measured to determine clearance between journal and bearing. Commonly used to measure crankshaft main-bearing and connecting rod bearing clearances.

Press-fit - A tight fit between two parts that requires pressure to force the parts together. Also referred to as drive, or force, fit.

Prussian blue - A blue pigment; in solution, useful in determining the area of contact between two surfaces. Prussian blue is commonly used to determine the width and location of the contact area between the valve face and the valve seat.

R

Race (bearing) - The inner or outer ring that provides a contact surface for balls or rollers in bearing.

Ream - To size, enlarge or smooth a hole by using a round cutting tool with fluted edges.

Ring job - The process of reconditioning the cylinders and installing new rings.

Runout - Wobble. The amount a shaft rotates out-of-true.

S

Saddle - The upper main bearing seat.

Scored - Scratched or grooved, as a cylinder wall may be scored by abrasive particles moved up and down by the piston rings.

Scuffing - A type of wear in which there's a transfer of material between parts moving against each other; shows up as pits or grooves in the mating surfaces.

Seat - The surface upon which another part rests or seats. For example, the valve seat is the matched surface upon which the valve face rests. Also used to refer to wearing into a good fit; for example, piston rings seat after a few miles of driving.

Short block - An engine block complete with crankshaft and piston and, usually, camshaft assemblies.

Static balance - The balance of an object while it's stationary.

Step - The wear on the lower portion of a ring land caused by excessive side and back-clearance. The height of the step indicates the ring's extra side clearance and the length of the step projecting from the back wall of the groove represents the ring's back clearance.

Stroke - The distance the piston moves when traveling from top dead center to bottom dead center, or from bottom dead center to top dead center.

Stud - A metal rod with threads on both ends.

T

Tang - A lip on the end of a plain bearing used to align the bearing during assembly.

Tap - To cut threads in a hole. Also refers to the fluted tool used to cut threads.

Taper - A gradual reduction in the width of a shaft or hole; in an engine cylinder, taper usually takes the form of uneven wear, more pronounced at the top than at the bottom.

Throws - The offset portions of the crankshaft to which the connecting rods are affixed.

Thrust bearing - The main bearing that has thrust faces to prevent excessive endplay, or forward and backward movement of the crankshaft.

Thrust washer - A bronze or hardened steel washer placed between two moving parts. The washer prevents longitudinal movement and provides a bearing surface for thrust surfaces of parts.

Tolerance - The amount of variation permitted from an exact size of measurement. Actual amount from smallest acceptable dimension to largest acceptable dimension.

U

Umbrella - An oil deflector placed near the valve tip to throw oil from the valve stem area.

Undercut - A machined groove below the normal surface.

Undersize bearings - Smaller diameter bearings used with re-ground crankshaft journals.

V

Valve grinding - Refacing a valve in a valve-refacing machine.

Valve train - The valve-operating mechanism of an engine; includes all components from the camshaft to the valve.

Vibration damper - A cylindrical weight attached to the front of the crankshaft to minimize torsional vibration (the twist-untwist actions of the crankshaft caused by the cylinder firing impulses). Also called a harmonic balancer.

W

Water jacket - The spaces around the cylinders, between the inner and outer shells of the cylinder block or head, through which coolant circulates.

Web - A supporting structure across a cavity.

Woodruff key - A key with a radiused backside (viewed from the side).

Notes

Chapter 9
Troubleshooting

This Chapter provides a reference guide to the more common problems which may occur during the operation of your vehicle.

Remember that successful troubleshooting is not a mysterious black art practiced only by professional mechanics. It's simply the result of a bit of knowledge combined with an intelligent, systematic approach to the problem. Always work by a process of elimination, starting with the simplest solution and working through to the most complex - and never overlook the obvious. Anyone can forget to fill the fuel tank or leave the lights on overnight, so don't assume that you are above such oversights.

Finally, always get clear in your mind why a problem has occurred and take steps to ensure that it doesn't happen again. If the electrical system fails because of a poor connection, check all other connections in the system to make sure that they don't fail as well. If a particular fuse continues to blow, find out why - don't just go on replacing fuses. Remember, failure of a small component can often be indicative of potential failure or incorrect functioning of a more important component or system.

Many times common problems can found - or at least your diagnosis can begin by starting down the right path - by checking Duramax diesel forums on the internet. Although any given problem could have many possible causes, more than likely other owners with a vehicle similar to yours will have encountered the problem, too.

Most driveability problems that can occur on Duramax diesel engine-equipped vehicles will require, at the least, a code reader or scan tool to determine where your diagnostic efforts should begin. Some problems will require a professional-grade scan tool with graphing capability; such problems are beyond the scope of this manual. For more diagnostic information pertaining to the fuel, emissions and engine control systems, refer to Chapters 3 and 6.

For more diagnostic information related to the mechanical condition of the engine, see Chapter 8.

Condition	Possible causes
Won't start	Out of fuel Air leak in fuel feed (suction) line(s) Restricted fuel line or filter Defective fuel supply pump (van models) Incorrect fuel Paraffin deposits in filter Defective injection pump Low compression Discharged batteries Inoperative glow plugs
Hard to start	Restricted air intake Air leak in fuel feed (suction) line(s) Blocked fuel line or filter External fuel leak Clogged or defective injection nozzle(s) Defective fuel supply pump (van models) Incorrect fuel Paraffin deposit in filter Defective injection pump Incorrect oil grade for climate Low compression Worn camshaft Inoperative glow plugs
Starts, then stops	Restricted air intake Excessive exhaust back pressure Out of fuel Blocked fuel return line Air leak in fuel feed (suction) line(s) Restricted fuel line or filter External fuel leaks Defective fuel supply pump (van models) Paraffin deposits in filter Defective injection pump

Condition	Possible causes
Rough idling	Blocked fuel return line Air leak in fuel feed (suction) line(s) External fuel leak Clogged or defective injection nozzle(s) Defective fuel supply pump (van models) Defective injection pump Broken or worn piston rings Leaking valve(s) Low compression Worn camshaft
Missing	Blocked fuel return line Air leaks in fuel feed (suction) line(s) Blocked fuel line or filter External fuel leak Clogged or defective injection nozzle(s) Defective fuel supply pump (van models) Incorrect fuel Defective injection pump Leaking valve(s) Low compression Loose timing chain Worn camshaft
Oil diluted	Defective injection pump Broken or worn piston rings Injector sleeve(s) leaking (LBY engine only) Water pump defective
Knocking	Clogged or defective injection nozzle(s) Incorrect fuel Defective injection pump Broken or worn piston rings Incorrect bearing clearance Damaged bearings

Condition	Possible causes
Low power	Blocked air intake
	Excessive exhaust back pressure
	Blocked fuel return line
	Air leak in fuel feed (suction) line(s)
	Blocked fuel line or filter
	External fuel leak
	Clogged or defective injection nozzle(s)
	Incorrect fuel
	Paraffin deposit in filter
	Defective injection pump
	Leaking head gasket
	Broken or worn piston rings
	Leaking valve(s)
	Worn camshaft
Black smoke when idling	Blocked air intake
	Blocked fuel line or filter
	Clogged or defection injection nozzle(s)
	Broken or worn piston rings
	Advanced timing
Black smoke under a load*	Blocked air intake
	Excessive exhaust back pressure
	Blocked fuel line or filter
	Clogged or defective injection nozzle(s)
	Incorrect fuel
	Defective injection pump
	Low compression
	Worn camshaft
	EGR valve stuck open

To some degree, black smoke under load is normal.

Condition	Possible causes
White smoke	Blocked fuel return line
	Air leak in fuel feed (suction) line(s)
	Blocked fuel line or filter
	Defective injection pump
	Incorrect oil grade
	Inoperative glow plugs
Excessive fuel consumption	Blocked air intake
	Excessive exhaust back pressure
	Blocked fuel return line
	Blocked fuel line or filter
	External fuel leak
	Clogged or defective injection nozzle(s)
	Incorrect fuel
	Defective fuel pressure regulator
	Leaking head gasket
	Broken or worn piston rings
	Leaking valve(s)
	Low compression
	Worn camshaft
No heat from heater	Thermostat stuck open
	Low coolant level

CONDITION	POSSIBLE CAUSES	CORRECTIVE ACTION
The engine cranks normally, but won't start	a) Incorrect starting procedure	Use the correct starting procedure
	b) Inoperative glow plugs	Refer to the glow plug section in Chapter 5
	c) Inoperative glow plug control system	Refer to the glow plug section in Chapter 5
	d) No fuel to the injection pump	Loosen the line coming out of the filter and crank the engine. Fuel should spray out of the fitting. Make sure the fuel is directed away from any open flame or other source of ignition. If fuel sprays from the fitting, go to step f.
	e) Blocked fuel filter	Replace fuel filter
	f) Inoperative fuel injection pump (low, or suction, side of the pump)	Connect a vacuum/pressure gauge to the fuel test port and check for suction (see Chapter 3, Section 2).
	g) Plugged fuel tank filter	Remove the fuel tank and clean or replace the filter.
	h) Incorrect or contaminated fuel	Flush the fuel system then add the correct fuel. To verify contaminated or poor quality fuel, connect a hose to the inlet of the fuel supply pump and route it to a container of known good quality fuel. If the engine starts and runs, drain and flush poor fuel from vehicle.
	i) Low compression	Check the compression to determine the cause. Repair as necessary.
	j) Air in fuel supply lines	See Chapter 3, Section 2
The oil warning light comes on at idle	a) Low oil level	Check oil level, adding as necessary.
	b) Oil pump pressure low	Refer to the oil pump inspection and repair procedure in Chapter 2 or Chapter 3.

CONDITION	POSSIBLE CAUSES	CORRECTIVE ACTION
The engine starts, but won't idle, and stalls	a) The glow plugs turn off too soon b) Insufficient fuel supply to the injection pump c) Low compression d) Incorrect, contaminated or poor quality fuel e) Air in the fuel	Refer to the glow plug section in Chapter 5 Connect a vacuum/pressure gauge to the fuel test port and check for suction (see Chapter 3, Section 2). Check the compression to determine the cause. To verify contaminated or poor quality fuel, connect a hose to the inlet of the fuel supply pump and route it to a container filled with known good quality fuel. Start the engine. If engine performance improves, drain and flush the system and refill with the correct fuel. Connect a vacuum/pressure gauge to the fuel test port and check for suction (see Chapter 3, Section 2).
Excessive surge at light throttle, under load	a) Torque converter clutch engages too soon b) Restricted fuel filter c) Restricted fuel return line	Have the transmission diagnosed. Replace the filter. Look for and repair the obstruction in the return line.
Engine starts, but idles roughly, in Neutral or Drive. There is no abnormal noise or smoke, and the engine is warmed up	a) Leaking injection line(s) b) Restricted fuel return system c) Air in the system d) Incorrect or contaminated fuel e) Defective injector f) Low or uneven engine compression	Wipe off the injection lines and connections. Run the engine and watch for leaks. Repair as necessary. Disconnect the fuel return line at the injection pump and redirect the hose to a metal container. Connect a hose to the injection pump connection and run it into the metal container. Start the engine and allow it to idle. If the engine idles normally, locate and repair the obstruction in the fuel return line. If the engine doesn't idle normally, remove the return line check valve fitting from the top of the pump and make sure it's not blocked. See Chapter 3, Section 2 Flush the fuel system and refill with the correct fuel. Check for the presence of stored Diagnostic Trouble Codes (DTCs) (see Chapter 6). Check the compression (see Chapter 4).
When cold, the engine idles roughly after start up, but smoothes out as it warms up (often accompanied by white exhaust smoke)	a) Incorrect starting procedure b) Air in the fuel c) One or more glow plugs are not working d) Insufficient engine break-in time	Refer to your owner's manual for the correct starting procedure. See Chapter 3, Section 2 Troubleshoot the glow plug system (see Chapter 5). Break-in the engine for 2,000 or more miles.
The engine misfires above idle, or runs roughly while driving, but idles okay	a) Air in the fuel b) Blocked fuel return system c) Blocked fuel supply d) Incorrect or contaminated fuel	See Chapter 3, Section 2 Locate and repair the obstruction in the fuel return system. Connect a vacuum/pressure gauge to the fuel test port and check for suction (see Chapter 3, Section 2). Flush the fuel system and refill with the correct fuel.
Noticeable lack of power	a) Blocked air intake b) Defective EGR system c) Blocked or damaged exhaust system d) Obstruction in fuel filter e) Blocked fuel tank vacuum vent in fuel cap f) Insufficient fuel supply from fuel tank to injection pump g) Obstruction in fuel tank filter h) Pinched or otherwise restricted return system i) Incorrect or contaminated fuel j) Low compression k) Turbocharger failure l) LLY models: Check for the presence of a P0202/P0207/2149 DTC (See Chapter 6).	Inspect the air cleaner element. See Chapter 6 Check the system and repair as necessary. Replace the filter. Remove the fuel tank filler cap. If you hear a loud hissing sound (a *slight* hissing sound is normal), the vacuum vent in the cap is plugged. Replace the cap. Connect a vacuum/pressure gauge to the fuel test port and check for suction (see Chapter 3, Section 2). Remove the fuel tank and clean or replace the filter. Inspect the system for restrictions and repair as necessary. Flush the fuel system and refill with the correct fuel. Check the compression to determine the cause. Replace turbocharger. Problem most likely caused by micro-abrasion of the injector electrical connector on cylinder no. 2 or cylinder no. 7. Repair kits with modified connectors and harness brackets are available through dealer parts departments.

CONDITION	POSSIBLE CAUSES	CORRECTIVE ACTION
Fuel leaks on the ground	a) Loose or broken fuel line or connection	Inspect the entire fuel system, including the tank, hoses, lines and injection lines. Determine the source and cause of the leak, and repair it as necessary.
Rapping noise from one or more cylinders (sounds like rod bearing knock)	a) Injector nozzle(s) sticking open or with very low nozzle opening pressure b) Mechanical problem	Remove the injector nozzles and have them tested/rebuilt. Clean or replace as necessary Diagnose and repair.
Louder than normal operating noise	Improper or poor quality fuel	Fill tank with proper grade fuel.
Louder than normal operating noise, accompanied by excessive black smoke*	a) Defective EGR system b) Defective injection pump	Refer to Chapter 6. Have the injection pump diagnosed by an authorized repair facility. *To some degree, black smoke under load is normal.*
Internal or external engine noise	Engine, fuel injection pump, alternator, water pump, valve train, vacuum pump, bearing(s), etc. smoke.	Repair or replace as necessary. If the noise is internal, see preceding diagnoses for noise, and for rough idle with excessive noise and/or
Engine overheats	a) Leaking cooling system or oil cooler system, or defective coolant recovery system b) Slipping or damaged belt c) Thermostat stuck closed d) Leaking head gasket	Inspect these systems for leaks and repair as necessary. Replace the belt and/or tensioner as necessary. Check and, if necessary, replace the thermostats. Check for the presence of exhaust gasses in the cooling system using a block tester. If there are, the head gasket(s) are usually the cause.
Excessive engine blow-by	Worn piston rings	Check the compression. If it's about 100 psi low, replace the piston rings.

Notes

Notes

Chapter 10
Wiring diagrams

List

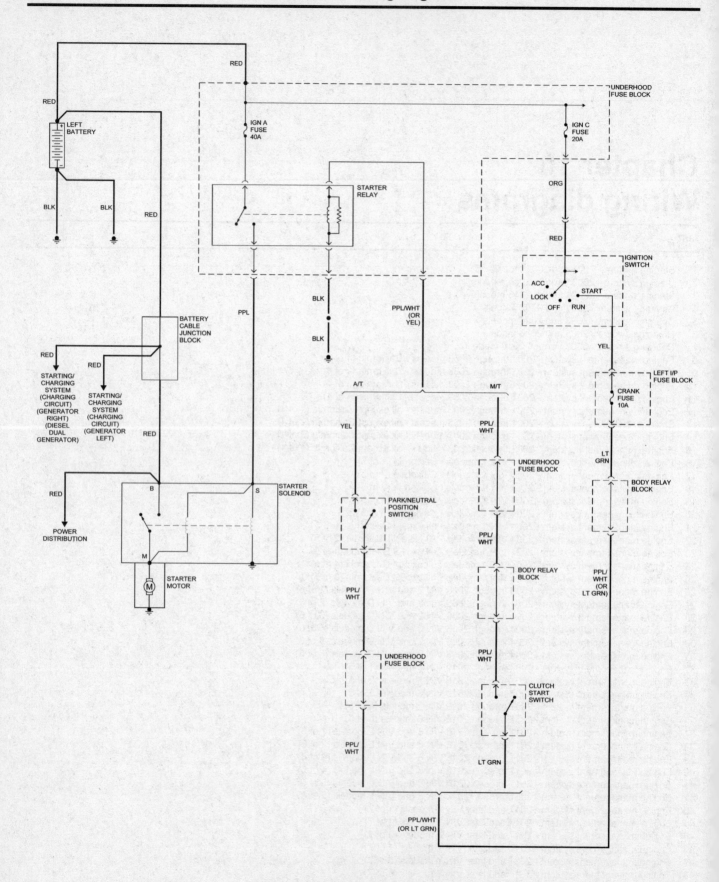

1. Starting system - 2001 and 2002 models

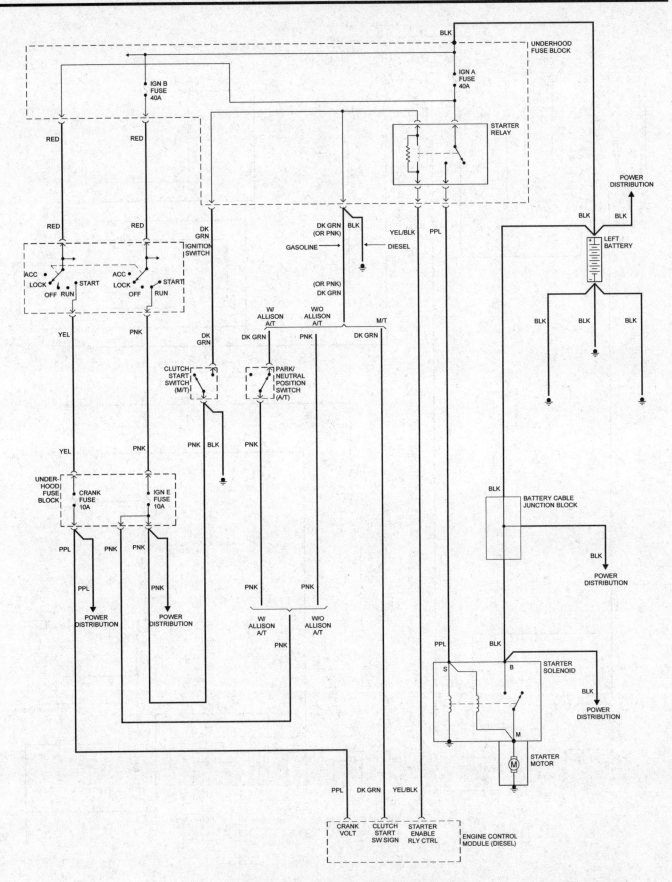

2. Starting system - 2003 through 2006 models

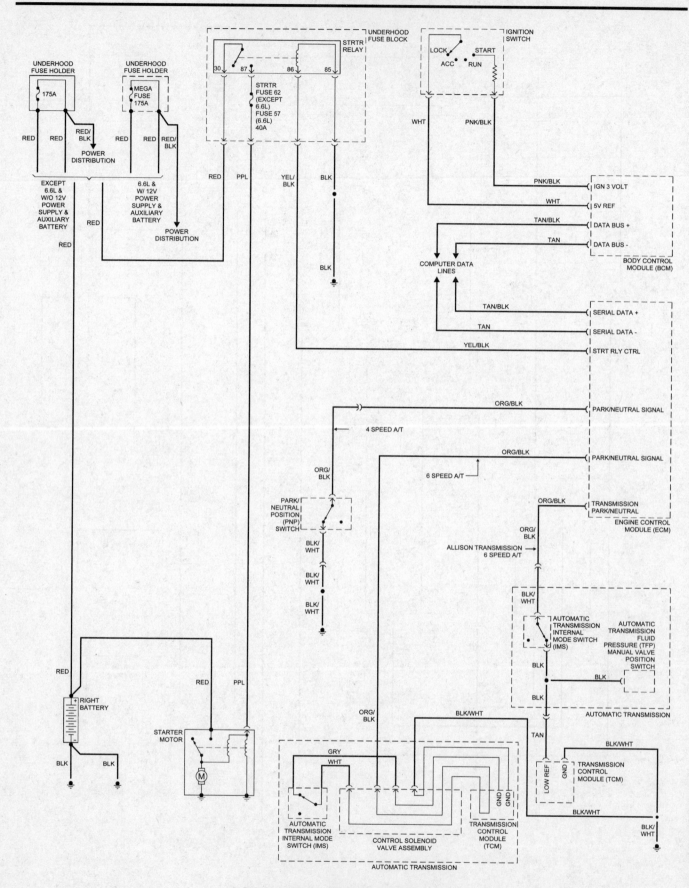

3. Starting system - 2007 through 2012 models

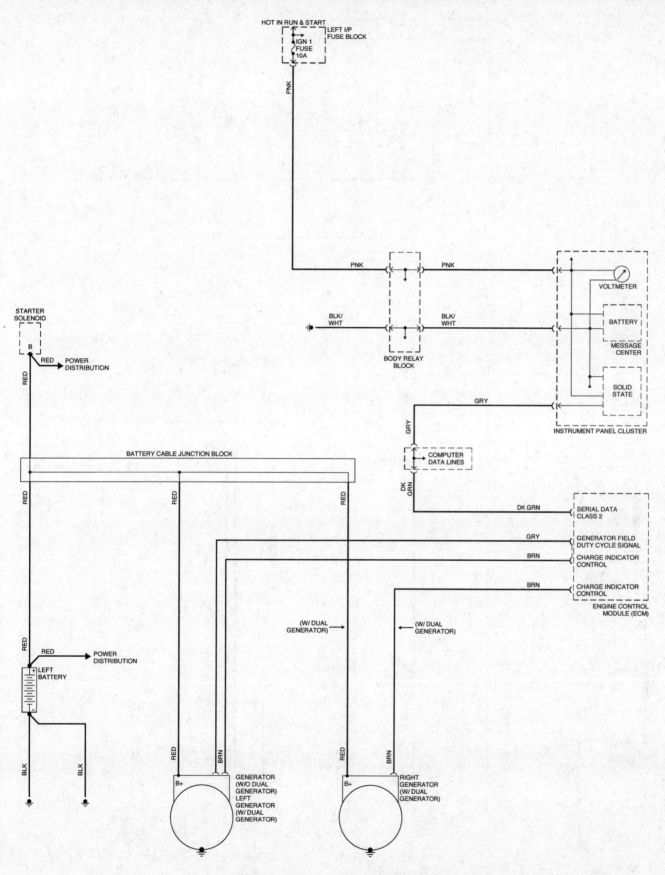

4. Charging system - 2001 and 2002 models

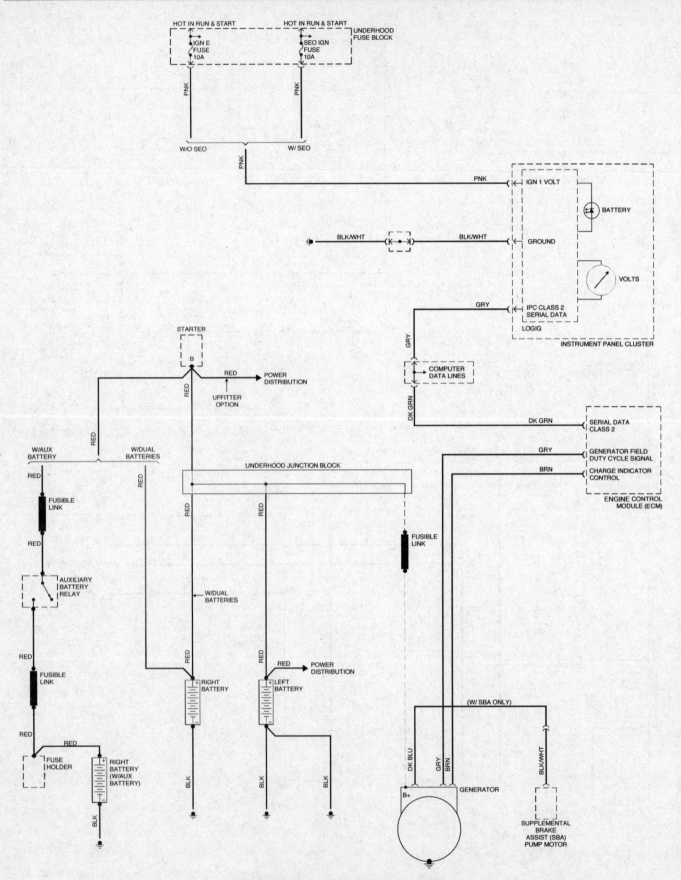

5. Charging system - 2003 and 2004 models

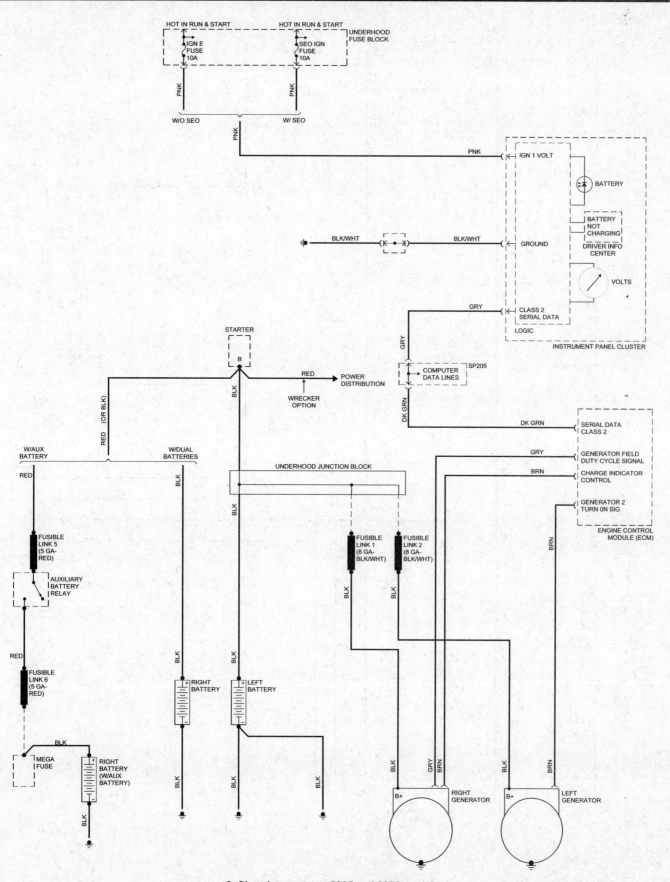

6. Charging system - 2005 and 2006 models

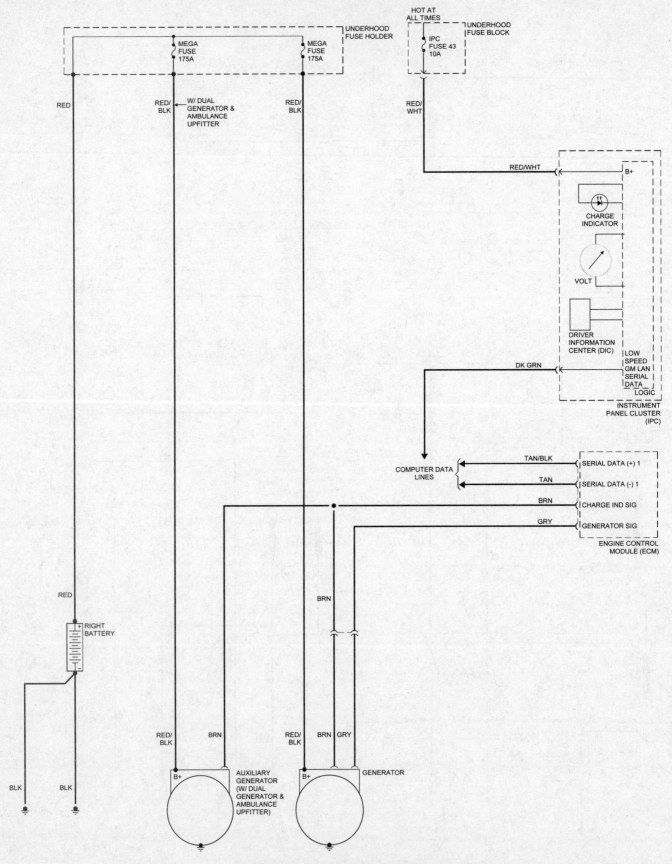

7. Charging system - 2007 through 2012 models

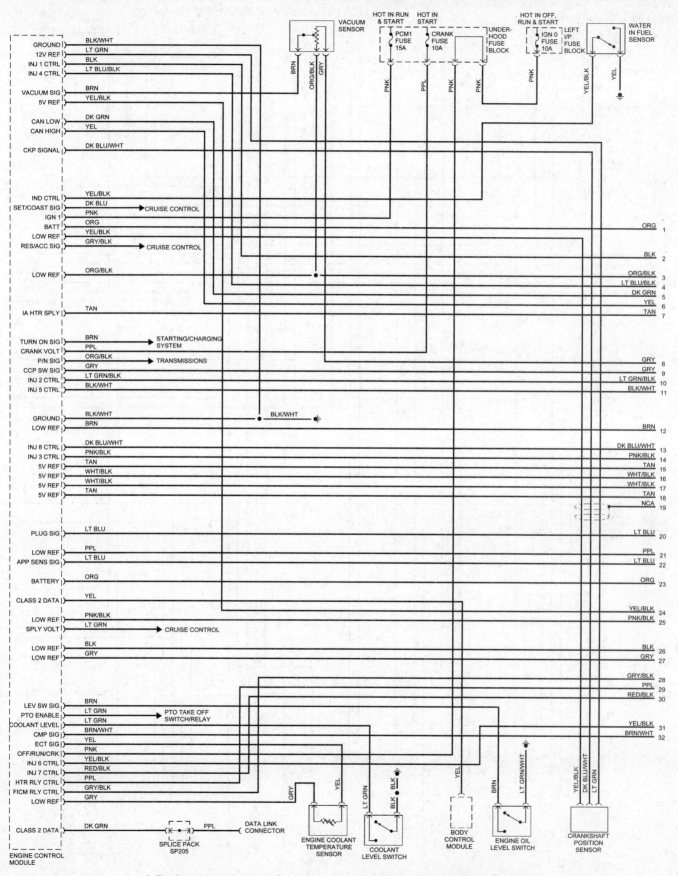

8. Engine management system - 2001 through 2003 models - California (1 of 4)

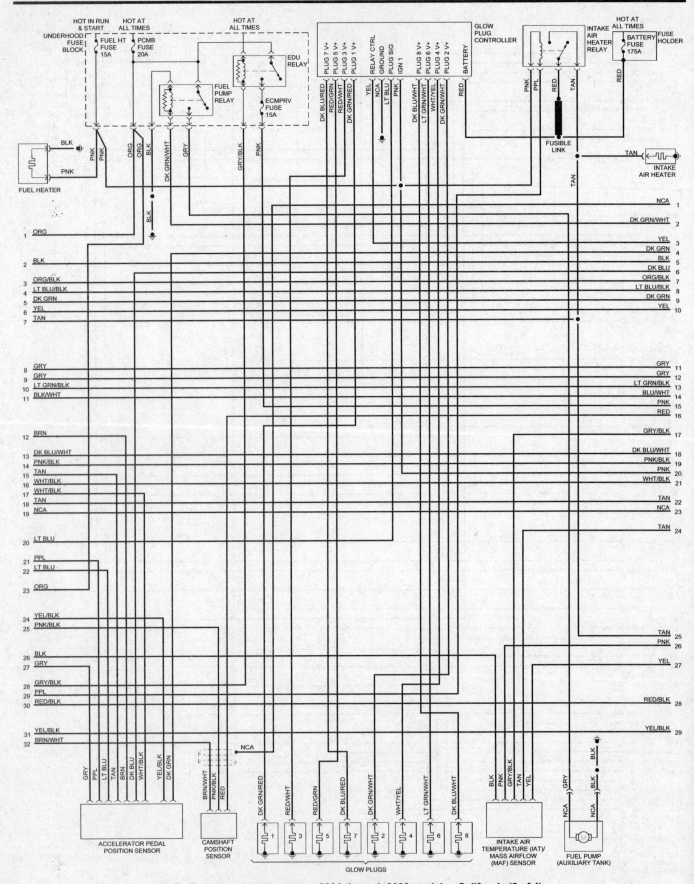

9. Engine management system - 2001 through 2003 models - California (2 of 4)

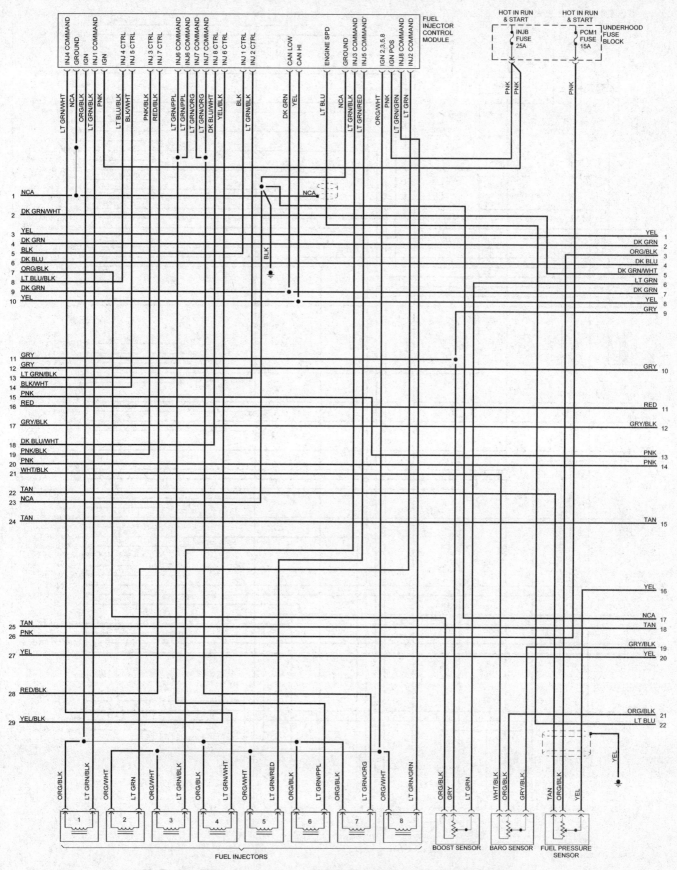

10. Engine management system - 2001 through 2003 models - California (3 of 4)

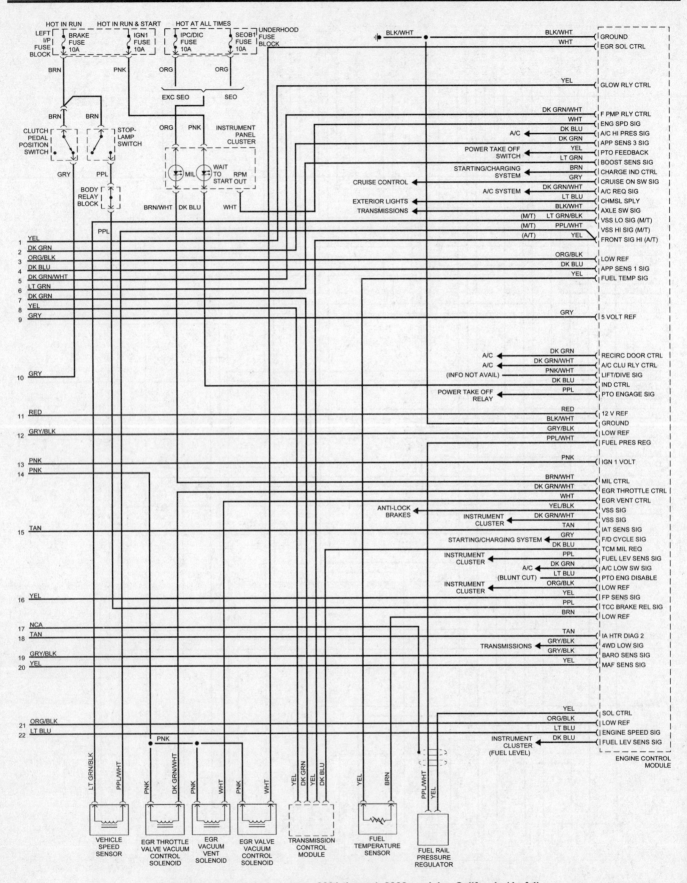

11. Engine management system - 2001 through 2003 models - California (4 of 4)

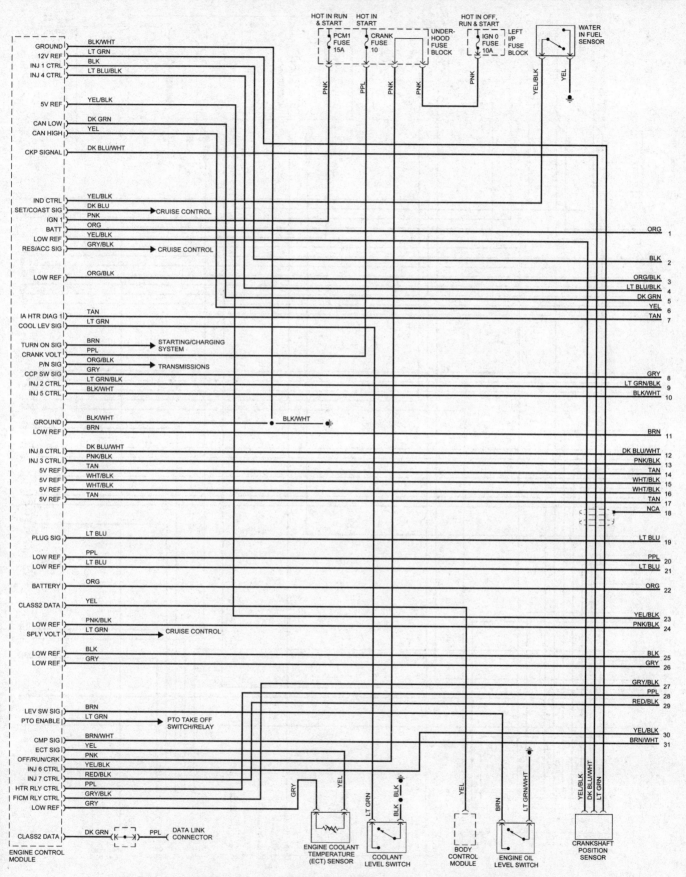

12. Engine management system - 2001 through 2003 models - all except California (1 of 4)

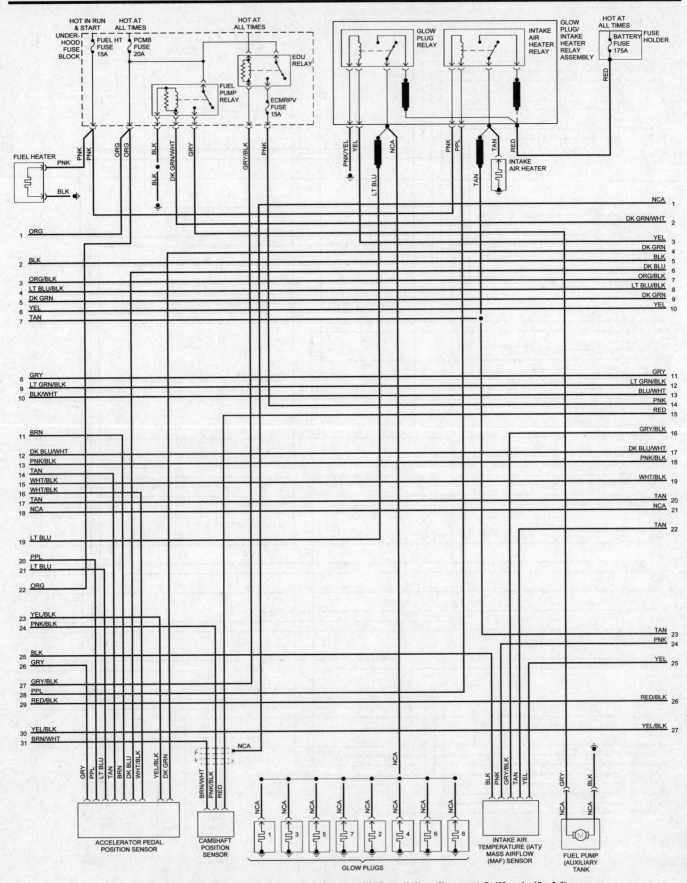

13. Engine management system - 2001 through 2003 models - all except California (2 of 4)

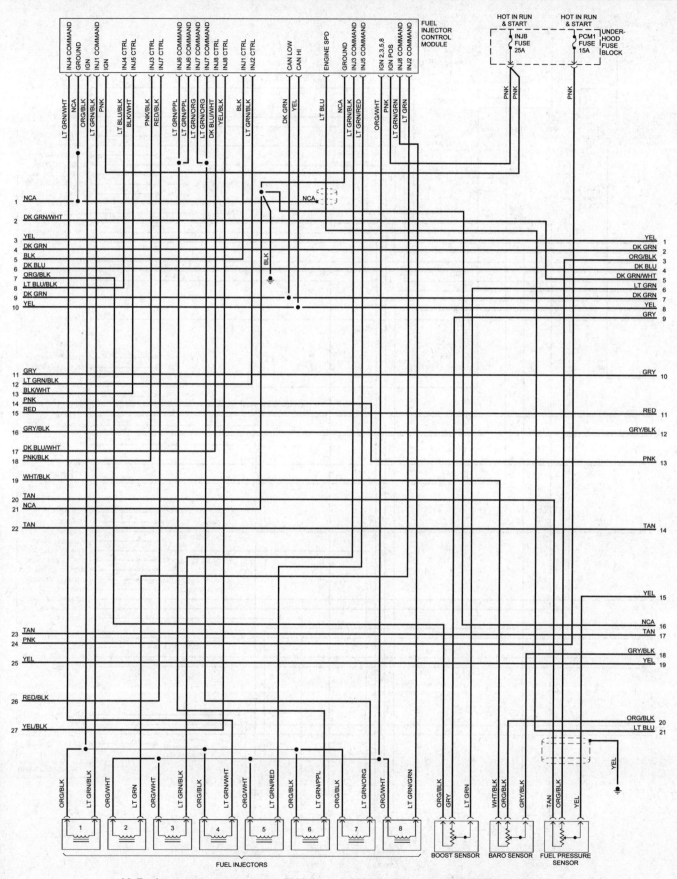

14. Engine management system - 2001 through 2003 models - all except California (3 of 4)

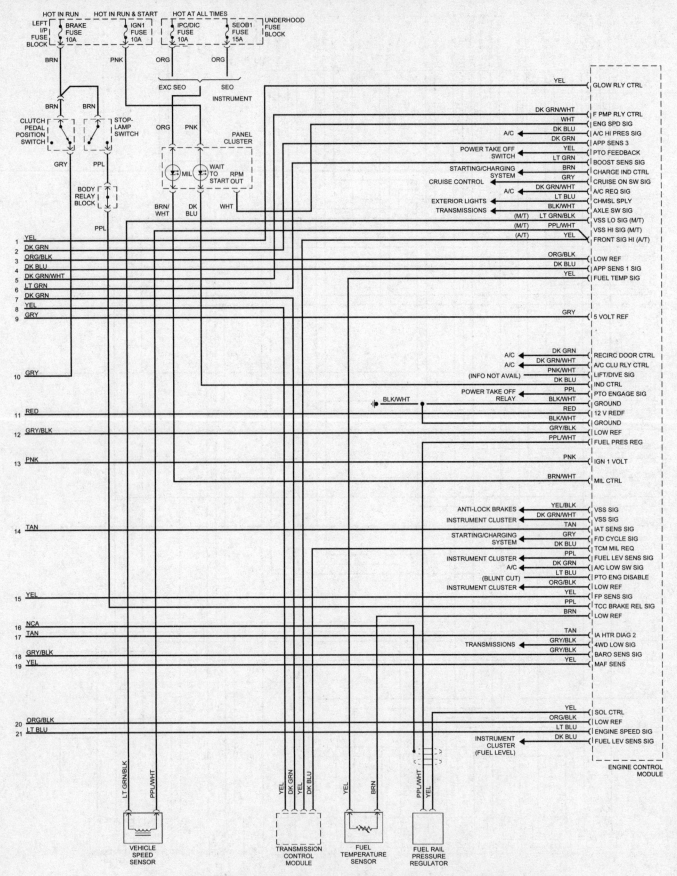

15. Engine management system - 2001 through 2003 models - all except California (4 of 4)

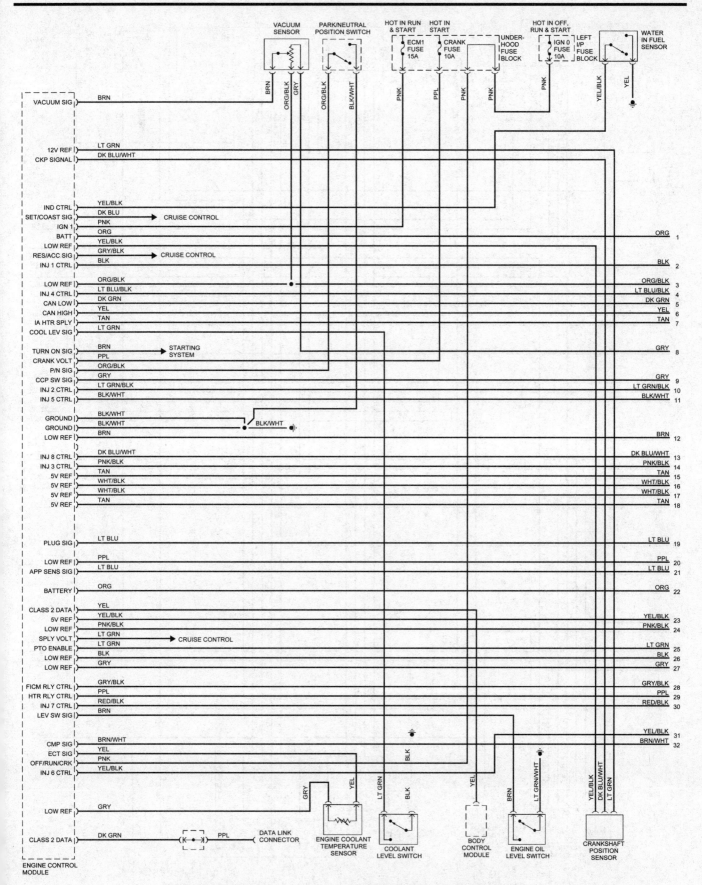

16. Engine management system - 2004 VIN 1 models - California (1 of 5)

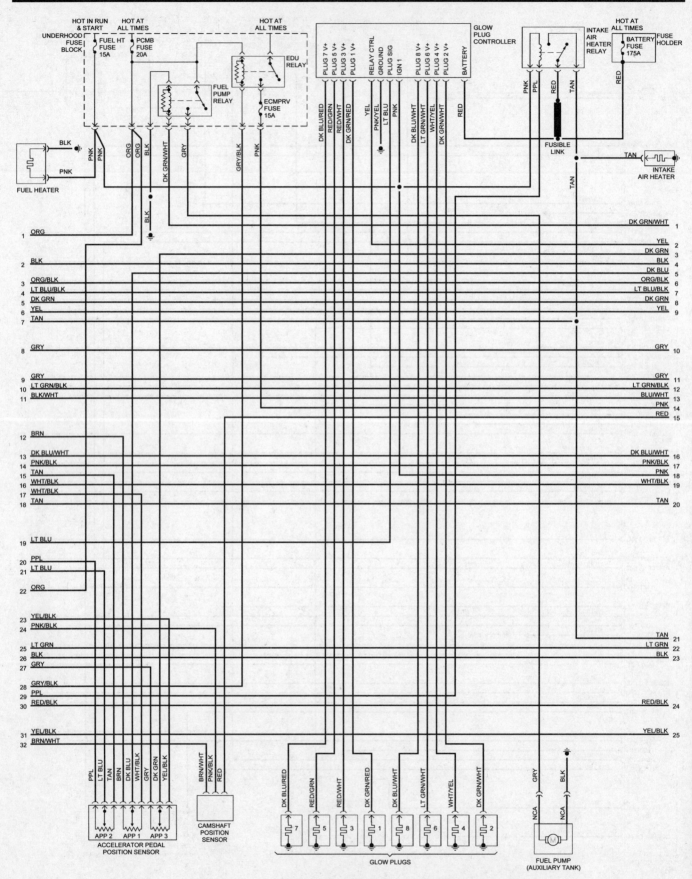

17. Engine management system - 2004 VIN 1 models - California (2 of 5)

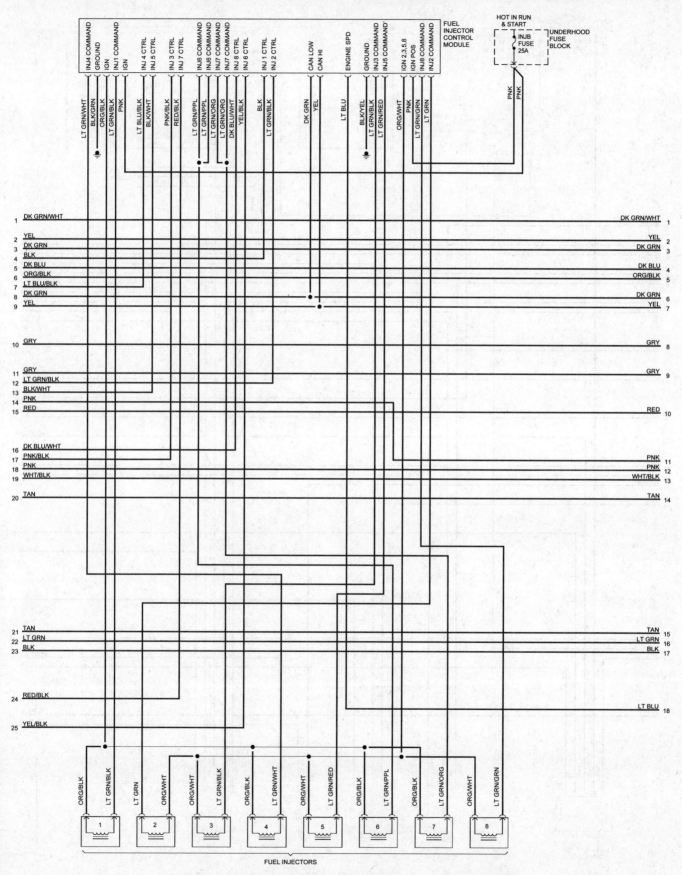

18. Engine management system - 2004 VIN 1 models - California (3 of 5)

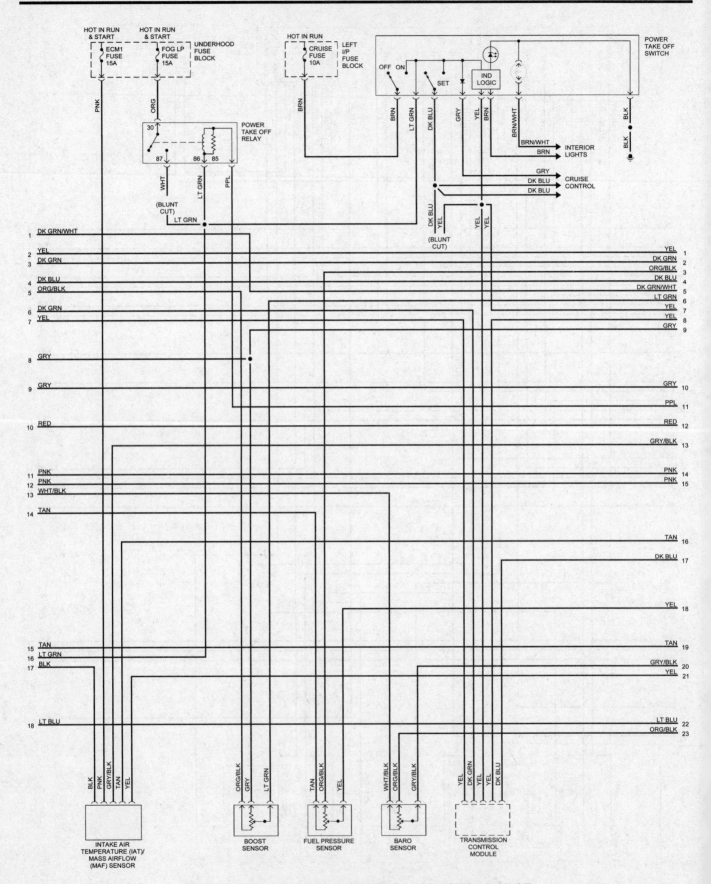

19. Engine management system - 2004 VIN 1 models - California (4 of 5)

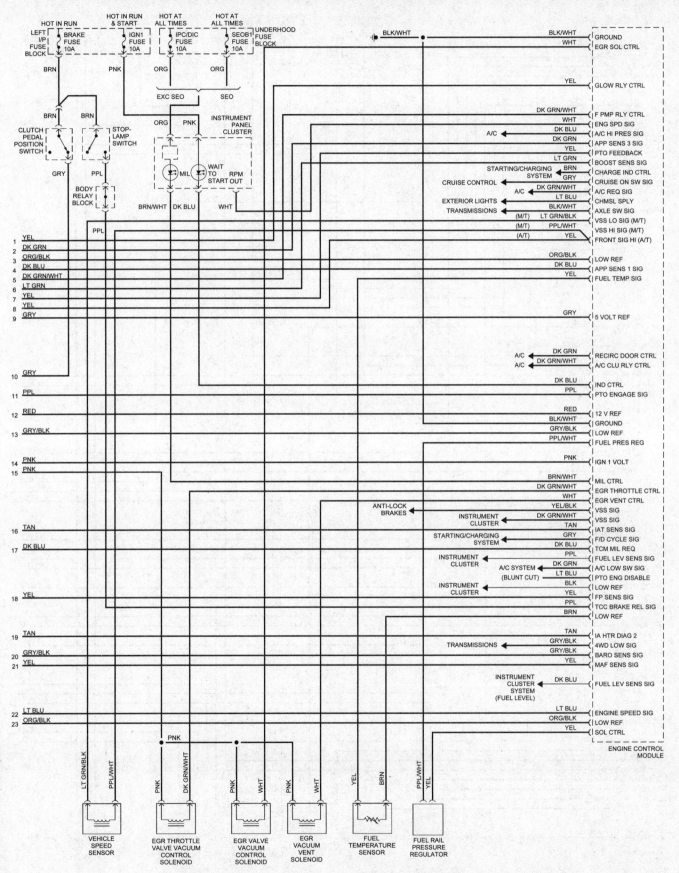

20. Engine management system - 2004 VIN 1 models - California (5 of 5)

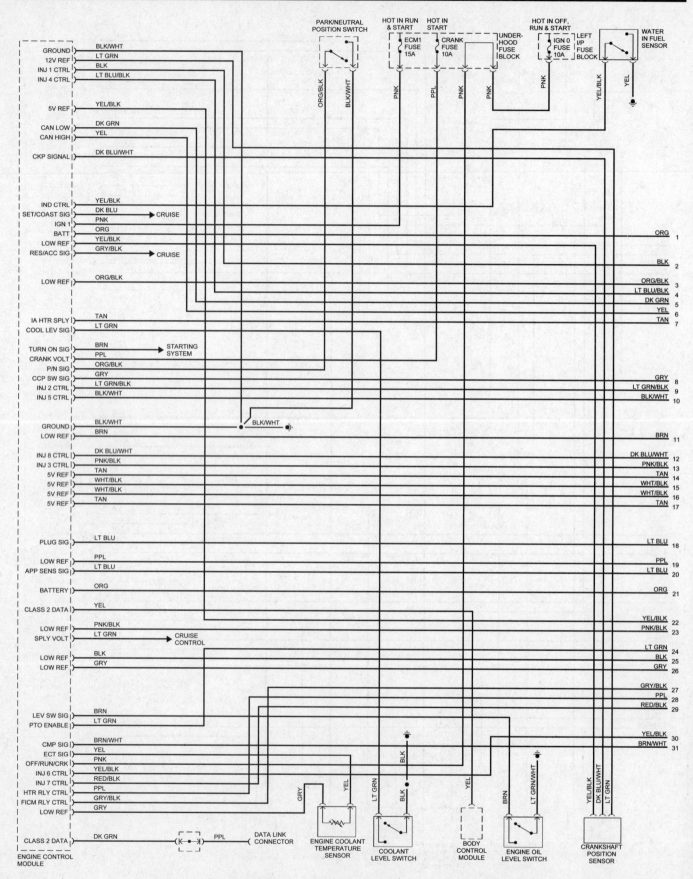

21. Engine management system - 2004 VIN 1 models - all except California (1 of 5)

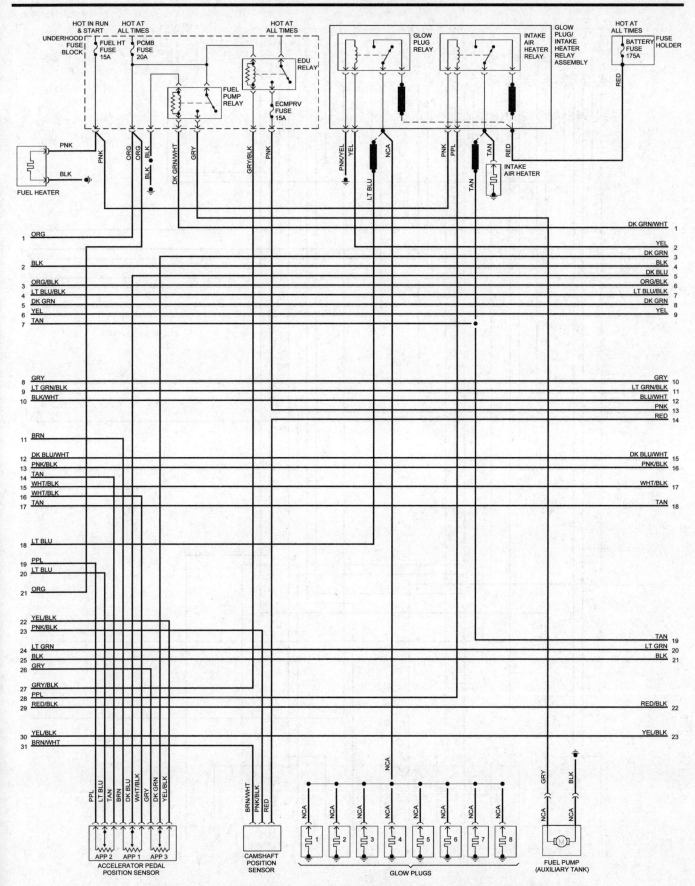

22. Engine management system - 2004 VIN 1 models - all except California (2 of 5)

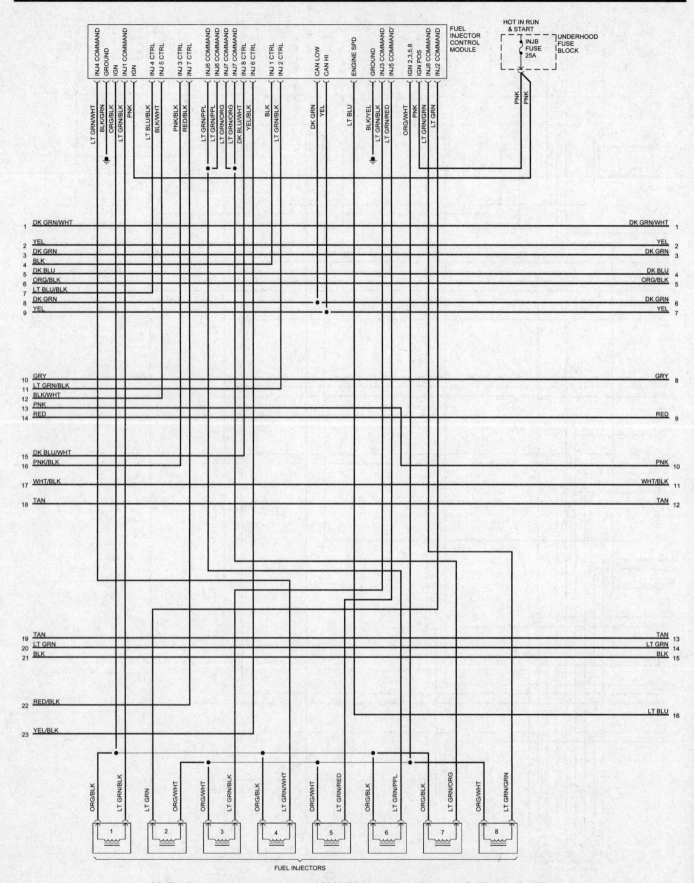

23. Engine management system - 2004 VIN 1 models - all except California (3 of 5)

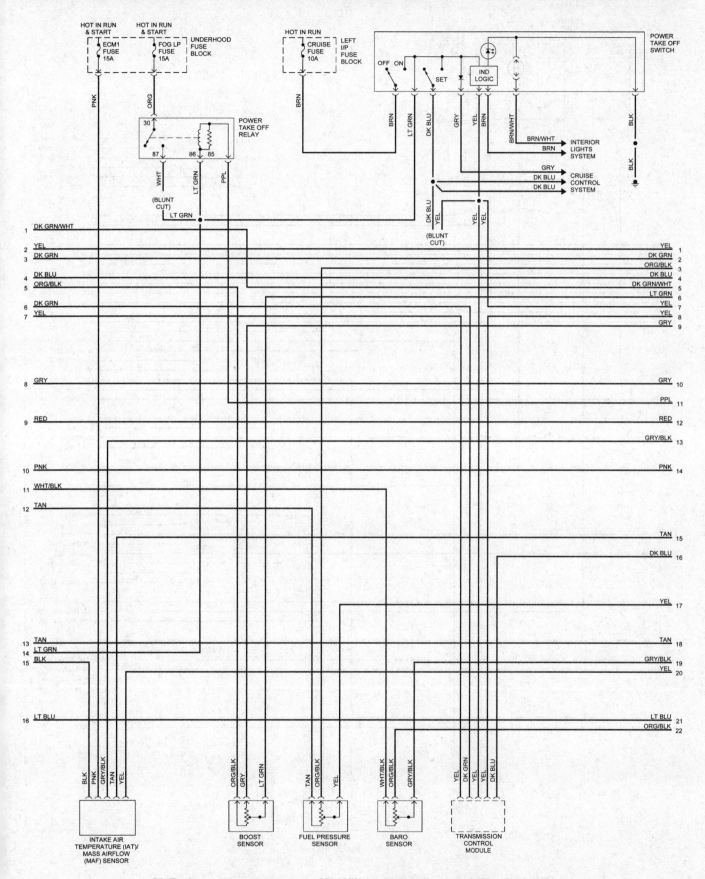

24. Engine management system - 2004 VIN 1 models - all except California (4 of 5)

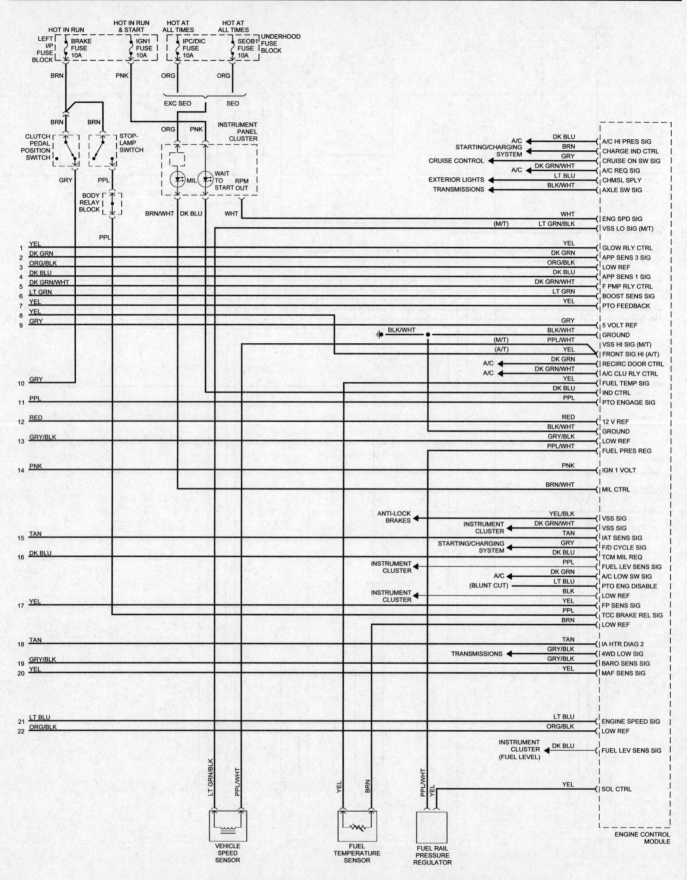

25. Engine management system - 2004 VIN 1 models - all except California (5 of 5)

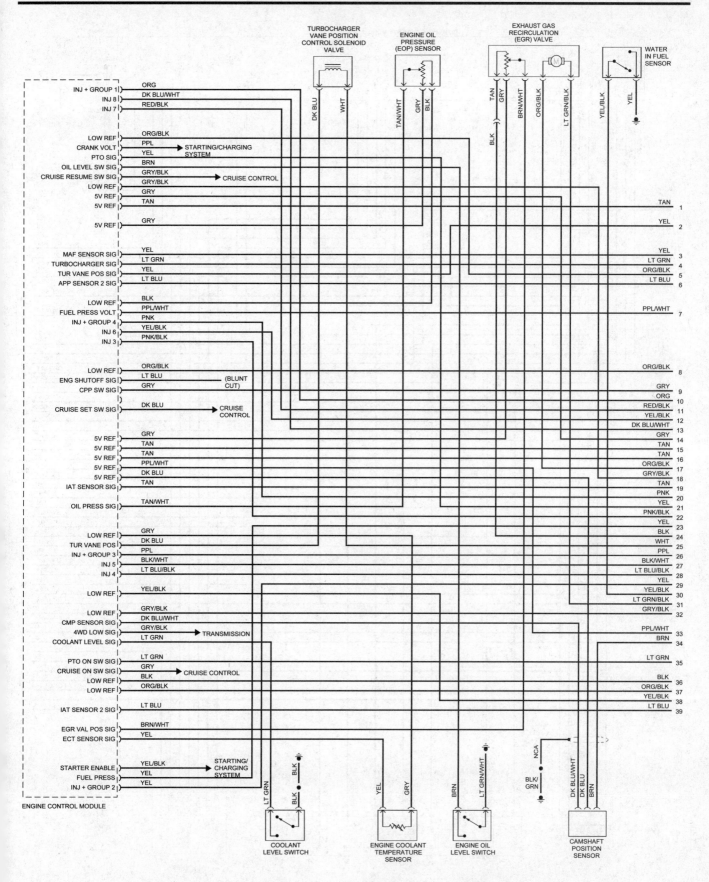

26. Engine management system - 2004 through 2006 VIN 2 and VIN D models (1 of 6)

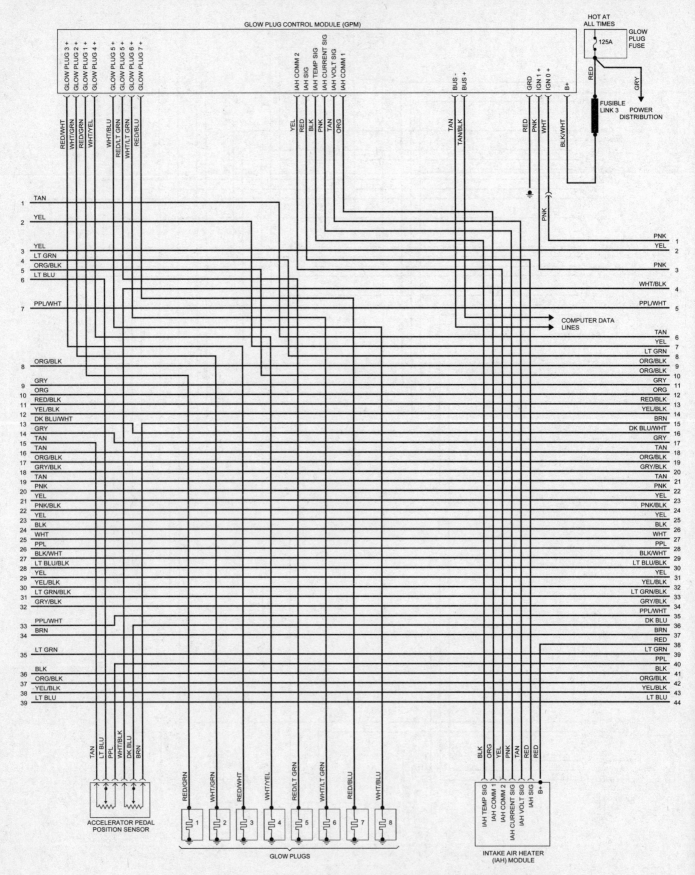

27. Engine management system - 2004 through 2006 VIN 2 and VIN D models (2 of 6)

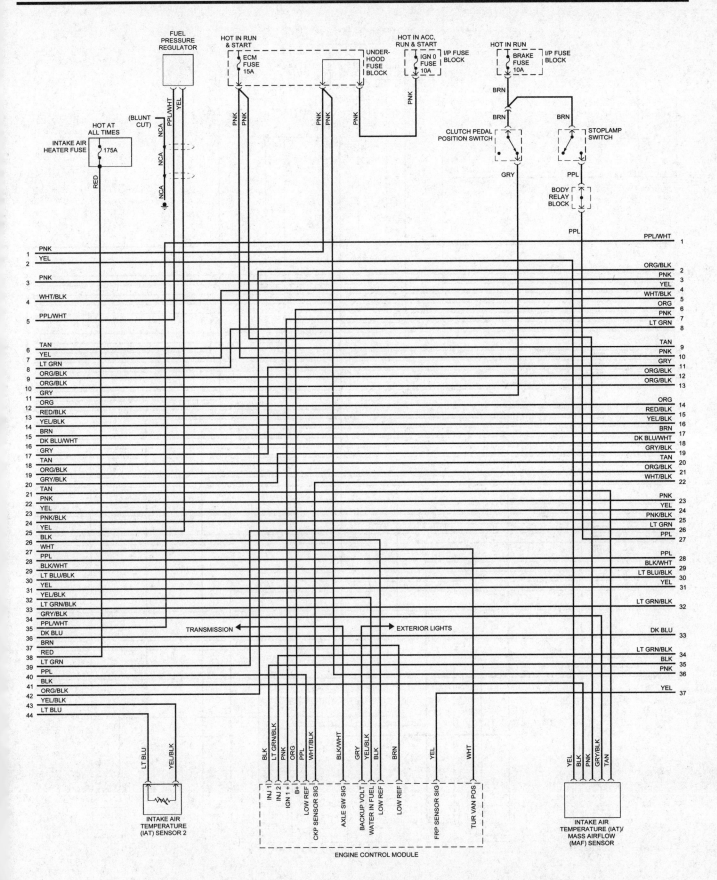

28. Engine management system - 2004 through 2006 VIN 2 and VIN D models (3 of 6)

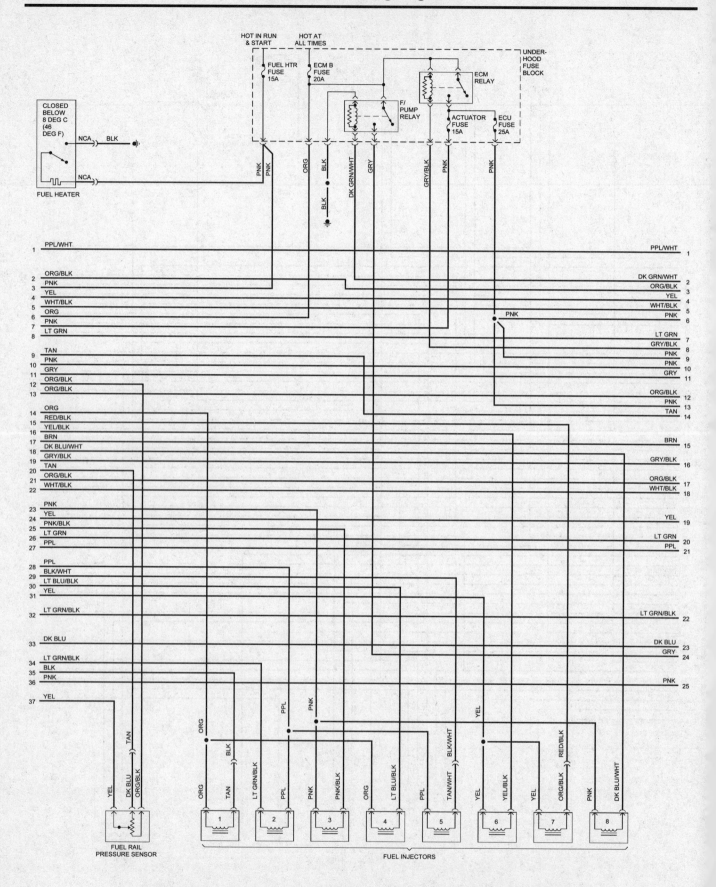

29. Engine management system - 2004 through 2006 VIN 2 and VIN D models (4 of 6)

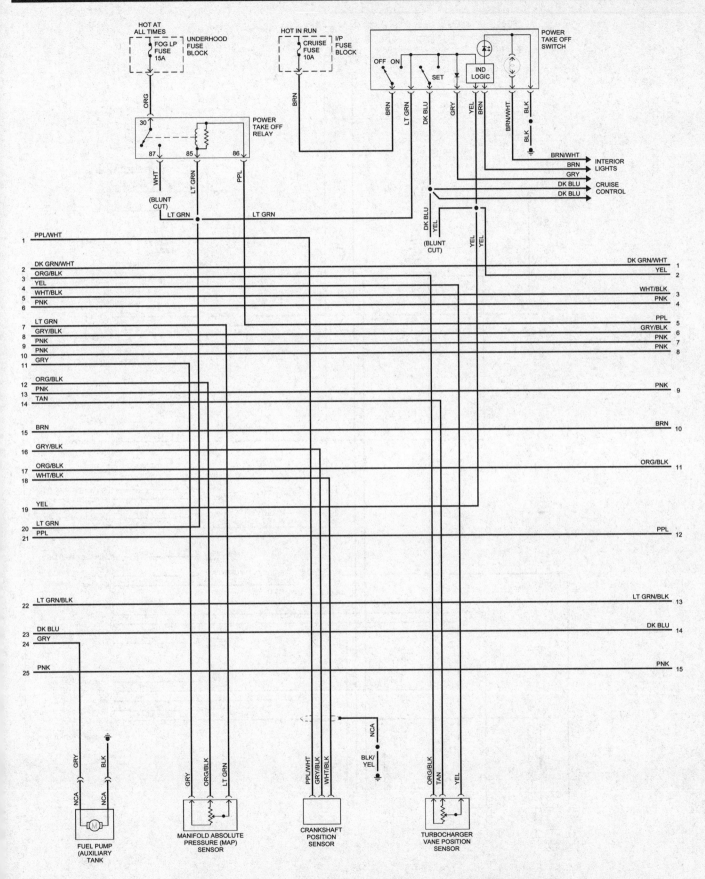

30. Engine management system - 2004 through 2006 VIN 2 and VIN D models (5 of 6)

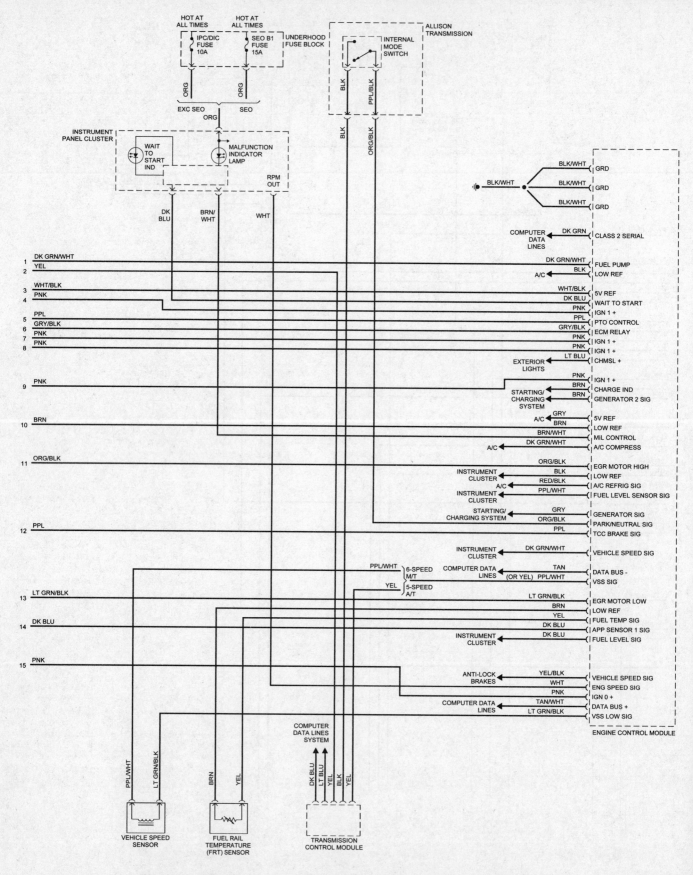

31. Engine management system - 2004 through 2006 VIN 2 and VIN D models (6 of 6)

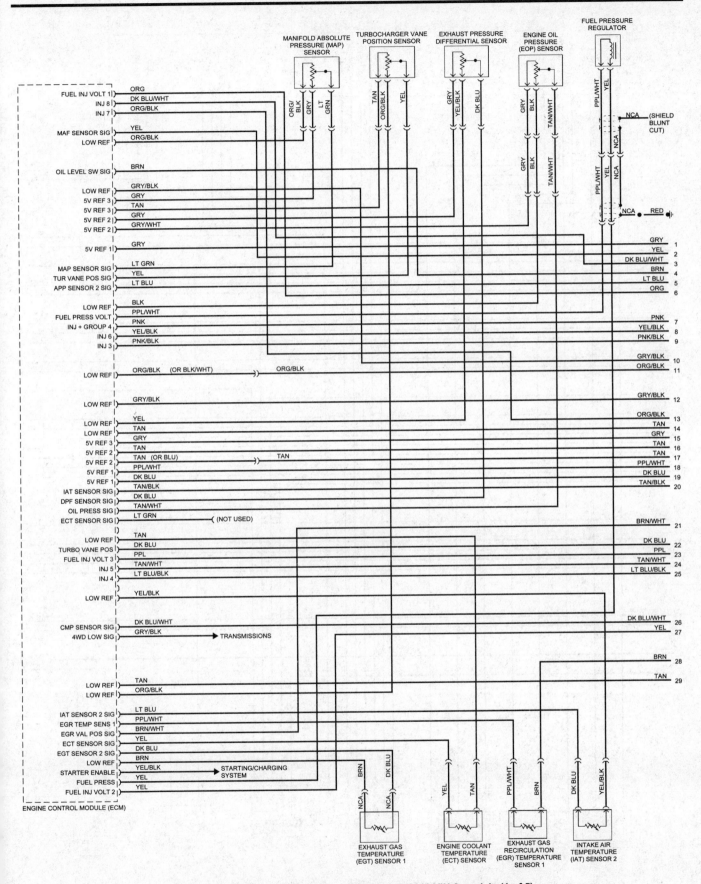

32. Engine management system - 2007 through 2010 VIN 6 models (1 of 5)

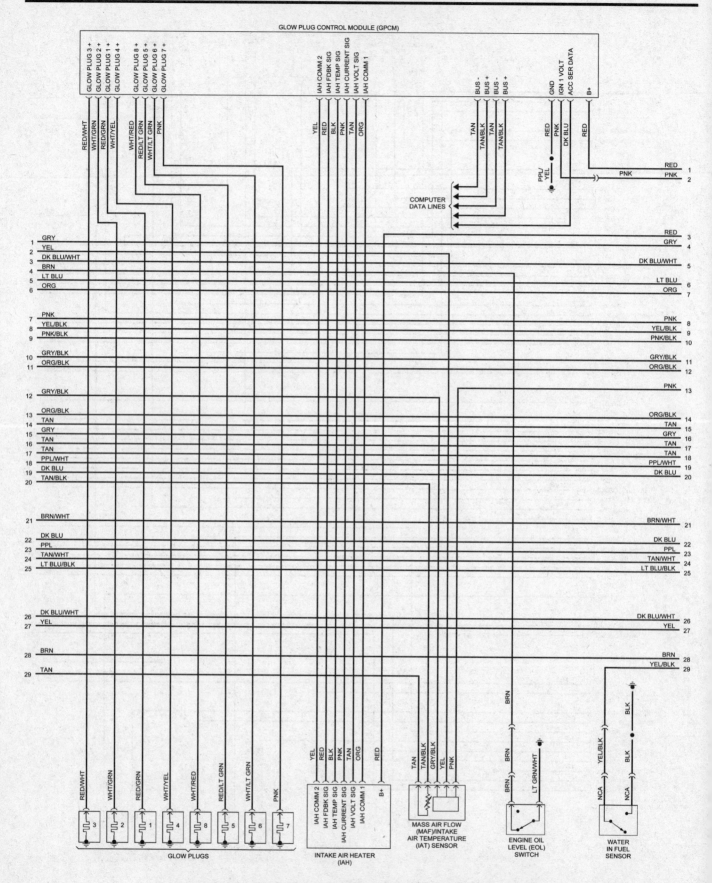

33. Engine management system - 2007 through 2010 VIN 6 models (2 of 5)

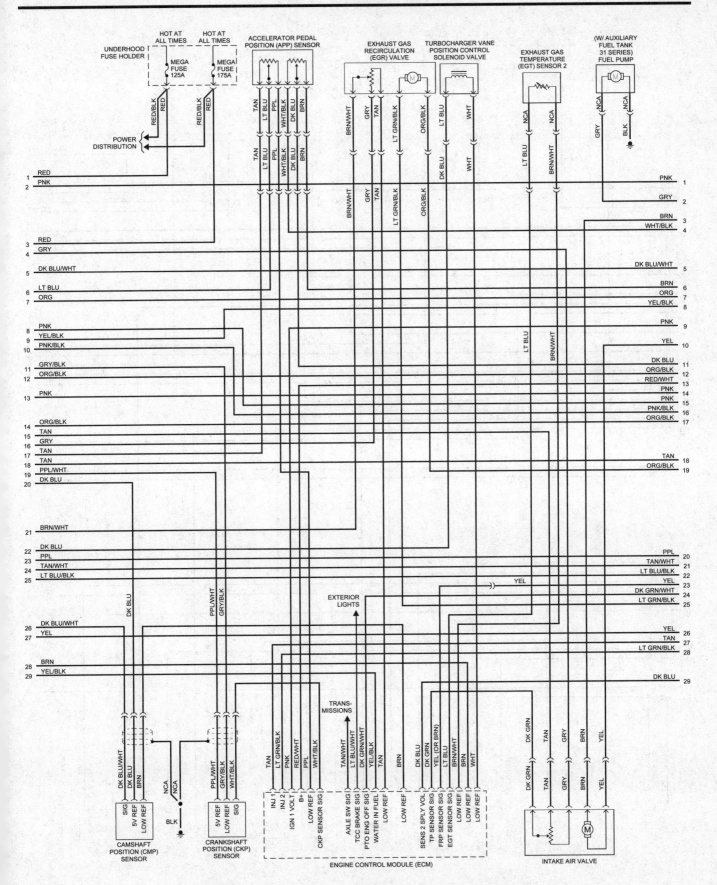

34. Engine management system - 2007 through 2010 VIN 6 models (3 of 5)

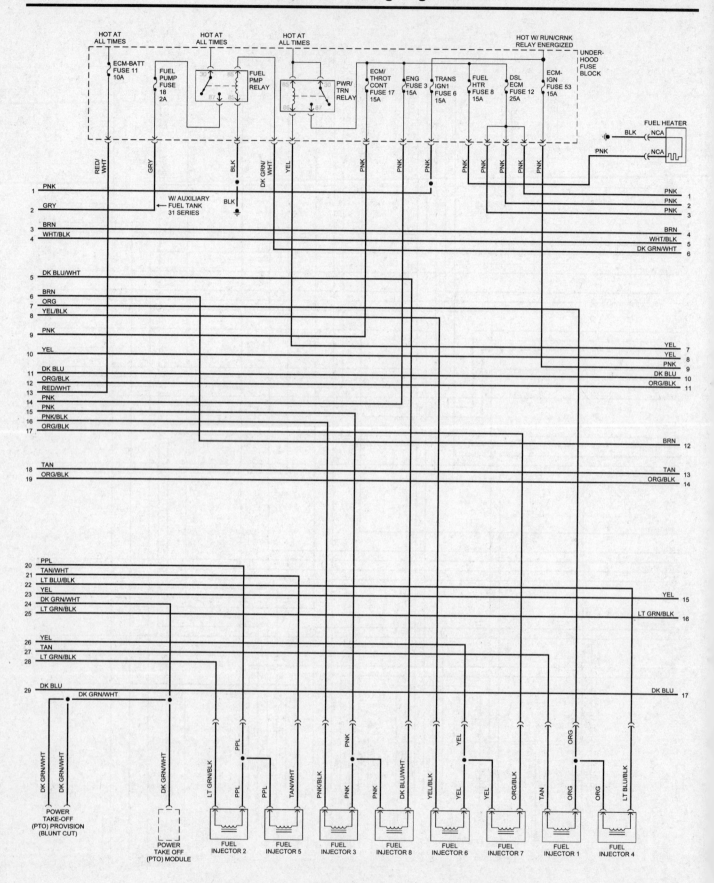

35. Engine management system - 2007 through 2010 VIN 6 models (4 of 5)

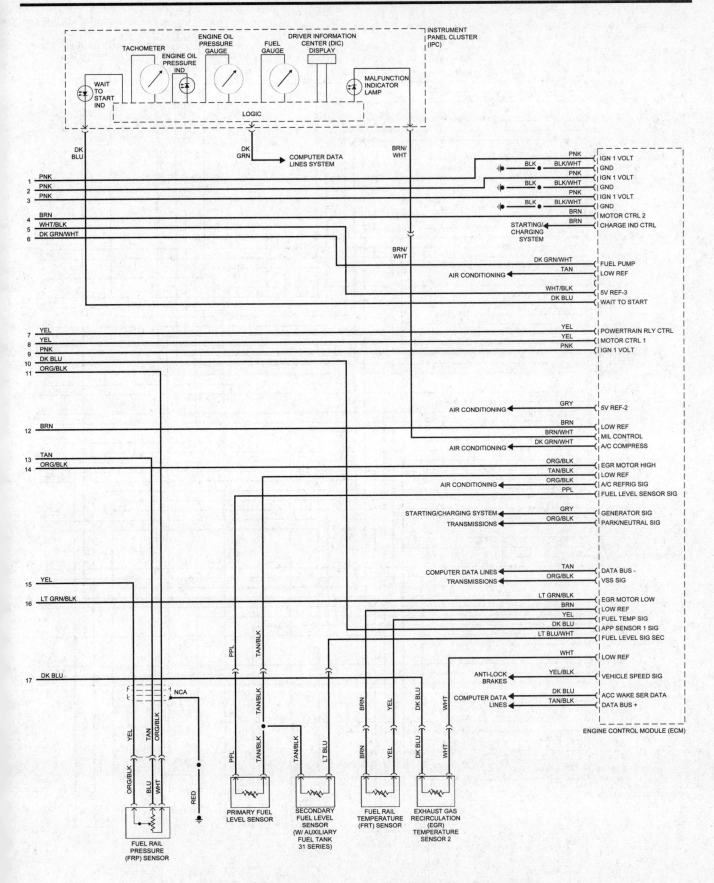

36. Engine management system - 2007 through 2010 VIN 6 models (5 of 5)

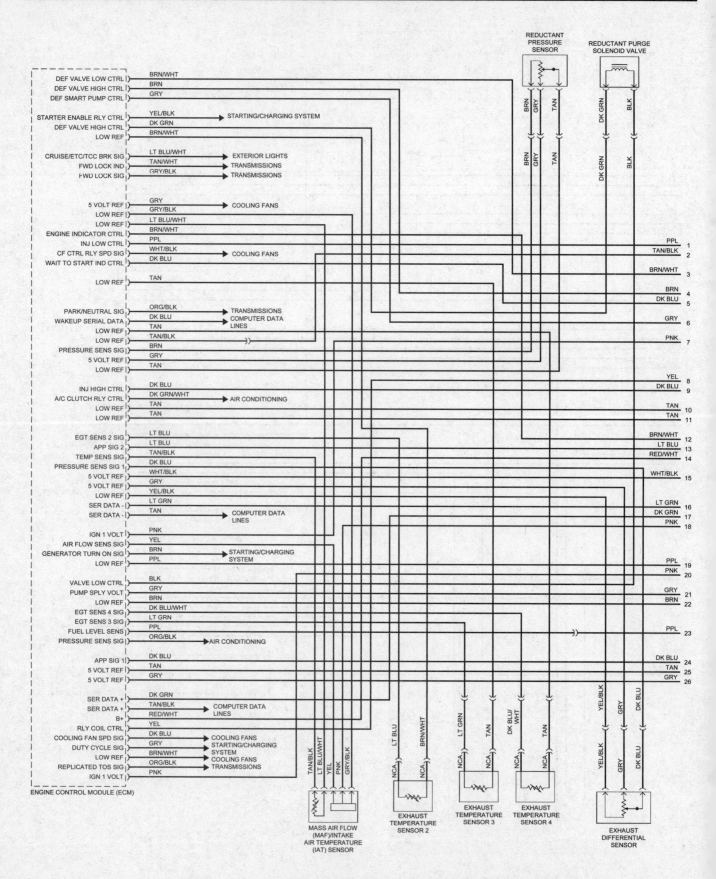

37. Engine management system - 2011 and later VIN 8 and VIN L models (1 of 6)

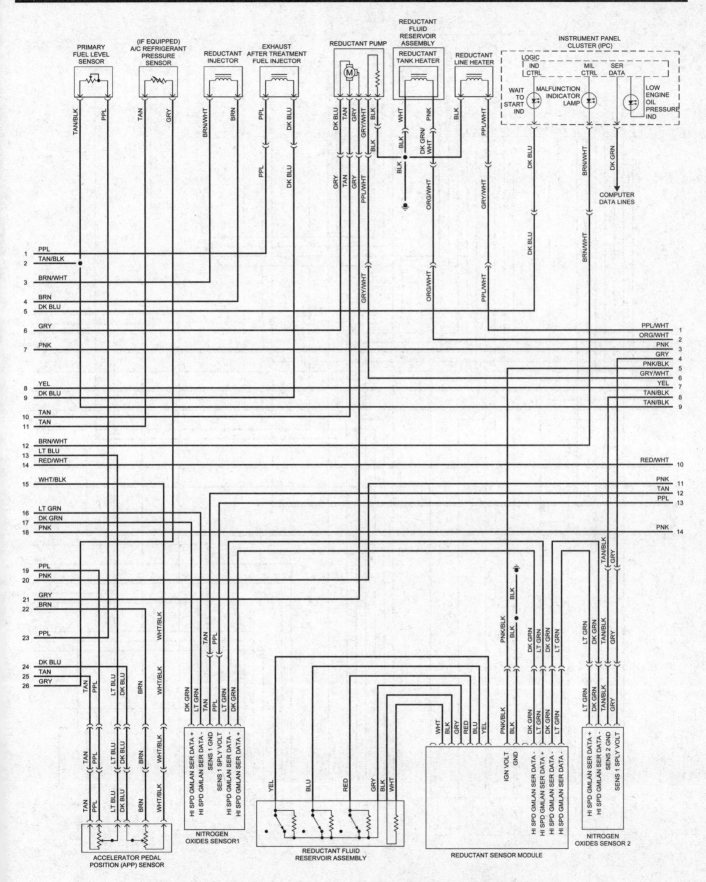

38. Engine management system - 2011 and later VIN 8 and VIN L models (2 of 6)

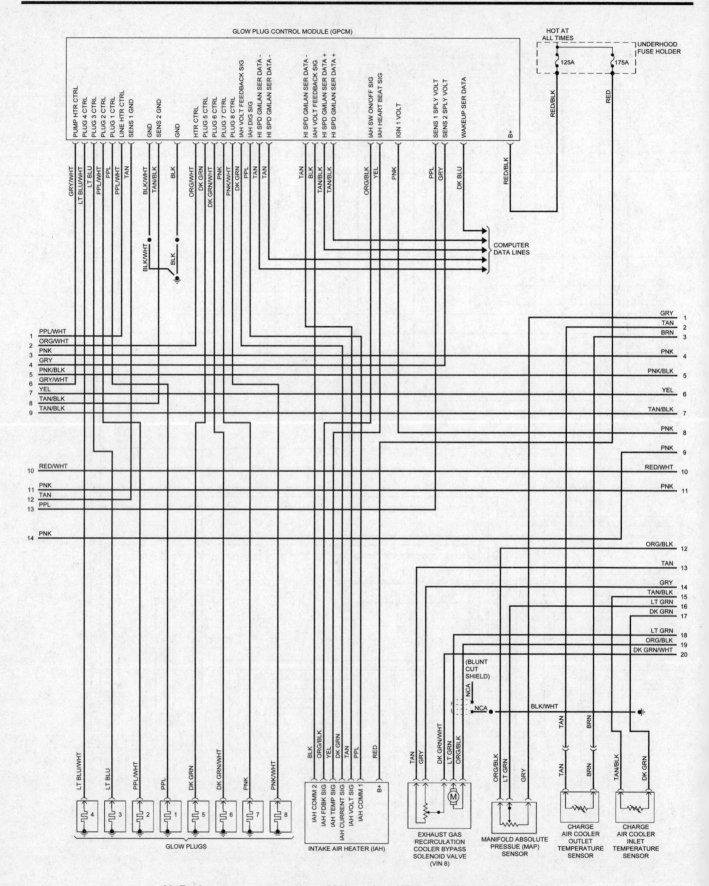

39. Engine management system - 2011 and later VIN 8 and VIN L models (3 of 6)

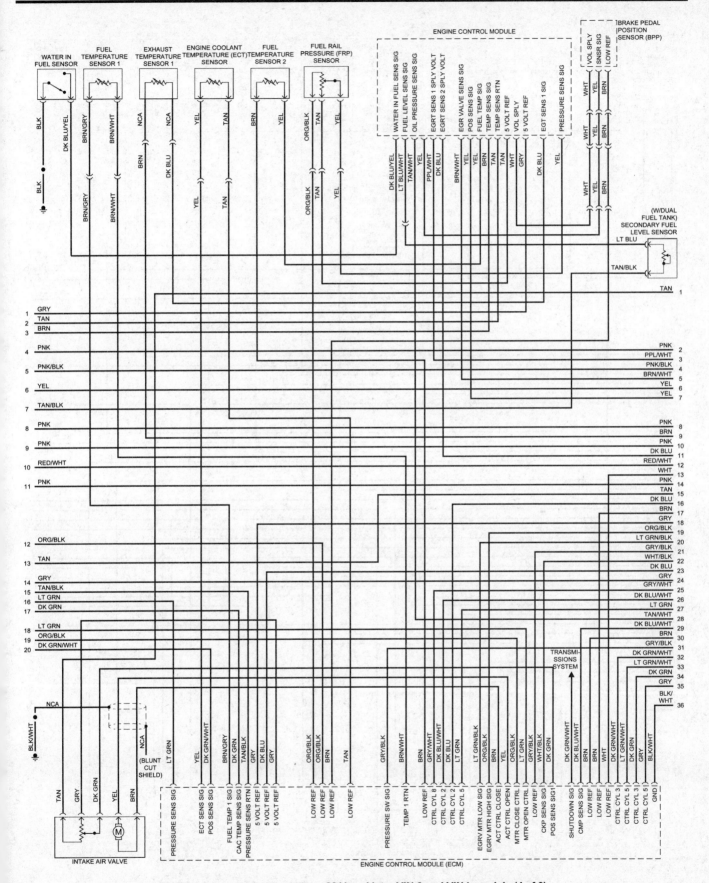

40. Engine management system - 2011 and later VIN 8 and VIN L models (4 of 6)

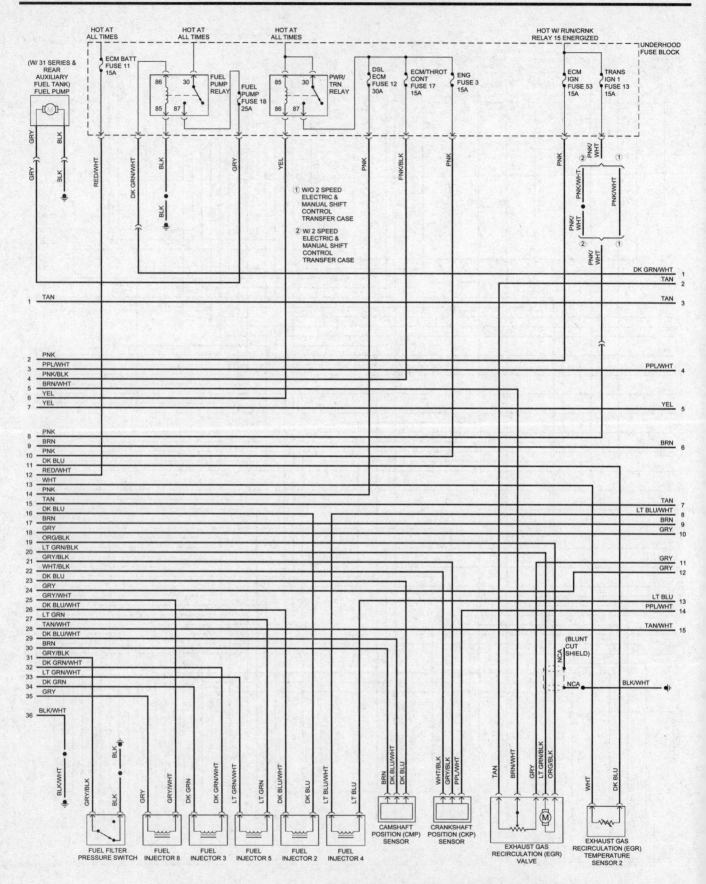

41. Engine management system - 2011 and later VIN 8 and VIN L models (5 of 6)

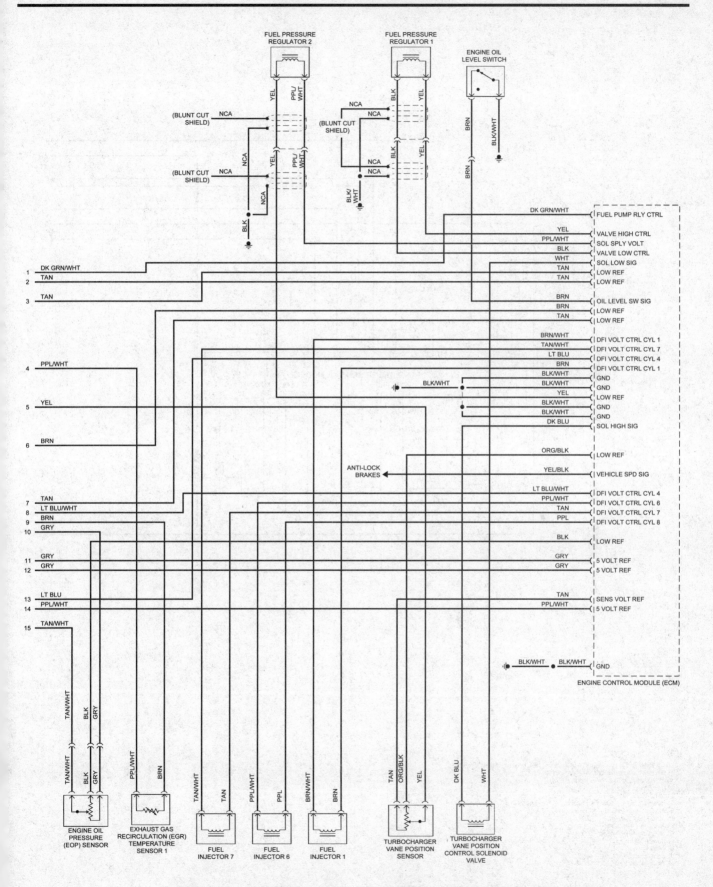

42. Engine management system - 2011 and later VIN 8 and VIN L models (6 of 6)

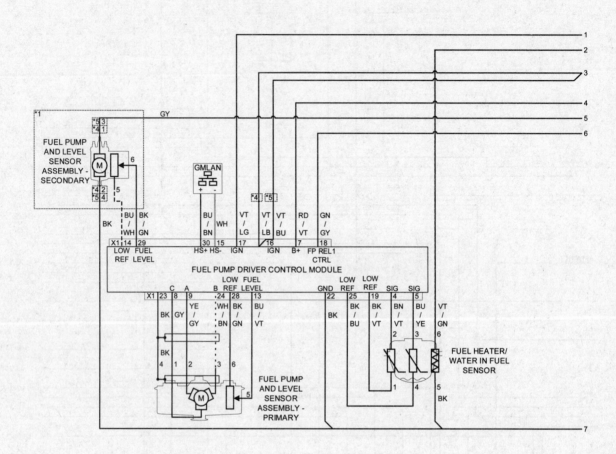

*1 With Dual fuel tank – Front Tank 23.5 Gal (89L), Rear Tank 40 Gal (151L)
*2 With electric exterior mirrors
*3 Without electric exterior mirrors
*4 Up to Model Year 2017
*5 From Model Year 2018
*6 Transfer case – Manual shift control – Two speed
*7 With Dual generators – 150 Amp and 220 Amp
*8 With Single generator – 150 Amp
*9 With Single generator – 220 Amp
*10 With Dual generators – 150 Amp
*11 Heavy duty
*12 Light duty
*13 Up to Model Year 2018
*14 From Model Year 2019

43. Engine management system - 2017 and later VIN Y models (1 of 7)

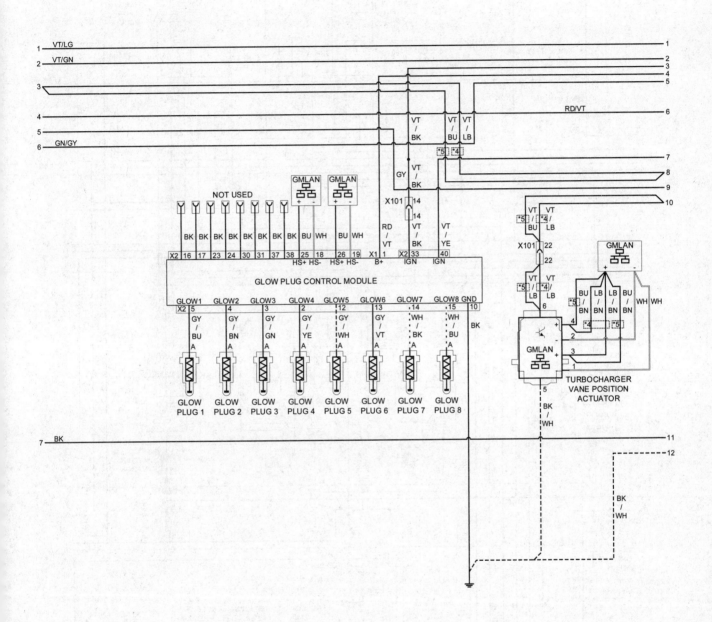

44. Engine management system - 2017 and later VIN Y models (2 of 7)

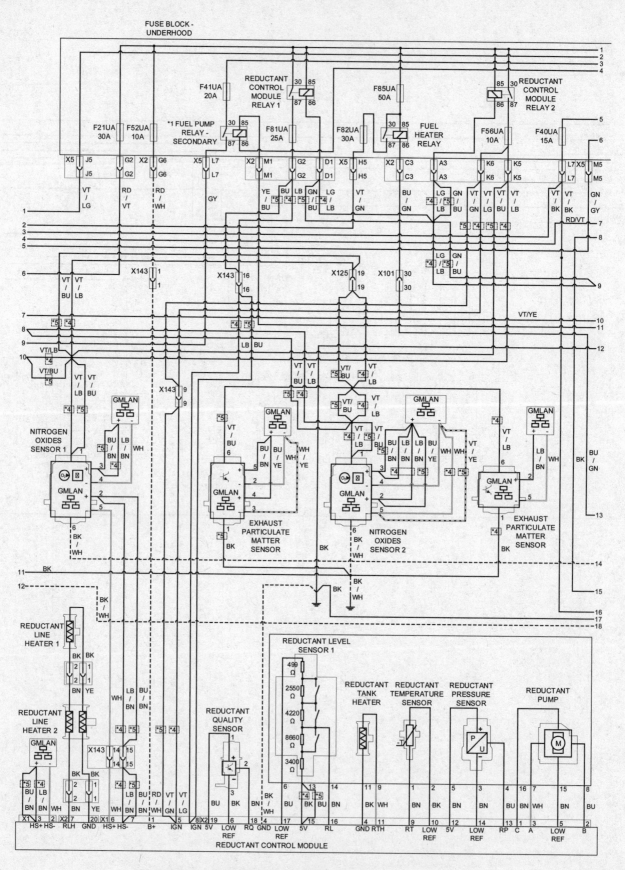

44. Engine management system - 2017 and later VIN Y models (3 of 7)

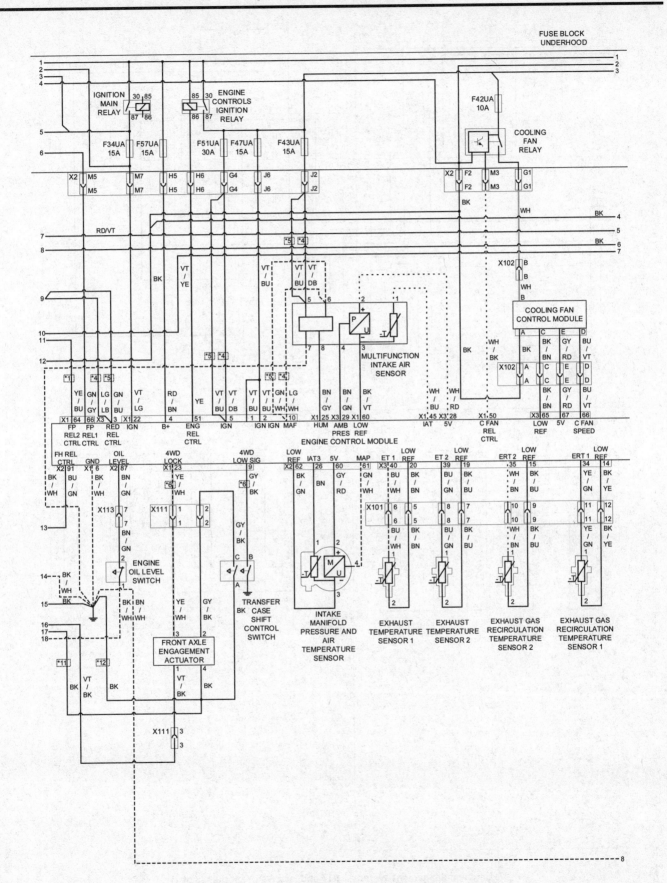

45. Engine management system - 2017 and later VIN Y models (4 of 7)

Chapter 10 Wiring diagrams

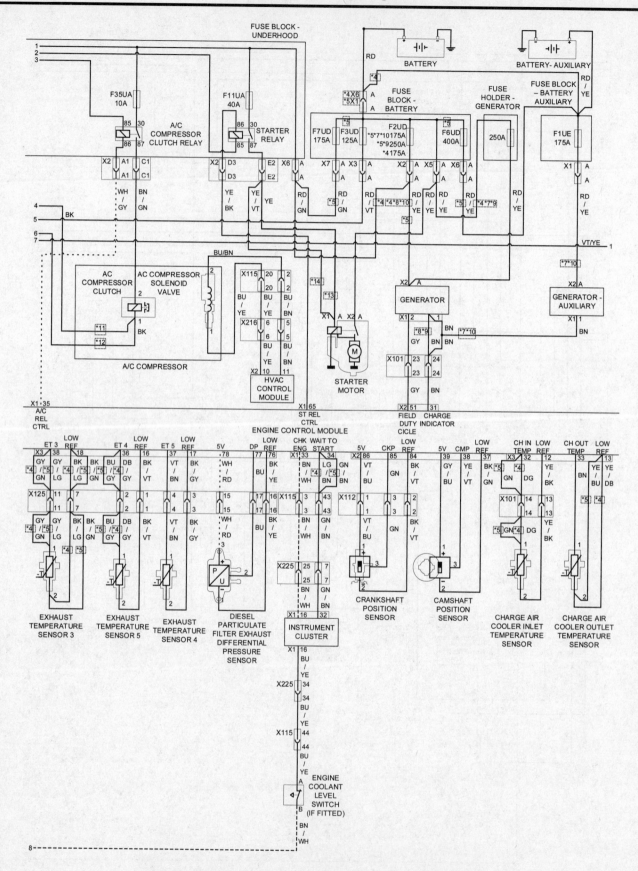

47. Engine management system - 2017 and later VIN Y models (5 of 7)

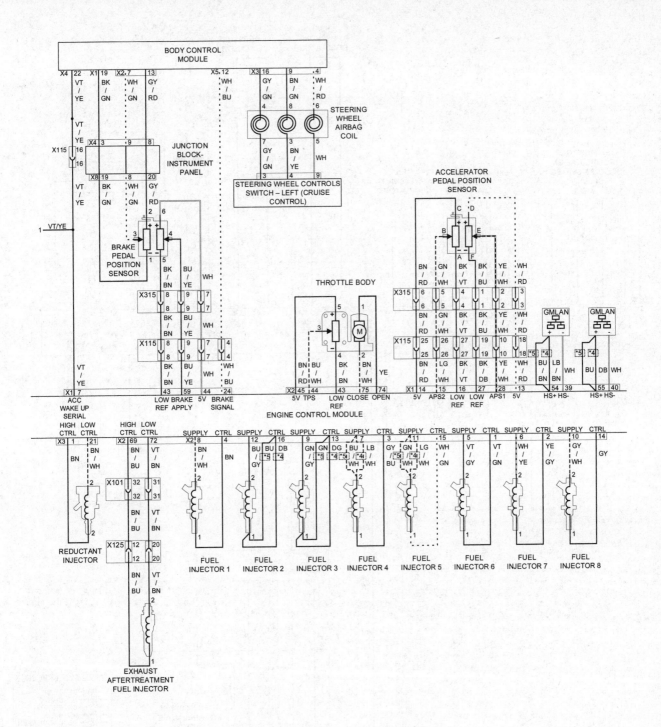

48. Engine management system - 2017 and later VIN Y models (6 of 7)

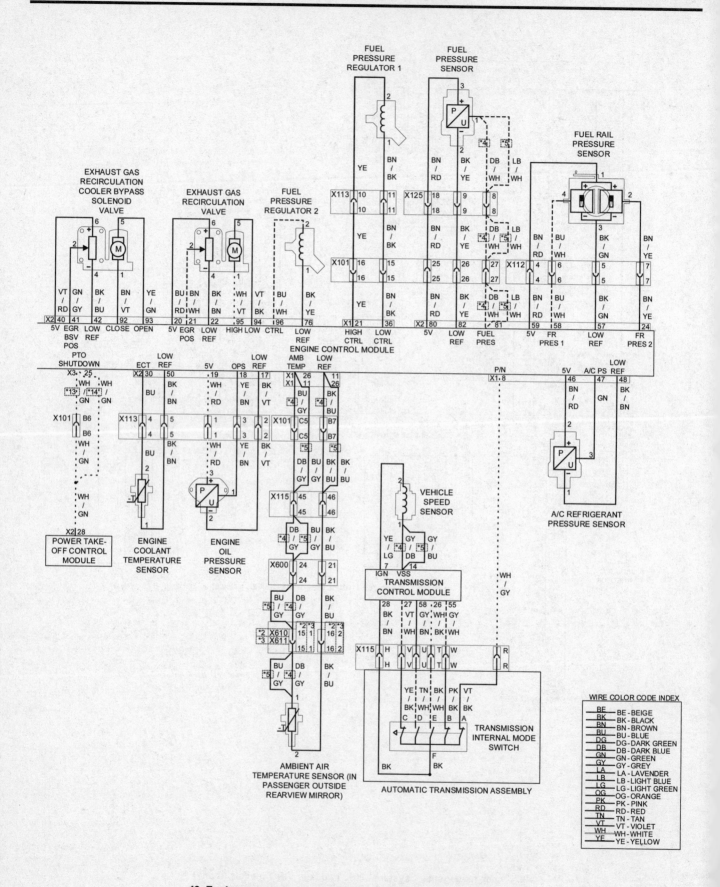

49. Engine management system - 2017 and later VIN Y models (7 of 7)

Notes

Notes

Index

Notes

Haynes Automotive Manuals

NOTE: If you do not see a listing for your vehicle, consult your local Haynes dealer for the latest product information.

ACURA
12020 Integra '86 thru '89 & Legend '86 thru '90
12021 Integra '90 thru '93 & Legend '91 thru '95
Integra '94 thru '00 - see HONDA Civic (42025)
MDX '01 thru '07 - see HONDA Pilot (42037)
12050 Acura TL all models '99 thru '08

AMC
Jeep CJ - see JEEP (50020)
14020 Mid-size models '70 thru '83
14025 (Renault) Alliance & Encore '83 thru '87

AUDI
15020 4000 all models '80 thru '87
15025 5000 all models '77 thru '83
15026 5000 all models '84 thru '88
Audi A4 '96 thru '01 - see VW Passat (96023)
15030 Audi A4 '02 thru '08

AUSTIN-HEALEY
Sprite - see MG Midget (66015)

BMW
18020 3/5 Series '82 thru '92
18021 3-Series incl. Z3 models '92 thru '98
18022 3-Series incl. Z4 models '99 thru '05
18023 3-Series '06 thru '10
18025 320i all 4 cyl models '75 thru '83
18050 1500 thru 2002 except Turbo '59 thru '77

BUICK
19010 Buick Century '97 thru '05
Century (front-wheel drive) - see GM (38005)
19020 Buick, Oldsmobile & Pontiac Full-size
(Front-wheel drive) '85 thru '05
Buick Electra, LeSabre and Park Avenue;
Oldsmobile Delta 88 Royale, Ninety Eight
and Regency; Pontiac Bonneville
19025 Buick, Oldsmobile & Pontiac Full-size
(Rear wheel drive) '70 thru '90
Buick Estate, Electra, LeSabre, Limited,
Oldsmobile Custom Cruiser, Delta 88,
Ninety-eight, Pontiac Bonneville,
Catalina, Grandville, Parisienne
19030 Mid-size Regal & Century all rear-drive
models with V6, V8 and Turbo '74 thru '87
Regal - see GENERAL MOTORS (38010)
Riviera - see GENERAL MOTORS (38030)
Roadmaster - see CHEVROLET (24046)
Skyhawk - see GENERAL MOTORS (38015)
Skylark - see GM (38020, 38025)
Somerset - see GENERAL MOTORS (38025)

CADILLAC
21015 CTS & CTS-V '03 thru '12
21030 Cadillac Rear Wheel Drive '70 thru '93
Cimarron - see GENERAL MOTORS (38015)
DeVille - see GM (38031 & 38032)
Eldorado - see GM (38030 & 38031)
Fleetwood - see GM (38031)
Seville - see GM (38030, 38031 & 38032)

CHEVROLET
10305 Chevrolet Engine Overhaul Manual
24010 Astro & GMC Safari Mini-vans '85 thru '05
24015 Camaro V8 all models '70 thru '81
24016 Camaro all models '82 thru '92
24017 Camaro & Firebird '93 thru '02
Cavalier - see GENERAL MOTORS (38016)
Celebrity - see GENERAL MOTORS (38005)
24020 Chevelle, Malibu & El Camino '69 thru '87
24024 Chevette & Pontiac T1000 '76 thru '87
Citation - see GENERAL MOTORS (38020)
24027 Colorado & GMC Canyon '04 thru '10
24032 Corsica/Beretta all models '87 thru '96
24040 Corvette all V8 models '68 thru '82
24041 Corvette all models '84 thru '96
24045 Full-size Sedans Caprice, Impala, Biscayne,
Bel Air & Wagons '69 thru '90
24046 Impala SS & Caprice and Buick Roadmaster
'91 thru '96
Impala '00 thru '05 - see LUMINA (24048)
24047 Impala & Monte Carlo all models '06 thru '11
Lumina '90 thru '94 - see GM (38010)
24048 Lumina & Monte Carlo '95 thru '05
Lumina APV - see GM (38035)
24050 Luv Pick-up all 2WD & 4WD '72 thru '82
Malibu '97 thru '00 - see GM (38026)
24055 Monte Carlo all models '70 thru '88
Monte Carlo '95 thru '01 - see LUMINA (24048)
24059 Nova all V8 models '69 thru '79
24060 Nova and Geo Prizm '85 thru '92
24064 Pick-ups '67 thru '87 - Chevrolet & GMC
24065 Pick-ups '88 thru '98 - Chevrolet & GMC

24066 Pick-ups '99 thru '06 - Chevrolet & GMC
24067 Chevrolet Silverado & GMC Sierra '07 thru '12
24070 S-10 & S-15 Pick-ups '82 thru '93,
Blazer & Jimmy '83 thru '94,
24071 S-10 & Sonoma Pick-ups '94 thru '04, including Blazer, Jimmy & Hombre
24072 Chevrolet TrailBlazer, GMC Envoy &
Oldsmobile Bravada '02 thru '09
24075 Sprint '85 thru '88 & Geo Metro '89 thru '01
24080 Vans - Chevrolet & GMC '68 thru '96
24081 Chevrolet Express & GMC Savana
Full-size Vans '96 thru '10

CHRYSLER
10310 Chrysler Engine Overhaul Manual
25015 Chrysler Cirrus, Dodge Stratus,
Plymouth Breeze '95 thru '00
25020 Full-size Front-Wheel Drive '88 thru '93
K-Cars - see DODGE Aries (30008)
Laser - see DODGE Daytona (30030)
25025 Chrysler LHS, Concorde, New Yorker,
Dodge Intrepid, Eagle Vision, '93 thru '97
25026 Chrysler LHS, Concorde, 300M,
Dodge Intrepid, '98 thru '04
25027 Chrysler 300, Dodge Charger &
Magnum '05 thru '09
25030 Chrysler & Plymouth Mid-size
front wheel drive '82 thru '95
Rear-wheel Drive - see Dodge (30050)
25035 PT Cruiser all models '01 thru '10
25040 Chrysler Sebring '95 thru '06, Dodge Stratus
'01 thru '06, Dodge Avenger '95 thru '00

DATSUN
28005 200SX all models '80 thru '83
28007 B-210 all models '73 thru '78
28009 210 all models '79 thru '82
28012 240Z, 260Z & 280Z Coupe '70 thru '78
28014 280ZX Coupe & 2+2 '79 thru '83
300ZX - see NISSAN (72010)
28018 510 & PL521 Pick-up '68 thru '73
28020 510 all models '78 thru '81
28022 620 Series Pick-up all models '73 thru '79
720 Series Pick-up - see NISSAN (72030)
28025 810/Maxima all gasoline models '77 thru '84

DODGE
400 & 600 - see CHRYSLER (25030)
30008 Aries & Plymouth Reliant '81 thru '89
30010 Caravan & Plymouth Voyager '84 thru '95
30011 Caravan & Plymouth Voyager '96 thru '02
30012 Challenger/Plymouth Saporro '78 thru '83
30013 Caravan, Chrysler Voyager, Town &
Country '03 thru '07
30016 Colt & Plymouth Champ '78 thru '87
30020 Dakota Pick-ups all models '87 thru '96
30021 Durango '98 & '99, Dakota '97 thru '99
30022 Durango '00 thru '03 Dakota '00 thru '04
30023 Durango '04 thru '09, Dakota '05 thru '11
30025 Dart, Demon, Plymouth Barracuda,
Duster & Valiant 6 cyl models '67 thru '76
30030 Daytona & Chrysler Laser '84 thru '89
Intrepid - see CHRYSLER (25025, 25026)
30034 Neon all models '95 thru '99
30035 Omni & Plymouth Horizon '78 thru '90
30036 Dodge and Plymouth Neon '00 thru '05
30040 Pick-ups all full-size models '74 thru '93
30041 Pick-ups all full-size models '94 thru '01
30042 Pick-ups full-size models '02 thru '08
30045 Ram 50/D50 Pick-ups & Raider and
Plymouth Arrow Pick-ups '79 thru '93
30050 Dodge/Plymouth/Chrysler RWD '71 thru '89
30055 Shadow & Plymouth Sundance '87 thru '94
30060 Spirit & Plymouth Acclaim '89 thru '95
30065 Vans - Dodge & Plymouth '71 thru '03

EAGLE
Talon - see MITSUBISHI (68030, 68031)
Vision - see CHRYSLER (25025)

FIAT
34010 124 Sport Coupe & Spider '68 thru '78
34025 X1/9 all models '74 thru '80

FORD
10320 Ford Engine Overhaul Manual
10355 Ford Automatic Transmission Overhaul
11500 Mustang '64-1/2 thru '70 Restoration Guide
36004 Aerostar Mini-vans all models '86 thru '97
36006 Contour & Mercury Mystique '95 thru '00
36008 Courier Pick-up all models '72 thru '82
36012 Crown Victoria & Mercury Grand
Marquis '88 thru '10
36016 Escort/Mercury Lynx all models '81 thru '90
36020 Escort/Mercury Tracer '91 thru '02

36022 Escape & Mazda Tribute '01 thru '11
36024 Explorer & Mazda Navajo '91 thru '01
36025 Explorer/Mercury Mountaineer '02 thru '10
36028 Fairmont & Mercury Zephyr '78 thru '83
36030 Festiva & Aspire '88 thru '97
36032 Fiesta all models '77 thru '80
36034 Focus all models '00 thru '11
36036 Ford & Mercury Full-size '75 thru '87
36044 Ford & Mercury Mid-size '75 thru '86
36045 Fusion & Mercury Milan '06 thru '10
36048 Mustang V8 all models '64-1/2 thru '73
36049 Mustang II 4 cyl, V6 & V8 models '74 thru '78
36050 Mustang & Mercury Capri '79 thru '93
36051 Mustang all models '94 thru '04
36052 Mustang '05 thru '10
36054 Pick-ups & Bronco '73 thru '79
36058 Pick-ups & Bronco '80 thru '96
36059 F-150 & Expedition '97 thru '09, F-250 '97
thru '99 & Lincoln Navigator '98 thru '09
36060 Super Duty Pick-ups, Excursion '99 thru '10
36061 F-150 full-size '04 thru '10
36062 Pinto & Mercury Bobcat '75 thru '80
36066 Probe all models '89 thru '92
Probe '93 thru '97 - see MAZDA 626 (61042)
36070 Ranger/Bronco II gasoline models '83 thru '92
36071 Ranger '93 thru '10 & Mazda Pick-ups '94 thru '09
36074 Taurus & Mercury Sable '86 thru '95
36075 Taurus & Mercury Sable '96 thru '05
36078 Tempo & Mercury Topaz '84 thru '94
36082 Thunderbird/Mercury Cougar '83 thru '88
36086 Thunderbird/Mercury Cougar '89 thru '97
36090 Vans all V8 Econoline models '69 thru '91
36094 Vans full size '92 thru '10
36097 Windstar Mini-van '95 thru '07

GENERAL MOTORS
10360 GM Automatic Transmission Overhaul
38005 Buick Century, Chevrolet Celebrity,
Oldsmobile Cutlass Ciera & Pontiac 6000
all models '82 thru '96
38010 Buick Regal, Chevrolet Lumina,
Oldsmobile Cutlass Supreme &
Pontiac Grand Prix (FWD) '88 thru '07
38015 Buick Skyhawk, Cadillac Cimarron,
Chevrolet Cavalier, Oldsmobile Firenza &
Pontiac J-2000 & Sunbird '82 thru '94
38016 Chevrolet Cavalier &
Pontiac Sunfire '95 thru '05
38017 Chevrolet Cobalt & Pontiac G5 '05 thru '11
38020 Buick Skylark, Chevrolet Citation,
Olds Omega, Pontiac Phoenix '80 thru '85
38025 Buick Skylark & Somerset,
Oldsmobile Achieva & Calais and
Pontiac Grand Am all models '85 thru '98
38026 Chevrolet Malibu, Olds Alero & Cutlass,
Pontiac Grand Am '97 thru '03
38027 Chevrolet Malibu '04 thru '10
38030 Cadillac Eldorado, Seville, Oldsmobile
Toronado, Buick Riviera '71 thru '85
38031 Cadillac Eldorado & Seville, DeVille, Fleetwood
& Olds Toronado, Buick Riviera '86 thru '93
38032 Cadillac DeVille '94 thru '05 & Seville '92 thru '04
Cadillac DTS '06 thru '10
38035 Chevrolet Lumina APV, Olds Silhouette
& Pontiac Trans Sport all models '90 thru '96
38036 Chevrolet Venture, Olds Silhouette,
Pontiac Trans Sport & Montana '97 thru '05
General Motors Full-size
Rear-wheel Drive - see BUICK (19025)
38040 Chevrolet Equinox '05 thru '09 Pontiac
Torrent '06 thru '09
38070 Chevrolet HHR '06 thru '11

GEO
Metro - see CHEVROLET Sprint (24075)
Prizm - '85 thru '92 see CHEVY (24060),
'93 thru '02 see TOYOTA Corolla (92036)
40030 Storm all models '90 thru '93
Tracker - see SUZUKI Samurai (90010)

GMC
Vans & Pick-ups - see CHEVROLET

HONDA
42010 Accord CVCC all models '76 thru '83
42011 Accord all models '84 thru '89
42012 Accord all models '90 thru '93
42013 Accord all models '94 thru '97
42014 Accord all models '98 thru '02
42015 Accord '03 thru '07
42020 Civic 1200 all models '73 thru '79
42021 Civic 1300 & 1500 CVCC '80 thru '83
42022 Civic 1500 CVCC all models '75 thru '79

(Continued on other side)

Haynes North America, Inc., 859 Lawrence Drive, Newbury Park, CA 91320-1514 • (805) 498-6703 • http://www.haynes.com

Haynes Automotive Manuals (continued)

NOTE: If you do not see a listing for your vehicle, consult your local Haynes dealer for the latest product information.

42023 Civic all models '84 thru '91
42024 Civic & del Sol '92 thru '95
42025 Civic '96 thru '00, CR-V '97 thru '01,
 Acura Integra '94 thru '00
42026 Civic '01 thru '10, CR-V '02 thru '09
42035 Odyssey all models '99 thru '10
 Passport - see ISUZU Rodeo (47017)
42037 Honda Pilot '03 thru '07, Acura MDX '01 thru '07
42040 Prelude CVCC all models '79 thru '89

HYUNDAI
43010 Elantra all models '96 thru '10
43015 Excel & Accent all models '86 thru '09
43050 Santa Fe all models '01 thru '06
43055 Sonata all models '99 thru '08

INFINITI
 G35 '03 thru '08 - see NISSAN 350Z (72011)

ISUZU
 Hombre - see CHEVROLET S-10 (24071)
47017 Rodeo, Amigo & Honda Passport '89 thru '02
47020 Trooper & Pick-up '81 thru '93

JAGUAR
49010 XJ6 all 6 cyl models '68 thru '86
49011 XJ6 all models '88 thru '94
49015 XJ12 & XJS all 12 cyl models '72 thru '85

JEEP
50010 Cherokee, Comanche & Wagoneer Limited
 all models '84 thru '01
50020 CJ all models '49 thru '86
50025 Grand Cherokee all models '93 thru '04
50026 Grand Cherokee '05 thru '09
50029 Grand Wagoneer & Pick-up '72 thru '91
 Grand Wagoneer '84 thru '91, Cherokee &
 Wagoneer '72 thru '83, Pick-up '72 thru '88
50030 Wrangler all models '87 thru '11
50035 Liberty '02 thru '07

KIA
54050 Optima '01 thru '10
54070 Sephia '94 thru '01, Spectra '00 thru '09,
 Sportage '05 thru '10

LEXUS
 ES 300/330 - see TOYOTA Camry (92007) (92008)
 RX 330 - see TOYOTA Highlander (92095)

LINCOLN
 Navigator - see FORD Pick-up (36059)
59010 Rear-Wheel Drive all models '70 thru '10

MAZDA
61010 GLC Hatchback (rear-wheel drive) '77 thru '83
61011 GLC (front-wheel drive) '81 thru '85
61012 Mazda3 '04 thru '11
61015 323 & Protegé '90 thru '03
61016 MX-5 Miata '90 thru '09
61020 MPV all models '89 thru '98
 Navajo - see Ford Explorer (36024)
61030 Pick-ups '72 thru '93
 Pick-ups '94 thru '00 - see Ford Ranger (36071)
61035 RX-7 all models '79 thru '85
61036 RX-7 all models '86 thru '91
61040 626 (rear-wheel drive) all models '79 thru '82
61041 626/MX-6 (front-wheel drive) '83 thru '92
61042 626, MX-6/Ford Probe '93 thru '02
61043 Mazda6 '03 thru '11

MERCEDES-BENZ
63012 123 Series Diesel '76 thru '85
63015 190 Series four-cyl gas models, '84 thru '88
63020 230/250/280 6 cyl sohc models '68 thru '72
63025 280 123 Series gasoline models '77 thru '81
63030 350 & 450 all models '71 thru '80
63040 C-Class: C230/C240/C280/C320/C350 '01 thru '07

MERCURY
64200 Villager & Nissan Quest '93 thru '01
 All other titles, see FORD Listing.

MG
66010 MGB Roadster & GT Coupe '62 thru '80
66015 MG Midget, Austin Healey Sprite '58 thru '80

MINI
67020 Mini '02 thru '11

MITSUBISHI
68020 Cordia, Tredia, Galant, Precis &
 Mirage '83 thru '93
68030 Eclipse, Eagle Talon & Ply. Laser '90 thru '94
68031 Eclipse '95 thru '05, Eagle Talon '95 thru '98
68035 Galant '94 thru '10
68040 Pick-up '83 thru '96 & Montero '83 thru '93

NISSAN
72010 300ZX all models including Turbo '84 thru '89
72011 350Z & Infiniti G35 all models '03 thru '08
72015 Altima all models '93 thru '06
72016 Altima '07 thru '10
72020 Maxima all models '85 thru '92
72021 Maxima all models '93 thru '04
72025 Murano '03 thru '10
72030 Pick-ups '80 thru '97 Pathfinder '87 thru '95
72031 Frontier Pick-up, Xterra, Pathfinder '96 thru '04
72032 Frontier & Xterra '05 thru '11
72040 Pulsar all models '83 thru '86
 Quest - see MERCURY Villager (64200)
72050 Sentra all models '82 thru '94
72051 Sentra & 200SX all models '95 thru '06
72060 Stanza all models '82 thru '90
72070 Titan pick-ups '04 thru '10 Armada '05 thru '10

OLDSMOBILE
73015 Cutlass V6 & V8 gas models '74 thru '88
 *For other OLDSMOBILE titles, see BUICK,
 CHEVROLET or GENERAL MOTORS listing.*

PLYMOUTH
 For PLYMOUTH titles, see DODGE listing.

PONTIAC
79008 Fiero all models '84 thru '88
79018 Firebird V8 except Turbo '70 thru '81
79019 Firebird all models '82 thru '92
79025 G6 all models '05 thru '09
79040 Mid-size Rear-wheel Drive '70 thru '87
 Vibe '03 thru '11 - see TOYOTA Matrix (92060)
 *For other PONTIAC titles, see BUICK,
 CHEVROLET or GENERAL MOTORS listing.*

PORSCHE
80020 911 except Turbo & Carrera 4 '65 thru '89
80025 914 all 4 cyl models '69 thru '76
80030 924 all models including Turbo '76 thru '82
80035 944 all models including Turbo '83 thru '89

RENAULT
 Alliance & Encore - see AMC (14020)

SAAB
84010 900 all models including Turbo '79 thru '88

SATURN
87010 Saturn all S-series models '91 thru '02
87011 Saturn Ion '03 thru '07
87020 Saturn all L-series models '00 thru '04
87040 Saturn VUE '02 thru '07

SUBARU
89002 1100, 1300, 1400 & 1600 '71 thru '79
89003 1600 & 1800 2WD & 4WD '80 thru '94
89100 Legacy all models '90 thru '99
89101 Legacy & Forester '00 thru '06

SUZUKI
90010 Samurai/Sidekick & Geo Tracker '86 thru '01

TOYOTA
92005 Camry all models '83 thru '91
92006 Camry all models '92 thru '96
92007 Camry, Avalon, Solara, Lexus ES 300 '97 thru '01
92008 Toyota Camry, Avalon and Solara and
 Lexus ES 300/330 all models '02 thru '06
92009 Camry '07 thru '11
92015 Celica Rear Wheel Drive '71 thru '85
92020 Celica Front Wheel Drive '86 thru '99
92025 Celica Supra all models '79 thru '92
92030 Corolla all models '75 thru '79
92032 Corolla all rear wheel drive models '80 thru '87
92035 Corolla all front wheel drive models '84 thru '92
92036 Corolla & Geo Prizm '93 thru '02
92037 Corolla models '03 thru '11
92040 Corolla Tercel all models '80 thru '82
92045 Corona all models '74 thru '82
92050 Cressida all models '78 thru '82
92055 Land Cruiser FJ40, 43, 45, 55 '68 thru '82
92056 Land Cruiser FJ60, 62, 80, FZJ80 '80 thru '96
92060 Matrix & Pontiac Vibe '03 thru '11
92065 MR2 all models '85 thru '87
92070 Pick-up all models '69 thru '78
92075 Pick-up all models '79 thru '95
92076 Tacoma, 4Runner, & T100 '93 thru '04
92077 Tacoma all models '05 thru '09
92078 Tundra '00 thru '06 & Sequoia '01 thru '07
92079 4Runner all models '03 thru '09
92080 Previa all models '91 thru '95
92081 Prius all models '01 thru '08
92082 RAV4 all models '96 thru '10
92085 Tercel all models '87 thru '94
92090 Sienna all models '98 thru '09
92095 Highlander & Lexus RX-330 '99 thru '07

TRIUMPH
94007 Spitfire all models '62 thru '81
94010 TR7 all models '75 thru '81

VW
96008 Beetle & Karmann Ghia '54 thru '79
96009 New Beetle '98 thru '11
96016 Rabbit, Jetta, Scirocco & Pick-up gas
 models '75 thru '92 & Convertible '80 thru '92
96017 Golf, GTI & Jetta '93 thru '98, Cabrio '95 thru '02
96018 Golf, GTI, Jetta '99 thru '05
96019 Jetta, Rabbit, GTI & Golf '05 thru '11
96020 Rabbit, Jetta & Pick-up diesel '77 thru '84
96023 Passat '98 thru '05, Audi A4 '96 thru '01
96030 Transporter 1600 all models '68 thru '79
96035 Transporter 1700, 1800 & 2000 '72 thru '79
96040 Type 3 1500 & 1600 all models '63 thru '73
96045 Vanagon all air-cooled models '80 thru '83

VOLVO
97010 120, 130 Series & 1800 Sports '61 thru '73
97015 140 Series all models '66 thru '74
97020 240 Series all models '76 thru '93
97040 740 & 760 Series all models '82 thru '88
97050 850 Series all models '93 thru '97

TECHBOOK MANUALS
10205 Automotive Computer Codes
10206 OBD-II & Electronic Engine Management
10210 Automotive Emissions Control Manual
10215 Fuel Injection Manual '78 thru '85
10220 Fuel Injection Manual '86 thru '99
10225 Holley Carburetor Manual
10230 Rochester Carburetor Manual
10240 Weber/Zenith/Stromberg/SU Carburetors
10305 Chevrolet Engine Overhaul Manual
10310 Chrysler Engine Overhaul Manual
10320 Ford Engine Overhaul Manual
10330 GM and Ford Diesel Engine Repair Manual
10333 Engine Performance Manual
10340 Small Engine Repair Manual, 5 HP & Less
10341 Small Engine Repair Manual, 5.5 - 20 HP
10345 Suspension, Steering & Driveline Manual
10355 Ford Automatic Transmission Overhaul
10360 GM Automatic Transmission Overhaul
10405 Automotive Body Repair & Painting
10410 Automotive Brake Manual
10411 Automotive Anti-lock Brake (ABS) Systems
10415 Automotive Detailing Manual
10420 Automotive Electrical Manual
10425 Automotive Heating & Air Conditioning
10430 Automotive Reference Manual & Dictionary
10435 Automotive Tools Manual
10440 Used Car Buying Guide
10445 Welding Manual
10450 ATV Basics
10452 Scooters 50cc to 250cc

SPANISH MANUALS
98903 Reparación de Carrocería & Pintura
98904 Manual de Carburador Modelos
 Holley & Rochester
98905 Códigos Automotrices de la Computadora
98906 OBD-II & Sistemas de Control Electrónico
 del Motor
98910 Frenos Automotriz
98913 Electricidad Automotriz
98915 Inyección de Combustible '86 al '99
99040 Chevrolet & GMC Camionetas '67 al '87
99041 Chevrolet & GMC Camionetas '88 al '98
99042 Chevrolet & GMC Camionetas
 Cerradas '68 al '95
99043 Chevrolet/GMC Camionetas '94 al '04
99048 Chevrolet/GMC Camionetas '99 al '06
99055 Dodge Caravan & Plymouth Voyager '84 al '95
99075 Ford Camionetas y Bronco '80 al '94
99076 Ford F-150 '97 al '09
99077 Ford Camionetas Cerradas '69 al '91
99088 Ford Modelos de Tamaño Mediano '75 al '86
99089 Ford Camionetas Ranger '93 al '10
99091 Ford Taurus & Mercury Sable '86 al '95
99095 GM Modelos de Tamaño Grande '70 al '90
99100 GM Modelos de Tamaño Mediano '70 al '88
99106 Jeep Cherokee, Wagoneer & Comanche
 '84 al '00
99110 Nissan Camioneta '80 al '96, Pathfinder '87 al '95
99118 Nissan Sentra '82 al '94
99125 Toyota Camionetas y 4Runner '79 al '95

Over 100 Haynes
motorcycle manuals
also available

7-12

Haynes North America, Inc., 859 Lawrence Drive, Newbury Park, CA 91320-1514 • (805) 498-6703 • http://www.haynes.com